Death
When A Loved One Passes
What to Do
How to Do It

Death
When A Loved One Passes
What to Do
How to Do It

Richard Jordan

Alford Press, llc

Death. When A Loved One Passes.

What to do. How to do it.

Copyright © 2012 by Richard Jordan

Publisher Alford Press, llc   First Edition 2012

ISBN: 978-0-9839235-2-7

All rights reserved. No part of this book shall be reproduced, stored in a data base or a retrieval system, or transmitted by any means, electronic, mechanical, photocopying, recording or otherwise, without prior written permission from the publisher.

Disclaimer:
Although the author and publisher have made every effort to ensure that the information in this book was correct at press time, the author and publisher do not assume and hereby disclaim any liability to any party for any loss, damage, or disruption caused by errors or omissions, whether such errors or omissions result from negligence, accident, or any other cause. This book is not and is not intended to be any type of legal advice. It is to serve only as a guide and is not intended to be a substitute for specific individual tax, legal, or estate settlement advice. You should always consult with a competent estate attorney or other professional source.

Available from the publishers at: RichardJordan.org , Amazon.com,
Barnes & Noble, Books-a-Million, and PhilGrace.com

Library of Congress Cataloging-in-Publication Data is on file.

Jordan, Richard 1948-

Cover Design by OIKEY1

Printed in the United States of America
Worldwide Distribution

To My Wife Judith

Thank You for all of your help and support.

Oikey1

INTRODUCTION

Death: We are here and then we are not here. We are going about our business and then we are not. We like to think that somehow everything stays the same. Life goes on, except without us. That is not really the case. On the one hand, life does go on, but we were important. We did have an impact. We were someone. We had stuff that needs to be taken care of. People cared about us even though we may have never met them. Remarkably, they still cared. We had an impact, no matter how small, on those around us. Like the ripple in the pond, we were here, we are not here, and we are still impacting others.

It is not until you sit down and take a good hard look at everything that must be done just to clean up after us that you realize how much work it can be. We have an obligation to make this as easy as we can for those who remain behind. Someone must come behind us and tidy up. We could at least gather up all important documents and place them in a safe place. We could at least write down our vital statistics. Make a list of property that we own, even if it does not seem like much. Someone has to tidy up when we leave and they really need our help. After all we are the ones who know they do not have to look for more property or "assets" because this is all there is. That's all folks. Nothing more to look at here. Tidy up and go back home to your families. Life is really short, sorry to take so much of your time, now go on home and enjoy what you have left.

There is a lot of work to do when someone passes on. If we do not take a little time now to tell them what we have and what we would like them to do with it, this may take them a year to sort everything out. Yes, the average amount of time it takes to tidy up after someone is one year. More than half of all adults never even leave a Will. A Last Will and Testament is really just the beginning. If you do not tell them, they will have to search for things that do not even exist. They will have to look for safe deposit boxes when you could have just left a note: "I have no safe deposit boxes". Instead they will have to get a certified copy of the Death Certificate and go to each local bank and fill out paper work searching for assets that may not even exist. Why? Because the law demands that someone tidy up. They must pay your bills, and it would be nice if you left them access to your bank accounts so they did not have to pay them out of their own pocket. They must collect your assets and it would be nice of you to at least leave them a list. They must pay your taxes. Yup. One of the first things someone will need to do is pay your bills and pay your taxes. Sounds like fun, doesn't it? So the least we can do is help them out a bit. A simple note: I own only one automobile and the keys are in the kitchen on the key rack. I own pretty much what you see at my home. I have one safe deposit box at Name of Bank. You will find all important documents in the box on the floor behind the bird cage. I have not been able to find the title to the house. I know I had one. I have been meaning to get another copy but I just kept putting it off. At least you can stop looking for it (or maybe you got lucky and actually found it?). Please give my good set of dishes, the ones with the flower pattern made by (brand name) to my sister (Name) because she always said how much she liked them. I have shopped online at name.com and 2name.com. The username is. . .and the password is . . .I have photos on CD's and DVD's on the book shelf in the living room.

I should have taken the time to clean up more often. You best just throw out all of those old magazines. I was saving the articles. Don't know why. I did not even have the time to find the title to the house. I really want to thank you for taking the time to come here and tidy up for me. I never really understood how much work it would be if I did nothing to help you. I am the only one who knows where everything is, and I don't seem to be able to find everything myself. Thanks for your help.

What The Book Covers

We have not tried to cover everything. The book was written to both Preplan a Funeral and organize an Estate for disposition. (Tidy Up). Some information is repeated so you do not have to hunt for it.

The book was also written to help you get started in your time of need if you were just informed that a loved one just passed. What do I do? How do I do it?

You may need to know more about what to do to tidy up. We cover as much as we can but sometimes just point out the main topics for the area. An example would be the subject of Wills. Everyone should have a Last Will and Testament. Many books have been written about how to draft a Will. You can go online and draft a legal Will for very little cost. Our purpose is not to teach you how to write a legal Will but to explain its importance and list some of the things you should not forget to include. Did you know it is important to include what you do not have as well as what you do have? Let me explain. If you do not have a pension plan the person(s) who tidy up after you must spend some time looking for pension plans. Wouldn't it just be easier to tell them? "I have only one pension plan. It is with Xyz Company, contact information is, the paper work is in the box with everything else on the floor behind the bird cage. And we try to forewarn you about relatives. Can they sell your body parts? No. It is illegal. If there is a Cremation, who owns the ashes? No one can own the ashes. They can only take possession for "proper disposition". Your friends and neighbors cannot just come over and load up their pickup truck with mementos. And how to take care of a situation if you have two heirs who both want your pretty dishes. Did you know that whoever comes to tidy up can, in most cases, just refuse and go home? Why not help them out so they stay and help you? Did you know they can be sued if they do not tidy up in what could be regarded as a "proper manner"? Because you did not take the time to help, they must inventory all assets and place a value on them. If they do this all by themselves without having a second party to offer a second opinion and or confirm the value of everything, they could end up in big trouble later on after the items were distributed. What if Uncle Buster thinks that stuffed squirrel was really owned by Teddy Roosevelt? He thinks it was worth more than the $3.00 you sold it for at the estate sale. You are in big trouble now bucko. If there were two of you and you both thought it was just a ratty old squirrel then at least you share liability and things will most likely work themselves out.

The Book Starts With A Time Line

1) The Time Line can also be used as a partial table of contents.

When you come to a listing, for example:

"Locate the Will." there will be a small amount of information following this listing right in the time line with references listed for more information. page -

-- Wills. This is where you can find information on Wills: What is a Will? How to write a will. Using software Online to formulate a proper Will. What should be included in a Will? Living Wills. What is the difference? Why are they both important? etc.

2) There is a **Glossary of Terms and Definitions** in the back of the book:

Use this to look things up quickly. If there is a major section of the book with more information about this subject, page numbers are also given here: example: Asset – describes what an asset is and some types of assets. There are also page numbers to read more about assets, types, how to locate assets, and how to secure assets, appraisals, sale of assets to pay the costs of the estate. Increase in the value of assets while held in the estate and taxes that may be due from the estate. This may in turn lead you to Taxes and the various taxes that may or may not be due. Personal income tax from January 1 until the date of death. Property tax. Estate tax and estate income tax (these are not the same thing). A Closing Letter from the Internal Revenue Service to the executor, if needed, verifies all federal estate taxes have been paid. Now you may proceed with distributions to the beneficiaries Yes, there is a lot of information and we try to help you by keeping it simple and giving you a place to begin.

Hundreds of volumes have been written on specific areas of the funeral industry. This guide brings many things together for you as a quick reference to help move you along with the preparations for a loved one and as a help to plan for your own passing. It is not our goal to cover everything.

Do you need to hire a competent estate attorney?

If you have real estate and need to transfer the title after death. If you have a business. If you have assets that you want to leave to specific persons or institutions. If you have the one crazy relative hiding in the woods that is just waiting for you to pass on so they can contest your will and try to pay for fish hooks and rifle bullets for another year. If you have any of these or if you just don't quite feel right about doing this without an attorney, then YES, by all means consult with a competent estate attorney. Initial consultation is usually FREE and it will give you peace of mind. Read through this book and if you begin to see more and more things that you just do not want to have to take care by yourself then make that call. There is no way we can cover everything in this small volume. Remember if you seek the advice of an attorney you can always just stop and find another attorney or make other arrangements.

It is our sincerest desire that this book helps make your life easier in this time of need.

Richard Jordan

Disclaimer:
Although the author and publisher have made every effort to ensure that the information in this book was correct at press time, the author and publisher do not assume and hereby disclaim any liability to any party for any loss, damage, or disruption caused by errors or omissions, whether such errors or omissions result from negligence, accident, or any other cause. This book is not and is not intended to be any type of legal advice. It is to serve only as a guide and is not intended to be a substitute for specific individual tax, legal, or estate settlement advice. You should always consult with a competent estate attorney or other professional source.

TABLE OF CONTENTS

Introduction	How to use this guide.	II
Table of Contents		VI
Section 1 **A Time Line - Index**	A Time Line Index of What to Do. This is the general order in which things are usually done.	XI
Section 2 **Time Line**	How to Tidy up. A Detailed Time Line. This walks you through the process and helps as a reminder of what needs to be done. From death to funeral is generally less than eight days but can be longer.	1
Section 3 **Key Areas** **Alphabetical Listing**	A More In-Depth Alphabetical Listing of most major areas of concern.	57
Asset List	Locating assets, insurance policies, property etc. You need to inventory, value and secure assets.	59
Attorney	Do I really need an attorney? Maybe.	71
Banks	Locating funds. Can I spend their money?	75
Safe Deposit Box	How to locate and how to open.	79
Be Careful - scams	Be careful before you sign for anything!	82
Beneficiary	Who gets what, how and when?	87

Burial	Direct Burial, Traditional burial, Home Burial	92
Business Ownership	The deceased owned a business. What now?	98
Cemetery	Cemeteries. General Information.	101
Cremation	Direct Cremation, Alkaline Hydrolysis (Green Cremation), Renting a Casket	104
Debt	What to do with debt and the Estate?	108
Documents	What documents do you need?	115
Estate – Close Estate	Closing the Estate.	128
Executor	Executor or Personal representative. What do they do? Their Responsibility & Liability	133
Executor – No Thank You	I do not want to be the Executor. Can someone make me? Yes, sometimes.	144
Free Funeral ?	Is there a Free funeral?	163
Funeral Goods & Services	What goods & services are not required? Which are required?	165
Funeral Procession	About the funeral procession.	176
Funeral Rule	FTC Consumer Protection – Funeral Rule	178
Hospice Care	Hospice, Palliative Care, & pain.	187
Identity Theft	Help prevent Identity theft.	190
Insurance	Life Insurance, Annuities, Filing claims	198
Living Will	A Living Will is a Medical Directive.	201
Medicaid	Medicaid. Some Medicaid information.	207

Mortgage	The home has a mortgage. What now?	210
Reverse Mortgage	The home has a reverse mortgage. What now?	211
Homes Underwater	The home is underwater. What now?	212
Prepay for Funeral	Prepay? Is it a good idea?	216
Preplan for Funeral	Preplan is not prepay. How to preplan.	219
Probate	Probate – What is it? Why?	241
Security for Estate	Providing security for the Estate.	246
Social Security	Social Security information and benefits.	254
Transportation	Transportation of the deceased. Local.	259
Transportation	Interstate & International.	259
Veterans	Veteran's information and benefits.	263
Vital Statistics	What you need.	269
Wills	Self Proving, Holographic, Pour-over etc.	274
Appendix Chart - Costs	A "ballpark" guide to goods & services.	285
Glossary & Index	An Alphabetized list of terms and definitions, crossreferenced.	293

SECTION 1

How to Tidy Up
TIME LINE INDEX

A Time Line Index of What to Do

TIME LINE DETAILS Table of contents

Pre-Death	Preparation	2, 219-240, 327-328
Hospice Care	A little background. Pain relief.	187-189
The Will	Locate the Will. Forward copies to . . .	15, 274-283, 450-453
Living Will	What is it? Is there one? What now?	3, 201-206
Health Care Directives	Organ Donor. Family says, No!	3, 201, 368
Vital Statistics	What you need now and later.	4, 269-274

XII | When a loved one passes.
What to do. How to do it.

Documents	Will, Bills, Contracts, Titles, etc.	115-128
Assets	Liquid assets, insurance, pension(s), 401(k), property, vehicles, homes out of state, etc.	5-8, 41-48, 57-70, 75-82
Digital Assets	Cell phones, Online Banking, Storage, the "Cloud", computers, etc.	40, 41, 250-254, 333-336
Mortgage	Mortgage, Reverse Mortgage, Underwater Home.	210-216, 444, 445
Identity Theft	Protect against. Minimize the Threat.	190-198, 246-253, 375, 376
Security	Secure the Estate. Assets, Digital Assets and Property.	246-253
Living Trust	Trust, Living Trust, Trustee, etc.	388
Business Ownership	LLC, Corporation, Partnership	47, 98-100
Real Property	Locate, ownership, Transfer Title	66, 382-385
When Death Occurs	An Expected Death	9, 328
	An Unexpected Death	10, 327
The First Weeks	Time Line. A practical guide.	9-50

The Will	Locate most current, Who to Notify, Disburse copies to . . .	15, 274-283, 450-453
Intestate. No Will.	What now?	377-381
Funeral? Not Required	Burial, Cremation or Alkaline Hydrolysis? Legal Requirements.	19
Executor	Defined, some of the Responsibilities	133-144
Executor: No thank-you.	So, You do not want to be the executor.	144-162
Free Funeral	Is there a Free funeral?	163-165
Funeral Expenses	To be paid at time of service.	14, 15, 51, 165-176
Funeral Goods & Services	Some usual goods and services.	165-176
Funeral Rule	Federal Trade Commission Consumer Rule. Protects the Consumer. How?	178-186
Funeral Costs - Prepay	Pre-paid or pre-planned (bank account).	216-219, 285-292
Casket	Purchase Online from Wal-Mart, Costco or another. Legal choices. Cost.	26, 167-169, 305-309
Urns, Headstones, Markers, etc.	Purchase Online from Wal-Mart, Costco or another. Legal choices. Cost.	27, 175, 445

XIV | When a loved one passes. What to do. How to do it.

Burial	Cemetery site, Crypt, Mausoleum.	18-20, 92-98, 300-303
Direct Burial	Your Choices. Legal Requirements.	19, 95, 337
Home Burial	Home burial? Laws vary by state.	92, 357, 373
Cremation	Your Choices. Legal Requirements.	21, 104-108, 324
Direct Cremation	With or without Graveside Service.	337
Services	Funeral Service, Memorial Service, Viewing, Visitation, Wake. Any or all?	29-32, 449
Obituary, Eulogy, Epitaph	What they are and how to Write.	344, 345, 405-407
Pallbearers and Ushers	What is Required. Etiquette.	31, 411
Transportation	Out of town guests. Funeral Service.	259-263
Last Day of the Funeral	Finish this part of the timeline.	32, 33
Executor Time Line	Probate, Inventory, Protect, Disburse &	33-55, 129-133
Documents	Locate, collect, protect. List.	115-128
Death Certificate	Twelve to Twenty Copies as needed.	329-331

Probate	Begin Probate. What is Probate?	34, 241-246
Attorney	Do I need an attorney?	71-74
Assets Held in Trust	Locate the Trustee and verify distribution.	439-444
Debt	Examine and pay if needed.	108-115
Joint Survivorship	Community Property, Joint Ownership.	48-51, 382-385
Taxes	Pay Taxes	433-435
Beneficiaries	Distribute the Inheritance.	38, 52, 87-91
Close the Estate	File Documents at Courthouse.	54, 55, 128-132

SECTION 2

How to Tidy Up

A Detailed TIME LINE

A Time Line – Death

This is a "general" time line that lists the most common things to do when a loved one passes. It is for both the loved one who has passed and for the family and friends who wish to pay their respects.

Read through the list and use what you need. Use this list as a guide.

Most people will not need to do everything on the list. It is a guide to help focus your effort. It is not meant to include everything that you may need to do. It is a general picture of things that need to be done and a reasonable order in which to do them. Do not worry if things seem to be out of order or if you add to this list or subtract from it. Remember it is only a guide to help you make plans and carry them out.

If you wait to do certain things on the list you may not honor the person's wishes. You may miss extremely important documents pertaining to prepaid, nonrefundable funeral plans in excess of $8,500 (the average cost of a funeral today). You may lose assets, or give away valuable assets that were meant to be left with a specific person. It is important that you do the best that you can for your loved one. If you are the executor you are legally libel and must account for your actions.

Pre-Death

It is best to begin preparation years before you need it. More than half of all Americans die without leaving a Will. Yes, it takes some thought and time but it will not get easier than right now. see *Funeral –Preplan*, page 219

One to Three Months Prior to Death: Many people realize death is approaching and express a degree of denial. They contemplate their life and revisit old memories. They may not want visitors or even family members around. They will sleep more and may already be under a doctor's care. Fortunately the body chemistry produces a mild sense of euphoria. Sometimes there is regret and bitterness. No matter, someone needs to spend time with the loved one and gather all of the necessary information.

Notify Family and Friends

A phone call is usually preferred for those who are close. Email is also acceptable.

Discuss - - - with the loved one. Everything . . .

Locate the Will

Read through it and use this book as a guide. Did they forget anything? We all seem to forget something. Does the Will need to be updated due to changes in circumstances. Are you now going to make certain liquid assets available for expenses due immediately after death? Review and make changes to the Will. Do you now feel you would like to consult with an attorney to get everything correct? Then do it now. Do these things as soon as possible and keep reading this guide. People can become unable to think clearly as time passes so it is important to begin now. see *Wills*, page 274

Is there a Living Will?

A Living Will allows a person to make health care decisions now in case they are unable to do so later on. It is a document that provides doctors and other health care providers information as to the circumstances under which they want life sustaining treatment provided, withheld or withdrawn. see *Living Will*, page 201

Are there any Health Care Directives? Advance Directives?

These are legal documents that allow a person to provide doctors and other health care providers information as to the circumstances under which they want life sustaining treatment provided, withheld or withdrawn. There may be some differences. see *Health Care Directives*, page 202

Does someone have Power of Attorney?

A written document in which one person (the principal) appoints another person to act as an agent on their behalf. They may legally sign a document for the principle. A limited power imposes limits on exactly what the representative may do in place of the principle. see *Power of Attorney*, page 415

Does someone have Durable Power of Attorney?

A durable power of attorney differs from a traditional power of attorney in that it continues the relationship if the principle becomes incapacitated. see *Power of Attorney*, page 415

Organ Donation

Even if someone signs a donor card, it is essential that their family also knows their wishes regarding organ donation. Let them know as soon as possible. The family may still be asked to sign a consent form in order for the donation to occur. If they say no, the hospital may refuse to accept the organ(s). If the donor has taken the time to register with the Secretary of State or with the Gift of Life, then their family does not have the right to object once they are in the registry. Sign the organ donor space on your driver license and carry an organ donor card. Make this information available to health care workers. see *Organ Donation*, page 408

Has an Executor, Personal Representative, Exectrix, or Administrator been named?

These are all names for a person who administers someone's estate. They should be named in the Will.

Has an alternate executor been named in case the first named predeceases the testator or cannot fulfill the obligations and duties? see *Executor*, page 133

Gather all Vital Statistics

Gather personal information of the deceased. see *Vital Statistics*, page 269

Locate all address books, boxes of previous Christmas card envelopes from previous years (names and addresses of friends).

Locate Important Documents

Locating documents can be time consuming. You may need to look for things even if they do not exist like other bank accounts. It is not unusual to have bank accounts in banks that the testator never personally visited. They may be out of state or out of the country. Is there any documentation? Where would you look? see *Documents*, page 115

Locate all Bills

Someone needs to keep paying the bills. Collect all bills and receipts. Buy a file folder. Store both paid and unpaid bills in a safe place, you will need to secure these to help limit the opportunity for Identity Theft. see *Identity Theft*, page 190, 246, 375

Insurance

Insurance Cards, statements, account numbers, online access user names & passwords. The executor must file Life Insurance Claims. Collect this information for them. You will need to secure these to help limit the opportunity for Identity Theft. see *Identity Theft*, page 190, 246, 375

Medical Equipment

Is it owned or a rental? If rental equipment is being used it will have to be returned. Name, address, phone, fax of the rental company. Do they pick up the equipment? Check for any cash deposits that should be returned.

Locate all Assets

All assets need to be secured to prevent theft. Real-estate, vehicles, stocks and bonds, brokerage accounts, annuity, Living Trust, Totten trust, collections, cash, holdings. see *Assets*, page 41, 57, 75

Digital Assets

Online banking, brokerage, websites, blogs, social networking, storage "in the cloud", art, patents, inventions, account numbers – user names – passwords and challenge questions. etc. see *Digital Assets*, page 40, 250, 333

Business Ownership

Do they own a business? If they do, steps must be taken to preserve and protect the business. What type of business structure is it? An LLC, Corporation, Partnership? Some business structures are simple and even have "Rights of Survivorship" where the spouse may have been named as a partner or in a community property state the spouse may have specific rights. This is where things can become very complicated very quickly. Now may be a good time to speak with a competent estate lawyer. see *Business*, page 47, 98

Locate all Real Property

Vacation homes, boats, airplanes, vacant land, vehicles, motorcycles, bicycles (some common bicycles are worth over $6,000). You will need to secure these before someone comes along and takes them as a memento. Collections from beanie babies to antique jewelry. Depending on the value an Appraisal may be needed later on. If you are in the process of preplanning, an estimated value may be all that is necessary right now. If you plan to insure these check with the insurance agent to see what kind of documentation you will need. see *Insurance*, page 198

Locate all Storage

Locate storage rental units, their location(s), keys, other access needed (combinations for locks, digital user names and passwords, biometric – eye scan thumb print contact information so you may gain access if needed. Some may be out of state. Digital storage of assets may be in the Cloud. see *Assets*, page 41, 57, 68, 75

Digital Assets

Locate ALL computers, hard drives, cell phones, answering machines, digital cameras, and copiers are very important as they contain very sensitive information in memory. Collect ALL CD's DVD's do not assume it is a movie just because someone printed "Movie" on the disk with a marker. These will all have to be viewed by someone. They may contain ANYTHING! They may contain video of hidden assets, collections, documents, and a whole other life no one ever knew about. They may contain maps and directions to hidden treasures that the loved one was keeping safe for their beneficiary(s) see Digital Assets, page 40, 333

Locate all Passwords & Usernames, Keys and Combinations

Tag keys as to what they are for. You will need to change the garage door opener code and any residence security codes. Keep a log of online access information: user names, passwords and challenge questions. Amazon.com, Facebook, PayPal, etc. see *Preplan*, page 219

Collect all Credit Cards

Locate and record contact and access information. Separate cards with joint ownership. You will need to secure these to help limit the opportunity for Identity Theft.

If you are pre-planning consider which accounts you may want to close. You will change your credit rating by closing some accounts. As a general rule, the older the account the more likely it will help your credit rating if you keep it open. Do some research before you just close everything. In any case, secure all credit cards, statements, usernames, passwords, and challenge questions for online access. Check all computers for bookmarks that may take you to online banking or personal credit card accounts.

Collect Driver's License and Insurance Cards

These are usually in a wallet or purse. They can walk away from the bedside of someone who is disabled. You will need to secure these to help limit the opportunity for Identity Theft.

Safe Deposit Box

Locate and record, contact information, any paperwork when the account was opened, key(s), their location, box numbers, account numbers, and access information. You will need to secure these to help limit the opportunity for Identity Theft. see *Safe Deposit Box*, page 79

Bank Accounts

Locate and record: All checking accounts, their contact and access information; all savings accounts, their contact and access information. Checkbooks, bank statements, money market accounts, online account access including user names, passwords and challenge questions. You will need to secure these to help limit the opportunity for *Identity Theft*. see page 190, 246, 375 - *Banking*, page 75

Retirement Accounts

Locate and record: All retirement accounts, their contact and access information. All pension plans their contact and access information. These may include 401k, IRA, and pension plans. You will need to secure these to help limit the opportunity for Identity Theft. see *Retirement Accounts*, page 424

Corporations, LLC's or any Business enterprise

Locate and record: All business ownership. It is not unusual today for many "Baby Boomers" to form a Limited Liability Corporation (LLC). page 98

Locate all Photographs

It is easier to locate and record the type of photograph: digital or hard copy, while you are gathering other information. Just keep notes as to the location and access information if needed to Photo albums, videos, and digital photos (some may be on a computer, hard drive, thumb drive or stored online in "the cloud" and will need to be saved to disk. Just because a CD or DVD has "Vacation 2003" printed on it with a marker does not mean that is what you will find on that CD or DVD. It could be anything. see *Digital Assets*, page 40, 250, 333

If you can, discuss the Funeral itself with the loved one

This is why it is necessary to gather and collect all documents and vital statistics. You may find that funeral, or cremation arraignments have already been made, and possibly prepaid. Were arrangements already made? When a loved one dies, family and friends will gather to celebrate their life and honor their memory. Often the celebrations involve one or a combination of a wake, funeral, and burial or cremation ceremony.

Before a loved one's passing, create a document (whether written or typed) that details how the funeral and burial process should take place. Ideally this should not be in the Will. If the testator has plans but no money to carry them out, you are under no obligation to do this. They may prefer the $25,000. casket with built in wet-bar. Use some discretion. see *Preplan*, page 219, 240

Funeral Preference

It's very difficult to lose a loved one. You're in a state of grief, and maybe a state of shock. The last thing you want to think about is planning the funeral. Many people prepay their funeral expenses. If you do not locate the paper work and make other arraignments the amount prepaid may not be refundable. This could amount to $10,000 or more. Have Funeral Arraignments been made? Burial, Cremation or Alkaline Hydrolysis? Prepaid or not? Important things to consider: Religious, Clergy, Church, veteran, funeral home, burial, visitation, reception, or wake. Where will the gathering be held? No Memorial service. Is there a cemetery plot, niche, crypt, or mausoleum? see *Preplan*, page 219, 240

When a Death Occurs

Someone must make the "first call". It doesn't seem to matter how prepared we are - or aren't - a loved one's death often leaves us feeling numb and bewildered. Shock and grief can be immobilizing. see *Grief*, page 364

An Expected Death

If no further medical intervention is required

No further medical intervention is normally required if the person passed while in a hospital, or under a doctor's care at a nursing home, assisted living facility or at a home residence with Hospice. You will most likely not need to call 911, the Police, or the Fire department after death has occurred.

If you have **health care professionals** involved in the care of the dying person they should be **notified** of the death, where the death took place and the circumstances of death. **You will need to call** the Doctor, Hospice Nurse or the health care professionals involved. Phone numbers can sometimes be found on the patient's medication.

If the person dies in a medical facility such as a hospital or hospice, the attending medical personnel will sign the death certificate and release the body for disposition. Hospitals, may release the deceased to a funeral home without input from the decedent's legal representative in order to conserve space. The legal representative has a right to move the body.

An Unexpected Death

If the person dies anywhere else call the police by dialing 911. If you are not sure what to do, call 911. What happens next will be determined by state law. In most cases a medical examiner or coroner, will be dispatched. If the medical examiner or coroner determines the person died of natural causes they will sign a death certificate and the body will be released.

If the medical examiner or coroner cannot determine the cause of death the body will be moved for an autopsy. When the autopsy is completed the medical examiner or coroner will sign the death certificate and the body will be released for disposition. see *Autopsy*, page 297

Remain in communication with the medical examiners, (coroners) office to determine the status of the death certificate and release date of the body.

When the Decedent is released where will the body go?

You will need to know exactly where the decedent will be moved for final disposition. Will this be a funeral provider or a crematory? It could also be a Home Funeral. If there is a Will the decedent's wishes should have been made known. If there was no Will (intestate) you should already have gathered contact information and have some idea of the funeral plans.

Organ and Tissue Donations

If the donor has taken the time to register with the Secretary of State or with the Gift of Life, then their family does not have the right to object once they are in the registry. The deceased should have signed the organ donor space on their driver license or carry an organ donor card to help identify their wishes. This information may have been written into a Will or Medical Directive. This information may also have been made available to health care workers. It is not necessary for all of these things to have been done. These are just some of the most common ways an organ donor can notify others of their wishes. see *Organ and Tissue Donations*, 204, 408

Death Certificate

Arrange to receive several copies of the death certificate. Twelve copies are not too many in most cases (the Funeral Home can request these for you). To estimate how many you need get one each for every bank or investment account, real estate owned either solely or jointly, each life insurance policy, each pension and retirement plan, and one for passport cancellation.

You will need certified copies to claim insurance proceeds and to transfer money out of bank, brokerage and mutual fund accounts. It is much easier to get a few too many than to try to get one or two more later on. Twenty is not an unreasonable number as it can be very time consuming to try to get these later. Death certificates cost between $8.00 and $25.00 per copy depending on where they are filled in the US. see *Death Certificate*, page 329

Notify the Immediate Family

Call immediate family members first: Parents, Children, Brothers, Sisters and Grandparents of the deceased. People from out of state will have to make arrangements if they are planning to attend a Funeral or Memorial Service. After a divorce or separation things can become more challenging. Do your best and try not to forget anyone. While you are calling ask about other members of the family and get their contact information. Predetermine where cards, flowers, or donations will be sent.

Do not worry about waking others. Research has shown that when people are not notified immediately they feel left out. The initial reaction from most people is shock. Have others assist you in notifying everyone, this is a lot to do right now by yourself.

Funeral Home, Crematory or Home Funeral: You will need to know exactly where the decedent will be moved for final disposition. Will this be a funeral provider or a crematory? It could also be a Home Funeral. If there is a Will the decedent's wishes should have been made known. If there was no Will (intestate) you should already have gathered contact information and have some idea of the funeral plans.

Ask for help. Decide who will look after minor children. Arrange for the immediate care of surviving spouse, children, pets, and anyone living with the deceased while you call. Keep a list of names and phone numbers of anyone who says they will help. You will need these later and will not remember where everything is located, so make a list now. Consider transportation, medical, and dietary needs. Keep a list of who was contacted and when. People will need to know how to follow up to obtain information regarding funeral and or other arrangements.

Notify the executor or administrator and any trustee named in a Will or Trust. The executor usually has full responsibility with regards to the funeral arrangements and should be named in the Will. If the deceased dies intestate (no Will) or there is no executor then an administrator, or the person in priority to be the administrator, has the right to possession of the body for the purpose of disposing of the remains. This will usually be the surviving spouse and then the next of kin.

Priority: What is the usual order of priority for disposition of remains? 1) An agent under a power of attorney for health care who has the right and duty of disposition. 2) The competent surviving spouse. 3) The sole surviving competent adult child of the decedent or, if there is more than one competent adult child of the decedent, the majority of the surviving competent adult children. (if they can all be notified and are able). 4) The sole surviving competent adult sibling of the decedent or, if there is more than one surviving competent adult sibling of the decedent, the majority of the surviving competent adult siblings (if they can all be notified and are able). 5) The surviving competent adult person or persons respectively in the next degrees of kinship. Next of kin. This is meant to be a general order but always check with your state statutes for a proper legal explanation.

Notify the Beneficiaries. They should each be sent a copy of the Will.

Notify the Employer: If the deceased was working someone needs to call their employer immediately. Ask about the deceased's benefits and any pay due, including vacation or sick time, disability income, etc. Find out if any dependents are still eligible for benefit coverage through the company. Find out if there is a life insurance policy through the employer, who the beneficiary is and how to file a claim. Get copies of the paperwork in case you cannot readily locate them.

Call all Life Insurance Companies: As you are going through the deceased's documents or preplan notebook, collect all insurance contact information and have someone start calling and ask how to file a claim. Write down all information and if you do not understand ask them to repeat it. There may be payment options: lump sum or yearly payouts.

Obituary: Publish an Obituary in the local newspaper. With the decline of readership in local newspapers publishing an obituary is no longer a guarantee of informing most people in the area. Families are now located in several states or overseas and a phone call is the best way to inform people. In a short time it will most likely be considered "proper" to use a social network or text the news. For the time being it is more considerate to phone someone and tell them. Email is still acceptable, but not everyone still looks at their email on a daily basis.

Notify all clubs and organizations the deceased was a member of but do not cancel these yet. Civic or Fraternal Organizations and Clubs. page 65

The First Week after Death

The family will typically spend the first week handling the burial or cremation arrangements. The funeral home requires payment long before an estate can be opened to allow you to pay expenses from the estate account.

The executor has full responsibility with regards to the funeral arrangements and should be named in the Will. If the deceased dies intestate (no Will) or there is no executor then an administrator, or the person in priority to be the administrator, has the right to possession of the body for the purpose of disposing of the remains. Some states require the body to be buried or cremated within 72 hours of the time the body is released from the place of death or released by the coroner or medical examiner if embalming is not desired. This amount of time may be extended if refrigeration is used. If you do not know, you can call your local public health department.

Paying for the Funeral: The most common way of paying for a funeral from an estate is simply paying the bill yourself, and then asking the estate to reimburse you. You will need to keep all receipts. Submit a receipt to the Executor (Personal Representative) of the estate for repayment. If it looks like you will not be reimbursed file a claim against the estate for payment. There is a time limit to file so do this immediately. In the case of limited assets, funeral bills, outstanding debts, and valid claims are paid first, then the expenses of administering the estate, then the Administration fees and executor fees, then Taxes, and finally the beneficiaries receive their inheritance.

Check for a Totten Trust. This would be mentioned in the Will. It is simply a bank account with the balance payable on death to a previously named beneficiary. Usually this is done to prepay for funeral expenses. see *Totten Trust*, page 443

The average cost of a funeral is $8,500. The average cost of cremation is $2,000 if arraigned through a cemetery or crematorium. This is average. Both can be done for much less. The average cost to the county for direct cremation is $350 if no one claims the body. These figures are general and can vary from state to state and county to county.

If you sign for any funeral services you are legally libel to pay for them no matter what you think or feel will happen or should happen later on.

Most people are under a great deal of stress and just want to do what they feel they should do now. If you sign for something you take the legal responsibility to pay for it. You may or may not be reimbursed by the estate later on. For example: If more money is owed for the funeral expenses, taxes, administration and debt than the assets are worth the estate may be insolvent (broke) and you will get nothing.

Banks seem so impersonal today but some will still honor your wishes. Take the purposed funeral expense estimate (do not sign for it) to the bank. The bank may pay normal and customary funeral expenses from the account of the person who died. Take the time to go and ask a bank manager.

The Will

Prepare legal papers, certificates and permits. Locate the original Trust and /or original Will of the decedent.

The Will is not read out loud to the family gathered in an attorney's office. It is the job of the estate attorney or executor to determine who is entitled to receive a copy of the Will and then send it to them. The executor and beneficiaries named in the Will should receive a copy. If there is a Trust the Trustee should receive a copy of the Will. If there is an accountant they also need a copy so they can understand what the Will provides with regard to the payment of claims filed against the estate and / or estate taxes due. It is usually not required to send a copy of the Will to someone who has been disinherited but may be advisable to speed the process along.

Once a Will is admitted to probate it becomes a public court record for anyone to see and read. You may also request to receive a copy of the Will by mail or fax for a fee. see *Will*, page 15, 274, 450

Executor, Personal Representative, or Administrator of the Deceased's Estate, Notify

Notify the executor or administrator and any trustee named in a Will or Trust. The executor has full responsibility with regards to the funeral arrangements and should be named in the Will. If the deceased dies intestate (no Will) or there is no executor then an administrator, or the person in priority to be the administrator, has the right to possession of the body for the purpose of disposing of the remains. see *Executor*, page 133

Beneficiaries

Notify the beneficiaries. They should each be sent a copy of the Will.

Joint Tenancy: Joint Tenancy with Right of Survivorship

Joint tenancy creates a Right of Survivorship. Under the right of survivorship, the death of one joint tenant automatically transfers the remainder of the property to the survivor(s). In community property states the surviving spouse is usually a joint tenant. It is fairly easy to clear the title by removing the name of the deceased. The executor can do this. see *Joint Tennant*, page 48, 382

Preparation for Burial, Cremation or Alkaline Hydrolysis

See that any **burial instructions** left by the decedent are carried out. Jewish funerals are traditionally performed within 24 hours, provided it is not on a Saturday. You should have located any documents by now that pertain to the person's last wishes. If not, look for paperwork outlining their wishes: cremation, burial or alkaline hydrolysis. Are there any instructions for their death? Are there any pre-paid funeral arraignments? Most are not refundable if not used. see *Prepaid*, page 216

Has a Cemetery Plot has been purchased for Burial or Final Disposition?

Someone needs to look for any paperwork or documentation that would suggest a burial plot has been purchased. Family members tend to follow family traditions. see *Cemetery Plot*, page 172, 313, 415

Has a Burial, Cremation or Alkaline Hydrolysis been Prepaid?

Sometimes a prepaid funeral has been arranged and partially or completely paid for. Sometimes a separate bank account has been set up for this purpose. see *Documents*, page 115 - *Prepaid*, page 216

Take care of Anyone Living with the Deceased

Arrange for their immediate care.

Take care of a surviving Spouse

Arrange for their immediate care.

Take care of Children

Arrange for their immediate care.

Take care of Pets

Find someone to take on the responsibility of permanent care of the deceased person's pets. Arrange for their immediate care.

Service Type

Will there be a service? What type of service: religious, military, fraternal, a Memorial Service with or without the body, a wake, or a graveside service? A service at graveside when there is a cremation is common. Will there be more than one service? etc. see *Funeral Preplan*, page 219

Location of Funeral or Memorial Service

Contact information: name, address, phone number, website (if any) and directions. Will it be at a Church, a Hall or other location?

Make Arrangements for Final Disposition

The executor or next of kin is responsible for payment of the funeral. Most funeral homes expect full payment at the time services are rendered.

Many funeral providers offer various "packages" by bundling common goods and services. When you arrange a funeral, you have the right to buy individual goods and services. You are not required to accept the "package deal" that may include items you do not want. see *Funeral Rule*, page 178, *Costs*, page 165

Burial

Burial Authorization

There is none. The executor has full responsibility with regards to the funeral arrangements and should be named in the Will. If the deceased dies intestate (no Will) or there is no executor then an administrator, or the person in priority to be the administrator, has the right to possession of the body for the purpose of disposing of the remains. This is usually the surviving spouse or next of kin. The Will should state clearly what the deceased wished to be done after they passed. If no funds are available from the estate you are under no obligation to follow these instructions. see *Burial*, page 92

Direct Burial

Select a casket. As cost is usually a concern you may have the funeral home place the deceased in the least expensive casket available or have one shipped to the funeral home from an outside vendor, online or local. Wal-Mart will even do this for you. Then ask for the body to be sent directly to the cemetery for burial. Embalming is not required or necessary. If a substantial refrigeration charge is added check with other funeral service providers. Some may charge less, while others may charge more. **A very dignified Memorial ceremony can be held at any location without the body present**. No service is necessary. see *Direct Burial*, page 95, 337

Grave site, mausoleum, crypt, pallbearers, casket, flowers, memorial book, guest book, funeral home, headstone, grave marker, burial vaults or grave liners, embalming, see *Funeral Goods & Services*, page 165

Arrange for the Cemetery Space if needed

The grave site or cemetery plot can be purchased directly from the Cemetery or from an online source. Many Cemeteries today can take care of the purchase online. If you plan ahead you will not feel so rushed and will be prepared to make a better decision.

Arrange for the Grave Liner, Cemetery Vault if needed

The burial vault, grave liner - concrete box, or burial container prevents ground collapse around the casket and allows easier maintenance of the lawn. Although they are not required by law in most states or localities, they are required by most (but not all) cemeteries. The cost of a grave liner is a few hundred dollars and up to a few thousand dollars. Then you pay a fee to have it lowered into the ground. This is usually another $100. You bury it. You almost never dig it back up. It deteriorates. "Green Funerals" try to limit the amount of material that does not decompose. Purchase the least expensive grave liner that you can find. Plastic and wood are also options. see *Vault*, page 446

Arrange for the Opening and Closing of Cemetery Space

There is a charge for this. The cemetery has to dig the space for the grave and fill it back in. They also charge you for paperwork and removing flowers The usual fee is $350 but the Cemetery can add on over fifty different "services" that you would most likely never need. Just be certain to check all paperwork and look for add on fees. Although most cemeteries and funeral homes are reputable many are not. The Federal Trade Commission (FTC) Funeral Rule holds Funeral Directors and Funeral Homes accountable but not Cemeteries.

There may be reasonable service charges for opening and closing the space. There may also be service fees for opening and closing a mausoleum, crypt, columbarium, niche, Urn garden or other space. Check these charges when you get your itemized good faith estimate from the service provider.

Burial (not direct burial)

Embalming Authorization

This document allows a body to be embalmed by a licensed professional. Embalming is the process of preserving a human body from decomposition. It's usually not required by law except in certain cases. The deceased can usually be placed in refrigeration until the burial. If the funeral home does not have a refrigerated holding room you should look at other funeral homes in the area. Embalming is not required, except in unusual cases when the deceased cannot be buried in a timely fashion. This is can be an extra charge of $800 or more that is not usually needed. see *Embalming*, page 341

Funeral Rule: The Funeral Rule prohibits funeral providers from claiming that any process or product can preserve remains in the grave indefinitely. They may not state that embalming or a particular casket or liner will preserve the body of the deceased for an unlimited time.

Cremation

Direct Cremation

A casket is not necessary. A cardboard container is used for the cremation. There is no requirement that customers hire a funeral home or cemetery to host a memorial service and a burial is optional. A Memorial service can be held at any location. There is usually no viewing, meaning there is no body present. Embalming is not required. see Cremation, page 21, 104, 324

Cremation Authorization

This document permits the crematory to cremate the body, as the process is irreversible. In most states, individuals are allowed to sign their own authorization prior to death. If not, the individual's assigned representative or next-of-kin will be required to sign it. page 324

Temporary Container

The crematory will return the ashes (cremains) in a temporary container. The most common dimensions for this type of container are approximately 8" tall x 4-1/4" deep x 6" wide; stamped "temporary container".

Urn

It is not necessary to purchase an Urn for the Ashes of a loved one. They are available from the service provider or online in many sizes and materials priced from around $75. An Urn can be made of any material. Metal, wood and stone are the most common. Sets of six mini Urns are also available. An Urn from a third party retailer may be purchased and shipped directly to the funeral home. The funeral home may not charge a fee for using these. see *Urn*, page 175, 445

If a Columbarium or Niche is going to be used remember not all Urns will fit inside every Niche. It is important to measure the Niche or Columbarium first. page---319, 401

Who owns cremation ashes? The answer – You can't own them. You may only take possession for their legal disposition.

Columbarium or Niche

If the Urn is to be placed into a columbarium or niche within a cemetery you must first consider the interior dimensions of the niche. Some of the Urns may not fit in every niche, it is important to make that determination prior to purchasing because Urns are generally not returnable. It is not required to place an Urn at a cemetery.

Alkaline Hydrolysis

Authorization

Alkaline hydrolysis disposition is not currently being used in every State in the US. It is considered a more "Green" disposition that reduces the remains to an ash by chemical means and not fire. see *Alkaline Hydrolysis*, page 294

Urn

It is not necessary to purchase an Urn for the Ashes, a white colored dust, of a loved one. They are available from the service provider or online in many sizes and materials priced from around $75. An Urn can be made of any material. Metal, wood and stone are the most common. Sets of six mini Urns are also available. An Urn from a third party retailer may be purchased and shipped directly to the funeral home. The funeral home may not charge a fee for using these. If a Columbarium or Niche is going to be used remember not all Urns will fit inside every Niche. It is important to measure the Niche or Columbarium first. see *Funeral Rule*, page 178

Columbarium or Niche

If the Urn is to be placed into a columbarium or niche within a cemetery you must first consider the interior dimensions of the niche. Some of the urns may not fit in every niche, it is important to make that determination prior to purchasing because Urns are generally not returnable. It is not required to place an Urn at a cemetery. page---319, 401

After the type of Disposition is chosen we need to transport the deceased and continue the process.

Disposition Permission

This document releases a body for disposition either in the form of burial or cremation. The document is signed by a medical professional or a medical examiner.

Deceased Transportation

This refers primarily to the transportation needed after the loved one passes away. Ideally, arrange direct transportation to the funeral home in charge of the services. In cases where distance or other factors prohibit this, a second transfer must be made later. see *Transportation*, page 259

Vital Statistics

Personal Information:

Finish gathering personal information of the deceased. Locate the executor or administrator, and attorney (if the decedent had an attorney). Locate the Trustee if there is a Trust. It is the executor's responsibility to send the trustee a copy of the will and see that they are making progress in the administration and distribution of the Trust. see *Vital Statistics*, page 269

Safe Deposit Boxes

Although many people keep their Will in their Safe Deposit Box it is not a good place for a will because it limits access when someone dies. see *Safe Deposit Box*, page 79

Medication and Medical Equipment

A health care provider may help with the safe disposal of medication and medical equipment, but it is the family's responsibility to do so. Some medical equipment may be rented and you will need to have the company pick it up. Collect any deposits that were placed on the equipment and close these accounts.

Attorney, notify

If the deceased did not have an attorney you may want to retain an attorney and possibly an accountant to provide any necessary advice or assistance to begin the probate procedures for any assets that were not titled in a Trust. A competent estate attorney will generally walk you through the closing of the estate. You will still do most of the work to keep costs down. Initial consultation is usually free. see *Attorney*, page 71

Clergy, notify

Did the decedent have any affiliation with a religious institution? Often a phone number can be found in an address book or in Contacts on a cellphone.

Employer, notify

Notify the employer's personnel department. Do not forget Wages, vacation time or other benefits owed to the deceased.

Service type and Location should have already been decided

Location of Funeral or Memorial Service

Contact information: name, address, phone number, website (if any) and directions. Time and place of Visitation and Funeral Service. Will it be at a Church, a Hall or other location? Does anyone need a ride?

Service Type

Will there be a service? What type of service: Religious, Military, Home Service or Fraternal? A Memorial Service with or without the body? A Wake or a Graveside Service? A service at graveside when there is a cremation is common. Will there be more than one service?

Flowers or Donations

Would you like floral displays or donations made to a charity of your choice instead? If you would rather have donations place this information in the Obituary. Also place this information in the Funeral program if you decide to have one made up. List the Church, religious organization or other charities that will benefit from memorial donations in your name. see *Flowers*, page 351

Obituary

The funeral notice should be sent to the newspaper four days before the funeral is to take place, to allow for next-day publishing. Call the local paper and place a notice in the obituary column. see *Obituary*, page 405

Eulogy

A formal speech praising a person who has recently died given by a member of the family, clergy, friend or business associate of the deceased. Eulogies may be given as part of funeral services. Provide information for the Eulogy. Prepare the Eulogy. see *Eulogy*, page :345

Epitaph

An Epitaph is the inscription on a person's headstone or plaque. Prepare an epitaph. Since this will be close to permanent it would be best to get a consensus as to what the Epitaph should be. see *Epitaph*, page 344

Casket

Select a casket. You may rent a casket for the viewing at a Funeral home and then use a much less costly casket for the actual burial. Some very nice caskets can be found online at 50% off the retail price with free next day delivery. see *Casket*, page 26, 167, 305

A Casket from a third party retailer may be purchased and shipped directly to the funeral home. The funeral home may not charge a fee for using these. see *Funeral Rule*, page 178

You may also rent a casket for a graveside service with a Cremation. The deceased is then removed before cremation. The actual Cremation may be done with a very dignified simple low cost container.

Vault, Grave Liner or Concrete Box, Outer Burial Container

Most states do not have laws requiring an outer burial container. The cemetery may require this because it does help prevent the ground from collapsing around the grave site. Also the human body has lots of hazardous materials that need to be contained and it makes for easier maintenance of the grounds. A burial vault completely contains the casket, while a grave liner generally covers only the top and sides of the casket and allows the bottom of the casket to be in contact with the earth. Purchased online it may be sent directly to the cemetery, but because cemeteries are not covered by the FTC's Funeral Rule, the cemetery may charge a fee for using a burial vault or grave liner you purchased elsewhere.

The cost of a grave liner is a few hundred dollars and up to a few thousand dollars. Then you pay a fee to have it lowered into the ground. This is usually another $100. You bury it. You almost never dig it back up. It deteriorates. Purchase the least expensive grave liner that you can find. Plastic and wood are also options. see *Vault*, page 174, 446

Urn

It is not necessary to purchase an Urn for the cremated Ashes of a loved one. They are available online in many sizes and materials priced from around $75. An Urn can be made of any material. Metal, wood and stone are the most common. Sets of six mini Urns are also available. An Urn from a third party retailer may be purchased and shipped directly to the funeral home. The funeral home may not charge a fee for using these. If a Columbarium or Niche is going to be used remember not all Urns will fit inside every Niche. It is important to measure the Niche or Columbarium first. page 175, 445

Niche

A Niche is an opening in a wall made especially for placing Urns containing cremated ashes. These are usually found in a cemetery. It is important to measure the Niche first because not all Urns will fit the opening.

Clothing

Select clothing and undergarments for the deceased. If they are too large the professionals setting up the Funeral Service will adjust them.

Jewelry and Glasses

Select these for the deceased. Are glasses to be worn or not? Both the jewelry and glasses may be returned before burial. Make your needs known to the funeral director. If you have any difficulties call your local Congressman. It is simple: Google (your city), (state) congressman. Call the phone number listed. They will be more than happy to help you in your time of need.

Cosmetology and Hairstyle

Select these for the deceased. Available services and pricing will vary from area to area.

Clergy at Funeral or Memorial Service

Select the Clergy and scripture readings for the service.

Music

Although you may not have direct input from your loved one regarding their wishes, take the time to gather information from other family members or close friends. They may be able to remember a favorite song or reading.

Select the Music for the service and the Organist, Pianist, or Vocalist. The cost of services can range from $50 to the more standard $150 for vocalist or pianist and up to thousands of dollars.

Register

A Register is a book made available for recording the names of people visiting the Funeral Home, Memorial Service or other Visitation to pay their respects to the deceased.

Memorial Cards

These go by many names: Memorial Tribute Cards, Memorial Funeral Cards, Remembrance Cards, Traditional Religious Prayer Cards also known as Mass Cards or Holy Cards. see *Funeral Goods & Services*, page 165

Floral Arrangements

To express your condolences, it's customary to send flowers to the funeral home, or, depending on the religion of the deceased, a Mass card. Donations to a charitable organization in lieu of flowers may have been requested. This should be noted in the Obituary. see *Flowers*, page 351

Food Baskets

Food baskets sent to the home of the deceased are most welcome at this time. It would also be kind to bring over casseroles or other easily prepared dishes so the bereaved has one less thing to worry about while they are mourning their loss.

Funeral Coach

Also called a Hearse. A funeral coach is used for transporting the casket in processions between the funeral home and the cemetery. There is only a front seat that can accommodate the driver and the funeral director.

Limousine

A luxury sedan that usually has a lengthened wheelbase and is driven by a chauffeur. It is used to transport family members in funeral processions from the funeral home to the cemetery.

Funeral Service Vehicles

These may include sedans or vans that are generally less expensive options to using a funeral coach and limousine.

Vehicle for Pallbearers

Often the pallbearers will be asked to ride in one of the vehicles driven by the funeral home staff to ensure they all arrive at the same time the deceased arrives at their destination. In this case they are transported in a limousine or service vehicle which follows closely behind the hearse.

Funeral Car list for Family and Friends

This is simply a list of which family members and / or friends will ride together in the limousine or service vehicles. Due to limited seating it is common for just a few family members to ride while the others follow behind in their own vehicles. If you are a family member or close friend get to the funeral home or church at least forty-five minutes before the service starts. You will begin to park behind the funeral limousine and others will be lined up in the order in which they arrive.

Transportation for Family Guests

Transportation and Lodging for out of town guests should be arranged at least two days before the funeral for family members and close friends. Contact names and numbers of local transportation companies and hotels or motels along with directions should be written down.

Catering

Catering for the funeral should be scheduled a few days before the service to allow enough time for food to be prepared and brought to the facility. Certain religions have dietary restrictions. If you are not certain speak with a close family member to be certain the food ordered is in accordance with the deceased's beliefs. All catering should be delivered and set up at least one hour before the funeral begins so that catering personnel are finished and out of the way.

Extra Chairs:

Getting extra chairs is easily arranged. There are usually different styles and prices. You can rent them from a caterer or a chair rental. They will deliver and pick up.

Clothing for you and Minor Children

Just take the time to make certain clothing is neat and clean.

Visitation or Viewing

Visitation or Viewing is usually held the night before or immediately prior to the funeral service. This is when people pay their respects to the grieving family in the form of a visit. This will allow friends and acquaintances to offer condolences to the family. Depending on the family's religion or heritage, this can either be done at home or at the funeral home. The casket may be open or closed. see *Visitation*, page 448

Wake

Traditionally, a wake is held on the night before a funeral. This is a gathering of family and friends to honor and recognize the deceased. Schedule a wake and visitation one day before the funeral service. see *Wake*, page 449

Funeral

Disposition and a Memorial Service can be two separate events if no viewing is involved. If a viewing is involved, the average funeral takes place within 2-4 days of death.

The Funeral can be held in many different places depending on the family's heritage and religion. It is most often held at a place of worship or the funeral home.

Pallbearers and Ushers

This is one of the highest honors that can be bestowed upon a family member or close friend.

Honorary Pallbearers do not actively assist in carrying the casket. They usually walk in front of the casket.

Pallbearers may or may not actually carry the casket. They may walk alongside a wheeled dolly carrying the casket. If you are selected and have a concern due to your age or health, just ask. List the names, addresses and phone numbers of selected pallbearers, honorary pallbearers and ushers. Most people will not need all three. see *Pallbearers*, page 411

Graveside Service

A graveside service may be held at the grave site just prior to burial of a casket or urn. The service may occur after or in place of a funeral service.

Some families will leave before the casket is lowered into the ground, while some prefer to stay. This is an individual choice.

After the service: it is common to gather at the home of a friend or family member. This is generally less somber and everyone has a chance to talk. Food is usually provided by friends or family members in a buffet style. Sometimes it is catered. If it is catered have the service workers set up an hour before the expected arrival of guests so they can be finished and out of the way.

Memorial Service or Tribute Service

At a memorial or tribute service, a casket or urn is usually not present. It can vary in ceremony and procedure according to community and religious affiliations. If the decedent's remains are present at a service held more than a few days after death it is almost always necessary to preserve the body through embalming. This is one reason a casket or urn is usually not present.

Clergy, Musicians, and those who have planned to read something or speak should be noted. List the names, addresses and phone numbers.

To Do Last Day of the Funeral

Food

Confirm any arraignments that have been made for food if an after service gathering has been planned.

Services

Confirm the funeral home or religious organization has everything in order, including any graveside service.

Honorariums

A payment given to a professional person for services for which fees are not legally or traditionally required. Arrange payment for the remaining honorariums not covered as well as catering services, and child or pet care that has been provided. If these have been paid by any other (such as the funeral home), be certain they are listed on the final bill.

Dispose of the Flowers when the service is over

Flowers may be given to a church or loved ones may be able to take them if they would like. Sometimes flower disposal is included in the fee for opening and closing the gravesite.

Check on the Family

In the weeks after the funeral, check on the immediate family members to see if they now need help for the short term? Knowing that you care will mean a lot to them.

Thank-You Cards

Although it is not necessary to send Thank-You Cards for a funeral, you may find it appropriate to send special thanks. A quick personal Thank-You Card will be appreciated. Send one to each Pallbearer, Honorary Pallbearer, Usher, Clergy, those who made donations and those who were really there to assist you in your time of need.

After the Service the Executor will need to finish the process of
Administering the Decedent's Estate and
Clear the Estate

These duties will be accomplished in a similar order as listed here. If you do things in a different order, that is perfectly fine. This list is to be used as a guide to help lead you through the process. You may not need to do everything listed here and you may also need to consult with a competent attorney to process legal disposition that is beyond the scope of this book. If you think you need help, then there is no embarrassment in getting qualified help. There is still a lot to accomplish.

Many things are listed above and should have been accomplished by now.

The Will should have been located by now

Death Certificate

Make certain someone obtained **certified copies of the death certificate.** If no one has done this, it needs to be done right now as it may be time consuming and they are necessary before other steps can be taken. Twelve copies are usually not too many. Twenty copies may be necessary. see *Death Certificate*, page 329

Start the Probate Process

The family will usually spend the first week handling the burial or cremation arrangements. You may file a petition to start the Probate process at any time after death. If it has not been done by now someone needs to file. It is usually the executor named in the Will that presents the decedent's Will for probate and at the same time qualifies as executor.

If you feel that you need help, meet with an estate lawyer who will further guide you through the process. We would at least speak with a competent estate attorney. The initial consultation is usually FREE and the advice could be a big help. Do not sign anything until you have a chance to think about it and talk with family members. This whole process of clearing the estate may take as long as one year. You have time to think, plan and make good decisions.

The person having custody of a Will must deliver the Will to the clerk of court or the executor named in the Will within thirty days of the testator's death. It may take one week to several weeks before a Judge issues an order appointing an Executor. see *Probate*, page 241

Executor, Personal Representative, Administrator, Exectrix, Court Appointed Administrator

An Executor is someone who administers an estate of a person who left a valid Will. If a person dies intestate, that is, without a Will, then the Personal Representative or Administrator will be appointed by the court. An Exectrix is a female executor.

No matter what they are called, they all oversee the disposition of property and possessions of a deceased person. An executor is entrusted with the large responsibility of making sure a person's last wishes are granted with regards to the disposition of their property and possessions. They identify the estate's assets, pay off its debts and then distribute whatever is left to the rightful heirs and beneficiaries.

Intestate: If the decedent dies without a Will (intestate) certain persons may qualify as the Personal Representative. see *Executor*, page 133

Notify the Executor, Personal Representative or Administrator of the Deceased's Estate

When the executor has been appointed by the court or named in the will they should be notified immediately. They will either accept this responsibility, decline taking on this responsibility or look into this further before deciding. Sometimes they have no choice and must accept this responsibility. Sometimes there is a more than one executor or an alternate executor has been named if for any reason the primary executor has predeceased the testator or must decline. see *Executor: No Thank-you*, page 144

When an executor has been located and they accept the position it now becomes their legal responsibility to administer the estate.

>**The Executor** (Personal Representative) may be held responsible for any damages they cause. You may be liable to the estate, the beneficiaries or both.
>
>**The Executor** must make rational decisions. They have a legal fiduciary responsibility to act with utmost honesty, impartiality, and scrupulousness on behalf of the deceased and the estate's beneficiaries. For an in-depth explanation of many of the executors responsibilities see *Executor*, page 133

I was named as the Executor. Do I have to accept this responsibility?

>Anyone can appoint you to be their Executor without asking your permission. The executor is named in the Will or if there is no Will, appointed by the court.
>
>In all likelihood the state will not force someone to act as executor or Personal Administrator for the deceased. They will use the Probate Court to handle the disposition of the deceased's estate. In this way they simply tax the estate for any and all "fees" due. This can change if the named executor is legally libel for some or all of the decedent's debt. Sometimes there is a more than one executor or an alternate executor has been named if for any reason the primary executor has predeceased the testator or must decline.
>
>Are you legally obligated to administer the decedent's estate because you are liable for the decedent's debt? Are you the decedent's spouse? Did you cosign a mortgage, a loan contract or in any way link your assets to the deceased through a business? Are you listed on a joint account? This may be a good time to speak with a qualified attorney because the laws governing these situations change frequently and can vary from state to state or even within a state.
>
>It may be an honor to be named someone's executor, but it is also a lot of administrative work that needs to be done properly. Most executors choose to

work with a competent estate attorney. This makes things much more manageable.

For a more in-depth look at declining the role of executor or personal representative see *Executor: No Thank-you*, page 144.

Most states require the Executor to Post a Surety Bond covering their actions.

This requirement can sometimes be waived if the Will states that the nominated Personal Representative or executor may serve without bond. Sometimes the state will require a bond anyway.

The Court has the power to remove and replace any Personal Representative or Executor for any cause deemed sufficient.

Letters of Administration

Letters of administration are a document issued by the probate court to authorize the administrator of an estate when there is no Will. It is a good idea to request additional copies of the Letters of Administration from the court.

Letters of Testamentary

Letters of testamentary are a document issued by the probate court to authorize the executor of an estate when there is a Will. It is a good idea to request additional copies of the Letters of Testamentary from the court you will most likely need them.

The Executor or Personal Representative needs to keep Accurate Records.

Record Everything: The executor should get a note book and keep a record of everything they do while administrating the estate. Any type of note book is fine. Keep copies of everything. Keep all receipts. Record the time and date of everything you do for the estate. This can be very informal. An example would be: June 14, 2013, morning, (name) and I had the collection of "rare" stamps looked at by (name) at the library. He has collected stamps for over forty years and told us the stamps are only worth $20 - $30 dollars for the whole collection. Someone sometime may want to know what happened to the "rare" stamps they used to look at when they were nine or ten years old. They were from all over the world and must be worth a fortune.

Photograph Everything Else: Be serious. Record EVERYTHING. Expect the best from people but prepare for the worst. There is a good reason why you do not visit some of your relatives very often.

Beneficiaries

All beneficiaries should be notified and receive a copy of the Will. This is done by the executor if someone else has not already done so. However, it is still the executor's responsibility to be certain they all have been notified. Keep records of who was notified, how they received a copy of the Will and when were they notified. You may send copies of the Will Certified Mail, Return Receipt Requested for about $5.50 each. The post office will have the recipient sign for the envelope and return the signed receipt to you or whatever person and address you choose. see *Beneficiaries*, page 87

Take Care of Anyone Living with the Deceased

Arrange for their immediate care. Keep a record of what was done. Keep receipts. Record any expenses so you may be reimbursed later on.

Take Care of the surviving Spouse

Arrange for their immediate care. Keep a record of what was done. Keep all receipts. Record any expenses so you may be reimbursed later on.

Take care of Children

Arrange for their immediate care. Was a guardian named in the Will or appointed by the court? Keep a record of what was done. Keep all receipts. Record any expenses so you may be reimbursed later on.

Take care of Pets

Arrange for their immediate care. Keep a record of what was done. Keep all receipts. Record any expenses so you may be reimbursed later on.

Gather all Vital Statistics

Begin or finish listing all vital statistics. This should include, father's name, mother's name, their place of birth if known and their country of origin. Mother's maiden name. Unions and organizations the deceased was a member of. This all may come in handy later on if you need to search for unpaid insurance benefits or wonder about filing a claim. Collect as much information as you can now because over the next year people may not be as cooperative. see *Vital Statistics*, page 269

Medical Equipment

Return rentals, collect deposits. Secure if owned, inventory and set a value. see *Medicare* and *Medicaid*, page 207, 392, 443

Digital Executor

Has a Digital Executor been appointed? In almost all cases Digital Executors have no legal authority but they are often very useful and necessary. The executor or personal representative has the legal responsibility for disposition of the estate. The Digital Executor helps with Digital Assets: online storage "in the cloud", online shopping sites, websites, blogs, online banking sites, CD's, DVD's (some contain important documents and may be password protected or encrypted. There may also be videos of other assets, movie videos, mp3 files, mp4 files, cell phones, iPhones, iPods, PSP, PS3, Wii, Xbox, PC, passwords, encryption, challenge questions, social networking websites. Digital Assets can be worth thousands or millions of dollars although most have no real monetary worth. All digital Assets must be protected and distributed. The Digital Executor can be very helpful. Most

Americans have a digital presence that needs to be located, collected, appraised, and protected.

The idea of a Digital Executor is fairly new and state law has not been updated in most cases. This means the Executor or Personal Representative still has all legal responsibility for the dispensation of the estate. They may not know how to find or even access Digital Assets worth hundreds of thousands of dollars. They may not even be aware off their worth. Today something as simple (to the untrained) as an "app" could be worth millions of dollars ONLY if it is turned into a more liquid asset quickly. If you have Digital Assets it is important to protect them with a Digital Administrator that could possibly act as executor of the estate. In any case if we all have digital assets the executor needs to access this information. The personal representative or executor must be made aware of the Digital Executor. If the Digital Executor is named a beneficiary, the Executor is obligated by law to inform them of the death and send them a copy of the will. see *Digital Assets*, page 250, 333

Digital Assets

Locate all Passwords & Usernames, Keys and Combinations.

Locate ALL computers, hard drives, cell phones, answering machines, Wii, PlayStations, laptops, tablets, eBook readers, hard drives, thumb drives and digital cameras. Copiers are very important as they contain very sensitive information in memory. Collect ALL CD's DVD's do not assume it is a movie just because someone printed "Movie" on the disk with a marker. These will all have to be viewed by someone. They may contain ANYTHING! They may contain video of hidden collections, documents or a whole other life no one ever knew about. They may contain maps and directions to hidden treasures that the loved one was keeping safe for their beneficiary(s) see *Digital Assets*, page 250, 333

Prevent Identity Theft

Identity theft is becoming more common today. There are many simple things that can be done to help protect the estate and surviving loved ones. Do not give away computers, copiers, cell phones, thumb drives, passwords and user names until the proper time, if ever. All digital assets should be protected. You do not want to just delete everything. First it really does not delete and second it may be a valuable asset. see *Identity Theft*, page 190, 246, 375

Property still has to be Secured and Protected

Locate all Real Property

Do not stop with the obvious. Many people own homes, condominiums, time shares, business interests, etc. in other states. It may have been left to the decedent in someone's Will and the paperwork was just placed in a closet or drawer.

Secure All Property: Real Property and Digital Property

Thieves: People are not allowed to just take things and load up the car or the pickup truck with a few mementos. It is the responsibility of the executor or personal administrator to secure and protect the assets. If you are the only one available it is your moral responsibility (and possibly legal responsibility) to secure the personal property for the executor to disburse. If you need to, call the local police department for help.

Personal items holding little monetary value are often distributed outside of probate. Before the executor may distribute these he/she should check to be certain this is even allowed in the state where the estate exists. If there is any kind of dispute concerning any item, no matter what the perceived value is, the item should be held for probate. The Executor, Personal Administrator, Administrator, Exectrix, etc. can be sued later in court for not performing their duty. By allowing the disputed item to go through probate you will get a definitive answer about who now owns and will take legal possession of the item. This is easy to do. Do not allow someone to talk you out of this. They will most likely be the very same one who comes back later to dispute your distribution of the property.

Apartments: If the decedent lived in a rental residence, terminate contracts, and cancel related payments including rental insurance. Arrange for personal belongings to be moved to a storage facility until they are distributed. Turn off electric, water, cable, satellite, cell phones, internet connection. Cancel magazine subscriptions and garbage collection. Have all mail forwarded. see *Mail*, page 390

Home Ownership: If the decedent lived in a residence that they owned, keep making payments on services necessary to maintain the property: electric, gas, water, lawn care, pest control, garbage collection. Pay all insurance premiums, taxes (state, local and federal tax). Decide what the property is worth. An appraisal may be necessary but websites like Redfin.com, Sawbuck.com, Trulia.com, and Zillow.com, can be enough to get you started. Find out what is owed on the property. Decide what you will do with the family residence if there is no direct survivor. Consult with family members and heirs because someone may have very strong feelings about keeping the home within the family and will not want it sold to a stranger. see *Mortgage*, page 210, 444

Joint Ownership: If there is joint ownership you will need to file a death certificate with the county where the real-estate is owned to clear the title of the deceased's name and register the survivor as the sole owner.

Locate all Assets

Continue to locate and secure all assets. see *Assets*, page 5, 41, 57, 75

Liquid Assets

A liquid asset is any asset that can be converted into cash quickly. This can include but is not limited to: cash, bank accounts, checks, easily-convertible securities, accounts receivable, precious metals, jewelry and some collections.

Bank Accounts

Locate and secure all bank accounts, checking and savings accounts, money market accounts, safe deposit boxes, accounts set up specifically for the payment of funds to provide funeral services (Totten Trust).

Totten trust: this is just a regular bank account with a designated "pay on death" inheritor. When the account is opened a friend, relative (most likely named as executor) is named as the beneficiary. Whoever opens the account can also close it at any time for any reason. They may also change banks and or change beneficiaries. The beneficiary does not need to know about the arrangement, and the depositor is entitled to deposit and withdraw funds from the account as they see fit. The idea is when the person dies the beneficiary collects the account balance and pays for the funeral expenses. This can work out very well if all parties are informed and kept up to date. see *Totten Trust*, page 437

Insurance

All Life Insurance Policies held by the deceased must be located. Automobile insurance policies may contain coverage if the death was the result of an automobile accident. If the death was accidental, there may be policies from a union, organization or other that cover accidental death. see *Insurance*, page 198

Locate any Property held in Trust

Only property owned, in the name of the Trust is subject to the terms of the Trust. If there is a living trust, confirm that the Trustee has been notified and is making progress in the administration and distribution of the Trust. A simple phone call is all that is needed. Log the date, time and major points of the conversation in your executor's notebook. Any notebook used for this purpose is fine. Get in the habit of keeping good records. This can be like a: "Dear Diary". What you did today in the name of the estate, name names and contact information as necessary. What was said and what was agreed on informally. You will need this later. You will need this later. Write that down. see *Trust*, page 439

Locate Important Documents

Put all documents, bills, vital statistics, bank account information, appraisals, contracts, real estate titles, vehicle titles, estate documents, passwords and their user names, keys, etc. in a safe and secure place. These need to be protected from fire, flood and theft. They do not all have to be kept in the same place. Just be certain you have access and they are safe and secure.

Prepare an Inventory of the Decedent's Estate.

You may have to use court approved forms. List the Asset, purchase price if known, current value and ownership. Is there a joint survivor? List the beneficiary if known and any other information that may seem interesting or necessary. It is much easier to add the details now than to do this again later on.

One person should never do the inventory by themself. Have a family member or heir assist in this. This helps to document accountability and limits the liability of a single person placing a value on assets. Keep family members and heirs informed about your progress and how items will be distributed. If the item must go through probate, say so. If an item needs to be appraised, say so. Your goal is to be fair, impartial and find out when someone may have a dispute over a certain item so you can deal with it. It is better to deal with any situations while you still have time and people are most cooperative.

Bills still have to be paid

Pay all bills necessary to maintain or secure a residence.

Receive payments due the estate, including interest, dividends, unpaid wages, vacation pay and other company benefits see *Debt*, page 108

Locate all Bills

Someone needs to keep paying the bills. Collect all bills and receipts. Buy a file folder, store both paid and unpaid bills in a safe place, you will need to secure these. You will need account numbers and contact information. Include all medical records and medical bills and receipts. It is not uncommon to be billed more than once for the exact same service. Someone will have to check all of these because they will have to be paid, but not twice.

If you are the executor, now is when you need to determine if the assets are worth keeping. Remember to keep all receipts and an accounting of the assets. Any beneficiary, heir, or the probate court can legally request and expect to receive an accounting of all assets from the time of death to the time of distribution of property. see *Debt*, page 108

Always record expenses YOU paid using personal funds. These charges can add up fast. Keep all receipts in a file folder. You need to be reimbursed by the estate IF it has any money to reimburse you. It may be insolvent and may not be able to repay you. Think about this before you pay out-of-pocket expenses.

Set up a Bank Account in the name of the Estate

An estate checking account needs to be set up to pay bills and keep an accounting of what was paid, for how much and when. Your month end bank statement should do this.

Notify all Known and Unknown Creditors

The probate court should supply the notification requirements for all known and unknown creditors. This may involve posting in newspapers or public posting at the courthouse. In some jurisdictions you must mail notices to creditors you know about and also mail the notice to beneficiaries and heirs. You may be able to find this information on the probate court website for the county in which you are distributing the estate. Google (name of the county where the probate court is located) (the state) probate.

Notification of all Known and Unknown Creditors starts a statute of limitation for future claims from creditors. You should start this process as soon as you can.

Lawsuits

Determine if there are any actions pending on behalf of the decedent. Also determine if the decedent's estate has an action for wrongful death of the decedent.

Locate all Storage

Pay ongoing storage claims until the contents can be inventoried and their value is determined. We have all seen the TV show "Antiques Roadshow". One small painting that looks like my grandma painted it after she had a few too many beers could be worth thousands of dollars.

Collect all Personal Identification Cards

Collect and protect all "plastic" cards: Driver License, Credit Cards, Insurance Cards, Membership Cards, Union Cards, Employment ID's, Hospital Cards, and Medical Cards. A more complete list can be found on see Document List, *Plastic Cards*, page 126

Safe Deposit Box

Locate all safe deposit boxes. The contents need to be inventoried and a value has to be placed on each item if it is to be distributed. All contents may not have to go through probate. Some of the contents may pass to a surviving spouse automatically. Is the safe deposit box in only on name? Is the deceased the sole owner of the contents? You may find it convenient to speak with a competent estate attorney.

Never check the contents of a safe deposit box by yourself. Protect yourself and inventory all assets with a family member or an heir. Make a written inventory and photograph all items. If it is in a safe deposit box, it is being protected for a reason. Photograph all sides of an item, especially the bottom where you may (or may not) find trademarks that can lead to authentication. Allow yourself enough time to do a proper inventory, photographic inventory and written inventory.

Do not leave anyone alone with the safe deposit box and the contents while you go back to the car because you forgot something. You are legally responsible and financially libel, not the family member or heir who may be worried someone else may get that nice broach with the pretty green and white stones.

Locate all Photographs

It is just easier to locate and set these aside while you are collecting other information and documents. Do not forget photo CD's and DVD's. Digital photos stored online. Make a note of their location and access information. Remember, just because a CD or DVD says "Vacation Photos" it may actually contain banking information or other digital assets.

Record the Will

Take the Will to the County Court of the deceased's primary residence. This should be done within thirty days of the death. page 453

Appraisals

Appraisals may be needed for art or collections to ascertain if any estate taxes are due. Collections of types of rope may be interesting but have no real monetary value. You can usually find out by doing a little research online. If you have a collection of 45 rpm Records and one just happens to be an original Elvis test audition, you just may have something worth a whole lot of money.

Business Ownership

Hopefully business ownership issues, continuation or liquidation, continuity issues, management issues, where the legal paperwork is located, passwords, combinations, key codes, digital assets, bank accounts, etc., was taken care of before the individual passed away. Preplanning can save everyone so much time, money and aggravation. If you are reading this and still have time; Please start making preparations now. This is just good business. Google: estate plan, business ownership for areas to look at. see *Business*, page 98

Decedent's Business

If the decedent owned a business, then steps must be taken to preserve and protect the business. What type of business structure is it? LLC, Corporation, Partnership? Some business structures are simple and even have "Rights of

Survivorship" where the spouse may have been named as a partner. In a community property state the spouse may have specific rights. This is where things can become very complicated very quickly. Now may be a good time to speak with a competent estate lawyer. Someone needs to continue running the business. Someone needs to protect and secure the business assets. Business issues involving an estate are beyond the scope of this book but you now know this is a good time to seek help from a competent estate attorney.

All financial institutions must be contacted to obtain a date of death value for assets located at the institution. Appraisals may need to be made to determine date of death values. If assets held by the estate after the date of death increase in value, taxes may have to be paid on profits earned by the estate. If it appears there will be an estate income tax due then the non-probate assets will also need to have their date of death values established. *Business*, page 98

Joint Survivor

The joint survivor still has access to accounts held jointly. These may be bank accounts, checking and savings accounts, money market accounts, etc. The survivor can usually remove the name of the deceased with a simple form and the death certificate of the deceased. Property held in joint tenancy, tenancy by the entirety, or community property with right of survivorship, almost always passes automatically to the survivor when one of the original owners dies. This will usually allow bank accounts, real estate, vehicles, and other property (especially in community property states) to pass to the survivor.

The titles of property held jointly are most often cleared with a minimum of paperwork and a copy of the death certificate.

If accounts are NOT jointly owned it is usually best to freeze these accounts to limit access. Check on all accounts from time to time to insure no one is tampering with them.

If an account is in a Trust check with customer service at the bank and ask what needs to be done.

Credit cards that are not joint accounts should be closed. The balance generally needs to be paid first to close the account. If this is the case request that they account be frozen. If they say this cannot be done have them change the account number. If they refuse simply call the customer service number found on the back of the credit card and tell them you lost the credit card and need a new account number. Check the card statements to see if any reoccurring bills are paid automatically, such as online services or movie sites. You may have Digital Assets stored online that could be worth (really they could be worth millions of dollars in rare instances) so be careful and seek out competent advice before closing these and wiping them out. Yes, you may ask your twelve year old nephew, but if he does not also have a business degree you may need more help. see *Digital Assets*, page 40, 250, 333

Immediately notify financial institutions if there is a concern about fraud on any account. The phone number can usually be found on the back of the credit card or online.

Notify Social Security

Make application for the social security death benefit. You may either do this yourself or ask the funeral home to do it for you. see *Social Security*, page 254, 428. http://www.ssa.gov/pubs/10084.html/

Notify any other Veteran or Government Agencies see *Veterans*, page 263

Notify the Post Office

The U.S. Postal Service has change of address cards that may be filled out.

A Change of Address (COA) request must be submitted by the addressee or by someone authorized to file on behalf of the addressee. When submitting a COA request, please note the following:

The person who submits this COA request states that he or she is the person, executor, guardian, authorized officer, or agent of the person for whom mail would be forwarded under this request form.

Anyone intentionally submitting false or inaccurate information on a COA request form is subject to punishment by fines or imprisonment or both under Sections 2, 1001, 1702 and 1708 of Title 18, United States Code (U.S.C.).

Transfer Real Estate

You need to file a death certificate with the local public land records showing that one of the owners has died and the surviving owner is now the sole owner of the property. This may be complex enough to warrant the use of a competent estate attorney.

Transfer Motor Vehicle Titles

Check with the State Department of Motor Vehicles (The State in which the deceased held a driver license) website. Use the "search" option for the website and search "death". In some states, if the Transfer on Death (TOD) Beneficiary accepts ownership and transfers ownership to another person, **two transfer fees** may be due.

In some cases to add a TOD beneficiary, the registered owner only needs to complete the new registered owner section on the back of the vehicle/vessel title. Check with the Department of Motor Vehicles website for the state in question for up to date procedures.

Investigate the Validity of All claims (if any) Against the Estate

It is now up to the executor or personal representative to determine what bills need to be paid. What bills can be satisfied in other ways. For example if you have a piece of property or a vehicle that is worth far less than what is owed and it is part of the estate. If there were no cosigners or others accepting responsibility for the debt then the family or heirs are usually not libel for the debt. If no heir or family member wants to take on this debt for sentimental reasons then there is probably no reason to continue making payments. This becomes the lenders problem and they would most likely pursue payment from the estate.

A large obligation, such as a home that is "underwater" may place the estate into insolvency. This simply means the estate has no money to pay all of the debt. Could a family member assume the note? Not all lenders allow this, but times are changing. This would be a good time to consult with a competent estate attorney. They will be paid by the estate. If there is no money, they will not be paid and will more than likely give you a lot of advice and help, just to line up business from surviving family members who are in need of estate planning. You should most likely take advantage of this now. You do not need to go through this again, and again.

A home headed for foreclosure should be dealt with BEFORE the individual passes. Spend some time. Make some plans and you may be able to separate it from a future estate.

There is a Statute of Limitation for claims from creditors.

Pay any Funeral Bills, outstanding Debts, and Valid Claims

Debts due an executor or personal representative generally may not be put ahead of other debts. Some states require that within a specific time frame (90 days seems to be average) the executor must file a claim against the estate, just like everyone else, to be paid from the estate. Their debt is usually not entitled to preference over others of the same class.

When a personal representative or executor receives a claim they may allow or disallow the claim. If they do nothing this is usually the same as allowing the claim. If the claimant disagrees they will usually pursue payment with the help of an attorney. When Closing an Estate Claims are usually paid in an order of priority. see *Priority for Debt*, page 110

Pay the Expenses of Administrating the Estate

This will most likely include expenses that needed to be paid before the estate could be opened. Funeral bills, utilities, property taxes, insurance, and storage fees, travel expenses, airfare, meals, lodging, car rental, office supplies, cost of documents, etc.

Administration Fees and Executor Fees

Pay the fees of the Executor and Attorney. Sometimes the Executor needs the money right away to pay for funeral expenses or other fees and expenses.

All Taxes Need to be Paid in Full or otherwise Dismissed

see *Taxes*, page 433

Distribute the Inheritance to the Beneficiaries in accordance with the instructions provided in the deceased's Will

This is the very last step in the process after everything else is paid. With good estate planning that is completed long before death, this process can be streamlined and less costly to the beneficiaries. Be responsible in life and in death.

Often by this time in the process, there is nothing left to distribute and even some of the families expenses cannot be repaid from the estate. An expensive item that has a lot of debt attached may place the estate in insolvency if claims are filled against the estate to pursue payment. If no claims were filled or the claims were filled after the **Statute of Limitation for claims from creditors** has passed, the estate may no longer be libel for payment. If this situation pertains to you, now would be a very good time to speak with a competent estate attorney.

Distribute Personal Property

Personal property includes items that belonged solely to the deceased. In a community property state these may directly pass to the surviving spouse. If you have any doubt as to the ownership of these items they should be probated to ascertain who now owns them. This may be a good time to seek legal advice from a competent estate attorney. These items could include season tickets, gun collections, real estate, jewelry, blogs, digital assets, inventions, patents, works of art etc. These items need to be disbursed by the executor.

Personal Property Memorandum

There may or may not be a Personal Property Memorandum that determines who gets what from the estate. All items may or may not be listed in the Will. The Probate Court may not have ruled on an item. If necessary submit the item for probate. To close the estate all items still need to be distributed and accounted for in a fair and just manner. If there is a surviving spouse it is most likely all personal property becomes theirs. If there are no guide lines then it becomes the responsibility of the executor to sell or distribute the items as they see best.

Remember to obtain receipts from all beneficiaries receiving assets. Have all beneficiaries sign and date a receipt. This is required and is also just good business practice. The executor must go before the court and PROVE they distributed the assets in an appropriate manner. They are libel and they need the receipts. Just explain this to Aunt Sally or Uncle Ted.

If they do not sign and date a receipt, they do not get the assets. Period. No exceptions.

If you think there may be a problem later on with the relative who conveniently forgets things, have the signatures notarized. The executor is libel and you can be held responsible to make up the financial difference even if you did everything correctly except get a signed, notarized receipt. Expect the best but always prepare for the worst. You and your family will sleep a lot better knowing that you did everything possible to protect the assets of the estate and your personal assets.

You may be held personally libel. Heirs or beneficiaries may take issue with how you managed things and ask the court to have you make restitution from your personal assets. Yes, this means they may be able to take your cars, bank accounts, property (your home) etc. Protect yourself. Write that down. Protect yourself. Every family and I mean *every family*, has a few of the usual suspects.

Closing the Estate

What Does It Take to Close a Deceased Person's Estate?

All Taxes must be paid. All outstanding debts must be satisfied.

All Disputes Must be Settled

All Beneficiaries must be taken care of

This is done last after all other fees, debts and taxes are paid. Some assets may have been sold to cover these other debts. Try to keep the family and heirs informed about what will be sold and why it is necessary. They may want to purchase it from the estate. You will be accountable to the court and others for the sale price. see *Close the Estate*, page 129

What Documents are Necessary to Close the Estate?

Confirm with the courthouse which documents are required to close the estate. You may find these online at the County website. Google (name of the county where the probate court is located) (the state) close probate

Notice to heirs and beneficiaries: You are usually required to mail or otherwise deliver a notice to heirs and beneficiaries that a final hearing is coming up. There are time limits on when to do this and you must prove to the court that you actually did this. Check with the court as to how they want this done.

Taxes: You may be required to submit copies of all taxes filed on behalf of the deceased and the estate. If a letter from the IRS is needed the estate will not be closed without it.

You may be required to prove the Will's validity by submitting the self-proving affidavit that was signed by the witnesses in front of a notary when the Will was signed. If this was not taken care of you may have to acquire notarized statements from one or more witnesses to the Will as to its validity.

Were you required to post a Bond? If you were you will also be required to show proof that you actually did this.

Proof of notification to Creditors: you will most likely need to file proof that you properly published and mailed the notice.

You need to get the courts permission to distribute or transfer all of the remaining assets to the heirs.

Remember, you will get signed, dated receipts. Notarized if you feel it is necessary or the amount of value is considered by you to be significant.

Once the IRS issues a closing letter, if one is necessary, the judge will allow closure of the estate. You may now go before the court with all necessary paperwork and receipts and ask the court to close the estate and release you from your duties.

56 | When a loved one passes.
What to do. How to do it.

SECTION 3

Key Areas
Alphabetical Listing

Assets

Estate Assets – Inventory and Value

Asset: Any item of monetary value owned by an individual or corporation, especially that which could be converted to cash. Assets are both **Intangible** such as investments and **Liquid** such as cash, bank accounts, precious metals and jewelry.

Joint Accounts: In most cases joint accounts and joint assets pass automatically to the other account holder(s).

Commingling of Assets: Issues about commingling of assets, personal property and bank accounts are more likely with unmarried couples living together. If they were married and a spouse dies without a Will or a Trust, under the probate laws the surviving spouse will be entitled to inherit most, if not all of that spouses assets. If you are cohabitating with another individual and they die, you are entitled to none of their assets if there is no Will or Trust. If the two unmarried partners have children from a previous relationship, there are issues as to whether the children will inherit anything or whether it will pass to the surviving partner or next of kin. If there is commingling of assets now may be a good time to speak with a competent professional.

Probate Asset: A probate asset is one in which title to the property does not transfer by operation of law upon the death of the owner and therefore requires court involvement. Once the estate has been probated the items are available for distribution.

Prenuptial Agreement: A prenuptial agreement typically handles issues relating to property and is drawn up before the marriage contract.

Collect and secure all important documents. This includes bank account, investment account and retirement account numbers and access information. Documents will provide the names and types of assets the executor or personal representative is looking for. See the document list. see *Documents*, page 115

Locating Assets with a Will: If there is a Will it should help in locating most, if not all of the assets. Some assets may be out of state or located in storage areas. There may be a letter to the executor or a notebook containing a list of assets and access information. The Will is legal and binding while a notebook or letter with information to help in the disposition most likely is not. If there is any confusion speak with a competent estate attorney. If worded properly and dated after the Will a notebook in the deceased's own handwriting may or may not be considered a Holographic Will taking precedence.

Locating Assets Intestate: without a Will can be much more of a challenge. Go through the asset list below. Feel free to add to it. Write down your ideas so you do not forget them. You have a lot on your mind.

Asset Search: The cost of the search can usually be paid for by the estate and the results can be shared with the heirs. Most asset searches cost less than $400. This will get a lot of questions answered and bring items that may or may not even exist out into the open.

Beneficiaries and Asset Searches: An heir can conduct an asset search of the deceased's property to verify that the executor or personal representative is not hiding or omitting information.

Responsibility for Assets and their Disposal: If the executor or personal representative is acting in good faith and suffers a loss in the value of the estate while they are working to distribute the assets the heirs or beneficiaries could sue in court. Assets from the estate should be kept separate from the executor's personal assets. An estate checking and/or savings account should be opened.

Asset List

Annuity: An annuity can be a contract between an individual and an insurance company that is designed to meet retirement and other long-range goals, under which the individual makes a lump-sum payment or series of payments. In return, the insurer agrees to make periodic payments to them beginning immediately or at some future date.

> Annuities typically offer tax-deferred growth of earnings and may include a death benefit that will pay a beneficiary a specified minimum amount, such as the total purchase payments. As a financial product, annuities are primarily used as a means of securing a steady cash flow for an individual during their retirement years.

Antiques: Collections, coins, stamps, beanie babies, beer cans, etc. Check on e-bay to get started. That old Bobby Vinton album may look really neat but only be worth $.99 ABBA's North American Tour 1979 - $4,000. Bee Gees, Their Greatest Hits, $700. Elvis Presley, Pot Luck album 1962 $5.00

> Double Fantasy by John Lennon (1980) - sold for $150,000. Happy hunting. Do not let people take something as a remembrance until you find out if the item is in the Will and has been left to someone for a particular reason.

Appraisals, existing: Any appraisals should point to an asset. If the appraisal ended in showing the asset had no value the appraisal needs to be located and secured for the court. If it were an appraisal for property that is now underwater the sand may again shift and the property may have value at a later date. Sometimes a forged work of art has value due to the renown of the forger. Appraisals may be needed for jewelry, coins, or gun collections along with art and property.

Appraisals, new: It is a good idea for the executor to get appraisals for valuable jewelry, furs, antiques, and collections. This may be needed for tax purposes and it will also help ensure that such items are distributed equitably or the estate gets fair value for them if they're sold.

Asset List: If you find a copy of this book (*Death When a Loved One Passes*) among the deceased's things look for a notebook listing assets, thoughts and instructions. We recommend that everyone should begin with a notebook and proceed through writing a Will. If they pass away before they complete their Will, the notebook may be all you have to work with. It is going to save you a lot of time.

Automobiles: Check the trunk area and under the trunk mat in the wheel well. Check the glove compartment and under the seats.

Auto Insurance: There may be money due the deceased depending on the amount and type of coverage.

Bank Accounts: Checking and savings accounts, Certificates of Deposit (CD's). Bank accounts can be anywhere in the world. A Certified Copy of the death certificate will be necessary to access the account. Banks are subject to both state and federal regulations and procedures can vary greatly from bank to bank and state to state. Some states have been known to automatically freeze joint bank accounts when one of the joint owners dies. Check with your bank and if necessary you may want to change your bank.

Brokerage Accounts: An account at a firm that conducts transactions on behalf of a client for a fee. A stock broker charges a fee to act as intermediary between buyer and seller. Accounts can exist solely online.

Business Ownership: limited liability corporation (LLC), partnership or corporate operating agreements. The deceased may have had an active role in a business or just a financial stake as a part owner.

Cemetery Plots: This paperwork should be readily available. Copies of contracts, contact information, account numbers and billing statements are necessary.

Certificates of Deposit (CD's): A Certified Copy of the death certificate will be necessary to access the account.

Clothing: Some designer clothing or old clothing and uniforms are considered collectables and may be worth a lot of money. Dealers buy period clothing. While you are going through the clothing look in all of the pockets as this is a common hiding place for valuables.

Clubs or Organizations: Tennis clubs, health clubs or country clubs.

Collections: There are all kinds of collections: porcelain or Bennie Babies, guns, coins, stamps, matchbook covers, etc. Sometimes the executor or family members will not understand the value of a collectible. This is one reason why a notebook listing all assets is very important. Hopefully the deceased prepared one for you. There are many software programs that help in creating a data base for collectors.

Company-Owned Life Insurance Policies

Credit: An up-to-date credit report of the deceased may help to locate assets and assess outstanding debts.

Credit Cards: Identify authorized users for each credit card and account. If another person is added to the account as an authorized user, depending upon the company specific terms, he or she may be agreeing to repay all of the debt when using the card.

Cremation Prepaid: This paperwork should be readily available. Copies of contracts, contact information, account numbers and billing statements are necessary. If it is not used at the time of death it is most often non-refundable.

Desk: Check in and under everything.

Digital Assets: Storage areas are also digital. see *Digital Assets* page 40, 250, 333

Disability Payments: If a disabled individual dies, his or her dependents may get Social Security survivors benefits.

Employer: Receive any Payments due the estate such as salary, vacation time, and wages due from an employer.

Federal Employment Benefits: If the deceased worked for the Federal Government benefits may be available to a beneficiary or to the family.

Frequent Flyer Miles: Depending on the amount and the type, this may be a nice asset.

Funeral Arrangements: Prepaid funeral arrangements either complete or partial. Funeral Plans that are pre-paid may include burial, cremation, or green cremation. The paperwork should be readily available. Copies of contracts, contact information, account numbers and billing statements should be included. If it is not used at the time of death it is most often non-refundable.

Gym Locker: Check for gym memberships (auto-pay?) and lockers.

Health Insurance: Some health insurance policies offer a limited amount of coverage for funeral expenses. You have to look through the policies or you may have to ask.

Heirlooms, Photographs, and other Irreplaceable items. While the executor is gathering information and documentation on assets they should not forget family keepsakes. Just because an item appears to have no monetary value does not mean that it does not have irreplaceable sentimental value to a family member. While the executor or personal representative is going through everything of the deceased's they should set aside everything that seems to fall into this category of irreplaceable items. A locket or lock of hair, a pressed flower in a book and the Family Bible all of these and many more items have tremendous value to loved ones.

Hidden Assets Search: Places you may want to look for assets include underwear drawers which are still an all-time favorite. You can look in the freezer. People hide many things wrapped in aluminum foil next to or under the frozen foods.

> **Can Safes:** If you search Amazon.com for "can safe" you will see many examples of what is available. Almost anything that comes in a can may be used as a safe. The bottom unscrews so items can be hidden inside. The can will generally be lighter (but not always) than a normal can. It may rattle when you shake it. Can safes are made to look like everything from soda cans to

shaving cream, peanut butter, cleansers, cans of fruit, cans of vegetables, automotive motor oil etc.

There are fake candle safes that have a cover in the bottom that screws on. Wall clock safes for under $10. Fake book safes. The water bottle safe contains water and looks very real. Batteries that twist apart. Fake computer mice that contain an internal area to hide things. A fake surge protector that can be plugged into a wall outlet and has a fairly large inner compartment to hide things. And of course the fake wall outlet safe. If you are looking for hidden items these may be some good places to start.

On the inside of the door frame, on the inside of the closets is a favorite place to hide things. People also hide things on the top shelf in the master bedroom closet in a shoe box. Under mattresses and behind headboards a small envelope could be taped containing a rare coin or stamp or a few old stock certificates worth over $1,000,000. Jewelry, cash, and papers in sometimes hidden in coat pockets. People still like to hide envelopes under drawers in a bedroom or desk.

Homeowners Insurance: This bill will still have to be paid if it comes due until it is no longer needed.

Household goods and Furnishings: Valuables that sit in an empty home are vulnerable to theft. It is one of the duties of the executor or personal representative to list, appraise secure and distribute all assets. The property should be secured by changing all of the locks and notifying the local police if no one will be living in the home. Make sure the residence looks occupied, is protected from intruders, and retains curb appeal. Pay necessary bills and taxes. Burglars today will steal whole kitchens and bathrooms out of an unoccupied home in a bad location.

> If it is an apartment, notify the apartment manager. If the executor does not feel comfortable leaving things in the home they should be moved to a secure storage area until the estate can be cleared. It is wrong to descend on the home of the deceased and take whatever you feel you would like but it is done every day. The executor has the responsibility to distribute the estate according to probate, the Will and their best judgment. The decisions made are not always popular. If you find yourself in situations that seem to be more

than you can or want to deal with now would be a good time to consult with a competent estate attorney or other professional who is knowledgeable.

Insurance: Look for all policies or what appears to have been a policy. Check for a credit union, union policy, former employers, or veteran's policy etc. If you locate an agent associated with any policy talk to them and see if they have any additional information on other policies the decedent may have had. Check life insurance, home owners insurance, health and disability insurance, auto insurance, etc. Sometimes policies have an option of setting up cash value accounts, which means that some of the premiums paid are set aside for the policy holder.

Interest and Dividends: The federal tax laws require brokerage firms, mutual funds, companies, and other entities to report on Form 1099 all interest or dividends they have paid to investors during the previous tax year. The Forms-Form 1099-INT for interest income and Form 1099-DIV for dividends-are supposed to be sent to investors by the end of January.

Jewelry: Estate jewelry requires a different understanding of gemstones, manufacturing techniques and signatures. Antique jewelry from a famous designer may be worth a lot more than the individual stones. Victorian or Art Nouveau jewelry may need an expert appraiser. The provenance of works of fine art, antiques and antiquities is of great importance, especially to their owner. The story sells the piece.

Keogh: A type of profit-sharing plan used by small business owners. Include the name of institution, contact information, account number and the amount of funds being paid out, if any.

Lawsuits: Lawsuits for wrongful death may be filed against an incompetent doctor, health care provider, careless driver or someone committing a crime among others. These lawsuits must be filed within a certain amount of time after death. Speak with a competent attorney. It can be important to gather and secure evidence.

Leases, leasing contracts: Include all paperwork. Apartment or property leases, rent to own types and any storage facility. Storage facility could be for an enclosed refrigerated locker or room or an outdoor storage area for cars, boats, planes (anything).

Legal rights: Did the deceased have any legal rights that may be transferable? Such as the right of access across another person's land or waterway. The right to use one half of season tickets from a divorce? There are many things to look into here. If they left a Will or a notebook it is much easier. We recommend that everyone should begin with a notebook and proceed through writing a Will. If they pass away before they complete their Will the notebook may be all you have to work with.

Life Insurance Policies: Each policy should be located. Include name of the carrier, policy number, named beneficiary, all access information and policy amount. These are most often missed when they are from a former employer. If you locate an agent associated with any policy talk to them and see if they have any additional information on other policies the decedent may have had.

Living Trusts: A legal arrangement whereby one person holds legal title to property for another person. There are many different kinds.

Loans: documents that list loans to others.

Memberships: Some memberships can be sold or transferred and are valuable assets. Some examples are country clubs, local annual golf memberships, theme parks, museums, travel, and health clubs, season tickets and annual passes to almost anything.

Money Market Accounts: Include locations, account numbers and access information.

Mortgage Accounts: Include locations, account numbers and access information. This bill will still have to be paid if it comes due until it is no longer needed. Locate the last mortgage statement. This can help to determine the worth of the property. Is there any insurance payable on death?

> **Escrow mortgage accounts:** Include locations, account numbers and access information.

Mutual Fund Accounts

Pets: Pets can and often are valuable assets. While "sparky" may just be a bird (or horse, dog, or cat etc.) to you, "sparky" may be an extremely rare or highly valued "pet". Are they a pet or an asset? In most cases they are both.

Pension Plans: A regular payment made during a person's retirement from an investment fund to which that person or their employer has contributed during their working life. Also a regular payment made by the government to some individuals who are disabled or of retirement age. A pension may be paid by a private company, government agency, or union. Each should name a beneficiary.

> Some pensions end at death while others are extended in whole or in part to the part to a surviving spouse or dependent children.

> If you are looking for a lost pension try: http://www.pbgc.gov/

Precious Metals: Just because it looks like gold, tastes like gold and smells like gold does not necessarily mean that it is gold. Many, many people have been fooled over the years by what appears to be valuable metals, jewelry, art, or artifacts. Have the item assayed or appraised. Keep an eye on it.

Railroad Retirement Act: If the deceased worked for a railroad and was covered by the federal railroad retirement act the family may be eligible for benefits.

Real Property Homes and Buildings: Locations, titles, mortgages, keys, pass codes and all access information should be included. Check bank statements, credit card receipts, utility bills and check books. There may be paid bills for a property that was not known about. Why were the bills paid? Did the deceased have a business interest or partial ownership? Some states require the title to real estate be transferred to the surviving spouse in order for title insurance to remain in force.

Rental Contracts: A rental contract will point to assets in many cases. What is the contract for? Even a rental contract for equipment can point to a business relationship or a property that was not known.

Retirement Accounts: IRAs, 401Ks, and any other pensions or retirement accounts. An IRA is considered dormant or unclaimed if no withdrawal has been made by age 70½. Each should name a beneficiary so any money due will pass directly to the beneficiaries named, without the hassles and expense of probate court. Many plans require the spouse to be named as beneficiary unless they sign a form giving up that right. A Certified Copy of the death certificate will be necessary to access the account.

Royalties, Copyrights or Patents: Much of the information necessary to locate these can be found online in documents or statements. see *Digital Assets* page 40, 250, 333

Safe Deposit Boxes: There could be more than one. Include all information as to the location, keys, contents list, contact person and all access information.

Savings Accounts: There could be more than one. Include all information as to the location, keys, contents list, contact person and all access information.

Savings Bonds: Savings bonds with a named beneficiary are not part of the estate. The beneficiary may cash the bond if they possess a certified copy of the death certificate.

>   Savings bonds without a named beneficiary may be cashed or reissued in the names of beneficiaries if stated in the Will.

Season Tickets: These can be very valuable. Do any rights pass to heirs on death or do they expire at death?

Security Deposits: There are many different kinds including utility companies, the electric company and property rentals.

Social Security One-Time Death Payment: A one-time payment of $255 can be paid to the surviving spouse if he or she was living with the deceased; or, if living apart, was receiving certain Social Security benefits on the deceased's record. If there is no surviving spouse, the payment is made to a child who is eligible for benefits on the deceased's record in the month of death.

Social Security Numbers: For every account the deceased had they were required to give their social security number and address. For any accounts that paid interest or a dividend, the institution is required to send to the deceased and to the IRS statements of the payments made so that taxes can be calculated and paid. Have all of the deceased's mail forwarded to the executor where they can watch for other assets.

Split Property Interests: Property can be transferred by a Will that is split between heirs. For example a vacation cabin can be split between heirs with one group using it for six months and then the other group using it for the next six months.

Stocks and Bonds: Today electronic transfers are most common. Hard copies are less common but you may still find them. Most people would leave the actual certificate with a broker or agent. Some old certificates are worth more to collectors than their actual monetary worth. An original stock certificate for Joe Namath's New York restaurant registers 100 shares, is green and white like the New York Jets colors, and includes a small football player graphic (approximate worth $99.) Certificates from old gold mines, land companies and railroads may be worth millions or a few hundred dollars. It is up to the executor to show due diligence in valuing these.

Stock Certificates: Stock certificates, savings bonds: online records of day trading, records of ownership online. You may also find hard copies of stocks and bonds but these are usually held for someone while the investor was given proof of ownership. Today electronic transfers are most common.

Storage areas can be lockers for furniture, cold lockers for clothes (and meat), and docks, hangers or outbuildings for large items. RV's are found secured in parking areas where a monthly rental fee is paid. Sometimes boats are stored on a trailer parked in the same area. Does a friend of the deceased own a large tract of land or building where they could be storing large items for the deceased? These are all things the executor needs to take into consideration. Storage areas include safe deposit boxes, home safes, hidden locations within the home and even under the mattress.

Suitcases and Brief Cases: Check them all. Check all of the pockets for documents and assets.

Tangible Personal Property List: This can be a list in the deceased's own handwriting that is dated and signed with witnesses attesting to your signature. This may or may not be valid for distribution of some assets depending on state and local laws.

Tax Returns: Tax returns will point to assets. Look at Schedules B and D, to find any receipts of interest, dividends or capital gains.

Timeshares: Include all paperwork, location, keys, access information, name of company, account numbers and contact information.

Titles to real estate, boats, vehicles, motorcycles: Any or all of these may have been stored with a friend because the deceased was not supposed to even have them for various reasons.

Transfer on Death Assets: Many assets (such as bank accounts) or benefits such as retirement savings accounts (e.g., IRAs) have their own beneficiary designations that allow the asset to pass payable on death (POD) or transfer on death (TOD). Check any trusts. Trusts should be mentioned in the Will but the executor may have to read the details of the trust in the trust documents available from the attorney who set up the trust. Joint ownership deeds and retirement statements that include beneficiary names and directives also need to be checked.

Trust Accounts: Location, contact information, account numbers and access information. A Certified Copy of the death certificate will be necessary to access the account.

Unions: A few unions provide death benefits.

Utility Bills, Service Agreements: Electric, gas, water, sewer, trash, pest control, lawn care, volunteer fire department, pet care, cable TV, phone, cell phones, etc. If bills were being paid for another property; why? Did the deceased own the property or have a business relationship with someone?

Vehicles: cars, boats, planes, RV's, motorcycles, or any other means of conveyance.

Veterans Benefits: There may or may not be benefits available. Surviving spouses may not be aware of benefits that could be available to them years after their veteran spouses were engaged in military service. see *Veterans,* page 263

Wages Owed: If the deceased was working up until the time of death, a surviving spouse or other relative can claim the final amount due from the employer. Also check for employee death benefits.

Workers Compensation: If the deceased was receiving benefits because of a work related injury make certain all benefits were paid. If the death occurred on the job or because of a work related injury or illness, family members will most likely qualify for worker's compensation death benefits.

Workshop or Hobby area: Check everything for hidden documents or assets. Sometimes the person was going to put the item away but never got around to it.

Search for Assets

Search Google: "name" state. Enter the person's name in quotation marks and add any defining information such as occupation or the State where they last lived. http://www.google.com/

Search the Government: Direct access to searchable information from the United States government, state governments, and local governments. http://www.usa.gov/

Search Missing Money: State treasurers currently hold $32.9 billion in unclaimed bank accounts and other assets. You can search for unclaimed assets at MissingMoney.com.

Unclaimed Property: Go directly to a government unclaimed property program by clicking on a state, territory, or province from the map or drop box below. You should search in every state where you have lived. http://www.unclaimed.org/

Search Vital Records: One of the most comprehensive resources for locating vital records online. United States Birth Certificates, Death Records & Marriage Licenses. Some Local Libraries allow you to use this and other websites for free. Call your local library for details. http://www.vitalrec.com/

Free People Search and **Public Information Search Engine.** People Search. Honestly Free! Search by Name. Find People in the USA. Free People Finder. A search tool that focuses on finding data related to individual people: names, addresses, and phone numbers. http://www.zabasearch.com/

Attorney

Attorney: Do we need an Attorney?

Attorneys just want my money. It sometimes appears like that, but then so do Churches, Car Salesmen, Plumbers, Landscapers, Restaurants, Barbers, etc. So it is common for a business to expect to be paid for services rendered. As we see it the real problem is paying top dollar for inferior service. No one likes to go out to a place that sells food and pay for something that is old, cold and full of mold. We get upset. The same is true of legal services.

> **Most attorneys** are competent, well-educated and concerned for your best interests. It is always up to you, the consumer, to use due diligence when purchasing the services of an attorney. You are buying the legal advice of the attorney and their office which is backed by their education, experience and Track Record. Ask friends and family. Go and get a cup of coffee at the county courthouse and make a friend or two. People love to talk about themselves and others. It seems like everyone in a particular business knows who the schmucks are in that business. That is a difficult thing to keep quiet. Get a cup of coffee. Make a friend. And ask people: *I am from out of town and need to settle an estate. Could you please tell me who is caring and competent?* Chances are they will tell you. Then Google the person's name and the name of their law practice. Ask around some more; maybe at a coffee shop or small restaurant across from the courthouse. Waiters and waitresses hear most everything and like to talk. Tip fairly well, within reason, when you leave.
>
> **Attorneys or Lawyers?** Potato, Potahto. The titles are interchangeable. What you should be concerned about is the Type of law they are experienced in. An attorney may have gone to school to study estate planning but has worked as a corporate lawyer writing opinions for the last thirty years. Now that estate law seems to be a

Hot market they may want to semi retire and cash in. Is this a bad thing? No, not necessarily. Just be aware of what you are purchasing. Someone who has spent the last ten years actually working with customers to probate estates may be in a much better position to assist you. It is your decision. The same is true of hiring a real estate attorney or a divorce lawyer to help you probate an estate. Look at the facts; make a good decision.

Do I need a Lawyer?

The answer used to be a simple; No. Now the answer is more often; "That depends." A few states now mandate by statute and court rules that an attorney is necessary for most probate proceedings. In most other state you still may do it yourself. You will need to check with the county probate court in the county in which probate will be filed. This is usually the county where the decedent had their primary residence.

You may get the paperwork necessary from the probate court in the county where the deceased passed or their website. Courthouse employees are not allowed to give legal advice. see *Attorney*, page 71

Should I Hire a Lawyer?

Yes, you probably should.

But since every case is different and not everyone really needs to hire an attorney, here is what we suggest. Gain a basic understanding of the whole process of what is involved in acting as an Executor or Personal Representative. Read this book. Information is power and you are holding a lot of information (power) in your hands right now. If you come to the conclusion that the estate is actually insolvent (broke, no money) then you may want to make a decision based on this information. If you come to the conclusion that the estate has assets and someone really needs to locate, inventory, appraise, record, and distribute the assets while at the same time locate, inventory, approve or disapprove and then pay all taxes and debts from the estate without becoming libel for simple mistakes. Then you have a legal right to do it yourself. We are not attorneys. We would rather do it ourselves.

Read through this book and you will come to many places where we make a simple suggestion: *This may be a good time to consult with a competent estate attorney.*

It can take over a year to settle a simple estate in 2012. As the population ages, courts will probably experience backlogs. There will most likely still be time limitations on how long you have to file this or that document. Can you stay ahead of everything? Why go it alone for the first eleven months and then come to find that you really need advice on any number of things. It would have been better and most likely less expensive, to consult with and work with an attorney from the beginning.

More law firms are focusing on funeral home, cemetery, and crematory malpractice. This is partially a result of the increased number of funerals. As the numbers double, the mistakes may also.

Read through this book and determine what your particular situation is. For some people it is really not very difficult to close an estate without an attorney. For others it would keep you awake nights with worry.

What happens if I hire a competent estate attorney?

In most cases the attorney you hire will act as your guide and direct you in what to do and when to do it. This may be a legal assistant working under the direct supervision of the attorney. They should keep up on all current legal decisions that may affect your estate. They should stay in close touch with you to see how you are doing. They should make themselves available to answer any and all questions.

An attorney working with you should be less expensive than an attorney doing everything for you. Working with a legal assistant should help to keep costs down. The only way to find out is to schedule an appointment (consultation) with the attorney and ask questions. Begin right now. Get a notebook and as you read through this book keep notes. Write down questions that need to be asked. Write down things you should do. Begin at the beginning and things will start to take shape.

Take this book and your notebook with you to the consultation. This will help to inform the attorney and their staff that while you do not know everything at least you know something and they may be able to work more closely with you. Translated: you may be easier to work with and get a better price.

Do I have to hire the same attorney who prepared the Will?

No, the executor named in the Will or administrator appointed by the court is free to ask the attorney who has possession of the original Will to hand it over, if they are holding it. They are also free to look for another attorney for any reason. It could be price or because you do not like the hat they wear.

Can I just hire someone to act as Executor?

Yes, but it is usually more expensive.

What if your attorney retires dies or sells the law practice?

Any documents that were with the attorney or their office belong to either the individual or their estate if deceased. You are not required to work with another attorney or law firm. If you have another attorney that you would rather work with, simply go and speak with them and they will collect the documents for you.

If you decide to hire a competent estate attorney

You will need many of the documents and vital statistics listed here. Locate, inventory, and secure as many as you can. see *Vital Statistics*, page 269 – *Documents*, page 115

Bank Accounts and Safe Deposit Boxes

Set up a Bank Account in the name of the Estate

An estate checking account needs to be set up to pay bills and keep an accounting of what was paid, for how much and when. Your month end bank statement should do this.

Immediately notify financial institutions if there is a concern about fraud on any account.

Savings accounts and Checking accounts

Some accounts may be local. Some accounts may be where the individual passed if this was a different location from their primary residence. Some accounts may be out of state at Banks or Credit Unions. Some accounts may even be overseas. It is not uncommon for people to have accounts in many other locations. If there is a Will then most if not all of these accounts should have been located. If there was no Will the executor may have a lot more work to do.

The executor, personal representative or administrator will locate and collect all bills. During this search they will most likely come across other documentation naming banks or credit unions. Post Office Box receipts may indicate mail piling up that has not been collected. Checkbooks and deposit receipts, certificate of deposit (CD) or receipt for a safe deposit box (and key) may be found.

Totten Trust

A Totten Trust is a regular bank account with a designated "pay on death" inheritor. When the account is opened a friend, relative (most likely named as executor) is named as the beneficiary. Whoever opens the account can also close it at any time for any reason. They may also change banks and or change beneficiaries. The beneficiary does not need to know about the arrangement, and the depositor is entitled to deposit and withdraw funds from the account as they see fit. The idea is when the person dies the beneficiary collects the account balance and pays for the funeral expenses. This can work out very well if all parties are informed and kept up to date.

Joint Accounts

If joint bank accounts, money market accounts, credit cards, or lines of credit from a Reverse Mortgage are jointly owned, the joint survivor continues to have full access to them. To clear the account of the deceased's name it is often only necessary to have a copy of the death certificate. Customer service at the institution will help you.

If you are going to clear joint accounts, always keep at least one joint account open for at least six months or more so you may deposit checks from refunds, or insurance payable to the deceased. Simply indorse the check on the back "For Deposit Only", PRINT the name of the deceased underneath and write the account number of where the deposit is going. With this and a deposit slip you should be good to go. You may clear this account after six months or more when you are certain all checks have been deposited. You have on average one year to close probate so it is not critical to clear this.

Joint account with absolute right of survivorship held by Spouse only: No tax waiver is usually required, and the surviving account owner will normally receive 100% of the funds upon the death of a co-owner.

If the right of survivorship is held by more than one person half of the funds may be released immediately with the other half held for later release. A Tax waiver may be necessary.

Automatic Deposit or Automatic Withdrawals

Check to see if there are any automatic withdrawals or deposits. What are they for? Are they necessary now? Automatic withdrawal for garbage collection at the deceased's residence may be necessary for a while. Continued debits or withdrawals for cable TV most likely will not be necessary if no one is now living at the residence. View each instance and decide one at a time. Keep records of everything you do in your notebook. Example: called (Name) bank, date, morning Reason . . .

Do not just stop payment for everything without first knowing and understanding what it is for.

Do not freeze either bank accounts or credit card accounts before you first see if there are any automatic payments and find out what they are for. Again: Digital Assets, websites, blogs, online storage, physical storage space or storage lockers, etc. If you stop payment you may lose the right to access or worse.

Digital Assets: most often digital assets are stored online and billed automatically to a credit card. Sometimes these are billed automatically to a debit card and this transaction will show up on the monthly bank statement. The deceased may no longer need a Netflix account (watch movies) but may still need to keep up payments to store valuable digital assets in "The Cloud" (online). You may encounter blogs, websites, contracts, business sales invoices that need to either be paid or debt that needs to be collected. Oops, sorry! is not an excuse if the executor or personal administrator fails to locate and secure these assets once located. If there is no Digital Administrator find someone to help that you can trust implicitly. Any competent estate attorney should have someone on staff to consult and help in this area. If they do not they are most likely not very competent.

Immediately notify the institution, company or business if there is a concern about fraud on any account.

Money Market Accounts

A type of bank account in which the bank pays a higher than usual interest rate in exchange for a high minimum balance and a restriction on the number of transactions made in any given month. Usually a Certified Copy of the Death Certificate and Letters of Administration or a Letter of Testamentary is necessary to gain access to the account if it is not a joint account with right of survivorship.

If it is a joint account it may pass to the survivor automatically. The account can be cleared with a certified copy of the death certificate any time. There may or may not be penalties for withdrawal or closing this account. Check with customer service at the bank where the account is located.

Certificate of Deposit

A certificate of deposit is a deposit of a specified amount of money in a bank, usually for a specified period of time at a fixed rate of interest. If it is a joint account it may pass to the survivor automatically. The account can be cleared with a certified copy of the death certificate any time. There may or may not be penalties for withdrawal or closing this account. Check with customer service at the bank where the account is located.

New Banking Accounts Located

If a bank is located find out if the institution is open or closed. The bank or savings institution may still exist under the same name or under a different name (common after bank mergers), or it may be closed.

If the bank was closed by the government, find out if the deposits and safe deposit boxes were transferred to another institution or to the FDIC. Some people never claim their insured deposit from the FDIC and, under federal law, forfeit the money. Under current rules in effect for failures as of June 1993, people have 18 months from the date of the failure to claim their insured funds from the FDIC. At the end of that period, the FDIC sends any unclaimed deposits to the state unclaimed property office. The depositor may be able to recover these funds from the state for 10 years.

The contents of any safe deposit box left unclaimed with the FDIC will be sent to state unclaimed property offices under the timetable outlined in the appropriate state law.

Federal Deposit Insurance Corporation (FDIC) Dormant Bank Accounts. Bank accounts are considered abandoned if a deposit or withdrawal is not made over a period of time, generally from one to five years. http://www.unclaimedassets.com/US3.htm

Bank accounts are considered abandoned after the owner or heirs fail to 'communicate an interest' in them. Failure to communicate an interest in a bank account can arise when you do not make a deposit or withdrawal over an extended period (as little as one year), when you fail to roll-over a CD, even when a statement or other official bank correspondence is returned by the post office as undeliverable. **http://www.lostbankaccount.com/**

http://www.unclaimed.org/ Go directly to a government unclaimed property program by clicking on a state, territory, or province from the map or drop box below. You should search in every state where you have lived.

Our site will assist you in thoroughly searching all participating states to find your family's missing, lost, and unclaimed property, money and assets. **http://www.missingmoney.com/Main/Index.cfm**

Safe Deposit Boxes

If the safety deposit box is in the sole ownership of the deceased most banks will require a Certified Copy of the Death Certificate and Letters of Administration or a Letter of Testamentary to gain access to the contents. On co-owned safety deposit boxes, the rules vary from state to state.

Register your spouse or child's name with the bank and ask them to sign the registration document so they can have access without securing a court order.

If you place the name of another individual on your Safe Deposit Box account they will have your permission to open the safe deposit box whenever they want. They will be able to go and remove everything against your wishes. Be careful. Speak to a competent estate attorney to safe guard yourself if you are even a little concerned.

The U.S. Internal Revenue Service can gain access to a domestic safe deposit box when they freeze all of a person's assets. A safe deposit box is a safe place to store assets; it is not a good way to protect assets from the Internal Revenue Service. It has been estimated that due to poor planning many baby boomers will give up more of their assets than was necessary.

Size: The smallest box is 2"x5" and 12 inches long. Rent is typically between $15 and $25 a year. There are larger safe deposit boxes and the fee is higher ($100/year +/-). A safe deposit box lease agreement (contract) may have been signed by more than one person. Everyone who has signed the lease contract (agreement) usually has the right to access the safe deposit box.

Contents: Most of the time people keep all important documents in a safe deposit box. They are also used to store gemstones, jewelry, coins, precious metals (gold or silver is common), property deeds, birth certificates, Wills, or deed to a burial lot, digital assets, insurance policies, stocks and bonds, and anything that is irreplaceable or treasured no matter what the monetary value. A lock of hair or a receipt for a Broadway show would both qualify.

If you feel that you would have a real problem if you lost something, chances are it should go into a safe deposit box (if it fits). Many people keep Wills, health care directives, and durable power of attorney in their safe deposit box. This keeps it safe but if it is needed and is locked in a bank that may not be open for a long weekend there may be a big problem. People need access to these documents immediately.

The rules governing a safe deposit box clearly make it the preferred place to store the Will. Health directives, organ donor information, and durable power of attorney may be better kept at home in a safe place where loved ones can access them immediately if necessary.

The State may Seal or Freeze the Box: Most states require the bank to "seal" safe deposit boxes for a few weeks after the death of an owner. Then the Tax people stop by the bank and look at the contents of the box to see if an inheritance tax is now due. Laws vary from state to state. In states where the surviving spouse is exempt from inheritance tax they retain access if the account was in both names. California law has not required the sealing of safe deposit boxes since the early 1980's. Some states still seal them.

Searching for a Will: Some states allow someone not listed on the signature card to view the contents of the safe deposit box with a bank manager present if they are searching for a Will or deed to a burial lot. If a Will is found it is photocopied and the original is submitted to the court to start probate. This varies from state to state.

If the executor thinks there may be a safe deposit box but has not located it look for records in the personal papers and bank records of the deceased. If you find the account numbers and branches of their banks call customer service and ask if there are any safe deposit boxes. They may or may not tell you. While you are looking through the paperwork also watch for keys, User names and passwords, combinations, account books, and address books. Many people keep an address book for Digital Asset information.

If you find no trace of a safe deposit box and still feel that there should be one because you cannot locate all necessary documents contact your state's unclaimed property office. If no one paid the annual fee on the safe deposit box, it would have been considered dormant once there was no activity for a period of time.

After a year or two depending on the state, all states must report all bank accounts or similar financial properties that are considered inactive. Wouldn't it have been nice if Ante Orler just left you a note (with the Will) that said, "By the way, that old safe deposit box we used to have. We got rid of it. Too costly. And we did not get another. Bye" "All important documents are now under the insulation in the attic. Go to the top of the attic steps and turn right…over by the dead mouse is . . ." It would have been a nice thing to do.

The executor or personal representative does not need to go to unusual and extreme measures to locate any asset. They need to show they made a usual and customary search. Keep records of what you did. Maybe now would be a good time to speak with a competent estate attorney. Spread the joy and share the liability.

Twitter and Facebook. Bank of America has a Twitter page and a Facebook page and both pages are managed and monitored by customer service representatives. Other financial institutions have also made the leap and use this social media to make a positive impact on their brand. Sweet!

Property Search Companies

A property search company can sometimes assist in finding and reclaiming safe deposit boxes and other assets. Contact the unclaimed property department at the institution first before approaching a property search company. Start with customer service.

They usually cost more than is necessary and you must give them all kinds of personal information that could be used for identity theft without any guarantee as to how they will safe guard this information. It may be a good time to speak with a competent estate attorney. Ask them what they think about hiring a property search company.

Be Careful

You sign for it and you may pay for it.

Be Careful and never go to any funeral service provider alone to make a major purchase. After a loved one passes many people feel like they are in a fog. Take a friend. Make good decisions.

> You honestly need to be careful. Read everything before you sign anything. Always leave with all U.S. Government required information (see *Funeral Rule* page 178) and think about everything, at least overnight. This is a stressful

time and you most likely want it to be over. Impatience or being too proud to ask someone to help you could cost you thousands of dollars.

With almost 80,000,000 Boomers approaching their own death experience it would just be good business if an intelligent, competent, caring attorney helped to supervise the purchase of funeral services in every city and town in America for a reasonable flat fee. Figure it out 80,000,000 x $1 is a lot of money.

Professional Services: When you seek the services of a professional make sure the "professional" is qualified to offer those services. We believe any licensed attorney that does not have financial planning licenses or credentials should not be offering their opinion or assistance for the management or investment of money. A professional bartender should not be working as your CPA and your CPA should not be giving you legal advice. Make sure the professional is competent and qualified to perform the service that you are hiring them to perform.

While saying that: Although the author and publisher have made every effort to ensure that the information in this book was correct at press time, the author and publisher do not assume and hereby disclaim any liability to any party for any loss, damage, or disruption caused by errors or omissions, whether such errors or omissions result from negligence, accident, or any other cause. This book is not and is not intended to be any type of legal advice. It is to serve only as a guide and is not intended to be a substitute for specific individual tax, legal, or estate settlement advice. You should always consult with a competent estate attorney or other professional source.

> That is correct. This book is a starting place to point out some of the things that you may need to do when a loved one dies. As you read from page to page it may become clear that you could really use some competent professional help. We took a poll and were amazed at how much needs to be done and how much can go wrong with just a few errors. Some of you are incredibly bright and will not have a problem. The rest of us may need help.

Airtight Seals and Gaskets: Thankfully, this is becoming less and less common. Protective gaskets that can cost less than fifty dollars are often sold as add-ons for up to several thousand dollars in additional charges. What is accomplished by an airtight seal? The consumer is often told that this seal will help to preserve the body of the loved one.

A casket sealed with a tight rubber gasket creates an environment that helps bacteria thrive. The body quickly decomposes to a noxious mass that releases gases capable of exploding the casket. Most cemetery workers pop the seal to allow air to vent and keep the remains from exploding the lid off the casket. The seal is also broken to allow air to vent when the casket is placed above ground. When placed in a tightly sealed container most bodies have a tendency to liquefy and create bloating gas which explodes the container releasing noxious gasses into the crypt or mausoleum. This is why many if not most mausoleums will not allow the gasket to be used.

> Without this airtight gasket there is normal dehydration and deterioration of the body.

Bait and Switch: Bait and switch is an illegal tactic in which a seller advertises a product with the intention of persuading customers to purchase a more expensive product. There usually needs to be an advertisement for the "bait" that is not available when you go to see it. If you just get talked into buying something else that is not bait and switch. It is just business.

Bill Collectors: It used to be when someone died they had some assets. Not so today. Many boomers will be in debt when they pass. They will leave this burden to family, friends or the state. Many children are concerned that if they serve as the executor of the Will or as Trustee of their parents Trust that may be held responsible for this debt. That is not likely. If you share debt you can be held libel. If the deceased was the sole debtor the estate is responsible for paying the creditor in almost all situations. If there are insufficient assets or there are no assets, the Trustee or the executor is not going to be held personally responsible. However, many bill collectors may try to manipulate the executor into paying the debt themselves. Bill collectors also try to get friends or relatives to pay the debt. Collectors that try to appeal to a consumer's moral obligation to pay the debt could be in violation of federal law.

> **FTC Consumer Alert: Paying the Debts of a Deceased Relative:** Who Is Responsible? After a relative dies, the last thing grieving family members want are calls from debt collectors asking them to pay a loved one's debts. As a rule, those debts are paid from the deceased person's estate.
>
> According to the Federal Trade Commission (FTC), the nation's consumer protection agency, family members typically are not obligated to pay the debts

of a deceased relative from their own assets. What's more, family members – and all consumers – are protected by the federal Fair Debt Collection Practices Act (FDCPA), which prohibits debt collectors from using abusive, unfair, or deceptive practices to try to collect a debt.

Under the FDCPA, a debt collector is someone who regularly collects debts owed to others. This includes collection agencies, lawyers who collect debts on a regular basis and companies that buy delinquent debts and then try to collect them.

Does a debt go away when the debtor dies? No. The estate of the deceased person owes the debt. If there isn't enough money in the estate to cover the debt, it typically goes unpaid. But there are exceptions to this rule. You may be responsible for the debt if you: co-signed the obligation; live in a community property state, such as California; are the deceased person's spouse and state law requires you to pay a particular type of debt, like some health care expenses; or were legally responsible for resolving the estate and didn't comply with certain state probate laws.

If you have questions about whether you are legally obligated to pay a deceased person's debts from your own assets, talk to a lawyer.

An excellent U.S. Government Federal Trade Commission website.

http://www.ftc.gov/bcp/edu/pubs/consumer/alerts/alt004.shtm

Insurance Death Benefits: A common way of handling expenses can be costly if you do not understand how it works. This is sometimes a good way for a family to pay for funeral expenses if they are not overpaying for goods and services. If you take the deceased's insurance policy into the funeral service provider they may ask you to sign over the policy to the funeral director. You should never sign away any more than the good-faith estimate provided by the funeral service. Funeral directors may want to take control of the entire death benefit. They tell you, "Trust me. I will return any money left over." They are a business. Their job as a business is to make a profit. Although many funeral service providers are reputable, many are not. Never be pressured into signing something. There are almost never any "sales, for today only". You are the customer. You are dealing with a salesperson that makes money when they sell you something. It is a business. Get some help from a friend or family member and show them this book so they can prepare themselves before you go and make a purchase together. Be careful.

Bronze Plaques: Bronze plaques are used by many cemeteries because they look nice and make it easier for maintenance crews to maintain the property. They are often sold by the inch. Check prices online for everything before you go and shop locally. Make certain that if you purchase an item online the local funeral service provider or cemetery does not charge you fees for its use. The may charge you a "leveling" fee, "perpetual care" fee, an "installation supervising" fee, or a "the sky is blue today" fee. This may make your previous "savings" very expensive.

Romantic Predators: They are both male and female. They come in all shapes and sizes and are known in retirement communities as opportunists who move from victim to victim. They will either take complete control of the retiree's finances or talk them into a business venture or "investment" that only drains their bank accounts and leaves them penniless. Often these same seniors are then too embarrassed to reach out and contact friends and family. This is exactly what the thief is counting on as they move to yet another victim. If you have been victimized call your local police department or sheriff's office. They will be more than glad to send someone out to speak with you or put you in touch with someone who can help. It may not be too late to get some or all of your money back. You are not the only one to be robbed so make the call.

Document Signing: Know what you are signing. If you are the spouse of someone with a medical situation you need to know and understand the implications of what is going to happen if: 1) everything goes as planned with no surprises. 2) Surprise! You do not qualify for the benefit and now you must pay the bill because you signed. 3) Surprise! Your spouse qualifies for Medicare or Medicaid but you do not and now you must pay the bill from your own funds because by signing you took responsibility for paying the debt. If you had talked with a professional in the well versed in the area of health care where you need assistance this may have been avoided. At the very least you would not be surprised.

> Most people do not understand anything about what they are signing; they are just told to, "Sign Here" and they do it. Most people who are telling you to, "Just sign here." do not understand what it is that you are signing or what they are required to explain to you by law. Their job is to have you sign the

documents. When you sign a contract be careful. You could have a lien placed on your home and it is a real concern that your home could be taken from you if you made an error in judgment. Be careful. Get some help.

Congressman: If you feel like you are being lied to or treated unfairly Google: congressman, (your county) (your state) get your congressman's phone number and call them to complain. Your local congressman and their staff will be more than happy to assist you in your time of need.

Beneficiary

Beneficiary or Heir

Beneficiary

A person or group entitled to receive funds or other property under a Trust, a Valid Last Will and Testament, or Insurance Policy.

Heir

When there is no Will. A person or group entitled to receive funds or other property when they are named by the court. Sometimes potential Heirs attempt do-it-yourself distribution and find out later they cannot clear titles or clear other legal problems.

Probate law generally defines heirs to be the spouse; their children and later heirs; parents; brothers and sisters; grandparents; and then others also considered next-of-kin. The exact order may vary from state to state. After going through a fairly long list of possible heirs the estate goes to the state if no heirs can be found. For instance a "laughing heir" statute exists in a few states. This statute names a person so remotely connected to the deceased that they would not feel any sorrow at the mention of the death.

Beneficiaries are Notified by the Executor

Executors sometimes send all beneficiaries a Citation or notice of the Will being submitted to probate with a copy of the Will attached. Some states allow for the signing of waivers. When the beneficiary signs and returns this to the executor they are waiving their rights to object to the Will and allowing it to be submitted for probate.

No Contest Clause: A no contest clause usually threatens to disinherit a beneficiary if they contest the Will. Unless you really just do not care or you feel there is nothing to be gained, you should really wonder why it was placed in the Will. Some clauses are very good and some are not legally enforceable. If someone took the time to add a "no contest clause" there may be a reason that is not obvious. That reason may be money.

If you have questions about the Will, disagree with its contents, or feel there was a later Will which would be in priority if located then you should most likely seek the advice of a competent estate attorney.

Incarcerated Beneficiaries

Someone who is incarcerated may receive assets from an estate. This is a special circumstance and it would be the obligation of the executor to protect the asset(s) until all decisions pertaining to them are made.

You will most likely need to talk to family and friends to clear this one. Would the funds go to reimbursement for restitution charges? Is this something that you want? If the person is serving a life sentence do they really need more than a small amount of money? Could these funds be used to hire an attorney for an appeal? Not a "fantasy appeal" that is meant only to rob you of your money, but is there even one chance to drive a sold appeal home that will be a benefit to the imprisoned person? How do you accomplish what you wish to accomplish without the state simply taking over the funds?

Special Needs Individuals

The same reasoning process would apply to anyone with special needs. What is the intent of the Will in naming them as a beneficiary? Can this intent now be accomplished? If the original intent was to pay for a Medical Education and the person is now mentally challenged then the situation is totally different and must be addressed. Things change every day. You must make good decisions based on your ability to react to those changes. There are many challenges in being an executor, do your best. You will most likely need to talk to family and friends to clear this one.

Children as Beneficiaries

Children can be named as beneficiaries. They may be given an asset outright or it may have been placed in a Trust. Both have their advantages and disadvantages. In most cases an adult will be named to manage money or property for a minor child. If there is also a guardian named for the minor children it may be the same person(s).

Parents usually leave everything to each other with the understanding the surviving spouse will take care of the children. Their children may then be named as alternate beneficiaries. If both parents pass at the same time a guardian should have been named. If this is a situation the executor is now facing and there is no Will or a Will and no guardian named at least speak with all family members to gather information to make a good decision pertaining to the children. Depending on the situation, now may be an excellent time to seek the advice of a competent estate attorney. Some people are very good coming into a difficult situation like this and some people really would rather not be bothered, but would never think of telling you.

If you do not arrange for property management for minor children the probate court will do it for you. This may be good or not so good. The courts, like people, usually do the best they can at the time using the information they are given. There will also be court supervision and attendant costs. The executor can most likely speak with everyone concerned on a one-to-one basis and get more honest input than the court and make a better decision.

If the "children" are eighteen years of age or older in most cases they are legal adults and may do as they wish with the property unless the Will or Living Trust specifies something else.

Life Insurance: Life insurance policies may name children as beneficiaries. The minor child (children) may be named as beneficiaries along with an adult custodian under the states Uniform Transfers to Minors Act (UTMA). Most insurance companies allow for this.

Trust or Living Trust: A trust account may have been set up for minor children. These can be very simple like the UTMA, or much more complicated. Trusts can make funds available for educational purposes either right now or at some time in the future. There may be restrictions as to the allowable schools and specific grades to be maintained among other restrictions. These need to be looked at on a case to case basis and a competent estate attorney may be of help.

Disinherited Family

Was the entire family disinherited in favor of a charity? Or for any reason? Were only one or two members of the family disinherited? If the executor or personal representative finds themselves in a situation like this you really need to go and speak with a competent estate attorney. Everything may look agreeable now but what happens in a month or two when one of the disinherited goes and talks with their neighbor who "is only trying to help"? How long can you be held personally libel for what the testator did and the way you handled it? Exactly, this varies from state to state and you really need some help to finalize this situation.

Special Administrator: A special administrator may be appointed by the probate court when there is a dispute between beneficiaries.

Beneficiary Payable on Death

When a beneficiary has been named on a bank account or retirement plan the accounts are most often automatically "payable on death". This allows them to pass without going through the probate process. Many times these accounts have been set up to make funds available to the executor for funeral expenses and other immediate needs. In almost every state stocks and bonds, and brokerage accounts may transfer "payable on death" to a beneficiary.

Beneficiaries and Debt

Beneficiaries should not pay any final bills out of pocket. They should wait for the Personal Representative or Executor to pay them out of the estate. If the beneficiary is left a car, boat or real property they will need to make a judgment call as to whether or not they intend to keep the item. If it is decided the item will not be kept then the debt should not be paid down.

Beneficiary Payable on Death: When a beneficiary has been named on a bank account or retirement plan the accounts are most often automatically "payable on death". This allows them to pass without going through the probate process. Many times these accounts have been set up to make funds available to the executor for funeral expenses and other immediate needs. In almost every state stocks and bonds, and brokerage accounts may transfer "payable on death" to a beneficiary.

Beneficiaries and Debt: Beneficiaries should not pay any final bills out of pocket. They should wait for the Personal Representative or Executor to pay them out of the estate. If the beneficiary is left a car, boat or real property they will need to make a judgment call as to whether or not they intend to keep the item. If it is decided the item will not be kept then the debt should not be paid down.

Burial

Ground Burial: The action or practice of interring a dead body in an underground chamber. Also called a funeral or interment.

Direct Burial or **Green Burial:** Direct Burial is the most common final disposition and is also called a Green Burial. It is the process of burying a body without the use of chemical preservation in a simple container to help preserve the earth. Costs associated with direct burial include grave opening and closing and perpetual care (maintenance) of the grave site. There are also charges for the purchase of a grave site

Home Burial: Most states allow burial on private land with few restrictions and laws for rural areas. There are usually more restrictions in areas with increased populations. You must check with your state's death care statutes before planning a home funeral or home burial.

Home funerals may also include a home burial but do not have to and a funeral home or crematory can assist if necessary. As cremated remains generally pose no public health concerns the regulations for scattering the ashes are different than burial.

Burial at Sea: Burial at sea when the deceased has not been cremated shall take place at a minimum of three nautical miles from land in water at least six-hundred feet deep. Certain environmentally protected areas such as the coast of central Florida to the east, and the coast of Florida to the west in most areas require a water depth of at least one-thousand, eight-hundred feet deep. The body must be prepared to sink to the bottom rapidly and permanently.

> **Permits** from may be required. Check with local law and customs first. The EPA requires information concerning the name of the deceased, the type of remains (cremated or non-cremated), date of burial, location of burial (longitude and latitude, depth of water and distance from shore, name of the port from which you departed, name of the vessel, and photo copies of any other necessary permits.
>
> **Burial of Cremated remains at Sea:** The disposition of Cremated ashes follow some of the same procedures as to permits. Always confirm what you think is alright with local laws. Cremated ash is a lot heavier than most people realize. It does not just blow away in a breeze but is more the consistency of a sand and dust. Be aware of the wind direction so the ashes do not blow back into the mourners faces. This does happen quite a lot unless you are prepared. http://www.epa.gov/region4/water/oceans/burial.html

Burials in Inland Waters are regulated by the Clean Water Act and permits are required from the proper state agency.

Flowers and Wreaths must be made of natural materials which readily decompose in the marine environment.

The Deceased: Who owns the body? Common law appears to say the corpse is the same as the person and cannot be owned. In most cases, the person in charge of the disposition of the body has a right to possess for disposition. If there is no Will the court appoints an administrator to take on this responsibility, but it takes time for the courts to act. The surviving spouse usually has the principal right to custody of the remains and to burial.

> The person next in line to assume the role of administrator would most likely have the right to possession for the purpose of disposition. Without a Will there is no specific person named (executor) to arrange the funeral and if family members disagree it may involve hurt feelings. In the case of the death of a child of divorced parents, the right to possess for disposition is usually awarded to the parent who had custody. When joint custody is a factor this may change.

> Whether the deceased is cremated or buried depends on what they specified. If no wishes have been expressed, the executor has sole decision over what to do with the body.

Lawful possession may be extended to the hospital if the person died on hospital premises. If the Coroner has jurisdiction they may have the right to possession for disposition. It depends on the circumstances.

> Following burial, the body is considered part of the ground in which it is placed and the law owns the body and has jurisdiction over it. An exception may be when an organ donor gives body parts away at death. It should be obvious they could not be reclaimed if they were in use.

Coroner: At times, the need to perform an autopsy or postmortem examination gives the local coroner a superior right to possess the dead body until such an examination is performed.

Hospital or Hospice: If the person dies in a medical facility such as a hospital or hospice, the attending medical personnel will sign the death certificate and release the body for disposition. Hospitals, may release the deceased to a funeral home without input from the decedent's legal representative in order to conserve space. The legal representative has a right to move the body within the law.

> A corpse may not be retained by a funeral home as security for unpaid expenses. They may not hold a body without authorization and demand payment as a condition precedent to its release.

Transportation for Disposition: Many states allow people other than death care professionals to transport a body. see *Transportation*, page 259

Burial Authorization: There is none. The executor has full responsibility with regards to the funeral arrangements and should be named in the Will. If the deceased dies intestate (no Will) or there is no executor then an administrator, or the person in priority to be the administrator, has the right to possession of the body for the purpose of disposing of the remains. This is usually the surviving spouse or next of kin. The Will should state clearly what the deceased wished to be done after they passed. If no funds are available from the estate you are under no obligation to follow these instructions.

Burial Certificate or Permit: A legal paper issued by the local government authorizing burial or cremation.

Direct Burial

> Select a casket. As cost is usually a concern you may have the funeral home place the deceased in the least expensive casket available or have one shipped to the funeral home from an outside vendor, online or local. Wal-Mart and Costco will even do this for you. Then ask for the body to be sent directly to the cemetery for burial. Embalming is not required or necessary. If a substantial refrigeration charge is added shop around for another funeral service provider. No service is necessary. A very dignified Memorial ceremony can be held at any location without the body present. A direct burial may include a graveside ceremony. All charges must be clearly listed on both the General Price List and the Itemized Statement of Services.

Arrange for the Cemetery Space if needed: The grave site or cemetery plot can be purchased directly from the Cemetery or from an online source. Many Cemeteries today can take care of the purchase online. If you plan ahead you will not feel so rushed and will be prepared to make a better decision.

If the funeral was preplanned a burial space is often included. If full body burial is desired, a grave plot (or mausoleum space) must be purchased. Things to consider are expenses, convenient access and personal meaning. Perpetual care will usually be an additional charge.

Arrange for the Grave Liner, Cemetery Vault if needed: The burial vault, grave liner, concrete box, or burial container prevents ground collapse around the casket and allows easier maintenance of the lawn. Although they are not required by law in most states or localities, they are required by most (but not all) cemeteries. The cost of a grave liner is from a few hundred dollars up to a few thousand dollars. Then you pay a fee to have it lowered into the ground. This is usually another $100. You bury it. You almost never dig it back up. It deteriorates. Purchase the least expensive grave liner that you can find. Plastic and wood are also options.

Arrange for the Opening and Closing of Cemetery Space: There is a charge for this. The cemetery has to dig the space for the grave and fill it back in. They also charge you for removing flowers and paperwork. A usual fee is $350 but the Cemetery can add on over fifty different "services" that you would most likely never need. Just be certain to check all paperwork and look for add-on fees. Although most cemeteries and funeral homes are reputable many are not. The Federal Trade Commission (FTC) Funeral Rule holds Funeral Directors and Funeral Homes accountable but not Cemeteries.

Burial (not direct burial)

Embalming Authorization: This document allows a body to be embalmed by a licensed professional. Embalming is the process of preserving a human body from decomposition. It's usually not required by law except in certain cases. The deceased can usually be placed in refrigeration until the burial. If the funeral home does not have a refrigerated holding room you should look at other funeral homes in the area. Embalming is not required, except in unusual cases when the deceased cannot be buried in a timely fashion. This is can be an extra charge of $800 or more that is not usually needed.

Burial - General Information

Grave Site Service: Some cultures consider it a sign of respect to deposit a ceremonial shovel of earth into the grave. This ceremony is initiated by a member of the family and followed by others. If you were close to the deceased, you may take your turn.

Burial Containers: Vault, Grave Liner or Concrete Box. Most states do not have laws requiring an outer burial container. The cemetery may require this because it does help prevent the ground from collapsing around the grave site. Also the human body has lots of hazardous materials that need to be contained and it makes for easier maintenance of the grounds.

Burial Vault: A burial vault completely contains the casket, while a **grave liner** generally covers only the top and sides of the casket and allows the bottom of the casket to be in contact with the earth. Purchased online it may be sent directly to the cemetery, but because cemeteries are not covered by the FTC's Funeral Rule, the cemetery may charge a fee for using a burial vault or grave liner you purchased elsewhere eliminating any savings. Eventually water or dirt from may find a way to get inside the casket.

The cost of a grave liner is a few hundred dollars and up to a few thousand dollars. Then you pay a fee to have it lowered into the ground. This lowering fee is usually another $100. You bury it. You almost never dig it back up. It deteriorates. If it is required, purchase the least expensive grave liner that you can find. Plastic and wood are also options. Plastic is as strong as concrete, less susceptible to water seepage, and durable. Stainless steel liners can be painted and decorated with gold, silver or bronze trims.

Decent Burial: Common Law recognizes there is a duty to both the deceased and to society for what is referred to as a "decent burial" without unnecessary delay.

When a person is buried the body is considered to be part of the ground in which they were placed and the law has jurisdiction over it. Articles of personal property such as jewelry that have been buried with the body may be taken by their rightful owner as determined by a Will or probate. They are considered material objects independent of the body. However, since the disturbance or removal of an interred body is subject to the control and direction of the court it is always best to ask the funeral service or crematory to return these items to you before disposition.

Chinese Burial: Cremation is uncommon and the burial is a matter taken very seriously in Chinese society. It is believed improper funeral arrangements can bring disaster and ill fortune to the family of the deceased. When a death occurs in a family they may cover all statues of deities in the house with red paper (not to be exposed to the body or coffin) and remove all mirrors (it is believed that one who sees the reflection of a coffin in a mirror will shortly have a death in their family). Traditionally the funeral ceremony will last for forty-nine days or longer.

Moving a Grave: The right to change the place of burial is not absolute and the court will take many factors into consideration before making a decision. Due to the cost to move the deceased from one state to another after burial ($10,000 average) the family will often place a headstone in the preferred cemetery with an acknowledgement that the gravesite is elsewhere.

Natural Disaster: After Hurricane Rita, vaulted caskets that had been buried for over twenty years were found intact dozens of miles from where they had been originally buried. If the individual had been placed in a wood casket they return to the earth pretty quickly.

Burial Plot Rentals: In some countries burial space is rented for just a few years because the cost of the land is so expensive most people just cannot afford to purchase a burial plot.

Business Ownership

When a Business Owner Passes Without a Business Succession Plan

Business Ownership

>Hopefully business ownership issues, continuity issues, management issues, where the legal paperwork is located, passwords, combinations, key codes, Digital Assets, bank accounts, etc. was taken care of before the individual passed away. Preplanning can save everyone so much time, money and aggravation. If you are reading this and still have time, Please start making preparations now. This is just good business. see *Business*, page 98

Death of an Owner: Unless documentation exists outlining exactly what happens when a business owner passes there is usually some confusion for the business associates and family. This is an instance where if no one has bothered to pre-plan the business could be lost simply because no one has the power to authorize things on a day-to-day basis to keep the business functioning. If a court order is needed it could take some time. This is an instance where it would be a very good idea to speak with a competent estate attorney who is knowledgeable about business relationships. You pay now or someone pays later.

Sole Proprietor: If the sole proprietor passes the estate becomes the owner of the business. If the deceased was the owner of a corporation the owners stock in the corporation usually passes to the deceased's estate. At this time the business owners spouse and surviving family may have no income. Life insurance policies need to be evaluated. Were there any powers of attorney? Are there any retirement plans that may be accessed? If a life insurance policy is pledged as security against contractual obligations it is a very good time to speak with a competent estate attorney. Really, at this point there are so many possibilities that most people should seek help. Who is in control? What powers do they have or are allowed to have? What happens if family members contest any decisions? What payments to the business are obligations to be paid from the deceased's estate?

Type of Business: Was the business a Limited Partnerships, C Corporations, S Corporations, Limited Liability Companies (LLC), General Partnerships, or Sole Proprietorship? Each may have different laws governing different aspects of procedure from this point on. If a family member was groomed to take over the business but never really wanted to, now may be the time they actually speak up. Do some family members just want to break up the business so it can be sold and they can cash out? If you are a business owner reading this you have absolutely no excuse not to speak with a competent estate attorney as soon as possible. So much grief and so many problems can be sorted out now, before there is a disaster. Take tomorrow off and just do it. The longer you wait, the more stress is involved.

Small Business: Many individuals today are employed by small business. What happens to these people and their families? Are they expected to work for free while "things work themselves out"? And who makes their house payments and their car payments? It is always easier to make decisions when you are not in poor health or an emotional crisis.

Key People: The correct people should have the legal right to keep the company functioning. The business should continue smoothly without major arguments and legal battles. At the owner's death or incapacitation a limited power of attorney and transfer of the business to a trust could take place. Life insurance can be purchased to help the owner met the companies goals. There are many things to look at: an employee stock ownership plan, a Trust, Key-man coverage, and power of attorney (its limitations or full control?). A revocable trust for holding the equitable interest may be a solution.

Buy Sell Agreements: If the business is a partnership a buyout, or buy-sell, agreement may be in order. These are a good idea and cover a lot of situations involving one partner wanting to leave the business for any reason. They may also be used to control who can buy into the business. Do you really want the partners spouse hanging around the office all day, every day accomplishing nothing but being a "part of the team?"

Business Succession: If there is no business succession plan and the business becomes an asset of the deceased's person's estate it generally takes a minimum six weeks before the court appoints an executor. This is if there are no situations or disagreements and no one wants to contest any decisions made.

Decedent's Business: If the decedent owned a business, then steps must be taken to preserve and protect the business. What type of business structure is it? An LLC, Corporation, Partnership? Some business structures are simple and even have "Rights of Survivorship" where the spouse may have been named as a partner or in a community property state the spouse may have specific rights. This is where things can become very complicated very quickly. Now may be a good time to speak with a competent estate lawyer.

Cemetery or Memorial Park

Cemetery or Memorial Park

Cemetery or Memorial Park: An area of ground set aside for burial or entombment of the deceased. Most often Memorial parks allow only flat markers, while cemeteries allow markers of varying heights. Cemeteries can be large landscaped lawns or small architected memorial gardens. A body can be buried directly in the ground (green burial), in a casket, in a vault: above or below ground, individually or communally. Most often Memorial parks allow only flat markers, while cemeteries allow markers of varying heights.

Memorial Garden: A memorial garden is usually a church garden with a section in which the cremated ashes are poured directly into the ground, and covered by grass or a ground-cover vine. These ashes are commingled with other ashes and with soil, in a tangible symbol of the communion of saints. A plaque on which the names and dates can be inscribed is usually nearby. A fountain in the memorial garden symbolizes

Baptism in living water and is often comforting to the bereaved. It is also common to have some benches, so people can sit and meditate.

Cemetery Sites: When purchasing a cemetery plot (grave site) keep in mind the location of the cemetery and whether it meets the requirements of the family's religion. Is it convenient and accessible? Are vaults or grave liners required by the cemetery? What restrictions are there on headstones and grave markers? What restrictions, if any, does the cemetery place on vaults or mausoleums purchased elsewhere? Is maintenance and record keeping included or are these additional charges? Is there an additional charge for perpetual care? What is the charge for opening and closing the grave?

Google: gravesites for sale This should give you access to the general cost of grave sites at cemeteries in your area. Some of the websites allow you to search by city and state. Things look different on the Internet than they do in person. Go and look at the cemetery and the actual location before making a purchase. The grave site may be next to the men's room. This may be either good or bad.

Mausoleum or Columbarium: If you plan to place your loved one's cremated remains in a mausoleum or columbarium you will purchase a crypt or niche. Then there will be charges for opening and closing the crypt, engraving, record keeping, perpetual care (endowment care, if maintenance is not included).

Mausoleum: A mausoleum a large tomb: an external free-standing building constructed as a monument. It contains burial chamber of a deceased person or persons. They are usually built above ground in cemeteries and are more common in areas with a high water table. Community mausoleums in cemeteries or churches can have hundreds of crypts, which are purchased individually. Many mausoleums are prefabricated and delivered to the site where they are assembled. There are additional fees. Entombment fees are charged to open and close the crypt or mausoleum. These range from $500 - $2,000, depending on the cemetery and time of entombment, with weekends and holidays being extra. Engraving the date of death can cost $50 to $200 or more. There may be perpetual care fees and record keeping fees. Be certain that all of this is understood before you sign the contract.

Endowment Care: A cemetery endowment care trust fund is designed to ensure that income will always be available for the continued maintenance and upkeep of the cemetery, even when all the interment spaces are sold. The cemetery owner should not be permitted to withdraw the principal of the endowment care trust fund. They should receive the income earned by the principal to offset maintenance expenses. This is good in a growing economy but what happens when the economy is stagnant and the owner has had enough?

Cremains: Cremains are another term for the decedent's ashes. Cremains can be placed in a cemetery or on private land, above or below ground. Cremains are often inurned in columbarium niches or scattered in nature. Your state's statues will dictate what is allowed.

Columbarium: A structure with niches (small spaces) for placing cremated remains in urns or other approved containers. It may be outdoors or part of a mausoleum.

Niche: A space in a columbarium or mausoleum for placing Urns containing cremated ashes. Not all niches are the same size and not all urns will fit in all niches. You need to be certain the urn will fit in the niche.

Funeral Rule: Cemeteries are not covered under the Funeral Rule enforced by the Federal Trade Commission (FTC) unless they sell both funeral goods and funeral services. Make certain you receive all pertinent advice in writing and then take it home with you so you can look it over for a day or two with an advisor. The advisor should go with you to the cemetery and/or funeral home and can be a friend or relative. While most funeral service companies (funeral homes, crematories) are honest, many are not. Do not allow yourself to be pressured into buying goods or services.

County Cemetery: Does your county have a cemetery that is still in use and not just of historic significance? Most county cemeteries have more lenient regulations covering eligibility. General rules can be as simple as: 1) Primary residence in County for five (5) years. 2) Tax payer in County for five (5) years. 3) Or having a request in granted in writing by the Cemetery Board. Google: public burial cemetery (your county) (your state)

State Cemetery: Some state cemeteries are restricted to former members of the legislature or a member who dies in office; a former elective state official or an elective state official who dies in office or other "prominent" people.

State Veterans Cemeteries: Many states have established state veterans' cemeteries. The regulations vary from state to state. Google: veteran cemetery (your state of choice)

National Cemetery: All veterans are entitled to a free burial in a national cemetery and a grave marker if space is available. Benefits also extend to their spouse and families. Be sure to check on transportation costs, if any, to the National Cemetery. There are usually no charges for opening or closing the grave, for a vault or liner, or for setting the marker in a national cemetery. See *Veterans*, page 263, 447

Commercial Veterans Advertisements: Be very careful of commercial cemeteries that advertise so-called "veterans' specials." What are you actually paying for? In some cases the grave plot is offered free for the veteran, but an adjoining plot for the spouse is priced at a higher than normal price. If the opening and closing charges, charges for the vault or liner, record keeping fees, cost of a grave marker, fees for perpetual care and all additional fees are considered you end up paying much, much more than a competitor in the same area. They are a business. They are selling you something to make money. It is like buying a used car, some dealers are better than others.

Cremation

Cremation

Cremation: In 2012 about half of all Americans choose cremation for their final disposition. Cremation, Direct Burial and Alkaline Hydrolysis Disposition are thought to be Green Disposition and better for the environment. The average cost of a funeral is $8,500 while the average cost of cremation is $1,000. There can be a service with a rented casket before the cremation.

Direct Cremation: A direct cremation package usually includes transportation, brief storage of the body, document processing (permits, death certificate), a container (usually cardboard) for the body prior to and during cremation, and a basic container (cardboard or plastic) for the ashes. This is the type (not guaranteed) of container the TSA suggests for airline passengers to carry on. The cost of direct cremation averages $1,000.

Cremation Process: Cremation reduces the body to ashes, (cremains), by fire, reaching temperatures of 1600°F -1800° F. The process takes between two and three hours. The ashes can then be buried, placed in a columbarium, or kept in your home. An urn may be purchased for the cremains rather than use the container provided by the crematory. You may also dispose of the cremains in any manner that complies with local health department or other regulations. While there are always some funeral service owners who manage companies that do not meet minimum standards most are reputable businesses with caring owners. If you would like more information check with your state funeral service board for guidelines and any reports on crematory inspections.

Cremation and Graveside Service: A common practice is to rent a casket for visitation and the funeral. The deceased is then removed from the casket for cremation. The service provider must offer an inexpensive pressboard, canvas, unfinished wood box or cardboard alternative to a casket.

Funeral Rule: Under the Funeral Rule funeral homes and crematories must have available an inexpensive pressboard, canvas shroud, unfinished wood box or cardboard alternative to a casket. They also must not tell a customer or prospective customer that state or federal law requires the purchase of a casket for direct cremation. They must provide written disclosure. The modern trend is for a more Green Cremation that includes an unfinished wood or pressed board alternative.

Cremation Authorization Form: Since cremation is irreversible a cremation authorization form must be filled out and signed by the executor, the personal representative or the next of kin agreeing to the process of cremation for the deceased. In most states, individuals are allowed to sign their own authorization prior to death.

Stopping a Cremation: In most all states at any time after executing a cremation authorization form and prior to the beginning of the cremation process, the authorizing agent who executed the cremation authorization form may modify the arrangements for the final disposition of the cremated remains of the decedent set forth in the authorization form or may, in writing, revoke the authorization, cancel the cremation, and claim the decedent's body for purposes of making alternative arrangements for the final disposition of the decedent's body. So if you or someone else changes their mind you may stop the cremation in most cases if it has not already been started.

Cremated Remains, Ashes, or Cremains: The portion of a body remaining after cremation. Who owns cremation ashes? Common law appears to say the ashes are the same as the person and cannot be owned. In most cases, the person in charge of the disposition of the body has a right to possess the ashes for disposition.

Urn: It is not necessary to purchase an Urn for the Ashes, a white colored dust, of a loved one. They are available from the service provider or online in many sizes and materials priced from around $75. An Urn can be made of any material. Metal, wood and stone are the most common. Sets of six mini Urns are also available. An Urn from a third party retailer may be purchased and shipped directly to the funeral home. The funeral home may not charge a fee for using these.

> If a Columbarium or Niche is going to be used remember not all Urns will fit inside every Niche. It is important to measure the Niche or Columbarium first.

Urn Garden: A garden containing urn burial sites.

Mausoleum or Columbarium: If you plan to place your loved one's cremated remains in a mausoleum or columbarium you will purchase a crypt or niche. Then there will be charges for opening and closing the crypt, engraving, record keeping, perpetual care (endowment care, if maintenance is not included). Check the spelling and dates before ordering engraving. Check the size of the Urn and the size of the space to be certain the Urn fits within the space the way you would like it to.

Columbarium: A structure with niches (small spaces) for placing cremated remains in urns or other approved containers. It may be outdoors or part of a mausoleum. There may be an opening and closing charge to place an urn. There most likely will be charges for maintenance or perpetual care, record keeping, engraving for a plaque and possibly others.

Niche: A space in a columbarium or mausoleum for placing Urns containing cremated ashes. Not all niches are the same size and not all urns will fit in all niches. You need to be certain the urn will fit in the niche.

Niche Garden: An outdoor garden containing structures with niches for urns.

Mausoleum: A mausoleum is a large tomb: an external free-standing building constructed as a monument. It contains burial chamber of a deceased person or persons. They are usually built above ground in cemeteries and are more common in areas with a high water table. Community mausoleums in cemeteries or churches can have hundreds of crypts, which are purchased individually. Many mausoleums are prefabricated and delivered to the site where they are assembled. There are additional fees. Entombment fees are charged to open and close the crypt or mausoleum. These range from $500 - $2,000, depending on the cemetery and time of entombment, with weekends and holidays being extra. Engraving the date of death can cost $50 to $200 or more. There may be perpetual care fees and record keeping fees. Be certain that all of this is understood before you sign the contract.

Transportation of Cremains: The TSA allows passengers to carry a crematory container as part of their carry-on luggage, but the container must pass through the X-ray machine. See *Transportation*, page 259, for more information on the transportation of an Urn or Ashes.

Veterans: Most veterans of U.S. military service and their qualified dependents are entitled to free burial in a Veterans Administration cemetery (space permitting); this includes cremated ashes. Transportation can be by U.S. Mail. see *Transportation*, page 259

Scattering the Ashes: Ashes may be scattered almost anywhere. You should get permission if it is on private property. Laws may be different for each state, county or city. Parks and recreation areas may have separate rules and regulations. You should check the rules. Ashes are not considered hazardous. Ashes are not a powder but more like light sand. When you are aboard a boat or in any high wind be careful when you scatter ashes because they may blow back on yourself or others. Cremains (ashes) may also be crushed into a diamond or launched into space.

Cremation Permit: A certificate issued by local government authorizing cremation of the deceased.

Crematory: A building housing a furnace for cremating remains.

Mercury Amalgam Dental Fillings: Along with energy consumption, mercury emissions from vaporized dental fillings are the most common concerns associated with cremation.

> According to the United Nations Environment Programme, the use of mercury in tooth fillings represents some 10% of global mercury consumption, thus being among the largest consumer uses of mercury in the world (AMAP/UNEP 2008). In the U.S., as demonstrated in this report, mercury use in dentistry amounts to over 32 tons[3] annually, which is considerably more than some recent estimates.[4] For comparison, in the European Union dental applications comprise the second largest use of mercury, amounting to some 20-25% of the annual consumption of mercury in the EU. With something less than twice the population of the U.S., the EU use of mercury in dentistry is somewhat more than twice the U.S. consumption (BIO 2012).
>
> www.chem.unep.ch/mercury/Atmospheric_Emissions/Technical_background_report.pdf
>
> http://www.zeromercury.org
>
> The significant releases to the environment of dental mercury in waste and through other pathways, as well as its persistence once it reaches the environment, are well established.
>
> Once in the environment, dental mercury can convert to its even more toxic form, methyl mercury.
>
> The answer seems to be in the continued filtration systems at crematories that reduce or eliminate the toxic chemicals contained in the deceased.

Debt

Estate Debt

Debt: Debts to pay. If a probate estate is opened, the probate estate is primarily liable for the decedent's debts. Debts owed to the estate such as rental property, leases, fees for service rendered are covered under *Assets*, page 5, 41, 57, 75

Executor and Funeral: An executor is responsible for organizing and paying for the funeral out of estate funds. The funeral costs are paid from the estate. If there is not enough money in the estate to cover the cost of the funeral or cremation the executor is not responsible for the costs.

Remember This: If you sign the contract at the funeral home agreeing to services YOU are responsible for paying the bill even if there is no money in the estate to do so. The problem is most funeral services or cremations are paid for during the first week after death before the executor can come to grips with what they are responsible for and what funds are available.

> If you arrange a funeral, you will be responsible for paying the bill, so first check where the money will come from and that there will be enough to cover expenses. Cremation is dignified and far less expensive than burial. Direct Burial or Direct Cremation is less expensive than what is called a traditional funeral.

Probate is a legal proceeding that pays the debts and transfers the property following death according to the terms of the Will or in the absence of a Will, to the heirs based on probate law. The estate will be probated whether or not there is a Will. All states have probate and every probate court has its own detailed rules about the documents it requires, what they must contain, and when they must be filed.

Before Bills are Paid: Before any bills are paid the executor or personal representative must first determine if there are enough assets to cover all bills and expenses. If there are not enough assets to cover all of the creditors then there is a priority of payment outlined in the state law that prioritizes the order in which creditors are paid. It is also true that if a surviving spouse or other survivors continue to live in the home the executor should continue to pay the mortgage, insurance and utilities. If there are vehicles that are still being paid off the executor should keep making payments from the estate and secure these for the beneficiary. If there is no money in the estate it may be a good time to speak with a competent estate attorney. see *Executor*, page 133

Bill Collectors: It used to be when someone died they had some assets. Not so today. Many boomers will be in debt when they pass. They will leave this burden to family, friends or the state. Many children are concerned that if they serve as the executor of the Will or as Trustee of their parents Trust that may be held responsible for this debt. That is not likely. If you share debt you can be held libel. If the deceased was the sole debtor the estate is responsible for paying the creditor in almost all situations. If there are insufficient assets or there are no assets, the Trustee or the executor is not going to be held personally responsible. However, many bill collectors may try to manipulate the executor into paying the debt themselves. Bill collectors also try to get friends or relatives to pay the debt. Collectors that try to appeal to a consumer's moral obligation to pay the debt could be in violation of federal law.

Community Property: In some community property states assets are considered to be joint property under certain conditions and debts are also considered to be joint debt under certain conditions. Check the state law.

> Laws change every day. It is always your responsibility to use due diligence and review the laws in your state and county.

Pay Bills: The executor pays off funeral expenses and administrative fees, then taxes and creditors. Assets may have to be sold to accomplish this. If there is anything left the executor is responsible for distributing any property to the beneficiaries. If you keep in contact with the beneficiaries it may not be such a shock to find out there is nothing left when an estate is insolvent.

Secure all Assets: As soon as the assets are identified and secured you will need to set up a checking account. see *Assets*, page 5, 41, 57, 75 - *Executor*, page 133

Set up a Checking Account for the estate to pay expenses from. Do not comingle your money with the estate's money.

Notify all Creditors. You will most likely need to file proof that you properly published and mailed the notification requirements for known and unknown creditors. The probate court should supply the notification requirements for known and unknown creditors and these can usually be found on their website. The requirements may vary from state to state or even county to county. This needs to be done quickly because it starts the time limit on creditors to file a claim against the estate.

Validate Debts: Are there any claims against the estate? You need to verify and validate these.

Credit Cards, Charge Cards: Identify authorized users for each credit card and account. If another person is added to the account as an authorized user, depending upon the company specific terms, he or she may be agreeing to repay all of the debt when using the card.

Cancel as necessary all of the decedent's memberships, driver's license, handicap permits, social security payments, library cards, etc. Before canceling memberships that include the right to season tickets, discounts or anything of value check to see if they can be transferred or sold.

> Cancel as necessary all of the decedent's credit cards, debit cards, etc. return all library books and cancel all subscriptions and cable. Pick up any dry cleaning, photos or vehicles in the shop for repair. If these are also "joint" accounts you may want to keep them open and remove the decedent's name.

Make Payments: see *Executor*, page 133

Insolvent Estate: If the total assets in an estate are not sufficient to pay all of the valid debts, claimants must be paid according to a priority schedule established by law.

Priority for Debt: Generally funeral expenses, costs and expenses of administering the estate, and taxes must be paid first. After paying taxes and creditors, the executor must give a full accounting to the court, detailing everything they did. Record expenses YOU paid using personal funds as these can add up fast. You need to be reimbursed by the estate. Your priority will be costs and expenses of administering the estate in most instances. The order of priority may change from state to state. The purpose of this book is to point you in the right direction and not to answer every question for every situation.

Tax: The personal representative or executor is responsible for paying all taxes. This includes, but is not limited to, the deceased's income taxes for the last year they were alive. This is from January 1 until the date of death. see *Tax*, page 433

Are you liable for the decedent's debt? Are you the decedent's spouse? Did you cosign a mortgage, a loan contract or in any way link your assets to the deceased through a business? Are you listed on a joint account? The general rule is that a person is not liable for the debts of another. A decedent's spouse, in a community property state, may be libel for all of the debt of the deceased spouse. This can include unpaid medical bills. A joint account holder most often will be held accountable for the other account holder, even if deceased. A person may be libel for another's debt if they cosigned a loan, acted as guarantor, and accepted the responsibility of payment for that loan when they cosigned the contract. If two people opened a credit card account together they are generally both held accountable even if one person never used the card.

> Who is responsible for a debt incurred by the decedent after the estate has been settled? No one is usually responsible unless their name was also on the debt. There is a period of time within which a creditor needs to file a claim. When that period of time ends in most every case the debt is cleared.

Unsecured Debt: Unsecured debts in the deceased's name only are not owed by the spouse. The estate will most likely be held responsible. Community estate property is usually liable for any debt incurred by either spouse during marriage (if the couple was living separate and apart before entry of a judgment of marital dissolution or legal separation). If you are concerned about a situation involving a beneficiary you should do more research or speak with a competent estate attorney. Credit cards are unsecured debt. The Credit CARD Act of 2009 requires credit card issuers to stop adding fees and penalties during the time the estate is being settled.

What if the deceased's property is under water? Many people owe more money on their home than the home can be sold for. Their home is said to be "underwater". Always check for a "payable on death" benefit within or attached to the mortgage.

If the property was owned solely by the decedent the mortgage debt is the responsibility of the estate. The mortgage will have to be satisfied along with all other debt before the estate can be closed. If the estate contains a home that is underwater, then you should consider abandoning the home and allowing it to be foreclosed upon by its lender(s), so that you incur no further expense on or liability with it. If the home is owned jointly or is in a community property state the surviving spouse (if any) has specific legal rights and these must be considered before anything is done. This is a good time to speak with a competent attorney.

What about a Reverse Mortgage? A reverse mortgage is a loan available to homeowners age 62 or older. It is a special type of home loan that lets you convert a portion of the equity in your home into cash. Homeowners can draw a lump sum or receive monthly payments as a revolving line of credit. The homeowner's obligation to repay the loan is deferred until the owner(s) die, the home is sold, or the homeowners cease to live in the property or breach the provisions of the mortgage. There are no monthly principal and interest payments but you are required to pay real estate taxes, home owner association fees, utilities, and hazard and flood insurance premiums. If the value of the property increases it is possible to acquire a second or third reverse mortgage. see *Reverse Mortgage* page 211, 444

> When the home is sold or no longer used as a primary residence, **the cash, interest, and other HECM finance charges must be repaid.** All proceeds beyond the amount owed belong to the surviving spouse or estate. Any remaining equity can be transferred to beneficiaries or heirs.

An Insolvent Estate: Is the estate really Insolvent? Are there other assets? Bank accounts, safe deposit boxes, collections, out of state property, or stocks or bonds purchased years ago? One piece of antique jewelry made by a now famous designer can be worth a small fortune at auction. A rare stamp or rare coin can be worth a great deal of money. We have all seen the TV shows or heard about someone who "found" a treasure that was overlooked. People usually keep the very best that they can. They drag it from place to place, hide it and protect it as best they can. So again: Is the estate really insolvent? Just because there is more owed on the home that it is worth does not rule out an oil painting hanging in the back bedroom that is worth millions. I can recall a case where an elderly lady died while living on the streets of a major city and she was actually an heiress worth millions of dollars.

>After all debts, taxes, costs and expenses of the estate have been paid, the executor or administrator must distribute the balance of the estate to the decedent's beneficiaries or heirs according to law. Distribute the remaining property in accordance with the instructions provided in the deceased's Will and Close Probate. The duties of the executor begin from the time of death and continue until the Probate Court releases them.

Probate, Simplified Procedure: Is there a simplified procedure for settling an estate with limited assets? Yes, in most states there is. There are various rules and regulations depending on the state and/or county but there will most likely be a dollar amount mentioned. An example could be: A simplified procedure for settling the estate may be available if the total value of the estate assets does not exceed ($40,000). In addition, at the time of death the decedent must not own any real estate other than survivorship property, and the estate assets must consist only of personal property and/or an unreleased interest in a mortgage with or without value etc. If a simplified procedure is available it may not be necessary to probate the estate.

Lawsuit: A lawsuit can still be filed by or against an estate. A wrongful death lawsuit can be filed by the estate and creditors can file a lawsuit to collect on a debt.

Beneficiary Payable on Death: When a beneficiary has been named on a bank account or retirement plan the accounts are most often automatically "payable on death". This allows them to pass without going through the probate process. Many times these accounts have been set up to make funds available to the executor for funeral expenses and other immediate needs. In almost every state stocks and bonds, and brokerage accounts may transfer "payable on death" to a beneficiary.

Beneficiaries and Debt: Beneficiaries should not pay any final bills out of pocket. They should wait for the Personal Representative or Executor to pay them out of the estate. If the beneficiary is left a car, boat or real property they will need to make a judgment call as to whether or not they intend to keep the item. If it is decided the item will not be kept then the debt should not be paid down.

FTC Consumer Alert: Paying the Debts of a Deceased Relative: Who Is Responsible? After a relative dies, the last thing grieving family members want are calls from debt collectors asking them to pay a loved one's debts. As a rule, those debts are paid from the deceased person's estate.

> According to the Federal Trade Commission (FTC), the nation's consumer protection agency, family members typically are not obligated to pay the debts of a deceased relative from their own assets. What's more, family members – and all consumers – are protected by the federal Fair Debt Collection Practices Act (FDCPA), which prohibits debt collectors from using abusive, unfair, or deceptive practices to try to collect a debt.
>
> Under the FDCPA, a debt collector is someone who regularly collects debts owed to others. This includes collection agencies, lawyers who collect debts on a regular basis and companies that buy delinquent debts and then try to collect them.
>
> Does a debt go away when the debtor dies? No. The estate of the deceased person owes the debt. If there isn't enough money in the estate to cover the debt, it typically goes unpaid. But there are exceptions to this rule. You may be responsible for the debt if you: co-signed the obligation; live in a community property state, such as California; are the deceased person's spouse and state law requires you to pay a particular type of debt, like some health care expenses; or were legally responsible for resolving the estate and didn't comply with certain state probate laws.
>
> If you have questions about whether you are legally obligated to pay a deceased person's debts from your own assets, talk to a lawyer.
>
> http://www.ftc.gov/bcp/edu/pubs/consumer/alerts/alt004.shtm

Documents

This is not meant to be an inclusive list of all documents. Rather it is to be used as a starting point or reference point. For more information on any document, look in the Glossary at the end of this book.

If the Family History says there was a Treasure Map of the families lost gold mine, hand drawn on an old t-shirt. This is now an important document if it is located.

This list should cover most documents the executor or personal representative will need.

Check the most likely places first, including wallets and purses, home safes, desk drawers and filing cabinets. Safe deposit boxes and storage areas, attics and basements, check all jacket pockets (people hide things in plain sight), check offsite gym lockers, and all cars. Everything needs to be checked. A spouse may "hide" something in the surviving spouses personal property (purses, handbags, golf bag) "knowing" the surviving spouse will find it if they pass first. This is very common and sometimes these things are not found for years. Look in freezers and at the bottom and cookie jars.

Also look for documents on the deceased's home computer or laptop, external flash drive, portable hard drive, tablet device, smart phone, CD's, DVD's, old floppy drives, laser disc, and old drives. Family members can sort through file cabinets for papers, but without User names, password, and challenge question information they may never find important online records. This is where a Digital Executor can really help. However, it is still the executor's responsibility to locate, appraise, safe guard and distribute all assets. see *Digital Assets*, page 40, 250, 333

If these documents are not mentioned a in a Will, listed as assets on last year's income tax return, or in old statements or "stuff" in a shoe box on the top shelf in the bedroom closet. Because we all know how safe the upper shelf is. If the decedent did not bother to inform the executor or personal representative that they own these assets, there is a good chance they never will be found. Begin watching the mail for real-estate tax bills and look through all checking accounts and Bank Books used to record all deposits and withdrawals. Insurance policy benefits, things in storage, retirement accounts and other assets may go unclaimed and be turned over to the state if they are not located.

Document List

Adoption Papers: legal records of a valid adoption.

Advance Directives: Living Will and Durable Health Care Power of Attorney and Organ Donor Cards are a few.

Annuity: An annuity can be a contract between an individual and an insurance company that is designed to meet retirement and other long-range goals.

Appraisals: Locate any appraisals made in the past and keep records of all appraisals made during the distribution of the estate. Any appraisals should point to an asset. If the appraisal ended in showing the asset had no value the appraisal needs to be located and secured for the court. If it were an appraisal for property that is now underwater the sand may again shift and the property may have value at a later date. Sometimes a forged work of art has value due to the renown of the forger.

Asset List: If you find a copy of this book (Death When a Loved One Passes) among the deceased's things look for a notebook listing assets, thoughts and instructions. We recommend that everyone should begin with a notebook and proceed through writing a Will. If they pass away before they complete their Will, the notebook may be all you have to work with. It is going to save you a lot of time.

Attorney(s): Are any attorneys named in address books or documents that may have more information or be holding more documents? Include all contact information, their purpose (real estate, divorce, estate, investment, etc.) and any other information that seems to be pertinent.

Auto Insurance: Bills will have to be paid if there are surviving family members.

Auto Loans: a personal loan to purchase an automobile.

Automatic Payments: Billed to a credit card or bank account. These must be located. Include name of company or institution, location and contact information, account numbers, username, password and challenge questions.

Brokerage Accounts: A brokerage account is a fund that a customer has entrusted to a securities brokerage.

Bank accounts locally or anywhere in the world: Do not exclude the existence of bank accounts "off shore" or in another country. This is becoming more common.

Birth Certificate: An official record of the date and place of a person's birth, usually including the names of the parents.

Business: Partnership, Limited Liability Corporation (LLC), or Corporate Operating Agreements.

Boat Loans: a personal loan to purchase a boat.

Business Credit Cards

Business Succession Plan: A legal plan for a business to survive after the death of an owner.

Cell Phone Bills: check for cell phone bills and phone records of called numbers.

Cemetery Plots: A plot is a piece of property to be used or in use as a place for burial within a cemetery.

Charitable Pledges: pledge cars or statements. A pledge is a vow or an earnest promise that binds one to perform in a certain manner. A financial pledge can be a legally enforceable commitment to pay a fixed amount of money during a given period of time. Churches and ministries can sell these pledges at a discount to lending institutions, so they can get their money right away.

> **A Faith Promise** is a commitment to give a certain amount only if the Lord provides it. A faith promise is a commitment to give only if the funds become available. It is understood that if God does not provide the funds there is no obligation to give. The estate may be held libel to pay a pledge.

Charitable Lead Trust: A trust that pays a charity income from a donated asset for a set number of years, after which time the principal goes to the donor's beneficiaries with reduced estate or gift taxes.

Charitable Remainder Trust: A trust that allows people to leave assets to a charity and receive a tax break but still retain income for life.

Checking Accounts, held locally or anywhere in the world

CD's (Certificates of Deposit): Include locations, account numbers, contact information and all access information.

Child-Support Payments: Include all records of payments made and court documents.

Children: Their health records and school records as available.

Citizenship, Naturalization Papers: a document stating that a naturalized person has been formally declared a citizen.

Clergy: Name of Church or religious institution, location, contact information and contact person.

Condominium Fees: Condominium fees cover the cost of assets held in common such as maintenance and recreation facilities. They can include almost anything.

Company Credit Cards: Many people use company credit cards for expenses.

Company-Owned Life Insurance Policies: A policy owned by a company on the life of an employee vital to the concerns of the company. Company-Owned Life Insurance Policies are sometimes called key person insurance.

Credit Card Accounts: Collect all credit card statements. Identify authorized users for each credit card and account. If another person is added to the account as an authorized user, depending upon the company specific terms, he or she may be agreeing to repay all of the debt when using the card.

Credit Report: Get a credit report from the big three credit reporting agencies in the United States: Experian, Transunion & Equifax.

Cremation Prepaid: This paperwork should be readily available. Copies of contracts, contact information, account numbers and billing statements should be included. If it is not used at the time of death it is most often non-refundable.

Debit Card Accounts: Debit cards are similar to credit cards, except debit cards extract money out of a checking or brokerage account. It is not a loan.

Death Certificates, certified copies: Twelve to twenty is a normal number.

Deeds to Property: Housing and land.

Digital Accounts: Include the website URL, all user names, passwords and challenge questions. Amount deducted, for what period of time ($b/month or year) and the reason (TV and movie viewing, cloud storage, website access, blog fee, web hosting, etc.).

Digital Estate: All digitally stored content and accounts owned by an individual at death.

Digital Wallet: software that allows you to pay for things using your cell phone. An individual's bank account is usually linked to the digital wallet.

Divorce / Separation Papers: persons from previous marriages may have claims.

Dormant Accounts: Note any accounts that "may have been." A bank account at a former address or a retirement account or insurance policy at a former employer should be researched.

Driver's License: Department of Motor Vehicles handles the driver's license, state ID cards and any vehicle registration papers are transferred to the new owners.

Executor, Personal Representative: Name of Church or religious institution, location, contact information and contact person.

Funeral Arrangements: Prepaid funeral arrangements either complete or partial. Funeral Plans that are pre-paid may include burial, cremation, or green cremation. This paperwork should be readily available. Copies of contracts, contact information, account numbers and billing statements should be included. If it is not used at the time of death it is most often non-refundable.

Government Employee: SF-50 (Standard Form 50).

Guardian: Name of Church or religious institution, location, contact information and contact person.

Health Directives: Living Will. All health directives should be readily available.

Heirlooms, Photographs, and other Irreplaceable items. While the executor is gathering information and documentation on assets they should not forget family keepsakes. Just because an item appears to have no monetary value does not mean that it does not have irreplaceable value to a family member(s). While the executor or personal representative is going through everything of the deceased's they should set aside everything that seems to fall into this category of irreplaceable items. A locket or lock of hair, a pressed flower in a book and the Family Bible all of these and many more items have tremendous value to loved ones.

Homeowners Association (HOA): Include all information: contact information, statements, fees due, etc. This bill will still have to be paid if it comes due until it is no longer needed.

Homeowners Insurance: This bill will still have to be paid if it comes due until it is no longer needed.

Immigration Services: if the decedent is not a U.S. citizen.

Independent Contractor 1099s: An independent contractor is an individual or business that provides services to another. They are not considered employees.

Investment Accounts

IRAs: An IRA is considered dormant or unclaimed if no withdrawal has been made by age 70½.

Insurance: Include all policies or what appears to have been a policy. Check for a credit union, union policy, former employers, or veterans etc. If you locate an agent associated with any policy talk to them and see if they have any additional information on other policies the decedent may have had. Check life insurance, home owners insurance, health and disability insurance, auto insurance, etc.

Key-Man Insurance Policy: An insurance policy owned by a company on the life of an employee vital to the concerns of the company.

Keogh: A type of profit-sharing plan used by small business owners. Include the name of institution, contact information, account number and the amount of funds being paid out, if any.

Letter of Instruction: Someone may leave a letter of instruction with a valid Will. The letter of instruction does not carry legal weight but informs the executor of their wishes. It could refer to funeral arrangements or any other instruction.

Leases, leasing contracts: Include all paperwork. Apartment or property leases, rent to own types and any storage facility. Storage facility could be for an enclosed refrigerated locker or room or an outdoor storage area for cars, boats, planes (anything).

Licenses: professional licenses: bar association, medical licenses, cosmetician, etc.

Life Insurance Policies: Each policy should be located. Include name of the carrier, policy number, named beneficiary, all access information and policy amount. These are most often missed when they are from a former employer. If you locate an agent associated with any policy talk to them and see if they have any additional information on other policies the decedent may have had.

Lines of Credit: Banks, casinos, bars and restaurants, etc.

Living Will: This should be readily available because it allows a designated person to make medical decisions for someone if they become incapacitated.

Living Trusts: A legal arrangement whereby one person holds legal title to property for another person. There are many different kinds.

Loans: documents that list loans to others.

Marriage License: The spouse may not be able to claim anything if they cannot prove they were married to the deceased.

Memberships: Some memberships can be sold or transferred and are valuable assets. Some examples are country clubs, local annual golf memberships, theme parks, museums, travel, and health clubs, season tickets and annual passes to almost anything. Look for any documentation pointing to these assets. It is up to the executor to show due diligence in valuing these.

Military Discharge Papers: Separation Documents, DD214

Military Records: Form DD214

Money Market Accounts: Include locations, account numbers and access information.

Mortgage Accounts: Include locations, account numbers and access information to any property. If there is a mortgage locate the last mortgage statement. This bill will still have to be paid if it comes due until it is no longer needed.

Escrow mortgage accounts: Include locations, account numbers and access information.

Mutual Fund Accounts: an account with a financial company that allows someone to invest in mutual funds.

Organ Donor Cards: These must be readily available. If they are in a safe deposit box they may not be accessible until it is too late.

Passport and/or Passport Card: According to the NPIC, National Passport Information Center, you do not have to do anything with the passport or passport card of the deceased. The passport of a person who has died can be kept as a memento if you choose, or you can return it for cancellation.

Pensions: You can track unclaimed pensions, 401ks and IRAs at Unclaimed.com.

Personal Representative, Executor: Name of Church or religious institution, location, contact information and contact person.

Pets: Pets can and often are valuable assets. While "sparky" may just be a bird (or horse, dog, or cat etc.) to you, "sparky" may be an extremely rare or highly valued "pet". Are they a pet or an asset? In most cases they are both. Locate any pedigree or documentation.

Pet Care: Include all pertinent information: veterinarian, diet, medication if any, etc.

Power of Attorney: This allows someone else to make decisions for the individual if they are incapacitated.

Prenuptial Agreement: A Prenuptial Agreement is a contract between two people before they are married and usually handles issues relating to property.

Durable Health Care Power of Attorney: This allows the person named to make health care decisions for someone if they are incapacitated. If the individual is incapacitated and the family members can't locate a health care power of attorney, they will have to go to court to get a guardian appointed.

A Qualified Domestic Relations Order can prove your spouse received a share of your retirement accounts.

Real Property Homes and Buildings: Locations, titles, mortgages, keys, pass codes and all access information should be included.

Rental Contracts: This bill will still have to be paid if it comes due until it is no longer needed.

Retirement Accounts: Retirement accounts are often missed, especially if they were from a prior employer. List all employer-sponsored plans or pensions.

401ks: There could be more than one.

Safe Deposit Boxes: There could be more than one. Include all information as to the location, keys, contents list, contact person and all access information.

Savings Accounts: There could be more than one. Include all information as to the location, keys, contents list, contact person and all access information.

Savings Bonds: Government savings bonds. If only one person is named on a savings bond, and that person is deceased, the bond becomes the property of their estate. If one of two people named on a bond is deceased, the surviving person is automatically the owner as if that survivor had been the sole owner from the time the bond was issued.

Self Employment Agreements: Independent Contractor 1099s.

Social Security: Include all correspondence, cards, and statements.

Stocks and Bonds

Stock Certificates

Storage Fees: Storage fees could be for lockers. boat docks, aircraft hangers, or property. They can be out of state. If there are storage fees there are most likely assets in storage.

Student Loans: All contact information and accounts.

Tax Returns, all: Tax returns can supply personal information and social security numbers may list assets that you should be looking for. A final personal income tax return most likely needs to be filled from January 1, through the date of death. There may also be a revocable living trust return that needs to be filed.

Timeshares: Include all paperwork, location, keys, access information, name of company, account numbers and contact information.

Titles to real estate, boats, vehicles, motorcycles: Any or all of these may have been stored with a friend because the deceased was not supposed to even have them for various reasons.

Trust Accounts: Location, contact information, account numbers and access information.

Trustee(s): Name of Church or religious institution, location, contact information and contact person.

Revocable Trust: A revocable living trust can be changed anytime during your lifetime and they are more private and harder to dispute. You retain ownership of the trust assets and can dissolve or change the trust as needed.

Irrevocable Trust: An irrevocable trust transfers asset ownership to the trust fund, making the fund the legal owner of those assets. They are more private and harder to dispute.

Totten Trust: A Totten Trust is just a regular bank account with a designated "pay on death" inheritor. When the account is opened a friend, relative (most likely named as executor) is named as the beneficiary. This should be readily available. Include the name, location of the institution, account number(s), contact information and access information. This is generally used to pay funeral expenses.

Utility Bills, Service Agreements: Include a copy of all, with contact information and account numbers. Electric, gas, water, sewer, trash, pest control, lawn care, volunteer fire department (in some areas if you do not pay they do not work), pool, pet care, cable TV, phone, cell phones, etc. Most of these bills will still have to be paid when they come due until the service is no longer needed.

Veteran's Administration: if the person was a former member of the military.

Veterans Benefits: Include all correspondence and statements.

Voter Registration: request a cancellation for a deceased voter.

Will, Last Will and Testament, The most current Will: A copy or the original should be readily accessible. Wills are often located in a safe deposit box. In 2013 this document may just as likely show up on a cell phone, in the Cloud, or on a personal computer, laptop or eReader.

Plastic Cards

These can access liquid assets in "the twinkling of an eye". Collect these, guard and secure these against theft, fire and flood.

Some major types of Plastic Cards

An Access Card or Access Control Card: is a plastic card used to gain/control access to premises or enter restricted areas. Usually associated with magnetic or chip cards and proximity cards with or without photo e.g. ID badges.

ATM Cards: These can access bank accounts using a PIN (personal identity number). Also called a debit card, bank card or cash card.

Driver's License

Credit Cards, Charge Cards

Employment ID's

Gift Cards: Many look like a credit card but they only hold a specified amount of credit and contain no personal identification. Since these are constantly changing, assume they have information that you should secure.

Insurance Cards: Include the name of the carrier, phone numbers, account numbers and contact information. Many people like to hang on to cards from a previous employer that expired years ago. Check each one.

Medical Cards: some contain patient and billing information.

Membership Cards: check for benefits that may be valuable (season tickets).

Microprocessor Card: A microprocessor card is a type of smart card. They contain memory and are used for identification and to secure confidential files among other things.

Optical Card: An optical card contains information recorded on an optical memory stripe, similar to compact disks. These are not very common but still need to be secured.

Online log-in information: User name, password, pin number if needed and challenge questions. While these are not strictly documents, they access documents and assets that are sometimes worth than everything else combined. see *Digital Assets* page 40, 250, 333

Passport Cards: The passport card may be in place of or in addition to a Passport. Check for both. According to the NPIC, National Passport Information Center, you do not have to do anything with the passport or passport card of the deceased. The passport of a person who has died can be kept as a memento if you choose, or you can return it for cancellation.

Photo ID Card: A photo ID card can be used by employees to gain access to a secure building. It is an identification card bearing a photographic image of the cardholder. The image can be an actual photograph or one captured wholly electronically.

Phone Card: A phone card stores a specific cash amount that allows the user to access telephone networks via a PIN number.

Prepaid Card: A prepaid card is any one of many cards paid for at point of sale allowing the holder to purchase goods or services in an amount up to the prepaid value. The identity of the purchaser is not always known.

Protected Memory Card: A protected memory card is a smart card that requires a secret code or PIN number to be entered before data can be sent or received from the chip.

Proximity Card: A proximity card or **Key Card** is placed near a reader and the information is read from the card. They are used for mainly for employee security access control.

Retail Store Cards: Retail store cards are used by some grocery stores to track purchases. Not every card refers back to a customer name, address, phone number and email. The store expects the customer to fill out the information but many customers just use the card without ever doing so.

SIM card: A SIM card (Subscriber Identification Module) is a smart card that connects to a GSM (Global System for Mobile Communication) and establishes a user's identity and account number.

Smart Card, Contact Smart Card, or IC card: A smart card has an embedded microchip that may be used to store information about the cardholder or record card transactions as they occur. They are the size of a credit card and contain one or more semiconductor chips.

Union Cards: Union cards may hold personal account information, Insurance Policy Information, or any other information depending on the card and its purpose.

Closing the Estate

What Does It Take to Close a Deceased Person's Estate?

All Taxes must be paid. All outstanding debts must be satisfied.

All Disputes Must be Settled.

All Beneficiaries must be taken care of.

This is done last after all other fees, debts and taxes are paid. Some assets may have been sold to cover these other debts. Try to keep the family and heirs informed about what will be sold and why it is necessary. They may want to purchase it from the estate. You will be accountable to the court and others for the sale price.

Assets and Debt: For an estate to close, the executor must pay off the deceased's debts, and the Internal Revenue Service (IRS) must release the estate from any further liability for taxes. Any taxes the deceased or their estate owes are priority claims against their assets during probate.

After the probate court has approved the final accounting the executor can make the bequests and give the beneficiaries whatever property and money they've inherited. This property may have to be sold to pay off the deceased's debts.

If the deceased had any outstanding credit card balances or auto loans, or if they owed any other sort of creditor, these will now be paid. If you have already gathered Vital Statistics, documents and asset information this will be much easier. If it was not completed until now go back to the beginning of the Time Line and follow the steps. If this is a search that is just beginning, it may be time consuming but if you follow our advice it will be a lot easier. Just keep doing one thing from the list after the other and you will finish. The court won't allow closure until these things are completed. Do not be afraid to ask for help.

If you need help from an Attorney or an Accountant now would be the time to consult with these professionals. You can also go back to your list and call other family members or close friends. Do not keep putting this off. Begin at the beginning and you will get things done.

Paying the Internal Revenue Service

The executor must file a Personal Income Tax return for the deceased from January 1 until the time of death. Federal Income Tax may not yet be settled from the previous years. This will also need to be corrected.

If the estate earns any interest on investments during the probate period or assets increase in value, the executor may have to file an Estate Income Tax return.

Some states charge a State Estate Tax if assets increase in value or the estate earns any interest on investments during the probate period. If you are in this position it may be a good time to consult with a competent attorney.

A Federal Estate Tax return must be prepared and taxes paid if the estate is worth more than five-million dollars in 2011.

Paying Creditors

All Bills should have been collected by now: rent or mortgage payments, insurance policies. Check for Mortgage Insurance policies. State law sets various time limits for creditors to collect from the estate. These vary from state to state. The executor will notify creditors that the debtor has passed away. In addition to ordinary bills the decedent owed at the time of death, other debts typically include expenses to keep up property; local, state and federal taxes; hospital and funeral expenses; and expenses of administration including probate court costs, bond premiums and fees charged by appraisers, attorneys and the administrator.

Checking Accounts can be used to see some of the payments made and when they were made. Online accounts may show up here but they are more likely to be found in credit card statements.

The estate may have insufficient funds to pay all creditors. If the total assets in an estate are not sufficient to pay all of the valid debts, claimants must be paid according to a priority schedule established by law. After all debts, taxes, costs and expenses of the estate have been paid, the administrator must distribute the balance of the estate to the decedent's heirs according to the law.

Always record expenses you paid using personal funds. These charges can add up fast. Keep all receipts in a file folder. You need to be reimbursed by the estate if it has any money to reimburse you. It may be insolvent and may not be able to repay you. Think about this before you pay out-of-pocket expenses. see *Executor*, page 133

Generally, costs and expenses of administering the estate, funeral expenses and taxes must be paid first. After paying taxes and creditors, the executor must give a full accounting to the court, detailing everything they did.

Appraisals: may be needed for art or collections to ascertain if any estate taxes are due. Collections of types of rope may be interesting but have no real monetary value. You can usually find out by doing a little research online. If you have a collection of 45 rpm Records and one just happens to be an original Elvis audition, you just may have something worth a whole lot of money.

What Documents are Necessary to Close the Estate?

Confirm with the courthouse which documents are required to close the estate. You may find these online at the County website. Google (name of the county where the probate court is located) (the state) close probate.

Notice to heirs and beneficiaries: You are usually required to mail or otherwise deliver a notice to heirs and beneficiaries that a final hearing is coming up. There are time limits on when to do this and you must prove to the court that you actually did this. Check with the court as to how they want this done.

Taxes: You may be required to submit copies of all taxes filed on behalf of the deceased and the estate. Once the IRS issues a closing letter, if one is necessary, the judge will allow closure of the estate.

You may be required to prove the Will's validity by submitting the self-proving affidavit that was signed by the witnesses in front of a notary when the Will was signed. If this was not taken care of you may have to acquire notarized statements from one or more witnesses to the Will as to its validity.

Were you required to post a Bond? If you were you will also be required to show proof that you actually did this.

Proof of notification to Creditors: you will most likely need to file proof that you properly published and mailed the notice. The probate court should supply the notification requirements for known and unknown creditors. If you are required to publish the notice keep copies to show the court. The court may also specify the number of copies to publish, where the ads must be published (local newspapers), and the length of time the ads must be published (generally a few days). Finish this as soon as possible because it starts the clock on the time limit creditors have to file a claim against the estate. It takes long enough to close an estate without needlessly prolonging it.

You need to get the courts permission to distribute or transfer all of the remaining assets to the heirs.

Remember, you will get signed, dated receipts. Notarized if you feel it is necessary or the amount of value is considered by you to be significant.

Once the IRS issues a closing letter, if one is necessary, the judge will allow closure of the estate. You may now go before the court with all necessary paperwork and receipts and ask the court to close the estate and release you from your duties.

This book serves as a general guide not as legal advice. You will need to get more detailed information that is beyond the intentions of this book to close the estate properly.

Executor

Executor - Personal Representative – Administrator – Exectrix - Court Appointed Administrator

Administrator: A person appointed by a court to take charge of the estate of a decedent, but not appointed in the decedent's Will.

Executor: An Executor is someone who the deceased named in their Will to administer their estate: They oversee the disposition of property and possessions. If a person dies intestate, that is, without a Will, then the Personal Representative or Administrator will be appointed by the court. An Exectrix is a female executor.

> No matter what they are called, they all oversee the disposition of property and possessions of a deceased person. An executor is entrusted with the large responsibility of making sure a person's last wishes are granted with regards to the disposition of their property and possessions. They identify the estate's assets, pay off its debts and then distribute whatever is left to the rightful heirs and beneficiaries.
>
> Most of the time, the executor also has the "right of possession" to the deceased for disposition of the remains. An exception is when an agent for the deceased has been granted Durable Power of Attorney. In most instances the durable power of attorney ends when the person dies but many states are now allowing the agent permission to oversee the final disposition of the body, including authorizing an autopsy and following your wishes for organ and tissue donation.
>
> It is usually best for one sibling to consult with and bring the other siblings into the decision-making process. Many times, family members feel that the

executor is not disclosing all of the deceased's assets. If it is difficult now, chances are it will be a lot more difficult later to answer and deal with all of the questions and hurt feelings. Being the executor is often a thankless responsibility. Everything is on you. Bringing everyone in to help in the decision making may allow others to see how difficult a job this can be. Use your best judgment. We all have family members that we see far too often when we see them at all. You are the executor. It is your responsibility. Do whatever you think is best within your legal responsibilities, regardless of the opinion of others.

Executrix: A female executor.

Multiple Executors: Yes, you may have more than one executor but this can be more of a hindrance than a help. Think about it. A Successor Executor is sometimes named, if the original nominee is unable or unwilling to take upon the responsibility or predeceases the deceased.

Personal Representative: Executor, Personal Representative, Administrator, Exectrix, Court Appointed Administrator, Independent Executor, Independent Administrator, Temporary Administrator, Guardian and Temporary Guardian, together with their successors.

Executor and Funeral: An executor is responsible for organizing and paying for the funeral out of estate funds. The funeral costs are paid from the estate. If there is not enough money in the estate to cover the cost of the funeral or cremation the executor is not responsible for the costs.

Remember This: If you sign the contract at the funeral home agreeing to services YOU are responsible for paying the bill even if there is no money in the estate to do so. The problem is most funeral services or cremations are paid for during the first week after death before the executor can come to grips with what they are responsible for and what funds are available.

Change Executor: Can the executor be changed and then changed again? An executor does not exist until the testator has died and the executor has submitted the Will for probate and been appointed as executor by the probate court. A testator has the absolute right to make, destroy, revoke or change any Will without seeking the permission of any other party. It would be nice if the testator destroyed any Will that they had revoked and maybe even made mention of this in a forward to the new Will. But they do not have to.

Decline being the Executor: Should you decline being the executor? see *Executor*, page 144

> You may no longer be viewed as impartial or unbiased. You may no longer be thought of as a friend. There is a beneficiary or heir that wants what they think is rightfully theirs. You are in the middle. The emotional involvement may be difficult to handle. The probate process can take on average one year if there is anything of value in the estate. If there is nothing of value there is no need for probate. If decisions that you make are contested during the process it may take a few years to close the estate. You may have a family, a career, a job, in effect you may have a life of your own to consider. Do not place your own family last, they deserve better. If you were chosen as a trustee it was most likely because the beneficiary needed to be protected and this may be a different situation.

Priority: If there is no Will (intestate) the probate court will appoint an administrator for the estate. The court usually appoints the surviving spouse of the decedent, if none, or if the spouse declines, the court will appoint one of the next of kin of the decedent. Before the court issues official Letters Testamentary naming an administrator (or executor), the appointed person must sign an acceptance statement that describes his or her duties and acknowledges that the court can fine or remove an administrator (or executor) for failure to perform those duties faithfully. This varies by state. Most states require the executor, personal representative or administrator to post a Bond covering their actions. Although the executor may not be officially assigned until the court appointment, that person should be made available immediately to secure assets, gather information and make arraignments for final disposition.

Business: see *Business Ownership*, page 47, 98

Evicting a Family Member

Evicting a Family Member: Most administrators do not anticipate having to evict a family member from the home. An increasing number of children are moving back into their parents' home after a divorce or job loss. The average age the adult male leaves home in the U.S. is now estimated to be 27 years old. It is very possible one of the beneficiaries of the estate may be living in the home at the time of death. They are not the sole beneficiary of the home and are in no position to purchase the home from the estate. They may also be quite argumentative and refuse to leave the home so it can be sold. The executor or administrator may have to go through the eviction process. If the family member has been living in the home for some time they may be considered a month to month tenant and throwing all of their personal items out on the lawn may be a violation of their rights. The family may feel it is less expensive and kinder to resettle the individual in an apartment in the individual's name. Do not sign a lease in your name for someone else. As executor you may have to formally evict the family member. Go to your local sheriff's department and get information on what forms to fill out and how long it takes in your area. After the home is empty it needs to be made ready for sale.

Evicting Adult Children: If you are preplanning your Will you may need to evict an adult child before things get too far out of hand. If you cannot just ask them to leave you already have some problems that are not being addressed. You may be able to just change all of the locks and hope they go away. If you need help during this ask a friend to stay at the house with you during this time. Pack up all of their things and have them ready to be picked up. It would not be wise to allow them to enter the residence again unless you have a friend with you that can guarantee they also leave. It is probably best to arrange a time for them to come and pick up their things and have them at the front entry when they stop by. Get help from friends and family members while doing this. Sometimes the adult child will be embarrassed enough to politely leave.

Put it in Writing: If they will not leave politely or you cannot forcibly suggest they leave politely, outline what you expect from them concerning behavior, payment of rent and what behavior is not tolerated. You should always have them pay something, even if it is a minimal amount. If you have them agree to only twenty dollars a week and they are in arrears it may help your case later on. Include what will happen if they fail to live up to the agreement: eviction. Write it out and have them sign it in front of a notary if possible.

Eviction Process: State laws concerning eviction vary from state to state. Google: eviction (your state), start reading and take notes. Visit the local sheriff's office and ask them if they have an eviction form to fill out and file. If you are afraid of your adult child they can tell you exactly how to get help. This puts law enforcement on notice and will help you. There are social services that help with evictions a lot more than anyone realizes and they are very good at it. It is still your home and you have the right to decide who lives there.

Digital Executor or Digital Administrator: People are naming a Digital Executor more often but state laws have not kept up with the need. The executor still has all legal responsibility for the dispensation of the estate including the distribution of all digital assets to the beneficiaries by providing them with the necessary content and/ or access information. Some digital assets may still need to be posted online after death and files may need to be deleted and hard storage scrubbed clean.

The executor has the legal responsibility for disposition of the estate. The digital executor helps with Digital Assets: online storage "in the cloud", online shopping sites, websites, blogs, videos, CD's, DVD's (some contain important documents and may be password protected or encrypted). Family photos all stored online, on DVDs or thumb drives. There are passwords, encryption, challenge codes, social networking websites. All digital Assets must be protected and distributed. The Digital Executor can be very helpful.

The executor of the estate may not know how to find or even access Digital Assets worth hundreds of thousands of dollars. They may not even be aware off their worth. Facebook's $1 billion acquisition of the mobile start-up Instagram changed a lot of things. Today something as simple (to the untrained) as an "app" could be worth a billion dollars only if it is turned into a more liquid asset quickly. If you have Digital Assets it is important to protect them with a Digital Administrator that could possibly act as executor of the estate. In any case if you have any digital assets (and we all do) you may need to allow your executor to access this information. Make the executor aware of the digital executor. If you name your digital executor as a beneficiary the executor is obligated by law to inform them of your death and send them a copy of your Will.

There are new business's that specialize in administering digital estates for a fee. There are few regulations so buyer beware holds true. Be careful.

Responsibilities of the Executor

Buy a notebook and a file folder: Immediately start writing everything down such as who you talked with at the insurance company and the bank. There is a lot to keep track of. Record all expenses paid. You need to be reimbursed by the estate. Keep all receipts for flowers, food, catering funeral expenses, any out of pocket expenses, transportation, pet care, etc. Set up an estate checking account as soon as possible. It is much easier to make payments from this account than to be reimbursed later on. The executor should not be comingling funds or assets. Keep accurate and complete records of why you did what you did along with dates, times and contact information. Keep track of your hours. It is not unusual for it to take over one year to close an estate and you will be compensated by the estate according to law before the estate is closed. If there is anything left of value. From 1995 through 2012 a lot of value was sucked out of what was to be retirement accounts and future estates. More and more homes are "underwater" and more estates are insolvent.

There is so much going on and you have a death to grieve over and mourn. Chances are you are not at your best. Write everything down. When searching for an insurance policy, write down what you have done. When you are interrupted and must come back to this later your notes will help to prevent you from doing everything all over again.

1) Obtain the Will (gain possession). If there is no Will (intestate) the probate court will appoint an administrator for the estate. The court usually appoints the surviving spouse of the decedent, if none, or if the spouse declines, the court will appoint one of the next of kin of the decedent. Before the court issues official Letters Testamentary naming an administrator (or executor), the appointed person must sign an acceptance statement that describes his or her duties and acknowledges that the court can fine or remove an administrator (or executor) for failure to perform those duties faithfully. This varies by state. Most states require the executor, personal representative or administrator to post a Bond covering their actions.

2) Obtain Certified Copies of the Death Certificate.

3) Secure all Assets. The executor is legally responsible for the proper distribution of all assets. If Aunt Minnie is leaving the wake with the good silver in her purse the executor can later be sued for not using reasonable care in securing the assets. Secure all personal information and documents. Securing all assets both in state and out of state is extremely serious. If someone is taking something that you consider valuable or a part of the assets named in the Will it may be necessary to call the police for some help. Legal help may be necessary if an asset is legally owned by a decedent and is in the possession of someone else at the time of death, or if property belonging to the decedent has been misappropriated or concealed by a third party. Sometimes collecting assets may require the administrator to complete a lawsuit or begin a new lawsuit to recover assets. It may also be necessary to file a suit to recover damages for wrongful death if the deceased was killed in an accident.

The surviving spouse, the sole heir, or a joint owner of the account may already have access to the account. No court-appointed documents are needed. This is not usually a problem. For a married couple going through a divorce this may become a problem for the executor trying to be reimbursed for funeral expenses from the estate.

Surviving Spouse: Rename the accounts the spouse will keep. If for some reason the name cannot be changed it may be best to close the account and reopen a new account in the spouse's name.

Unsecured Debt: Unsecured debts in the deceased's name only are not owed by the spouse. The estate will most likely be held responsible. Community estate property is usually liable for any debt incurred by either spouse during marriage (if the couple was living separate and apart before entry of a judgment of marital dissolution or legal separation). If you are concerned about a situation involving a beneficiary you should do more research or speak with a competent estate attorney.

4) Set up a Checking Account for the estate to pay expenses from. Do not comingle your money with the estate's money.

5) Bank Accounts: The executor should inform the deceased's bank of their passing, so that the bank will put a hold on all funds and transfer them into an estate account. Any checks the executor receives that are made out to the estate are given to the bank and deposited into the account. The executor cannot touch any funds in the estate account until Letters Testamentary are received by the bank. The bank will also allow the executor to access any safety deposit boxes.

6) Locate and notify all Beneficiaries named in the Will and all other people who may have a legal interest in the Will. This may or may not include children from a previous marriage, a former spouse and others. They should each be sent a copy of the Will.

7) Probate Assets: Determine if there are any probate assets. Probate is a legal proceeding that pays your debts and transfers your property following your death according to the terms of your Will or in the absence of a Will, to your heirs based on probate law. Your estate will be probated whether or not you have a Will. All states have probate and every probate court has its own detailed rules about the documents it requires, what they must contain, and when they must be filed. see *Probate*, page 241

8) Assets: Locate, inventory, secure and place a value on, or appraise all assets of the deceased. Items in general do not have to be appraised item by item in all cases. For example: Household furniture: dining room table and six chairs $1,500, two bedrooms with beds and dressers $2,000, shop tools and power equipment $2,500 etc. A diamond necklace with six large diamonds and four small diamonds should have a closer appraisal. This is necessary for tax purposes and for a correct sale value if necessary. You will need to get more detailed information that is beyond the intentions of this book to close the estate properly.

Securities that are named with a single beneficiary should be transferred as soon as possible to reduce or eliminate the executor's responsibility for those holdings.

9) Receive any Payments Due the estate. Salary, vacation time, and wages from an employer. Interest and dividends.

10) Credit Unions: You can contact the three major credit reporting agencies: Experian, Equifax and Transunion. Check the Deceased's credit report. It will list all the credit accounts in the Deceased's name. This will help in locating assets and liabilities. Make sure to ask the credit agency to mark the accounts as "deceased" to avoid any possibility of identity theft. You will need Letters Testamentary and a certified copy of the Death Certificate.

11) Notify all Creditors. You will most likely need to file proof that you properly published and mailed the notification requirements for known and unknown creditors. The probate court should supply the notification requirements for known and unknown creditors and these can usually be found on their website. The requirements may vary from state to state or even county to county. This needs to be done quickly because it starts the time limit on creditors to file a claim against the estate.

12) File Claims for all Benefits. Insurance, social security and employer. etc.

13) Cancel as necessary all of the decedent's memberships, driver's license, handicap permits, social security payments, library cards, etc. Before canceling memberships that include the right to season tickets, discounts or anything of value check to see if they can be transferred or sold.

Cancel as necessary all of the decedent's credit cards, debit cards, etc. If these are also joint accounts you may want to keep them open and remove the decedent's name. Identify authorized users for each credit card and account

14) Validate Debts: Are there any claims against the estate? You need to verify and validate these.

15) Make Payments: Generally funeral expenses, taxes and the costs and expenses of administering the estate must be paid first. The IRS considers the deceased person and their estate to be separate taxpaying entities. You will need a separate tax-identification number to file tax returns for the estate if the estates income is over a few hundred dollars. (It used to be $600). This is for dividends, interest and capital gains on the decedent's assets during the administration of the estate. A final federal personal income tax return will need to be filed. A final state personal income tax return will need to be filed. see *Tax*, page 433

If a person is both the sole beneficiary of the estate, and the estate is not subject to Federal Estate Tax, it usually does not make sense to take any fees as all fee income is subject to Income Tax.

16) Pay other Debt: If the estate includes vehicles, maintain insurance premiums and loan payments until the vehicles are transferred to a beneficiary. Continue to pay property taxes, utilities and keep homes as if they are being lived in until you can legally transfer them to beneficiaries or heirs. These payments must be kept current. Continue to pay bills on properties that are out of state, storage lockers, and rental space for boats, RVs, airplanes and motorcycles.

If there are sufficient cash assets in the estate to pay debts, they will be paid out of cash. If there is not enough cash, then estate property will be sold (personal property first and then real estate) to raise the cash needed.

17) Insolvent Estate: If the total assets in an estate are not sufficient to pay all of the valid debts, claimants must be paid according to a priority schedule established by law.

18) After all debts, taxes, costs and expenses of the estate have been paid, the executor or administrator must distribute the balance of the estate to the decedent's beneficiaries or heirs according to law.

19) Distribute the remaining property in accordance with the instructions provided in the deceased's Will and Close Probate. The duties of the executor begin from the time of death and continue until the Probate Court releases them.

Hire a Probate Lawyer: The Executor, Personal Representative or Administrator does not have to do everything by themselves. They are allowed to hire a probate lawyer when necessary and pay the legal fees out of the estate.

Hire an Executor: Can I just hire someone to be the Executor? Yes. You can hire a professional executor. Banks and trust companies are available to serve as an executor of a Will. The fee professional executors charge varies, but it is usually a flat fee and a percentage of value of the probate property. The company may also charge an additional fee for handling non-probate property. It can get expensive.

> Even when a professional serves as executor, an attorney will usually be retained and there may now be two professional fees paid from the estate. If an attorney is serving as both executor and attorney they may wave one fee but charge for both attorney fees and executor fees at the higher rate. You will pay for time and service. It is usually best to speak with and work with an attorney. You do the work of the executor with the help of an attorney to keep you on target and answer questions. As with anything else shop around.

Remove the Executor: Can the beneficiaries or heirs have the executor or personal representative removed? Yes. If a beneficiary or heir feels that an executor is breaching their fiduciary duties in a way that does not comply with the wishes of the deceased, they may petition the probate court to have the person removed as executor.

This book is not intended to be all inclusive and it is not intended to be a "How To" in place of good legal advice from a competent attorney. It is, however, intended to be a window into what an executor will have to deal with should you decide to become the executor or administrator. Use this as a guide and please seek competent legal advice as needed.

Executor? No, Thank You

So you want to be an Executor or Personal Administrator?

No, Thank-you.

It may be an honor to be named someone's executor, but it is also a lot of administrative work that needs to be done properly. Most executors choose to work with a competent estate attorney. This makes things much more manageable.

Do the Executor - Personal Representative - or Personal Administrator get paid? *Yes.* How much?

These fees are dictated by the state. Sometimes this is a "reasonable" fee and sometimes it is listed as a percent of the estate (2%-4% up to one-hundred thousand dollars, 2.5% on a million dollars is reasonable, and decreasing as the estate gets larger).

If you are traveling from out of state you may have expenses for time lost from work, airfare, hotel or motel, meals away from home and car rental. You may also incur attorney fees to get help in disposing of the estate according to the law. Probate usually takes over six months and can take upwards of a year. You must keep excellent records and keep all receipts. The court may ask for them if you are to be reimbursed. The Will must also be carefully reviewed to look for any guidance as to what the Personal Representative should be paid.

Will the Estate Reimburse Me for my costs? *Maybe, Maybe Not*

Executor and Funeral: An executor is responsible for organizing and paying for the funeral out of estate funds. The funeral costs are paid from the estate. If there is not enough money in the estate to cover the cost of the funeral or cremation the executor is not responsible for the costs.

Remember This: If you sign the contract at the funeral home agreeing to services YOU are responsible for paying the bill even if there is no money in the estate to do so. The problem is most funeral services or cremations are paid for during the first week after death before the executor can come to grips with what they are responsible for and what funds are available

Insolvent Estate: If the estate owes more than the available assets then there will be no money available to pay you. In addition to ordinary bills the decedent owed at the time of death, other debts typically include expenses to keep up property; local, state and federal taxes; hospital and funeral expenses; and expenses of administration including probate court costs, bond premiums and fees charged by appraisers, attorneys and the administrator.

Probate, Simplified Procedure: Is there a simplified procedure for settling an estate with limited assets? Yes, in most states there is. There are various rules and regulations depending on the state and/or county but there will most likely be a dollar amount mentioned. An example could be: A simplified procedure for settling the estate may be available if the total value of the estate assets does not exceed ($40,000). In addition, at the time of death the decedent must not own any real estate other than survivorship property, and the estate assets must consist only of personal property and/or an unreleased interest in a mortgage with or without value etc. If a simplified procedure is available it may not be necessary to probate the estate

Funeral Expenses: Funeral expenses are usually paid by someone, out-of-pocket and they will later submit receipts to the estate for payment. With any payout from a life insurance policy or pension plan these bills have a good chance of being reimbursed later on. There are time limits for filing a claim with the estate for repayment.

Insufficient Funds: The estate may have insufficient funds to pay all creditors. If the total assets in an estate are not sufficient to pay all of the valid debts, claimants must be paid according to a priority schedule established by law. After all debts, taxes, costs and expenses of the estate have been paid, the administrator must distribute the balance of the estate to the decedent's heirs according to the law.

Priority for Debt: Generally, funeral expenses, taxes, and then the costs and expenses of administering the estate, must be paid first. After paying taxes and creditors, the executor must give a full accounting to the court, detailing everything they did.

Public Aid: In most states, some forms of public aid allowances are available from the state, county, city or a combination to obtain a dignified burial for the indigent. Your state Department of Social Services may be able to help.

How much does Probate Cost?

Probate: Probate is a legal proceeding that transfers your property following your death according to the terms of your Will or in the absence of a Will, to your heirs based on probate law. Your estate will be probated whether or not you have a Will. All states have probate and every probate court has its own detailed rules about the documents it requires, what they must contain, and when they must be filed. Probate pays debts and transfers assets to beneficiaries. see *Probate*, page 34, 241

Court Fees: Court fees are dictated by state law and can range anywhere from a few hundred dollars to over a thousand dollars.

Personal Representative (Executor or Administrator) and their Attorney Fees: These fees are dictated by state law. Some states reference a "reasonable fee" while others reference a reasonable fee that is equal to a percentage of the value of the estate being probated. It could be more if allowed by the court.

A typical fee is a flat amount for the first $100,000 of property plus a percentage of the value of the assets above $100,000. If the estate is large and had competent preplanning it may be less expensive to find an attorney that charges by the hour.

Accounting Fees: Accounting fees will depend upon the overall value of the estate and the type of assets owned. Will the accountant or the executor file taxes?

Appraisal Fees: Appraisal fees may be necessary to determine the value of real estate, jewelry, antiques, art work, collections, vehicles, etc. at the time of death. They can be a few hundred or a few thousand dollars.

Bond Fees: If the Last Will and Testament does not specifically waive the posting of a bond by the executor or Personal Representative, then in most cases they will need to pay for and post a bond in an amount determined by the probate judge. Sometimes even if the bond is waived the state law will require the executor to post a bond.

Miscellaneous Fees: Postage and the cost of documents: 12 death certificates at $25 each = $300. You may need 15-20 certified copies of death certificates. You may need a few copies of Letters Testamentary to prove you are the legal executor. There are costs for relocating and securing property, storage fees, and the cost of insuring and storing personal property. Out of state property: what is the value? How much is owed? Should you go and look at the property? Out of state property may be probated by another probate court depending on how the property is titled. These may all be out-of-pocket expenses to be paid by the estate if funds are available.

Other Costs: Travel expenses to the deceased's residence, airfare, meals away from home, car rental, attorney fees to get help in disposing of the estate according to the law, time lost from work, out of state living expenses for days or weeks (do you need to sell a home for the estate?), airfare back and forth to an out of state residence as the estate goes through probate.

Who is responsible to pay these fees? Fees and costs should be paid from the estate of the deceased. If the estate appears to be small there will usually be a rush to open probate so funds can be accessed to pay bills. An executor needs to be appointed as quickly as possible in order to access any bank accounts. As executor do not comingle your funds with those of the estate.

While this process is ongoing, bills still need to be paid: taxes, utilities for properties both in state and out of state, insurance, auto payments and mortgage payments if these are assets going to a beneficiary. As executor you will be responsible to deliver an asset to a beneficiary or dispose of it. You are legally responsible to handle this properly. Funeral arraignments are generally paid at the time of service. **The general rule is: if you sign for any funeral arraignments then you are responsible for making payment no matter what happens later on.**

If expenses are not paid on time soon after death, there may be interest or late fees. If you do not pay storage fees or insurance fees for real property and it is lost due to accident etc. you may be held libel.

Taxes: There may be additional costs to the estate, such as property taxes, the deceased's personal income taxes for the last year they were alive. Estate taxes, estate income tax (different than estate tax), state estate tax, state personal income tax, etc. see *Tax*, page 433

Funeral Expenses

How are these paid? The family will typically spend the first week handling the burial or cremation arrangements. **The funeral home requires payment long before an estate can be opened to allow you to pay expenses from**

the estate account. The most common way of paying for a funeral from an estate is simply paying the bill yourself, and then asking the estate to reimburse you. You will need to keep all receipts. Submit a receipt to the Executor (Personal Representative) of the estate for repayment. If it looks like you will not be reimbursed file a claim against the estate for payment. There is a time limit to file so do this immediately. In the case of limited assets costs and expenses of estate administration, family allowance, exempt property, homestead claims, and limited funeral expenses have high priority of payment. Debts are paid and then Beneficiaries are paid last if anything is left.

Funeral Cost: The average cost of a funeral is $8,500. The average cost of cremation is $1,000 if arraigned through a cemetery or crematorium. This is average. Both can be done for much more or much less. Direct Cremation costs can be reduced to less than $600 or $400 in some cases. Yes, you need to shop around. A loved one passes on Monday and in most cases you have about two weeks to be finished with the burial or cremation including payment and paperwork. If the deceased has already made funeral arraignments it is much simpler. If they prepaid for these arraignments or used a Trust account to pay for these arraignments it is even easier. If you do not know, ask. Look for paperwork. see *Documents*, page 115

The executor is responsible for the funding of and organizing the final disposition of the body in most cases. The funds are paid from the estate; if there is not enough money in the estate to cover the funeral, the executor is in most cases not responsible for the costs. There are a few states that can actually appoint someone to take responsibility and make payment. We will most likely see more of this as the population ages and has fewer assets left in their estate. There is far greater flexibility in dealing with the remains in cremation as opposed to the traditional burial. Direct Cremation costs can be reduced to less than $600 or even $400 in some cases.

Insurance Policies: In many cases the funeral home or crematorium will ask the customer to just sign over the insurance policies to them and then they will refund whatever is left over. DO NOT DO THIS. Get a written agreement as to the total cost. In many instances the funeral home will charge a fee for services and then charge a larger fee of thousands of dollars and just list it as "Cemetery Fees" since cemeteries are not held responsible under the "Funeral Rule" there is no way to really find out what these "Fees" were for. Although most service providers are honest this can and does happen. If you have a situation do not hesitate to call your local State Representative (Congressman), they have a full time staff to help you and will be more than happy to help in your time of need. Google: congressman (your state)

The Body: The executor has full responsibility with regards to the funeral arrangements and should be named in the Will. If the deceased dies intestate (no Will) or there is no executor then an administrator, or the person in priority to be the administrator, has the right to possession of the body for the purpose of disposing of the remains. The Will should state clearly what the deceased wished to be done after they passed. If no funds are available from the estate you are under no obligation to follow these instructions.

If there are no available funds. With the loss of a job people almost always lose the life insurance that was part of their benefit package. Whoever does the final disposition of the body will want to be paid at the time of service. Whoever signs the contract will be agreeing to pay in full the entire bill for services no matter what relationship they have with the family and this is not always reimbursed at a later time. Sometimes there simply is no money in the estate and Taxes are always paid first.

If you arrange a funeral, you will be responsible for paying the bill, so first check where the money will come from and that there will be enough to cover expenses. Cremation is dignified and far less expensive than burial. Direct Burial or Direct Cremation is less expensive than what is called a traditional funeral.

Having to finance a burial or cremation can be a burden that many, perhaps most, families are unprepared to face. Some customers are required to put up collateral when they are asked to make payments for funeral services. The funeral service may feel payments are more likely to be made if they hold the title to a family vehicle that can be repossessed and sold.

Are Children Responsible for the Funeral Costs of Indigent Parents?

Yes and No – It depends

It depends on the laws of the state in which the death occurred and the laws of the state in which the adult child now resides. Most of the time the answer is No, the adult child is not responsible for the funeral costs. However as more and more deaths occur after the deceased has cashed out all or most of the assets including insurance, pensions, and retirement accounts, states are changing the law to place this burden somewhere else. As mentioned above if you arrange a funeral, you will be responsible for paying the bill. Be careful what you sign. Some states like Arizona have or had statutes that allowed funeral homes to bill and collect funeral expenses from adult children who had no contact with the parent and lived out of state. This may have changed so you really need to do your homework on this issue. It will become more of a problem and not less of a problem as the 80,000,000 Baby boomers age over the next 15 years.

Many people know that if there is no money to bury someone then the city or county pays for it. This is still true some of the time.

Many people have cashed in insurance policies, which leaves them with no money for burial expenses. Other family members either cannot or will not take responsibility for the burial of loved ones. In some cases they are not making payments after arranging for burial services. And younger people just do not seem to care. If no one claims the body, there are procedures in place for disposition of the remains.

The legal responsibility for burial falls to the deceased person's closest relative, such as a spouse, adult child or parent. In many cases the first in line to be billed for the funeral is the person who signed for and was given Durable Power of Attorney. Before you apply for an indigent burial determine who is responsible for the funeral arrangements. If you make arrangements and sign for them you will be held responsible for payment no matter who should have done what.

How long will Probate take?

Hidden assets may take days, weeks, months or years to locate. If someone disagrees with the disposition, an appraisal, or the sale of assets it could take longer. The Will defines the powers of the executor. If the executor or personal representative is not given all of the powers necessary to buy, sell, mortgage, or deal with the property it will usually take much longer to probate the estate. One year is not unreasonable. see *Executor*, page 133

What are the duties of an Executor - Personal Representative - Administrator?

The Body: The executor has full responsibility with regards to the funeral arrangements and should be named in the Will. If the deceased dies intestate (no Will) or there is no executor then an administrator, or the person in priority to be the administrator, has the right to possession of the body for the purpose of disposing of the remains.

Can body parts or organs be sold to pay off the estate? *No.* see *Organ Donor*, page 204

Assets: The executor must locate and protect all assets until they can be distributed to the beneficiaries or sold to pay debts. This includes Digital Assets, Liquid assets, Real Property and Vehicles, etc. see *Assets*, page 5, 41, 57, 75

Probating the Will: The executor must work with the Probate Court if the estate goes through probate. Whether or not the Will is probated will depend on the laws of the state and the value of the estate. The law usually requires the Will to be filled in the appropriate probate court even if the Will does not have to be probated.

Notify: The executor must notify the beneficiaries of the Will. Notify the Trustee, if any, and supply all parties with copies of the Will. If there is an attorney involved they may have already done this.

The Executor must look for and collect on all insurance policies, social security benefits, retirement accounts, pension plans, bank accounts, safe deposit boxes. The executor must also secure all property from theft, cancel credit cards, notify all banks and close all accounts. They must pay all bills and pay all taxes due from the estate. The executor may need to set up an estate bank account to keep the estates funds separate from their own. In effect the personal representative or executor must take care of the deceased's affairs. This is one of the reasons preplanning is so very important.

The executors will most likely stay in contact with the beneficiaries while doing all of this.

The personal representative or executor is responsible for paying all taxes. This includes, but is not limited to, the deceased's income taxes for the last year they were alive. This is from January 1 until the date of death. see *Tax*, page 433

The executor then pays off funeral expenses and administrative fees. Creditors are next. Assets may have to be sold to accomplish this. see *Debt*, page 108

If there is anything left the executor is responsible for distributing any property to the beneficiaries. see *Executor*, page 133

What if I really screw up the job? Can I be sued?

Can I be held personally libel? *Yes*

The executor or personal representative may be held responsible for any damages they cause. You may be liable to the estate, the beneficiaries or both.

The executor must make rational decisions. They have a legal fiduciary responsibility to act with utmost honesty, impartiality, and scrupulousness on behalf of the deceased and the estate's beneficiaries.

What if I do a really great job? Can I still be sued? *Yes*

Not everyone may agree with how you handle the estate. You may find it necessary to sell off certain assets to pay off creditors. If you have choices and sell off one asset instead of another a beneficiary may disagree enough to take you to court and try to recover what they feel is rightfully theirs.

I know I can be sued for almost anything today. I haven't spoken to family members in a long time; will they think I took all the money? Most people really have no idea what is going to happen when a loved one passes. Most people will assume that there was some money and do not understand that things must take place in a specific order before the estate can be distributed. Always try to avoid situations at a later date by keeping beneficiaries informed. If there is any dispute over an item no matter what the cost, probate the item. An old teapot that is worth $1.85 may cause you more grief and legal fees later on than anything else. If you just have the item added to what the court probates, then the court decides as to the disposition and not you.

Can I just hire someone to be the Executor? Yes.

You can name a professional executor. Banks and trust companies are available to serve as an executor of a will. The fee professional executors charge varies, but it is usually a flat fee and a percentage of the probate property. A professional executor is usually not necessary if you work with a competent estate attorney.

As the population ages most people will find that as they get older even what seemed doable a few years ago, can now become frightening. We have said over and over: preplan, do it properly, and be responsible for your death as well as your life. If you decide to look into a professional executor shop around. see *Executor*, page 133

Can a will be changed without notifying the executor of the most current existing will? *Yes*

An executor does not exist until the testator has died and the executor has submitted the Will for probate and been appointed as executor by the probate court. A testator has the absolute right to make, destroy, revoke or change any Will without seeking the permission of any other party. It would be nice if the testator destroyed any Will that they had revoked and maybe even made mention of this in a forward to the new Will. But they do not have to.

How is the Executor or Personal Representative Named?

Anyone can appoint you to be their Executor without asking your permission. Surprise! The executor is named in the Will or if there is no Will, appointed by the court. In most cases you may decline.

Who is next of kin?

The person or persons most closely related by blood or marriage to another person. This could be the son or daughter of a divorced parent that you have not had contact with for years. What legal responsibility does the child of a divorced parent have to the estate? Most likely none.

Are there assets? Millions of dollars in assets? Is everything upside down and they now owe more than the estate is worth? This is the time to seek advice from someone you can trust who may not have a vested interest in the outcome.

What happens to the body if there is no next of kin?

Public employees will handle the body, personal property and money of those who have died. The body is prepared for disposition. Workers haul away personal property, photographs, digital assets, little treasures and mementos. Auctioneers disperse the property from county warehouses.

What happens to the body if there is a Will but there are no visible assets?

If no one comes forward and makes the arrangements themselves they are most likely not responsible for the funeral expenses. The body is considered unclaimed and they are abandoning the body and have no say in how the body is buried or cremated. The city or county government in which the body is located will bury the body and charge the decedent's estate with the cost. More families today are fragmented or have financial problems. With the average cost of a funeral in the U.S. at $8,500 it is no longer reasonable for one family member to step forward and assume responsibility for someone they have not even seen in years.

As more states and localities run out of funding they may no longer be able to pay for this service. We saw this happen in Detroit, Michigan and other cities in recent years. When the states run out of funds the local cities or counties are burdened with the expense. As this happens more pressure is put on families to pay for these costs. Remember: If you arrange for the funeral and sign for it you most likely will be held legally responsible for the costs involved.

An Insolvent Estate

An Insolvent Estate: Is the estate really Insolvent? Are there other assets? Bank accounts, safe deposit boxes, collections, out of state property, or stocks or bonds purchased years ago? One piece of antique jewelry made by a now famous designer can be worth a small fortune at auction. A rare stamp or rare coin can be worth a great deal of money. We have all seen the TV shows or heard about someone who "found" a treasure that was overlooked. People usually keep the very best that they can. They drag it from place to place, hide it and protect it as best they can. So again: Is the estate really insolvent?

Just because there is more owed on the home than it is worth does not rule out an oil painting hanging in the back bedroom that is worth millions. I can recall a case where an elderly lady died while living on the streets of a major city and she was actually an heiress worth millions of dollars.

I am the next of kin. Can I be forced to be the executor or court appointed administrator? *It is not likely*

In all likelihood the state will not force someone to act as executor or personal representative for the deceased. They will use the Probate Court to handle the disposition of the deceased's estate. In this way they simply tax the estate for any and all fees due. However, I think more and more states will be looking for some family member or next of kin to pay for the disposition of the body. For a simple dignified direct cremation the average cost to the state or local government is $300. The average cost of a funeral in the U.S. in 2012 is $8,500. Direct Burial is less.

This can change if the named executor is legally libel for some or all of the decedent's debt. see *Debt*, page 108

Legally Obligated: Are you legally obligated to administer the decedent's estate because you are liable for the decedent's debt? Are you the decedent's spouse? Did you cosign a mortgage, a loan contract or in any way link your assets to the deceased through a business? Are you listed on a joint account? This may be a good time to speak with a qualified attorney because the laws governing these situations change frequently and can vary from state to state or even within a state.

Debts and the Deceased: The general rule is that a person is not liable for the debts of another. A decedent's spouse, in a community property state, may be libel for all of the debt of the deceased spouse. A joint account holder most often will be held accountable for the other account holder, even if deceased. A person may be libel for another's debt if they cosigned a loan, acted as guarantor, and accepted the responsibility of payment for that loan when they cosigned the contract. Also when two people sign up for a credit card together, both are libel for the debt, even if one person never used the card.

What if the deceased's home is under water?

If the property was owned solely by the decedent the mortgage debt is the responsibility of the estate. The mortgage will have to be satisfied along with all other debt before the estate can be closed. If the estate contains a home that is "underwater," that is, its net proceeds of sale would not pay of the balance of its debt; you should consider abandoning the home and allowing it to be foreclosed upon by its lender(s), so that you incur no further expense on or liability with it. If the home is owned jointly or is in a community property state the surviving spouse (if any) has specific legal rights and these must be considered before anything is done. This is a good time to speak with a competent attorney.

Many people owe more money on their home than the home can be sold for. Their home is said to be "underwater". Always check for a "payable on death" benefit within or attached to the mortgage.

It will be much easier to administer an estate if you live locally. Living even a few hours' drive away can complicate things a great deal.

What about a Reverse Mortgage?

A reverse mortgage is a loan available to homeowners age 62 or older. It is a special type of home loan that lets you convert a portion of the equity in your home into cash. Homeowners can draw a lump sum or receive monthly payments as a revolving line of credit. The homeowner's obligation to repay the loan is deferred until the owner(s) die, the home is sold, or the homeowners cease to live in the property or breach the provisions of the mortgage. There are no monthly principal and interest payments but you are required to pay real estate taxes, home owner association fees, utilities, and hazard and flood insurance premiums. If the value of the property increases it is possible to acquire a second or third reverse mortgage.

When the home is sold or no longer used as a primary residence, **the cash, interest, and other HECM finance charges must be repaid.** All proceeds beyond the amount owed belong to the surviving spouse or estate. Any remaining equity can be transferred to beneficiaries or heirs.

Payments may be received as:

Tenure: Equal monthly payments as long as at least one borrower lives and continues to occupy the property as a principal residence.

Term: Equal monthly payments for a fixed period of months selected.

Line of Credit: A line of credit allows unscheduled payments or installments, at times and in an amount of your choosing until the line of credit is exhausted. At this point it may make sense to speak with a competent attorney who is well versed in estate planning. If the home is valued at a high level you may want to draw up a Last Will and Testament, set up a pay on death bank account, pre-purchase simple funeral arrangements, place cash in accordance with the executors need to administer the future estate and in general be responsible in life and in death.

Modified Tenure- combination of line of credit and scheduled monthly payments for as long as you remain in the home.

Modified Term- combination of line of credit plus monthly payments for a fixed period of months selected by the borrower.

Am I legally obligated to administrate the deceased's insolvent estate? *Yes, sometimes*

You are most likely legally obligated to administer the decedent's estate if you are liable for the decedent's debt. Are you the decedent's spouse? Did you cosign a mortgage, a loan contract or in any way link your assets to the deceased through a business? Are you listed on a joint account? This may be a good time to speak with a qualified attorney because the laws governing these situations change frequently and can vary from state to state or even within a state.

The general rule is that a person is not liable for the debts of another. A decedent's spouse, in a community property state, may be libel for all of the debt of the deceased spouse. This can include unpaid medical bills. A joint account holder most often will be held accountable for the other account holder, even if deceased. A person may be libel for another's debt if they cosigned a loan, acted as guarantor, and accepted the responsibility of payment for that loan when they cosigned the contract. If two people opened a credit card account together they are generally both held accountable even if one person never used the card.

Should I go ahead and administer an Insolvent Estate?

If you are not libel for the deceased's debts, then there is no reason you should administer an insolvent estate. **IF the estate is actually insolvent.** See Insolvent Estate above.

How am I notified that I have been chosen to be executor? Do I get a call? Registered letter?

This can vary. First the Will must be located. If a Will cannot be found does anyone know the name of the person(s) who drew up the Will? They should have a copy of the Will. If the executor is named in the Will they may be notified by any means available. Ideally the Executor should be notified by the testator (person writing the Will) before they pass on. There is nothing like the final passing of a close friend or loved one and then the SURPRISE ! You have been named as the executor of the estate. This is just not good manners. You may not be required to accept but remember you were chosen for a reason. The person may have been rushed and never got around to discussing this with you. They respected you enough to want your help and assistance. Do your best for them and you will sleep much better in the nights to come.

I just do not want to get involved. What next?

If you have a legal obligation to become the executor because of comingled debt or court order, now would be a good time to speak to a competent attorney familiar with estate law.

If you are not legally obligated to become the executor first find out what you can very quickly because someone must make arrangements. Were you the only Executor or personal representative named? Was a Successor Executor named? If there are others, you may choose to change your mind. If you still decide to not become the administrator, executor, or personal representative whatever else they choose to call it, just say no, thank you. Do not sign anything without consulting with an attorney, and ask to be kept informed.

Can I go and look for the money and then turn down being the executor?

Yes, a lawyer or anyone appointed as Executor can quit. Now would be a good time to speak with a competent estate attorney and see just what options you really have. You may have a lot more choices. Get some good information and then make a good decision. The law varies from state to state and sometimes within a state.

OK I am the executor and now I am in way over my head. What can I do? Help!! I just want to give up and quit and go home.

An Executor can "renounce probate", which means they no longer wish to be an Executor. If an Executor doesn't apply for Probate, family members, beneficiaries and other interested parties can apply to the Court to be appointed an Executor. A creditor is considered an interested party in most all cases.

Many people get to this point because everything is a surprise to them. They are not accountants, or attorneys. They are mothers and fathers, sisters and brothers. It is one of the main intentions of this book to help make this process easier for everyone. Now is the time to speak with other family members and a competent attorney who comes highly recommended and is well versed in estate law in the state where the deceased lived. Do not be embarrassed to get help. You owe it to everyone, including yourself to get competent help and do the best job that you can in this difficult time.

There are over 80,000,000 baby boomers in the United States. There is a greater chance than ever that the majority of family members will be living in another state. There is a greater chance than ever that the deceased has taken out a Reverse Mortgage on their home, or more money is owed on their home than it is worth even if you could sell it. There is a greater chance than ever that insurance policies have been cashed in, no Will has been drafted, and no arrangements have been made by the deceased for a proper burial or cremation.

It used to be when someone died they had some assets. Not so today. Many boomers will be in debt when they pass. They will leave this burden to family, friends or the state. The probate courts will backlog with all of the legal ramifications and the states will have to address this issue sooner or later.

Laws change every day. It is always your responsibility to use due diligence and review the laws in your state and county. If you feel like you are in over your head, you are not alone.

Free Funeral

Are Any Funerals Free?

Free Funeral: Funeral expenses are usually paid out of the estate of the deceased. If the estate is insolvent or the deceased was indigent, most cities or counties have funds set aside for the disposition of the deceased that are very poor. As these funds run low there is going to be more of an effort to assign this cost to next of kin.

Liability of Next-of-Kin: In some states a person may be liable for funeral or burial expenses based on his or her relationship to the decedent, such as a husband and wife, or a parent and child even if you have not seen or heard from the relative for years and years. Some statutes designate the persons charged with the duty of burial but do not impose financial responsibility for burial or funeral expenses. Others impose financial liability on designated people in the order in which they are named in the statute.

No Next-of-Kin: Public employees will handle the body, personal property and money of those who have died. The body is prepared for disposition. Workers haul away personal property, photographs, digital assets, little treasures and mementos. Auctioneers disperse the property from county warehouses.

An individual, charity or institution that is not normally obligated to pay for the disposition of remains can elect to do so. Remember if you sign the contract with the funeral or cremation service provider for goods and/or services you are obligated to pay the cost. You signed for it and you will be held accountable to pay for it. In many cases these expenses are turned over to the executor and you are reimbursed out of the decedent's estate. This is not true in every case. The estate may not have any money to pay you. Be careful, if you make arrangements and sign for goods and/or services you will be held responsible for payment no matter who should have done what.

Local churches, service organizations and charities often have funeral funds available for those who were active members.

Memorial Societies: Memorial societies work with death care providers to create fixed-cost packages. Some may be better than others. Be careful and shop around.

Cremation and Burial Societies: Some are very good and some are not. They offer low cost cremation and burial services. Some are for specific religious groups or veterans groups. Be careful and shop around.

Direct Burial and Direct Cremation: Many funeral homes and crematories offer direct burial and direct cremation which provide the minimum level of death care required. It can be very dignified and meaningful while keeping expenses down. Goods and or services may be added with or without the service provider. A memorial service at an outside facility or public park, for instance.

Federal Statue: Federal statutes authorize the payment of expenses for the burial or disposal of the remains of certain persons in federal custody, persons dying on or in federally owned property or facilities, and certain federal employees who die in the line of duty. Also, federal statutes authorize payment of interment of employees of the Immigration and Naturalization Service who die while in a foreign country in the line of duty.

Veterans: U.S. Veterans of the Armed Forces who received an honorable discharge may be entitled to a burial in the local National Cemetery at no cost. The Veterans Administration will reimburse a portion of the burial or cremation expenses if the veteran's death is service connected. The VA may also assist with burial, cremation, and plot expenses for eligible veterans. see *Veterans*, page 263

Donating the Body to Medical Study: The body may be donated to a medical college. Go online and check with a facility in your area to find out their rules and regulations. Usually it is very simple: You give your permission by filing out a copy of the Bequest Form and the deceased is picked up. Cremation is often provided free of charge, with ashes returned to the family. If a family member cannot be located in many cases the ashes are kept for one year and then scattered. Sometimes there is a small fee of $100 or less. **Can body parts or organs be sold to pay off the estate?** *No.* see *Organ Donor*, page 204

Funeral Goods & Services

Funeral Home

Will there be a service? What type of service: religious, military, fraternal, a memorial service with or without the body, a wake, or a graveside service? A service at graveside when there is a cremation is common. Will there be more than one service?

Private Service: A private service is by invitation only and may be held at a place of worship, a funeral home or a family home. Only selected relatives and a few close friends attend a private funeral service. Sometimes a public viewing is held either earlier or later in the day.

The average cost of an average funeral in the U.S. is $8,500. The "cost" may be advertised as $6,000 but this usually only covers the amount paid to the funeral service provider. The cost of the cemetery plot, mausoleum or columbarium, crypt, niche, cemetery vault liner, opening and closing fee, headstone or bronze grave marker, granite vase, ceramic pictures and headstone photos, care and maintenance or perpetual care, record keeping fee, honorariums for music, clergy, church rental, guest book or memorial book are most likely extra.

The funeral service industry is a $21 billion a year industry in 2011 and growing. Funeral directors are not clergy, they are business owners. They are in business and expect to make a profit. Unfortunately in these times when anything and everything is all about ME, families may be talked into spending every dollar of insurance money on a funeral. This most often hurts the families that can least afford it while the average "wealthy" family will chose to have a modest Direct Funeral or Cremation. Do not allow yourselves to be talked into something that is unnecessary or unwanted. A funeral should not be a burden left for the surviving family. After the loss of a loved one many people describe their state of mind as being similar to walking around in a fog. Always have a friend or professional you can trust, help you with the arraignments. Show them this book and then the two of you can make better decisions. Federal law requires that funeral service prices be provided over the phone.

Package Deals: A package of services may be more expensive than just purchasing the goods and services that you actually want or need. Ask to see the price list and make an informed decision.

You do not need to spend a lot of money to have a meaningful dignified service. Who owns the local funeral service provider? Many local family-owned service providers are owned by corporate chains. They often keep the original name but change pricing and policy after the buyout.

Prepay for Funeral Services: Is it a good idea to prepay for your funeral services? Usually it is a better idea to set up a trust to cover your expenses. A Totten Trust seems to work out very well for most. It may also be advisable to prepay for some services like a cemetery plot, direct burial or direct cremation and set aside money in a trust for the cost of a service and other expenses. When you finish with this book you should have a much better idea of what you want to do.

Caskets

Casket: A casket is often the single most expensive item to be purchased. Prices can range from less than one thousand dollars to more than ten thousand dollars. You do not need to buy the most expensive casket. It is a common practice to rent a casket for the viewing and then bury the least expensive casket available.

Materials and Cost: Caskets are made from almost any material. Common materials are wood, metal and plastic. Copper or bronze caskets can cost over ten thousand dollars. Wood caskets constructed from walnut, mahogany, cherry, oak, birch or poplar have a higher markup and are the ones most funeral homes will show customers. A pine or cedar casket can be purchased for $500. The eighteen gauge steel caskets that most people are familiar with can cost $5,000 or more at a local funeral home. The same casket can be purchased online for $995, and this price includes free shipping to your local funeral home.

Airtight Seals and Gaskets: Protective gaskets are sometimes sold as add-ons for up to several thousand dollars in additional charges. What is accomplished by an airtight seal? The consumer is often told that this seal will help to preserve the body of the loved one. A casket sealed with a tight rubber gasket creates an environment that helps bacteria thrive. When placed in a tightly sealed container most bodies have a tendency to liquefy and create bloating gas which explodes releasing noxious gasses into the crypt or mausoleum. Most cemetery workers pop the seal allowing air to vent into the casket to keep the remains from exploding the lid off the casket. The seal is also broken to allow air to vent when the casket is placed above ground.

Without this airtight gasket there is normal dehydration and deterioration of the body. Many of the newer Green Cemeteries do not allow seals or gaskets.

Caskets and other funeral service supplies can be purchased online from Wal-Mart, Cost-co, Sears, other online retailers and direct from the manufacturer. Everyone should shop online first to get an idea of cost and quality while you are under no pressure to purchase anything. When you have some facts you will be in a much better position to make an informed decision. If you do not see any low-cost container in the display room, ask to see one anyway. Many funeral service providers keep them in another area of the building because it has been shown that most people buy one of the first three caskets they see and it is usually the mid-priced one they purchase. Now would be a good time to look at other service providers. Some are very reputable and caring; some are not. You are a customer. They are in business to sell you something. Always go to price products and services with another person. If you are unsure of yourself or would just like some professional help, now would be a good time to speak with a competent estate attorney. They may be able to save you enough money to pay their fee. Win-win.

Direct Burial: The body is buried shortly after death, usually in a simple container. No viewing or visitation is involved, so no embalming is necessary. A memorial service may be held at the graveside or later. Direct burial usually costs less than the "traditional," full-service funeral. Costs include the funeral home's basic services fee, as well as transportation and care of the body, the purchase of a casket or burial container and a cemetery plot or crypt. If the family chooses to be at the cemetery for the burial, the funeral home often charges an additional fee for a graveside service.

http://www.ftc.gov/bcp/edu/pubs/consumer/products/pro19.shtm

Direct Cremation: The body is cremated shortly after death, without embalming. The cremated remains are placed in an urn or other container. No viewing or visitation is involved, although a memorial service may be held, with or without the cremated remains present. The remains can be kept in the home, buried or placed in a crypt or niche in a cemetery, or buried or scattered in a favorite spot. Direct cremation usually costs less than the "traditional," full-service funeral. Costs include the funeral home's basic services fee, as well as transportation and care of the body. A crematory fee may be included or, if the funeral home does not own the crematory, the fee may be added on. There also will be a charge for an urn or other container. The cost of a cemetery plot or crypt is included only if the remains are buried or entombed.

http://www.ftc.gov/bcp/edu/pubs/consumer/products/pro19.shtm

Alternative Container: Funeral providers who offer direct cremations also must offer to provide an alternative container that can be used in place of a casket. see *Funeral Rule*, page 178

Casket Rental: It is very common to rent an appropriate casket for a graveside or memorial service to be held before cremation or burial. The remains are then transferred before cremation or burial. Jewelry is returned to the family if requested.

Funeral Rule: To protect consumers, the Federal Trade Commission wrote and enforces The Funeral Rule. The funeral rule clearly says funeral homes must accept delivery of merchandise purchased from other retailers at no extra charge to the consumer. Cemeteries are not under the funeral rule and can charge you a fee for using merchandise from another retailer. see *Funeral Rule*, page 178

Casket Price List: The casket price list is a printed or typewritten list which the funeral home presents to you before you discuss or are shown a casket. This list will provide a brief description of each casket and alternative container (such as a cardboard or pressed wood box) regularly offered by the funeral home. The Funeral Rule states funeral homes must give you a written list with all the prices and services offered, including the least expensive. It must state the retail price of each item offered. see *Caskets*, page 26, 305

Cosmetology and Hairstyle: If there is a viewing or an open casket these services may be necessary.

Funeral Transportation

Funeral Transportation: Transportation expenses can include permits, transportation from out of state, and transportation from the place of death to the funeral service or crematory, and then to the church, cemetery or burial place. There can be additional charges for a hearse, chauffeured limousine, flower vehicle, service vehicle for the pallbearers, from the funeral service or crematory, and then to the church, cemetery or burial place.

Transportation within the U.S.: Transportation of the deceased within the U.S. averages $1,500. Actual airfare is additional.

Transportation Overseas: $4,500 - $11,000 on average and this includes airfare.

Funeral Ceremony and Viewing: $1,000.

Embalming: Embalming is rarely required when the person will be buried within 24 to 48 hours. The Centers for Disease Control has consistently shown that embalming does not serve any public health purpose. Cost is $750 and up. see *Embalming*, page 341

Burial Clothes: Prices usually begin at $150 for a man's suit and $100 for a ladies dress.

Preparation Fees: $150 - $550.

Refrigeration Fees: $50 to $100 a day.

Funeral Rule: To protect consumers, the Federal Trade Commission wrote and enforces The Funeral Rule. The funeral rule clearly says funeral homes must accept delivery of merchandise purchased from other retailers at no extra charge to the consumer. Cemeteries are not under the funeral rule and can charge you a fee for using merchandise from another retailer. see *Funeral Rule*, page 178

Price List: The funeral Rule states funeral homes must give you a written list with all the prices and services offered, including the least expensive.

The Casket Price List: Information and Use (FTC)

If you do not list the retail price of each casket on your General Price List, you must prepare a separate printed or typewritten Casket Price List (CPL). (11)

Information to be Included

The CPL must include the following basic information:

- The name of your business;

- The caption: "Casket Price List;"

- The effective date for the Casket Price List; and

- The retail price of each casket and alternative container that does not require special ordering, with enough information to identify it.

You must give enough descriptive information about each casket on the CPL to enable consumers to identify the specific casket or container and understand what they are buying. For example, the CPL could describe the exterior appearance (including the gauge of metal or type of wood), the exterior trim, and the interior fabric. You also may give any other information, such as a photograph or manufacturer name and model number. However, a photograph or model number alone is not a sufficient description under the Rule.

According to the Funeral Rule:

- You have the right to choose the funeral goods and services you want (with some exceptions).

- The funeral provider must state this right in writing on the general price list.

- If state or local law requires you to buy any particular item, the funeral provider must disclose it on the price list, with a reference to the specific law.

- The funeral provider may not refuse, or charge a fee, to handle a casket you bought elsewhere.

- A funeral provider that offers cremations must make alternative containers available.

The Funeral Rule, FTC An excellent government website.

http://business.ftc.gov/documents/bus05-complying-funeral-rule

Memorial Service

Use of Church: averages $200.

Catering: Catering costs can range from $10 per person and up. Many reputable caterers list their prices online.

If the family chooses to go to a restaurant after the memorial service or funeral it allows others to serve the food and clean up but it can get expensive. If the reception is held in a religious facility or someone's home and friends are allowed to bring food and drink it will minimize the expense. When people ask how they can help ask them to provide specific food or drink for the reception.

Music Honorarium: usually $150.

Amount to Clergy: $200.

Flag Cases: Flag cases are used to preserve and display the American flag of a veteran who has passed away. $50 and up.

Memorial Book: usually $40 - $80.

Guest Register Books: $25 and up.

Cemeteries

Cemetery Plot

Pricing: You will most likely get a better price if you purchase a cemetery plot before you need it. Later on you just call the cemetery a few days to a week before the day you plan to have the service or use the plot and they will have it ready. A headstone (if allowed) can also be purchased early and placed on the plot. The date of death is added when the person passes. Prices range from under one thousand dollars to over ten thousand dollars. Does the price include maintenance and grounds keeping?

Pre-purchased: Someone needs to look for any paperwork or documentation that would suggest a burial plot has been purchased. Family members tend to follow family traditions. Check with the local cemetery to see if the deceased purchased a plot if you are in doubt.

eBay: There were over four hundred cemetery plots listed for sale online the other day on eBay. Why do people resell cemetery plots? People change. Families change due to divorce and remarriage. People move to other areas of the United States and no longer want to be buried in that plot way across country but they just never got around to selling the plot. Many people are choosing cremation instead of the charges and fees involved with burial. Many people are trying to "go green". There are as many reasons as there are people for no longer needing a cemetery plot purchased years ago. A word of caution: Always go and visit the cemetery plot in person. It is amazing how great a picture can look online and how much different it looks when you go and see it for yourself. The plot could be right beside the men's room. This may or may not be best for you.

Grave Space, Single Grave Plot: $1,000 - $2,000 and up.

Cemetery Arrangements: Cemetery arrangements are most often made separately from funeral arrangements. Most Americans have traditionally selected cemeteries based on family traditions and religion. After several generations and many lifestyle changes cemetery plots are available for resale.

What you need to know: Cemeteries are not required to keep even the basic tenants of the Funeral Rule. They may add additional charges and fees if you purchase a burial vault (grave liner) somewhere else. See what restrictions, if any, the cemetery places on a burial vaults (grave liner) purchased elsewhere. Does this even make any difference to you? Does the cemetery allow headstones? Many do not and allow only grave markers because it reduces the cost of maintenance and grounds keeping. Just be certain to ask a lot of questions and do not allow yourself to be pressured into buying something before you have time to think about it.

Perpetual Care: Is perpetual care included in the purchase price? Is there a yearly fee or ten year fee? Check to see if there is a separate endowment care fee or maintenance and grounds keeping fee.

Opening and Closing Fees: The cemetery has to dig the space for the grave and fill it back in. They also charge you for removing flowers and paperwork. A usual fee is $550. but the Cemetery can add on over fifty different "services" that you would most likely never need. Just be certain to check all paperwork and look for add on fees. Although most cemeteries and funeral homes are reputable many are not. The Federal Trade Commission (FTC) Funeral Rule holds Funeral Directors and Funeral Homes accountable but not Cemeteries.

Vaults and Liners: A burial vault completely contains the casket, while a grave liner generally covers only the top and sides of the casket and allows the bottom of the casket to be in contact with the earth. Purchased online it may be sent directly to the cemetery, but because cemeteries are not covered by the FTC's Funeral Rule, the cemetery may charge a fee for using a burial vault or grave liner you purchased elsewhere. Green cemeteries do not use vaults or grave liners.

> The cost of a grave liner is a few hundred dollars and up to a few thousand dollars. Then you pay a fee to have it lowered into the ground. This is usually another $100. You bury it. You almost never dig it back up. It deteriorates. If one is required, purchase the least expensive grave liner that you can find. Plastic and wood are also options.

Mausoleum or Columbarium: Cremated remains placed in a mausoleum, columbarium or niche may also be charged an opening and closing fee. You will also most likely be charged a fee for endowment care for maintenance. Sometimes a record keeping fee and perpetual maintenance fee is added.

Columbarium Niche: $1,500 and there are additional opening and closing fees.

Community Mausoleum: prices start at less than $1,000.

Mausoleum Crypts: The price for a single mausoleum crypt can range from $2,500 to over $28,000. A double crypt is almost double the price.

Free-standing single and double crypt granite Mausoleums: $12,000 and up when delivered to the cemetery and assembled on site.

Mausoleum: $30,000 - $300,000 and up.

Bronze Grave Markers: Bronze grave markers cost from $400 to $1,200 and up.

Opening and Closing the Grave: $1,000.

Headstones: $500 - $2,000. Statues range in price from a few hundred dollars to several thousand dollars. Not all cemeteries accept headstones or statues.

Granite Vases: $45.

Ceramic Pictures & Headstone Photos: $175 and up.

Cemetery service providers may say they are not responsible for headstones purchased from an outside dealer but they are responsible if it is damaged due to worker negligence after they accept it.

Crematory

Cremation

Cremation: With a rental casket and service a modest cremation can be had for $2,000.

Direct Cremation: A direct cremation package usually includes transportation, brief storage of the body, document processing (permits, death certificate), a container (usually cardboard) for the body prior to and during cremation, and a basic container (cardboard or plastic) for the ashes. Cost averages $600 to $1,000 without casket rental and viewing.

Urn: It is not necessary to purchase an Urn for the Ashes, a white colored dust, of a loved one. They are available from the service provider or online in many sizes and materials priced from around $75. An Urn can be made of any material. Metal, wood and stone are the most common. Sets of six mini Urns are also available. An Urn from a third party retailer may be purchased and shipped directly to the funeral home. The funeral home may not charge a fee for using these.

If a Columbarium or Niche is going to be used remember not all Urns will fit inside every Niche. It is important to measure the Niche or Columbarium first.

You may also purchase a place in an urn garden.

There may or may not be a fee to scatter ashes in an Ash Garden.

Funeral Procession

Funeral Procession Etiquette

Funeral Procession: When the funeral ceremony and the burial are both held within the local area, friends and relatives might accompany the family to the cemetery. Immediate family members may be riding in a limousine at the front of the procession.

> The procession is formed at the funeral home or place of worship. Usually the pallbearers and honorary pallbearers will arrive at least one half hour early so their cars can be placed at the front of the procession. All others will be parked in the order in which they arrive. Pallbearers may have been provided with a funeral service vehicle to ride in so they all arrive together at the place

of burial. The funeral attendant usually places a magnetic flag, which reads "Funeral" on each car. In a large procession the flag may be placed on every third car. If you will not be driving in the procession, you will be directed to park in another area.

When the funeral service is over, the pallbearers will transport the casket outside and place it in the hearse. A funeral attendant should direct you to get in your vehicle and be ready to follow those ahead of you in the procession line. You will drive slowly with your headlights on, close to the car in front of you. Do not allow enough room for anyone not in the procession to cut in front of you as it is illegal to cut through or into a funeral procession, but it is sometimes done because people just do not know or are not paying attention. The procession may be driving through red lights. They will usually have a funeral service vehicle stop in the intersection with hazard lights flashing to stop oncoming traffic. You are supposed to follow the car in front of you until you reach the cemetery.

When You Encounter a Funeral Procession: Be respectful and yield the right of way once the lead car has entered traffic, such as going through an intersection. The entire procession will follow without interruption even if their traffic light is red and yours is green, you must stop and allow the procession to continue through the intersection until all cars in the procession have passed. Watch for the last vehicle in the procession: it typically has 2 or more flags and a hazard lights flashing. Once it passes by, you may resume the normal flow of traffic.

Do not cut into or cut off a procession. Do not honk at a car in a funeral procession. Do not pass a funeral procession on the right side on a highway, unless the procession is in the far left lane. There are traffic fines and penalties that are usually imposed on people who disrupt a funeral procession. The traffic court is not kind in such instances.

Funeral Rule

Funeral Rule: The Funeral Rule was written for the Protection of consumers, you and me.

Federal Trade Commission (FTC) Funeral Rule.

The Funeral Rule requires the funeral provider to give consumers accurate, itemized price information and various other disclosures about funeral goods and services. In addition, the Rule prohibits the funeral provider from:

Misrepresenting legal, crematory, and cemetery requirements;

Embalming for a fee without permission;

Caskets: Requiring the purchase of a casket for direct cremation;

Requiring consumers to buy certain funeral goods or services as a condition for furnishing other funeral goods or services; and

Engaging in other deceptive or unfair practices.

If you violate the Funeral Rule, you may be subject to penalties of up to $10,000 per violation.

These guidelines do not amend or modify the Rule. They explain the requirements of the revised Funeral Rule and discuss how to prepare documents required by the Rule — the General Price List, the Casket Price List, the Outer Burial Container Price List, and the Statement of Funeral Goods and Services Selected. The guidelines also include sample price lists and a sample itemized statement form. These guidelines represent the FTC staff's view of what the law requires. They are not binding on the Commission.

Who Must Comply With the Funeral Rule?

All "funeral providers" must comply with the Rule. You are a funeral provider if you sell or offer to sell both funeral goods and funeral services to the public. Funeral goods are all products sold directly to the public in connection with funeral services.

Funeral services are: services used to care for and prepare bodies for burial, cremation, or other final disposition; and services used to arrange, supervise, or conduct the funeral ceremony or final disposition of human remains.

Pre-need: The Rule's requirements, as described on the following pages, apply to both pre-need and at-need funeral arrangements.

You also must comply with the Rule if you sell pre-need contracts on behalf of one or more funeral homes, but do not yourself provide funeral goods and services. In such a case, even though you don't provide the funeral items, you are an agent of a funeral provider and therefore are covered by the Rule.

The General Price List: The General Price List (GPL) is the key stone of the Funeral Rule. It must contain identifying information (see page 6), itemized prices for the various goods and services that you sell (see pages 9-13), and other important disclosures (see pages 6-9). The GPL enables consumers to comparison shop and to purchase, on an itemized basis, only the goods and services they want.

The Casket Price List: Information and Use. If you do not list the retail price of each casket on your General Price List, you must prepare a separate printed or typewritten Casket Price List (CPL). (11) From the Funeral Rule.

Information to be Included

The CPL must include the following basic information: the name of your business; the caption: "Casket Price List;" the effective date for the Casket

Price List; and the retail price of each casket and alternative container that does not require special ordering, with enough information to identify it.

You must give enough descriptive information about each casket on the CPL to enable consumers to identify the specific casket or container and understand what they are buying. For example, the CPL could describe the exterior appearance (including the gauge of metal or type of wood), the exterior trim, and the interior fabric. You also may give any other information, such as a photograph or manufacturer name and model number. However, a photograph or model number alone is not a sufficient description under the Rule.

The Outer Burial Container Price List: Information and Use. If you sell outer burial containers and do not list the retail price of each such container on your General Price List, you must prepare a separate printed or typewritten Outer Burial Container Price List (OBC Price List).(12) The term "outer burial container" refers to any container designed to be placed around the casket in the grave. Such containers may include burial vaults, grave boxes, and grave liners. From the Funeral Rule.

Information to be Included on the OBC Price List

The OBC Price List must contain the following basic information: the name of your business; the caption: "Outer Burial Container Price List;" the effective date of the price list; the retail price of each outer burial container you offer that does not require special ordering, with enough information to identify the container; and the following disclosure (discussed earlier on pages 8-9):

In most areas of the country, state, or local law does not require that you buy a container to surround the casket in the grave. However, many cemeteries require that you have such a container so that the grave will not sink in. Either a grave liner or a burial vault will satisfy these requirements.

You do not have to include the phrase "in most areas of the country" in the disclosure if your state or local law does not require a container to surround the casket in the grave.

You must give enough descriptive information about each outer burial container in your OBC Price List to enable consumers to identify the specific container. You need list only those containers that you usually offer for sale and that do not require special ordering. "Special ordering" means purchasing an outer burial container that is not in stock and not part of your regular offerings to your customers. However, the Rule does not require you to offer any particular outer burial containers; in fact, it does not require you to sell any outer burial containers.

Statement of Funeral Goods and Services Selected: Cost Information and Disclosures. The Statement of Funeral Goods and Services Selected (Statement) is an itemized list of the goods and services that the consumer has selected during the arrangements conference. (13) The Statement allows consumers to evaluate their selections and to make any desired changes.

Telephone Price Disclosures: You must give consumers who telephone your place of business and ask about your prices or offerings accurate information from your General Price List, Casket Price List, and Outer Burial Container Price List. You also must answer any other questions about your offerings and prices with any readily available information that reasonably answers the question. (17)

Note: You cannot require callers to give their names, addresses, or phone numbers before you give them the requested information. You can ask callers to identify themselves, but you still must answer their questions even if they refuse to do so. You cannot require consumers to come to the funeral home in person to get price information.

Record Keeping: You must keep price lists for at least one year from the date you last distributed them to customers. You also must keep a copy of each completed Statement of Funeral Goods and Services Selected for at least one year from the date of the arrangements conference. You must make these documents available for inspection by FTC representatives upon request. (24) From the Funeral Rule.

For complete information visit the Federal Trade Commission (FTC) Funeral Rule website at:

http://business.ftc.gov/documents/bus05-complying-funeral-rule/#comply

The Funeral Rule was written because there was a need for it. Take the time to go online and look through the whole Funeral Rule.

The Funeral Rule: Facts for Consumers.

Paying Final Respects: Your Rights When Buying Funeral Goods & Services

When a loved one dies, grieving family members and friends often are confronted with dozens of decisions about the funeral — all of which must be made quickly and often under great emotional stress.

What kind of funeral should it be? What funeral provider should you use? Should you bury or cremate the body, or donate it to science? What are you legally required to buy? What about the availability of environmentally friendly or "green" burials? What other arrangements should you plan? And, practically, how much is it all going to cost?

Each year, people grapple with these and many other questions as they spend billions of dollars arranging funerals for family members and friends.

Many funeral providers offer various "packages" of goods and services that make up different kinds of funerals. The Federal Trade Commission, the nation's consumer protection agency, wants you to know that when you arrange for a funeral, you have the right to buy goods and services separately. That is, you do not have to accept a package that may include items you do not want.

The Funeral Rule

The Funeral Rule, enforced by the FTC, makes it possible for you to choose only those goods and services you want or need and to pay only for those you select, whether you are making arrangements when a death occurs or in advance. The Rule allows you to compare prices among funeral homes, and makes it possible for you to select the funeral arrangements you want at the home you use.

The Rule does not apply to third-party sellers, such as casket and monument dealers, or to cemeteries that lack an on-site funeral home.

The Funeral Rule gives you the right to:

Buy only the funeral arrangements you want. You have the right to buy separate goods (such as caskets) and services (such as embalming or a memorial service). You do not have to accept a package that may include items you do not want.

Get price information on the telephone. Funeral directors must give you price information on the telephone if you ask for it. You don't have to give them your name, address or telephone number first. Although they are not required to do so, many funeral homes mail their price lists, and some post them online.

Get a written, itemized price list when you visit a funeral home. The funeral home must give you a General Price List (GPL) that is yours to keep. It lists all the items and services the home offers, and the cost of each one.

See a written casket price list before you see the actual caskets. Sometimes, detailed casket price information is included on the funeral home's General Price List. More often, though, it's provided on a separate casket price list. Get the price information before you see the caskets, so that you can ask about lower-priced products that may not be on display.

See a written outer burial container price list. Outer burial containers are not required by state law anywhere in the U.S., but many cemeteries require them to prevent the grave from caving in. If the funeral home sells containers, but doesn't list their prices on the General Price List, you have the right to look at a separate container price list before you see the containers. If you don't see the lower-priced containers listed, ask about them.

Receive a written statement after you decide what you want, and before you pay. It should show exactly what you are buying and the cost of each item. The funeral home must give you a statement listing every good and service you have selected, the price of each, and the total cost immediately after you make the arrangements.

Get an explanation in the written statement you receive from the funeral home that identifies and describes any legal, cemetery or crematory requirement that compels the purchase of any funeral goods or services for which you are being charged.

Use an "alternative container" instead of a casket for cremation. No state or local law requires the use of a casket for cremation. A funeral home that offers cremations must tell you that alternative containers are available, and must make them available. They might be made of unfinished wood, pressed wood, fiberboard, or cardboard.

Provide the funeral home with a casket or urn you purchase elsewhere. The funeral provider cannot refuse to handle a casket or urn you bought online, at a local casket store, or somewhere else — or charge you a fee to do it. The funeral home cannot require you to be there when the casket or urn is delivered to them.

Make funeral arrangements without embalming. No state law requires routine embalming for every death. Some states require embalming or refrigeration if the body is not buried or cremated within a certain time; some states don't require it at all. In most cases, refrigeration is an acceptable alternative. In addition, you may choose services like direct cremation and immediate burial, which don't require any form of preservation. Many funeral homes have a policy requiring embalming if the body is to be publicly viewed, but this is not required by law in most states. Ask if the funeral home offers private family viewing without embalming. If some form of preservation is a practical necessity, ask the funeral home if refrigeration is available.

Cost Considerations

The casket and the funeral home's fee for the basic services of the funeral director and staff are typically the most expensive items in a full-service funeral. Comparison shop before you decide on a casket and funeral home; you may find a wide variation in pricing. If cost is a consideration, look at lower-price caskets and outer burial containers offered by the funeral home, local casket providers, or online retailers. Caskets and outer burial containers with warranties may not be worth the extra cost because no casket or container can delay the decomposition of human remains indefinitely, and the Funeral Rule prohibits statements to the contrary.

If you do not want to hold a viewing, you can avoid charges for embalming and "other preparation of the body," and the charges for a viewing. Most states do not require embalming except in special cases. The Funeral Rule requires that an explanation of any charge for embalming be included in the written statement you receive immediately after making the funeral arrangements.

Immediate burial and direct cremation usually are the least expensive options. The cost of permits, preparing death notices, and coordinating cemetery or crematory arrangements must be included in the price for direct cremation and immediate burial. If you choose cremation, ask if the direct cremation price includes any crematory fee. If you want additional services, including the use of staff and facilities for a memorial service, the funeral home may charge an additional fee.

In most states, you are not legally required to use a funeral home to conduct a funeral. These functions may be handled by a religious or other organization, or by your family. In addition, veterans, their immediate family members, public health workers, and some civilians who provide military-related service are entitled to burial in a national cemetery with a grave marker. Burial for the veteran is usually free, but the family is responsible for all funeral home expenses, such as the funeral ceremony or memorial service, and transportation to the cemetery. Many states have low-cost cemeteries for veterans.

The Funeral Rule in Brief

You have the right to choose the funeral goods and services you want (with some exceptions).

The funeral provider must give you a General Price List (GPL) that states your right to choose what you want in writing.

If state or local law requires you to buy any particular good or service, the funeral provider must disclose it on the statement it provides describing the funeral goods and services you have selected, with a reference to the specific law.

The funeral provider cannot refuse to handle a casket or urn you bought elsewhere — or charge you a fee to do that.

A funeral provider who offers cremations must make alternative containers available.

You can't be charged for embalming that your family didn't authorize, unless it's required by state law.

For complete information "Facts for Consumers," visit the Federal Trade Commission (FTC) Funeral Rule website at:

http://www.ftc.gov/bcp/edu/pubs/consumer/products/pro26.shtm

The Funeral Rule was written because there was a need for it. Take the time to go online and look through the whole Funeral Rule.

Hospice Care

Hospice Care - Comfort and Pain Relief

Hospice Care: Hospice is a philosophy of care that focuses on patient comfort rather than curing illnesses. Choosing hospice care in no way means a patient is giving up hope. Hospice care neither prolongs life nor hastens death. Hospice offers a variety of bereavement and counseling services to families before and after a patient's death. Hospice includes pain management.

> Hospice care neither hastens nor postpones dying. Hospice deals with the emotional, social and spiritual impact of the disease on the patient and the patient's family and friends. Treating the whole person is essential to patient comfort. Hospice care is comfort care for patients in the last six months of life and recognizes the person's hope for continued life. The goal of hospice care is to improve the quality of a patient's last days by offering comfort and dignity while controlling the patient's pain and discomfort.
>
> Choosing hospice care in no way means a patient is giving up hope. Hospice care may be provided in your home or in a special facility. More than 90% of the hospice services provided in this country are based in patients' homes. The dying process takes time. Patients and their loved ones need support, information, and medical care. Social workers and chaplains need time to work with patients and their loved ones to bring them to a place of acceptance.

Pain: Pain is probably the most feared symptom at the end-of-life but not every illness that leads to death causes pain. Pain can affect every part of your life. A patient may not be able to eat or sleep. They may not want to talk with loved ones. Pain may consume their daily life. Physical pain can take away peace of mind, comfort, enjoyment and most of all hope.

Pain is not a normal part of growing older; it is your body's way of telling you something needs attention. It is not common for people who receive pain medication to become addicted. If you are experiencing pain, tell someone. You can receive help.

Patients can be kept lucid and alert and also be pain free in almost every case during the end-of-life experience. Hospice includes pain management and most patients can attain a level of comfort they consider acceptable.

Cost of Hospice Care: Home hospice care usually costs less than care in hospitals, nursing homes, or other institutional settings. This is because less high-cost technology is used and family and friends provide most of the care at home. Medicare, Medicaid in most states, the Department of Veterans Affairs, most private insurance plans, HMOs, and other managed care organizations pay for hospice care. Also, community contributions, memorial donations, and foundation gifts allow many hospices to give free services to patients who can't afford payment. Some programs charge patients according to their ability to pay. Some hospices provide services without charge if a patient has limited or no financial resources. Google: hospice (your city or county and state)

Hospice patients receive care in their personal residences, nursing homes, hospital hospice units and inpatient hospice centers.

Medicare: To get payment from Medicare, the agency must be approved by Medicare to provide hospice services.

Medicaid: In 1986, laws were passed to allow the states to develop coverage for hospice programs. Most states have a Medicaid hospice benefit, which is patterned after the Medicare hospice benefit.

Insurance: Most private insurance companies include hospice care as a benefit. Look for benefits for hospice and also home care. Ask someone if you cannot find the benefit, it may be included somewhere else.

Discussing Hospice Care: It is appropriate to discuss hospice care or any other care at any time during a life-limiting experience. By law the decision belongs to the patient. If they become incapacitated their medical directive (if any) will speak for them as to decisions they have made. The patient, family members, medical professionals, clergy and friends may speak freely about hospice care. It is a philosophy of care that focuses on patient comfort rather than curing illnesses that includes pain management.

Recovery: If a hospice care patient shows signs of recovery they may be returned to regular medical treatment. If the patient's condition improves and the disease seems to be in remission, patients can be discharged from hospice and return to aggressive therapy or go on about their daily life. If the discharged patient should later need to return to hospice care, Medicare and most private insurance will allow additional coverage for this purpose.

Palliative Care (Pain Relief): If you chose not to have life-prolonging intervention it does not mean that you cannot alleviate pain or be made comfortable. Instead of prolonging life, palliative care focuses on quality of life and dignity by helping a patient remain comfortable and free from pain until life ends naturally.

Palliative Care Programs: Palliative care is a program of action to make a patient comfortable by treating the person's symptoms from an illness. Hospice and palliative care both focus on helping a person be comfortable by addressing issues causing physical or emotional pain, or suffering. The goals of palliative care are to improve the quality of a seriously ill person's life and to support that person and their family during and after treatment.

Hospice Care focuses on relieving symptoms and supporting patients with a life expectancy of months not years. **Palliative Care** may be given at any time during a person's illness, from diagnosis on and is being used by other healthcare providers, including teams in hospitals, nursing facilities and home health agencies in combination with other medical treatments to help people who are seriously ill. Most hospices have a set of defined services, team members and rules and regulations for palliative care.

Identity Theft

Identity Theft and Prevention

Secure all Assets: As soon as the assets are identified and secured the executor will need to set up a checking account.

Bank Accounts: Protect and secure all bank accounts.

Collect and secure all important documents: This includes bank account, investment account and retirement account numbers and access information. Documents will provide the names and types of assets the executor or personal representative is looking for. See the document list see *Documents*, page 115

Immediately notify financial institutions if there is a concern about fraud on any account.

> Many cases of deceased identity theft are committed by a family member. The identifying information of a deceased family member should be secured and only be made available on a *need*-to-know *basis*. The documents and data can be turned over to a responsible family member when the estate is closing.
>
> The United States and the world have changed so much in just the last twenty five years that many people still do not think they will be taken advantage of. Thieves steal from the sick and elderly because it is easier. People steal the identities of the deceased because it is easier than stealing from the living. It is important that you take corrective steps to make sure that you or your loved one are not victims of exploitation or identity theft.

Durable Power of Attorney: In estate planning, a durable power of attorney is often chosen as a way to plan for those times when an individual is incapacitated. With a durable power of attorney, you are able to appoint an agent to manage your financial affairs, make health care decisions, or conduct other business for you during your incapacitation. A durable power of attorney may be general or limited. A general durable power of attorney may allow your agent to do every act which may legally be done by you. A limited durable power of attorney cover specific events, like selling property, making investments, or making health care decisions.

Durable Power of Attorney and Fraud Watch: Durable Power of Attorney can allow another person to watch over a family member so that they have the authority to follow up with their financial institutions and/or advisors and monitor their accounts to make sure that large sums of money are not being transferred or being paid out. This can be limited so the individual with durable power of attorney can watch over but not touch (withdraw) the assets. An attorney could help you with this. Too many eighty and ninety year old men still believe they are twenty-four. Men especially tend to see themselves as the person they were when they were at their peak of power and health. A part of them still believes they are that same age. Really; this is true and it is not that funny.

Notify all Creditors: Request a copy of the decedent's credit reports from the three major credit bureaus: Experian, Equifax and TransUnion. The executor or personal representative will need these to locate assets and debts. Notify the three credit reporting bureaus that the individual has passed away (Experian, Equifax and TransUnion). Request that the credit report is flagged with the note: "Deceased, Do Not Issue Credit." Contact all CRAs, credit issuers, collection agencies, and any other financial institution that need to know of the death. Specific information on how to do this can be found on each of their websites.

Medical Records Identity Theft: Medical records identity theft continues to be an effective way to steal someone's identity. Medical records are easier to steal from any local office. Security can be lax or nonexistent. Check your medical records regularly. Requesting and obtaining your medical records can be time-consuming and expensive, but it can reveal serious medical fraud issues. At a minimum, keep a list of the names and contacts for doctors and other healthcare providers you have visited in the past and refer back to this list in the event of an issue.

Mail: The U.S. Postal Service does not need to be informed of a person death. The mail needs to be forwarded to the executor's home address or a post office box for at least a year. The bills and financial statements that come in the mail are often the most reliable way to find all of the deceased person's assets and debts. All insurance companies are required by law to send a statement once a year and this may identify previously unknown policies and accounts.

All mail should be sent certified, return receipt requested. Keep copies of everything mailed including notes on what was mailed and when.

The U.S. Postal Service has change of address cards that may be filled out.

A Change of Address (COA) request must be submitted by the addressee or by someone authorized to file on behalf of the addressee. When submitting a COA request, please note the following:

The person who submits this COA request states that he or she is the person, executor, guardian, authorized officer, or agent of the person for whom mail would be forwarded under this request form.

Visitation and Wakes: When opening the deceased's home for visitation secure all assets. Friends and family have just suffered a loss and thieves take advantage of this. They look very normal, dress nicely and come to rob and steal from you. We recommend that the deceased's home or anyone's home is not open for public visitation or viewing. Use a Church or local facility. Be very careful. see *Security*, page 246

Credit Cards, Charge Cards: Identify authorized users for each credit card and account. If another person is added to the account as an authorized user, depending upon the company specific terms, he or she may be agreeing to repay all of the debt when using the card.

If there is a surviving spouse or other joint account holders, make sure to immediately notify relevant credit card companies, banks, stock brokers, loan and lien holders, and mortgage companies of the death. They may require a certified copy of the death certificate and letters testamentary to do this, as well as permission from the survivor, or other authorized account holders. Only send a copy of the death certificate if they will not close the account without it.

Power of Attorney: Sometimes durable power of attorney continues after the death for the sole purpose of priority in regards to disposition of the body. Otherwise if needed, inform the banks and institutions active durable powers of attorney are null and void and advise them of the individual that will be contacting them as the Personal Representative of the estate or Trustee of a living Trust.

Deceased Do Not Contact Registration: To stop unwanted pre-approved credit card offers contact Direct Marketing Association. DMA sometimes receives calls from family members, friends or caretakers seeking to remove the names of deceased individuals from commercial marketing lists. We understand how difficult this process can be.

> To assist those who are managing this process, DMA created (in October 2005) a Deceased Do Not Contact List (DDNC) which all DMA members are required to honor. The Deceased Do Not Contact List is available to companies and nonprofit organizations for the sole purpose of removing names and addresses from their marketing lists.
>
> https://www.ims-dm.com/cgi/ddnc.php

Memberships: Cancel as necessary all of the decedent's memberships, driver's license, handicap permits, social security payments, library cards, etc. Before canceling memberships that include the right to season tickets, discounts or anything of value check to see if they can be transferred or sold.

Credit: Cancel as necessary all of the decedent's credit cards, debit cards, etc. return all library books and cancel all subscriptions and cable that are no longer needed. Pick up any dry cleaning, photos or vehicles in the shop for repair. If these are also joint accounts you may want to transfer the account and remove the decedent's name. If you close an account, ask that it be listed as: "Closed. Account holder is deceased." This may affect the joint account holder's credit rating.

Notify all clubs and organizations the deceased was a member of. This is not limited to country clubs, civic organizations, fraternal organizations, video rental, public library, fitness club. Do not just close memberships without first checking to see if there are certain benefits such as reduced dues and fees or season tickets that may be sold or transferred to someone else.

Driver's License: Department of Motor Vehicles handles the driver's license, state ID cards and any vehicle registration papers are transferred to the new owners.

Immigration Services: if the decedent is not a U.S. citizen. Contact and inform them the individual is deceased.

Licenses: professional licenses: bar association, medical licenses, cosmetician, etc.

Passport and/or Passport Card: According to the NPIC, National Passport Information Center, you do not have to do anything with the passport or passport card of the deceased. The passport of a person who has died can be kept as a memento if you choose, or you can return it for cancellation.

> If you choose to have the passport cancelled and returned to you or destroyed, you may return the passport to the Consular Lost and Stolen Passport - CLASP unit. A copy of the Certificate of Death is required along with the passport. **If you want the cancelled passport returned, you must include a letter stating that request.** Mail the passport, Certificate of Death, and letter requesting cancelled/returned passport (if applicable) to the following address:

Attention CLASP, 1111 19th St NW, Suite 500, Washington, DC 20036

Social Security: Social security needs to be contacted and informed of the death. see *Social Security*, page 254

Veteran's Administration: if the person was a former member of the military.

Veterans Benefits: Include all correspondence and statements. Benefits need to be discontinued if they stop at the person's death. see *Documents*, page 115

Voter Registration: request a cancellation for a deceased voter.

Obituaries and Identity Theft: Identity theft continues to be one of the fastest growing crimes in the United States. The FTC estimates that as many as 9 million Americans have their identities stolen each year. Due to this proliferation of identity theft it is recommended that the full date of birth or even the year of birth not be given. Unfortunately there are people who read through obituaries for names and addresses and then buy social security numbers, credit histories and other personal data online. They will apply for and get credit cards in the name of the deceased and run up charges quickly. Surviving family members are unlikely to be held liable for the debt but may still spend a lot of time and money straightening out the fraud. Why is the Federal Government allowing this to not only persist, but get worse? We will most likely lose some of our freedom as our society becomes more digital and no one wants to step up. The FTC estimates that as many as 9 million Americans have their identities stolen each year. This is a very real, serious problem for millions of Americans. Please do not allow yourself to become a victim.

Writing an Obituary: Today an obituary should only include the full name, and plans for a memorial service and internment. Families are now located in several states or overseas and a phone call is the best way to inform people. Do not include: Mothers maiden name, address, ancestry, occupation, date-of-birth and date-of-death or any personal information that can be used to steal an identity. Do not include the deceased's address. This is a formal invitation to thieves to stop by while everyone is at the funeral service. You can still honor the person without giving up their personal information. see *Obituary*, page 405

An Excellent Free Government Resource on Identity Theft
http://www.ftc.gov/bcp/edu/microsites/idtheft/consumers/about-identity-theft.html

Another excellent resource: http://www.idtheftcenter.org/

Digital Estate

All digitally stored content and accounts owned by an individual at death. The digital estate of the deceased needs to be located, reviewed and distributed as required by a valid Will or the probate court.

Digital Assets

Many of the assets are the same as those listed under: Assets page 5, 41, 57, 75, but the access is online. Sometimes a bank account or a brokerage account is located in another state and access is online with passwords, user names and challenge questions. Locate all Passwords & Usernames, encryption, Keys, PINs, Combinations and challenge questions. if you are preplanning do not leave this information in your Will because it is going to be made public after your death.

There are software programs that may be able to unlock and reset current passwords. Google: password recovery

Locate: All computers, laptops, tablets, PC, Macs, eBook readers, storage, hard drives, cell phones, iPhones, iPods, iPads, answering machines, Wii, PlayStations, PSP, PS3, Xbox, thumb drives and digital cameras. Copiers are very important as they contain very sensitive information in memory.

Online Websites: Websites that may have value or contain user information that should be cleaned include but are not limited to: brokerage sites, gambling sites, online shopping sites, email accounts, blogs, photo storage sites, online subscriptions with automatic renewal, online banking, online bill paying, online credit card access, mortgage providers, college savings accounts, retirement plans, automatic bill paying for (anything) utilities and cell phones, and online tax software that may have copies of the deceased's returns.

There are more people than ever using paperless billing and statements online. These and all online accounts need to be analyzed. Make copies of everything and then most accounts will need to be cleaned and closed. Be careful before you clear or close accounts. Do they have any special privileges like ordering season tickets? Can this be resold or reassigned to someone else? In any case, be careful before you delete or clear anything. If you need help now would be a good time to seek out a competent individual.

There may also be videos of other assets, movie videos, mp3 files, mp4 files, and social networking websites. Collect All CD's DVD's do not assume it is a movie just because someone printed "Movie" on the disk with a marker. These will all have to be viewed by someone. They may contain ANYTHING! They may contain video of hidden collections, documents or a whole other life no one ever knew about. They may contain maps and directions to hidden treasures that the loved one was keeping safe for their beneficiary(s).

Royalties, Copyrights or Patents: Much of the information necessary to locate these can be found online in documents or statements.

Stocks and Bonds: Today electronic transfers are most common. Hard copies are less common but you may still find them. Most people would leave the actual certificate with a broker or agent. Some old certificates are worth more to collectors than their actual monetary worth. An original stock certificate for Joe Namath's New York restaurant registers 100 shares, is green and white like the New York Jets colors, and includes a small football player graphic (approximate worth $99.) Certificates from old gold mines, land companies and railroads may be worth millions or a few hundred dollars. It is up to the executor to show due diligence in valuing these.

All digital Assets must be protected and distributed. The Digital Executor can be very helpful. Most Americans have a digital presence that needs to be located, collected, appraised, and protected.

Computers: Before you dispose of any computer you should wipe the hard drive clean of all data. When you use the "delete" function or "empty recycle bin" you do not remove data. You are only removing the sign post pointing to it. The data is still there and can be recovered. A digital executor or a knowledgeable trustworthy individual may be able to help with this. If you cannot do this you may want to remove the hard drives and dispose of them separately.

Copiers: The internal hard drives on home and office copy machines retain sensitive information. This information is almost never scrubbed clean and could be a jackpot for an identity thief. Before you dispose of any home or office copier, remove and destroy the hard drive, or internal memory. If the machine is leased, software can be purchased to scrub (wipe clean, permanently remove) the data. The executor should never give away the old copier or computers, hard drives, storage devices of any kind without first permanently removing all data so that it is considered unrecoverable. Be careful not to remove data that you need or want. A digital executor is often necessary to help in doing this.

Shredder: The executor may want to purchase a good cross-cut shredder for the purpose of disposing of bills and receipts. Shred documents containing personal information, such as credit card statements, bills and even some junk mail. Thieves will look through the garbage you throw away to obtain the decedents personal information.

This website is a one-stop national resource to learn about the crime of identity theft. It provides detailed information to help you deter, detect, and defend against identity theft.

http://www.ftc.gov/bcp/edu/microsites/idtheft/

Insurance

Insurance Policies: Copies of life insurance policies are among the most important documents for the family to have. Family members need to know the name of the carrier, the policy number and the agent associated with the policy. Life insurance policies granted by an employer upon retirement are overlooked most often. Place this information in your notebook and make it available to the executor.

> The proceeds of insurance policies will be paid at your death to whomever you named as beneficiaries of the policies. Your will does not control the pay-out of the life insurance proceeds. It is usually not a good idea to name the estate as the beneficiary of your policy because it subjects the proceeds to probate costs and delays.

Life Insurance: You may need life insurance if you are likely to die leaving a large debt and you want it paid without eating into the capital of your estate. You want to create a fund to pay funeral costs, taxes, and probate fees or you want to leave money you wouldn't otherwise have to a family member, friend, or charity

Insurance Policy or Annuity: An insurance policy or annuity is a contract between the company that sold it and the person who bought it. The proceeds do not go through the probate process. The policy beneficiary, not the executor, generally files the claim with the insurance company and collects the benefits directly. Executors may be called upon to help beneficiaries claim the payments they're entitled to and it is still the responsibility of the executor to "keep an eye" on things for proper distribution.

Type of life insurance policy: This could be term, whole life, or variable life. Credit insurance pays off credit cards, mortgage insurance or furniture on death. Who are the beneficiaries and what is the amount of the payout? Annuities are contracts with insurance companies that usually provide retirement income to the policy owner. Sometimes this includes payments to a beneficiary.

Annuity: Annuities can be fixed or variable. Some annuities have a death benefit. If the deceased had annuities with death benefits, who are the beneficiaries and what is the payout? To file a claim go to the insurance company website that issued the annuity and request a claim form. Find the steps for filing a claim. Many companies allow the beneficiary to make initial contact with a copy of the death certificate and then they send a packet of instructions and forms to be filed out. If more than one adult beneficiary was named, each should submit a claim form.

Annuity and Tax: The earnings on annuities are usually not taxed until they are distributed. Tax laws change all of the time so check these for your state and local.

Executor: The personal representative or executor must review the decedent's automobile, homeowner's liability, and other insurance to assure coverage continues until assets are distributed. Check for Mortgage Insurance policies. State law sets various time limits for creditors to collect from the estate and these vary from state to state. Check all policies and installment payments promptly. Some may carry insurance clauses that will cancel them if they are not paid. The executor will notify creditors that the debtor has passed away. If death was accidental, there may be accidental death policies that apply. Check all credit cards for accidental death insurance. Automobile insurance may cover deaths that occurred as a result of an automobile accident.

> If you are unable to locate a policy, you may need to complete a "Lost Policy" form. Your insurance company can provide this for you. Insurers are only required to pay a policy when the beneficiary makes a claim. Legally it seems

insurance companies are not required to determine if a policy holder is still alive, check their records for a beneficiary and pay on the policy. They do not have to look for you or notify you. You have to look for them and make your claim. If funds are not available and you anticipate a delay in making payments, consult with creditors for extensions of time.

Employer: Contact the deceased's employer as the estate may be entitled to life insurance, pension fund contributions, accrued vacation and sick pay, unpaid commissions, disability income, credit union balances and other benefits. If the death was work related file a claim for Workers' Compensation benefits through the deceased's employer.

File a Claim: To file a claim the executor may need a claim form, a death certificate or copy of one and possibly a Letter of Testamentary (proves who is executor of the estate). Contact the insurance company. Keep records of your conversations as to who you spoke with and in general what was said. Record all contact information, account numbers, beneficiary information and anything else that you think is pertinent.

Look at the insurance company's website to see the procedure for filing a claim. Many allow the beneficiary to make initial contact with a copy of the death certificate and then they send a packet of instructions and forms to be filed out. If more than one adult beneficiary was named, each should submit a claim form.

Insurance Agent: Is there an insurance agent associated with the policy? If there is, contact them.

Locating an Insurance Policy or Annuity: Sometimes parents purchase an insurance policy for a minor child and then forget about it. Fifty or sixty years later the policy is still in effect and has grown to a substantial amount. How do you locate this "lost" policy? You begin at the beginning with the paper trail. Check old checkbooks, bank statements and credit card statements to see what bills were paid and to what companies. All insurance companies are required to report the status of a policy at least once a year. If you cannot locate any policy information, have the mail forwarded to a location where you can collect it and watch for statements. If it is a large policy the insurance company would most likely have contacted the Medical Information Bureau (MIB) and the executor can contact them to see what is on file for the deceased.

The Medical Information Bureau (MIB) "Will Provide One Free MIB Consumer Report Every Year" Under the Fair and Accurate Transactions Act (FACTA), at your request, MIB will provide you one free MIB disclosure report every 12 months. To request your free report: Call 1-866-692-6901 OR Visit our on-line disclosure request form on our website. http://www.mib.com/html/request_your_record.html

Payout: Most of the time you may choose to receive the money in a lump sum, in installments over your lifetime or for a fixed number of years, or in installments of a specified amount until the proceeds run out.

Insurance and Beneficiaries: If life insurance is made out to a named beneficiary who is not the executor, that money cannot be used for funeral expenses or other debts.

Living Will

Living Will – Health Care Directive

Living Will: A Living Will allows you to make health care decisions now in case you are unable to do so in the future. It documents instructions for your medical care in the event you are unable to communicate due to a severe injury, terminal illness or other medical condition. A Living Will can also be called a health care declaration, advance directive, or medical power of attorney. It is not a Last Will and Testament or a Living Trust. It has been estimated that more than one third of Americans have had to make a decision whether or not they should keep a loved one alive using "extraordinary means."

Health Care Power of Attorney: A health care power of attorney gives someone you choose the power to make decisions if you if you are incapacitated. These papers should be readily accessible. If you are incapacitated and your family members cannot locate a health care power of attorney, they may have to go to court to have a guardian appointed.

Medical Directives, Health Care Directives or Advance Directives: An advance directive is a written statement of a person's wishes regarding medical treatment. It is a legal document detailing a person's health care wishes, including the individual to whom they give the legal authority to act on their behalf and what types of treatment they do and do not want to receive in the event they are unable to speak or communicate. The living will and the power of attorney constitute what are called advance directives. A divorce has no effect on your written directions for health care.

Durable Power of Attorney: In estate planning, a durable power of attorney is often chosen as a way to plan for those times when you are incapacitated. With a durable power of attorney, you are able to appoint an agent to manage your financial affairs, make health care decisions, or conduct other business for you during your incapacitation. A durable power of attorney may be general or limited. A general durable power of attorney may allow your agent to do every act which may legally be done by you. A limited durable power of attorney cover specific events, like selling property, making investments, or making health care decisions.

> The durable power of attorney for health care is a limited durable power of attorney created only for the purpose of making health care decisions. There may be slight legal differences depending on the state you reside in or become incapacitated in.
>
> The durable power of attorney for health care can do everything that a living will can do. In addition, it gives your agent the power to actively remind your physician of your wishes. Your agent will make all of your health care decisions in the event you become incapacitated. The agent must follow your wishes and must consider your physician's recommendations. Any decision must also be within the range of accepted medical practice.
>
> In most instances the durable power of attorney ends when the person dies but many states are now allowing the agent permission to oversee the final disposition of the body, including authorizing an autopsy and following your wishes for organ and tissue donation.

As the Durable power of attorney you will most likely be the first in line to be held, legally responsible to pay for the disposition of the body in the event of death. Even if there are no assets in the estate after taxes and fees are paid you may be next in line to pay from your own resources. Now might be a good time to speak with a competent estate attorney. Yes, a few states can compel someone to pay for a funeral under certain circumstances.

Protective Medical Decisions Document (PMDD): A durable power of attorney for health care designed to meet state requirements and protect the signer. It is available from the Patients' Rights Council. Federal regulations require every hospital and health program that receives any Medicare or Medicaid funds to inform you, upon admission, of your rights regarding an advance directive. As a result, many facilities are giving patients a Living Will or Durable Power of Attorney to sign at the time of admission. They feel this "covers" them. The PMDD specifically prohibits euthanasia and assisted suicide.

Changing Health Care Directives: Health care directives and powers of attorney may be changed or revoked whenever you want as long as you have the legal capacity to do so. An irrevocable trust is generally speaking irrevocable and cannot be changed.

Legally Incapacitated: A person is legally incapacitated when they are temporarily or permanently impaired by mental and/or physical disability, illness, or by the use of drugs to the extent they lack sufficient understanding to make rational decisions or engage in responsible actions. A health care directive takes effect when your doctor determines that you lack the capacity to make your own health care decisions. This does not give your agent the authority to override what you want in terms of treatment if you have the capacity to make your own decisions. Even if you later become incapacitated your agent must act in your best interest to follow your wishes as you have expressed them in your health care directives.

Naming a Power of Attorney: Family members are chosen most often. They should not have financial problems or drug use problems. They should not have a criminal record. They should be someone you can trust. Many individuals do not have family members to turn to serve as their power of attorney. In such a case you may want to consider naming two agents so there are checks and balances or you may want to consider designating an institution to serve as a corporate Trustee. Most of these financial institutions are regulated and there are several people acting on your behalf. You should consult with a competent estate planning attorney or other estate professional.

Designation of Patient Advocate: A written statement of a person's wishes regarding medical treatment. A health care directive.

Medical Power of Attorney: A written statement of a person's wishes regarding medical treatment. A health care directive.

Palliative Care (Pain Relief): If you chose not to have life-prolonging intervention it does not mean that you cannot alleviate pain or be made comfortable. Instead of prolonging life, palliative care focuses on quality of life and dignity by helping a patient remain comfortable and free from pain until life ends naturally.

Do-Not-Resuscitate (DNR): If a medical emergency occurs, this form alerts emergency personnel that you do not wish to receive cardiopulmonary resuscitation (CPR). Your doctor can add a DNR order to your medical record. You should also obtain an easily identifiable Medic Alert bracelet, anklet, or necklace.

Organ and Tissue Donation: Even if someone signs a donor card, it is essential that their family also knows their wishes regarding organ donation. Let them know as soon as possible. The family may still be asked to sign a consent form in order for the donation to occur. If they say no, the hospital may refuse to accept the organ(s). If the donor has taken the time to register with the Secretary of State or with the Gift of Life, then their family does not have the right to object once they are in the registry. Sign the organ donor space on your driver license and carry an organ donor card. Make this information available to health care workers.

> Anyone over eighteen years of age can become an organ or tissue donor. This will not interfere with their own health care and it will not, within reason, delay their own funeral arrangements. You may change your mind at any time, simply notify people you have changed your mind and if you have checked Organ Donor on your driver's license, contact the department of motor vehicles in the state where the license was issued to change the designation. The most important thing to do is to sign up as an organ and tissue donor in your state's donor registry. www.organdonor.gov

For reasons why you should think about this before making a decision read:

What You Lose When You Sign That Donor Card By Dick Teresi
http://online.wsj.com/article/SB10001424052970204603004577269910906351598.html

http://blog.beliefnet.com/watchwomanonthewall/2012/03/what-you-lose-when-you-sign-that-donor-card.html

Google: What You Lose When You Sign That Donor Card By Dick Teresi (you will get some good pro and con)

Organ transplantation is a twenty billion dollar a year business. Organ transplantation—from procurement of organs to transplant to the first year of postoperative care—is a $20 billion per year business. Recipients of single-organ transplants—heart, intestine, kidney, liver, single and double lung and pancreas—are charged an average $470,000, ranging from $288,000 for a kidney transplant to $1.2 million for an intestine transplant, according to consulting firm Milliman. Neither donors nor their families can be paid for organs.

Your Cost: Your family pays for your medical care and funeral costs, but not for organ donation. Costs related to donation are paid by the recipient, usually through insurance, Medicare or Medicaid. Costs for the donation of organ or tissues are covered by the local organ procurement organization in many cases and the assumption is they are reimbursed.

First Person Consent: Recently, several states have passed legislation establishing "first-person consent" whereby the family cannot override an individual's documented desire to be an organ donor. Some states have established first-person consent registries for people interested in being deceased organ donors.

Organ Donor Cards: Many Organ Donor Cards can be downloaded, printed, signed and carried with you. On Facebook Time Line, under Life Event there is a Health and Wellness section with a place for the individual to indicate that they have decided to be an organ donor, provide their state and/or country and even a story about why they have chosen to be an organ donor.

Financial Power of Attorney: A financial power of attorney gives a trusted person authority to handle your finances and property if you become incapacitated and unable to handle your own affairs. In most cases this is a good idea and if you have wisely chosen an agent they will manage your financial affairs as you would have. Can they steal from you? Yes. You are giving them the right to act in your place. It would be a good idea to see a competent attorney to discuss this. If you do not have a durable financial power of attorney and you are alone and incapacitated your family may have to go to court to have a guardian or conservator appointed. This can be expensive and take time. Even if you are married, have a living trust or joint tenancy a durable power of attorney may make it easier for your family if you become incapacitated. In many situations property may not be sold without the joint tenant's signature because an incapacitated spouse cannot consent to a sale.

If you have assets that you are concerned about, you should most likely discuss this with a competent attorney.

Living Trust: In most cases a living trust allows someone to distribute assets at the time of your death but does not allow for someone to make financial decisions for you if you become incapacitated.

Companies like http://www.docubank.com/ offer immediate access to healthcare directives & emergency medical information. They keep all of your health care directives online for you to access 24/7. We are not recommending them, just pointing out they exist.

Medicaid

Medicaid: Medicaid is a need-based program that provides health-care benefits to families based on income and other criteria. Each state operates a Medicaid program that provides health coverage for lower-income people, families and children, the elderly, and people with disabilities. The eligibility rules for Medicaid are different for each state, but most states offer coverage for adults with children at some income level. In addition, beginning in 2014, most adults under age 65 with individual incomes up to about $15,000 per year will qualify for Medicaid in every state. Less than 10% of seniors typically have long term care insurance, yet 90% worry about long term care costs.

> **Hospice Care:** In 1986, laws were passed to allow the states to develop coverage for hospice programs. Most states have a Medicaid hospice benefit, which is patterned after the Medicare hospice benefit.
>
> **Burial Funds** are funds specifically set aside and clearly designated for an individual's or their spouse's burial, cremation or other burial-related expenses. Medicaid allows you to put aside your own money for funeral and burial expenses without having that money counted as part of your assets when Medicaid determines your eligibility for medical or long-term care coverage. Medicaid does not count the value of a burial plot the individual owns. The amount Medicaid allows to be set aside for the funeral or burial account is around $3,500. If you are married, you may also be able to set aside $3,500 for the funeral or burial expenses of your spouse but the exact amount, and the rules that govern these funds vary from state to state. Some states reduce this to a maximum of $1,500 if the individual is receiving certain benefits.
>
> **Medicaid and Tax:** The IRS tax code does not coordinate with the Medicaid laws. Medicaid does not coordinate with the IRS Tax code concerning "gifting". Medicaid laws look at "gifting", the amount of the gift and the date the gift was made. Medicaid does not like it when someone tries to give all of

their money to their family or friends so they can then qualify for low income assistance. Many estate planning laws coordinate and many are in opposition.

Medicaid and Beneficiaries: If an individual is receiving Medicaid or Supplemental Security Income (SSI) they are only authorized to have $2,000 or less in their bank account. If they then inherit a substantial amount of money, that money will become part of their estate and if the amount exceeds $2,000 they will most likely lose their government benefits. If they try to refuse the inheritance that could be considered a divestment and may affect their benefits. It may be best to have those funds go directly into a special needs trust for the individual with a guardian to oversee the funds.

Some states provide death benefits to recipients of Medicaid. Google: Medicaid (state). Call your local Medicaid information help line for assistance. They are available to help you.

Many people believe they can transfer all of their wealth to their children and qualify for Medicaid. Medicaid is welfare through the state and federal government and closely scrutinizes what people do with their money prior to entering a nursing home and applying for benefits.

Estate Recovery Mandate

The 1993 Estate Recovery Mandate requires state Medicaid programs to place liens on property owned by Medicaid patients after their death. Many families of Medicaid recipients expect to receive a death benefit and end up facing heavy liens from the state upon their loved one's death.

States must pursue recovering costs for medical assistance consisting of:

1) Nursing home or other long-term institutional services.

2) Home- and community-based services.

3) Hospital and prescription drug services provided while the recipient was receiving nursing facility or home- and community-based services.

And At State option, **any other items covered by the Medicaid State Plan.**

At a minimum, states must recover from assets that pass through probate (which is governed by state law). At a maximum, states may recover any assets of the deceased recipient.

How is "estate" defined?

At a minimum, states must pursue recoveries from the "probate estate," which includes property that passes to the heirs under state probate law.

Alternatively, states can expand the definition of estate to allow recovery from property that bypasses probate -- for example, property owned in joint tenancy with rights of survivorship, life estates, living trusts, annuity remainder payments, or life insurance payouts.

How much is subject to recovery?

At a minimum, states must recover amounts spent by Medicaid for long-term care and related drug and hospital benefits, including any Medicaid payments for Medicare cost sharing related to these services.

At their option, states may recover costs of all Medicaid services paid on the individual's behalf.

Recoveries may not exceed the total amount spent by Medicaid on the individual's behalf, nor the amount remaining in the estate after the claims of other creditors delineated in state law have been satisfied.

Medicaid's primary function is to help the poor receive health care. Most people don't have health insurance that covers long term care costs. A major source for payment of long term care costs, including both nursing home costs and, to an increasing extent, home care costs, is the Medicaid Program. Now might be a good time to contact a knowledgeable estate attorney.

Mortgage

Mortgage and Reverse Mortgage

Mortgage: When a person dies the mortgage passes to the joint tenant if there is one. Real property held in joint tenancy can be transferred by recording an affidavit of death of a joint tenant with the local county recorder's office. A home solely titled in the name of the decedent will require probate to transfer title of the home. Probate can easily take a year or more if there are no situations (someone contesting a decision made by the executor, for example).

Married, Community Property: Some states limit a spouse's ability to transfer property acquired during the marriage as an extra protection for the surviving spouse. Even if only the decedent's name is listed on the property title, depending on state law, they may be able to transfer only one half interest in the property. The surviving spouse may also be able to claim a forced share of the estate if this amount is more than what is provided in the will.

Intestate: If the decedent left no Will and the property is held in joint tenancy it passes to the joint tenant in almost all cases. If the decedent owned property in joint tenancy in more than one state, who inherits the property is determined by the intestacy laws of two or more different states. If one state is a joint property state and one state is not and the property was not held in joint tenancy, now may be a good time to speak with a competent professional. Usually any assets held in joint tenancy such as: bank accounts, safe deposit box contents, stocks and bonds, real-estate, and community property usually pas directly to the sole survivor.

Assume the Mortgage: Not all lenders allow assumptions by family members following the death of original mortgagors, but many do. Unless other arraignments are made the lender will foreclose on the house if payments stop.

Reverse Mortgage

Reverse Mortgage

Reverse Mortgage (HECM): A reverse mortgage is a special type of home loan available to homeowners age 62 or older that lets you convert a portion of the equity in your home into cash. The equity that you built up over years of making mortgage payments can be paid to you. FHA's Home Equity Conversion Mortgage (HECM) program may be available to you. The reverse mortgage can become due when all homeowners have passed away or moved out of the home for 12 consecutive months. Taxes and insurance must be paid.

Fraud Alert: If you are interested in a reverse mortgage, beware of scam artists that charge thousands of dollars for information that is free from HUD!

Payments may be received as:

Tenure- equal monthly payments as long as at least one borrower lives and continues to occupy the property as a principal residence.

Term- equal monthly payments for a fixed period of months selected.

Line of Credit- unscheduled payments or in installments, at times and in an amount of your choosing until the line of credit is exhausted.

Modified Tenure- combination of line of credit and scheduled monthly payments for as long as you remain in the home.

Modified Term- combination of line of credit plus monthly payments for a fixed period of months selected by the borrower.

Home Equity Line of Credit (HELOC): In order to qualify for a HELOC, banks require that borrowers meet certain income and credit qualifications. Borrowers must have adequate income, and they make monthly payments on the principal and interest. Unlike a reverse mortgage, monthly mortgage payments are required in order to stay current on the loan.

Reverse Mortgage (HECM): A reverse mortgage is different, because it pays the homeowner and there are no monthly principal and interest payments. With a reverse mortgage, you are required to pay real estate taxes, utilities, and hazard and flood insurance premiums.

Homeowners can draw a lump sum or receive monthly payments as a revolving line of credit. The homeowner's obligation to repay the loan is deferred until the owner(s) die, the home is sold, or the homeowners cease to live in the property or breach the provisions of the mortgage. If the value of the property increases it is possible to acquire a second or third reverse mortgage.

HECM to Purchase a New Home: Many people are not aware that a reverse mortgage can be used to purchase a primary residence. The HECM for Purchase includes the same fees and requirements of all FHA reverse mortgage products. The borrower buys a new home and takes a reverse mortgage on the home in a single transaction. There are no mortgage payments while they remain in the home.

Underwater Homes

Underwater Homes: A home is said to be "underwater" when more is owed on the home than the home is worth. A reverse mortgage is a "non-recourse" loan which means that **the HECM borrower (or their estate) will never owe more than the loan balance or value of the property, whichever is less; and no assets other than the home must be used to repay the debt.** Non-recourse means simply that if the borrower (or estate) does not pay the balance when due, the mortgagee's remedy is limited to foreclosure and the borrower will not be personally liable for any deficiency resulting from the foreclosure.

Is the lender entitled to any or all monies owed on the unpaid balance before the beneficiaries are paid?

The mortgage must be paid or the lender may foreclose on the home or property. This does not necessarily mean the whole principle must be paid in full. The payments on the note must be kept current. If the payments stop the lender has the right to foreclose and reposes the property and sell it. Usually the payments are made by the estate pending disposition of and closing the estate.

The estate is also responsible to pay any insurance, utilities, and security fees to cause no harm to the value of the property. If more money is owed on the property than it is worth the executor may decide to allow the lender to have the property back and foreclose. However, if it is a family home or someone in the family or an heir wants the property they most likely should be allowed to purchase it from the estate or they may contest the executor's decision to sell the property and hold up the disposition of the estate. Not all lenders allow a family member to assume the loan.

Cosigners: If a family member or members co-signed the mortgage everything changes. The loan is generally due and payable when the borrower(s) no longer live in the house for 12 consecutive months or pass away.

Abandon the Home: If the net proceeds of sale would not pay off the debt you may consider abandoning the home and allowing the lender to foreclose so that you incur no further expense or liability with the home. Before you decide to abandon the home it would be a really good time to speak with a competent estate attorney, real-estate attorney or other professional. How will this affect your credit? In your state can you simply refuse to accept the inheritance? Can you surrender possession to the lender?

Home Repairs: What is the appraised value of the home? Are any taxes owed on the home? You can get an idea of a home's worth by going online to websites like Zillow.com, Redfin.com, and realestate.yahoo.com. Elderly people tend to not make repairs until they are overdue. A prudent course of action would be for you to pay for a home inspection before selling the home. This will give you a good idea of how the roof, waste water and electrical systems are. The American Society of Home Inspectors (ASHI.org) may be a good place to start.

Non-Recourse Loans: With the HUD (Department of Housing and Urban Development), FHA-insured (Federal Housing Administration) HECM (Home Equity Conversion Mortgage) reverse mortgage, the borrower can never owe more than the value of the property and cannot pass on any debt from the reverse mortgage to any heirs. The sole remedy the lender has is the collateral, not assets in the estate, if applicable.

The executor may sell the home. If a member of the family or an heir chooses to pay off the loan in order to prevent selling the house the full amount of the loan has to be repaid even if the balance of the loan is higher than the value of the house. However, if the heirs decide to sell the house to repay the loan, the HECM product has a non-recourse policy which states that the heirs will not be required to pay more than the value of the home, even if the loan balance exceeds the value of the home. Now may be a good time to consult a competent professional.

The HECM reverse mortgage was created to allow seniors to live in their home for the rest of their lives without worrying about being evicted or foreclosed on for non-payment. This can and will change if the homeowner does not keep the home in good condition and meet other obligations, such as property insurance and property tax payments.

Home Disposition

Reverse Mortgage Lien: A reverse mortgage lien is often recorded at a higher dollar amount than the amount of money actually disbursed at the loan closing. This recorded lien is at times misunderstood by some borrowers as being the payoff amount of the mortgage. The recorded lien works in similar fashion to a home equity line of credit where the lien represents the maximum lending limit, but the payoff is calculated based on actual disbursements plus interest owing.

Reverse Mortgage and Heirs

Automatic Transfer to an Heir: If there is only one name on the title of the home the reverse mortgage does not automatically transfer to the surviving, non-borrowing spouse, in the event the borrower passes away or moves. If there are adult children living in the home with the reverse mortgage borrower the loan is due and payable when the borrower(s) no longer live in the house for 12 consecutive months or pass away.

Heirs: Ownership in most cases will pass to the surviving spouse if their name is also on the title of the home. If there is no surviving spouse or joint tenant the property may belong within the estate of the deceased. The value of the property when the owner(s) no longer meet the requirements of the loan is determined by the homes appraised value minus cash, interest and finance charges to be repaid. When the home is sold or no longer used as a primary residence, the cash, interest, and other finance charges must be repaid. All proceeds beyond the amount owed return to the estate. This means any remaining equity can be transferred to heirs.

Inheritance: In most states when the home is left to an heir from the estate of the deceased the heir is responsible for repaying the loan. The home may be resold to repay the lender. It is still considered a non-recourse loan in most cases.

Home Sales for Home with a Reverse Mortgage: If the house is sold by the estate the reverse mortgage is paid off from the proceeds from the house and any extra money is returned to the estate.

Advice: If you have a financial interest in the home or anything else worth what you consider to be a lot of money go and speak with a competent professional. It will most likely be less expensive for you in the long run. Do things once and sleep nights.

HUD (Department of Housing and Urban Development)

http://portal.hud.gov/hudportal/HUD?src=/program_offices/housing/sfh/hecm/hecmhome

Prepay

Should I Prepay for Funeral Expenses?

Prepay for Funeral Expenses: Is it a good idea to prepay for your funeral services? Usually it is a better idea to set up a trust to cover your expenses. A Totten Trust seems to work out very well for most. It may also be advisable to prepay for some services like a cemetery plot, direct burial or direct cremation and set aside money in a trust for the cost of a service and other expenses. When you finish with this book you should have a much better idea of what you want to do.

After a loved one passes it can be a very stressful time to make decisions about financing a funeral.

Pre-plan or Pre-pay: You can pre-plan without pre-paying. If you decide to pre-pay, you are the customer. They are the funeral service business. They are in business to make money. There is nothing wrong with that, just understand it is a business. Shop around for the best service and the best price.

Most pre-paid Funeral Services are not refundable if not used so make certain those that come later to tidy up have all the necessary access to the information. Include the original paperwork with your documents.

Be Careful: 1) If you prepay a funeral home for services and it goes out of business, or declares bankruptcy, you may not get your money back. 2) If you move to another city or state you may not be able to get a refund. You may have to be transported after death back to the area in which you repurchased in order to use the services. 3) Not all expenses may be covered. 4) You may not be able to change the plan at all (irrevocable). 5) You may only be able to change the plan by paying penalties. 6) Are you paying for merchandise only or are you paying for merchandise and the funeral service? 7) Some prepaid plans actually cost you more in payments than what is paid out at your death. 8) In some states consumers forfeit 10% just to get out of the plan. What happens if you can no longer make the payments? 9) What about cemetery charges? Are you only prepaying for the funeral without the cemetery charges? 10) If you prepay for a casket and that model is discontinued ten years later what happens? Is there an add-on fee for "something similar"? 11) What happens when prices increase? 12) What happens if at the time of death the family could not find the policy only to discover it later on? In many cases it is nonrefundable and not transferable. Like anything else, there are some very good prepaid plans and there are some very bad prepaid plans. Go online and research what you are buying before you sign anything.

How to Prepay Funeral Expenses

Joint Savings Account: Save for funeral expenses in a joint savings account. If you have the discipline just keep the money in a joint savings account and do not touch it. The money can be accessed by the joint holder of the account and is available now. You must be able to trust this person to not withdraw the funds prior to paying for the funeral expenses.

Payable-on-Death Account (POD): You can set up a payable-on-death account at your bank and deposit funds into it to pay for your funeral and related expenses. A payable on death bank account is a regular bank account that names a specific person as the beneficiary. The immediate transfer of assets is triggered by the death of the client.

Totten Trust: A Totten Trust is just a regular bank account with a designated "pay on death" inheritor. When the account is opened a friend, relative (most likely named as executor) is named as the beneficiary. Whoever opens the account can also close it at any time for any reason. They may also change banks and or change beneficiaries. The beneficiary does not need to know about the arrangement, and the depositor is entitled to deposit and withdraw funds from the account as they see fit. The idea is when the person dies the beneficiary collects the account balance and pays for the funeral expenses. This can work out very well if all parties are informed and kept up to date.

Funeral Insurance Policy: The vast majority of final expense life insurance policies will typically have a cash value of somewhere in between $5,000 and $50,000. You do not have to spend all of this money on a funeral. It should be spent by the survivors to help them financially through this time of need. Do not sign over an insurance policy to a funeral service provider for any more than the "Good Faith estimate". It is our suggestion that you never sign over an insurance policy to anyone without the advice of a competent estate attorney. Some people "overspend" on a funeral or burial because they think of it as a reflection of their feelings for the deceased.

Purchase a good quality funeral insurance policy from a reputable insurance company. You can check prices, complaints and reviews online. Your actual cost may vary due to your age and health. Read the fine print and check for restrictive clauses that may limit or eliminate the payout. If you are paying premiums and only get back what you paid in you may be better off rethinking this particular policy.

Trust-based Pre-Payment Plans: Trust-based Pre-Payment Plans sound good but you have to be careful and read the fine print. Some are much better than others. If you need help ask an insurance agent or trusted family member. Get some information, think about it and discuss it with a friend before deciding. Sometimes if you move to a different town or state the money in trust cannot be moved prior to death.

Prepaid Funeral Contracts: There are basically two distinct kinds of prepaid funeral contracts: revocable and irrevocable. Irrevocable is something that cannot be undone or changed. You bought it and you own it. A revocable contract may allow you to cancel the policy for no penalty or a penalty fee. It may allow you to make changes to the policy for a fee. Read the fine print. You should know and completely understand what you are buying before you sign a contract for goods or services. It is a legal contract and when you sign it, you bought it. Be careful. It may be a good idea to speak with a competent estate attorney before you sign anything.

Sometimes prices are guaranteed and sometimes they may change over time. This is spelled out in the contract. How much do you have to pay and when? What happens if you miss one or two payments? Can you pay off the whole amount without a penalty? Yes, sometimes there is prepayment penalty if you are not going to pay all of the interest. They stay up late nights thinking of these things.

Pre-plan Your Passing

Help Others Manage Your Paperwork

What to Do Now

To Pre-Plan is really very simple.

1) **Inventory:** Someone needs to make a list.

2) Value: The list should contain all assets and all debts. Each item should be followed by its estimated worth (assets) or the current amount owed (debts).

3) Location: A location should be shown for each item. If a bank this should be the local branch. If you are giving the location of a Will or document this should be where the document is now.

4) Access: This should include access information: keys, account numbers, passwords and user names, lock combinations, security access cards etc. This is extremely sensitive information and could be used to empty all of the money from your accounts. Secure this information in a theft proof, fire proof, and flood proof location. Do not leave it on a table or chair while you are working on it where it may be available to others. Your accounts could be emptied electronically in just a few minutes. If you even suspect fraud, contact the bank or institution immediately.

5) Disbursement: Who gets what? If someone always commented on how nice that little figurine looked maybe you would like to leave it to them; maybe not. After each item list anyone that you would really like to have it when you pass away. This information then goes into your Will.

The last thing loved ones need to do is go on a scavenger hunt.

Paperwork

> **It is really all about the paperwork or Digital Information when we plan to help others tidy up behind us.** It is so much easier to leave a notebook with INFORMATION that is useful. We recommend a notebook because all of the pages stay together and you can add to it as you think of things over the years. It is easy to update and work on. There really does not have to be any order. Think of it like this. The Executor or Personal Representative that comes in to help can spend days or weeks looking for any indication of a Trust fund or you can write in your notebook. "Trust funds. I don't have any. Thought about it but did not get around to it yet; maybe later in the year. If I do set one up; I will leave a note." or "I have a Totten Trust at Name of bank, local branch, address, and phone. I set it up with (name of contact, maybe

tape the business card to the page). We put $5,000 in this trust payable on death to: (name, address, phone number, email) and the executor of my estate. This money is to be used for my immediate funeral needs so you do not have to pay this yourself. You are quite welcome." Even if you set up this Totten Trust and named a spouse, still include all information in the notebook. You may forget. Your spouse may forget. Someone is going to read this notebook, so leave them directions.

Another page could read: "I was thinking about Pensions today. I checked into all of the places I used to work and do not recall ever having a pension plan that was not closed after I quit working there. I still have a retirement account at: name, account number, address, phone number, email, and website". If you have a statement of the account you can fold it in half and staple or tape it to the sheet of paper in your notebook. This makes it easy for you to keep records and for those that come behind trying to help you with your paper work; it is all in one place. It may be a bit disorganized. That is fine. It is all in one place. They can take it and sit down in a comfortable chair to read through it and make notes if need be. It is so much more considerate to tell someone "I do not have any pension plans. You do not have to look for them". The alternative is for the executor to spend days or weeks looking for things that do not exist.

It is very important to tell people what you do not have as well as telling them what you have.

You do not have to remember to list everything but if you list the main things by going through this checklist your personal representative will understand that you are helping and most likely do not have any assets that you have not listed.

The main purpose of this list is to help you inventory your assets, debts and documents. Answer yes/no if you have any of these. We will later collect copies of documents and records and detailed information of their location, account numbers, passwords, etc. . For now a simple yes/ or no and more general location (example: bank name or top drawer my dresser) will save many weeks of searching for an executor.

Notebook: List all Assets, Debts and Documents

Treat this information as if it were Cash. You are recording all of your account access information that can be used to withdraw all of the money in your accounts. You need to keep this information secure from theft, fire and flood.

Go through the following list and check off the items that you have. In the last column briefly write their current location. For example, bank name – safe deposit box. This is all the information you need to place here. When you are finished you will go back over the list and make notations in your note book in more depth. Add to the list whenever you want.

Assets, Debts Documents	I have/ I do not have	Location
Name	Yes or No	What is the current location?

Advance Directives
Living Will
Conservator
Power of Attorney
Durable Health Care
Power of Attorney

Organ Donor Cards
Annuity
Auto Loans
Authorization to Release
Protected Healthcare
Information form
Brokerage Accounts

Bank Accounts
Bank accounts locally or anywhere in the world

	I have: Yes/No	Location
Cell Phone: a cell phone is considered a document		
Checking Accounts		
Savings Accounts		

Insurance

Life Insurance Policies
Health Insurance Policies
Home Owners Insurance
Mortgage Insurance Policies
Accident Insurance Policies
Auto Insurance Policies
Long Term Care Policies

Business Relationships

Business Partnership
Limited Liability Corporation (LLC)
Corporate Operating Agreements

CD's (Certificates of Deposit)
Cemetery Plots
Charitable Pledges
Charitable Lead Trust
Charitable Remainder Trust
Child-Support Payments
Coins
Collections: list what you consider a collection and would like to stay together.
Copyright
Credit Card Accounts
Debit Card Accounts: Credit Cards
Deeds to Property
Firearms

	I have: Yes/No	Location
Government Benefits		
Guardians for Adults		
Guardians for Children		
Health Directives		
Home		
Home alarm system		
Home Gate Access Code		
Home Mailbox		
Home Safe		
Home: locked boxes, drawers or cabinets.		
IRAs		
Insurance Agent		
Insurance Cards		
Life Insurance Policies		
Investment Accounts		
Living Trust		
Living Will		
Loans		
I Loaned Money to:		
I Borrowed Money from:		
Mortgage Accounts		
Escrow Mortgage Accounts		
Memberships		
Membership Cards		
Mutual Fund Accounts		
Online log-in information	see **Digital Assets** below	
Passport: Passport Card		
Pets		
Pensions		
Power of Attorney		
Qualified Domestic Relations Order		
Real Property homes and buildings		
Recipes		
Rental Contracts		

	I have: Yes/No	Location
Retirement Accounts		
401k		
Safe Deposit Boxes		
Key to Safe Deposit Box		
Savings Accounts		
Savings Bonds		
Season Tickets		
Social Security Death Benefit		
Sports Equipment		
Stamps		
Stocks and Bonds		
Stock Certificates		
Storage Agreements		
Storage Lockers & (keys)		
Tax Returns for the last three years. Federal & State		
Timeshares		
Trade-marks		
Trust Accounts		
Revocable Trust		
Totten Trust		

Utilities
- Cell Phone Provider
- Cable TV
- Electric
- Garbage
- Gas
- Internet
- Water

Vehicles
- Autos
- Boats, water craft
- Airplanes
- Motorcycles
- Bicycles

Digital Assets	Will: Last Will and Testament	
	User Name = User	**Password & challenge questions** = PW & CQ
Airlines		
Frequent Flier Miles	User	PW & CQ
Answering Machines		
Blogs	User	PW & CQ
Blogger	User	PW & CQ
Brokerage Account	User	PW & CQ
CDs		
Cell Phones	Pin number	
Computers		
Passwords & User names	User	PW & CQ
Names or locations of important files on your hard drive.		
Copiers		
Credit Card accounts	User	PW & CQ
Data Storage Online (CLOUD)	User	PW & CQ
Digital Cameras		
Digital Wallet	User	PW & CQ
DVDs		
Email Accounts. The executor will need access.	User	PW & CQ
Gmail accounts	User	PW & CQ
Facebook	User	PW & CQ
Floppy Disc		
Google Docs	User	PW & CQ
Hard Drives (encrypted?)		
External Drives		
Flash Drives		
Internal Drives		
Thumb Drives		
iTunes	User	PW & CQ
Images and Photos	User	PW & CQ

Insurance Accounts	User	PW & CQ
LinkedIn	User	PW & CQ
Magazine Subscriptions Online	User	PW & CQ
Manuscripts		
Memberships	User	PW & CQ
Movie Subscriptions Online	User	PW & CQ
Music Subscriptions Online	User	PW & CQ
Netflix	User	PW & CQ
Newspaper subscriptions online	User	PW & CQ
Pandora	User	PW & CQ
PayPal	User	PW & CQ
Photos		
Family Photos		
Photo Sharing Sites	User	PW & CQ
Retirement Plan	User	PW & CQ
Safe Deposit Box online	User	PW & CQ
Second Life: Virtual Land	User	PW & CQ
Virtual Land	User	PW & CQ
Virtual Assets	User	PW & CQ
Social Media Profiles		
Facebook	User	PW & CQ
Flickr	User	PW & CQ
YouTube	User	PW & CQ
Twitter		
Travel booking - online	User	PW & CQ
URLs you own	User	PW & CQ
Utility Bills paid online	User	PW & CQ
Video Game Sites	User	PW & CQ
Videos	User	PW & CQ
Websites	User	PW & CQ
Word Press	User	PW & CQ
You Tube	User	PW & CQ

Where I do Banking Online		
Bank	User	PW & CQ
Credit cards	User	PW & CQ
PayPal	User	PW & CQ
Bills Paid Online		
Automobile	User	PW & CQ
Cable	User	PW & CQ
Cell Phone	User	PW & CQ
Electric	User	PW & CQ
Gas	User	PW & CQ
Phone	User	PW & CQ
Water	User	PW & CQ
Where I have shopped online		
Amazon.com	User	PW & CQ
eBay	User	PW & CQ
Social Networking Sites		
Facebook	User	PW & CQ
LinkedIn	User	PW & CQ
Twitter	User	PW & CQ
Online Services where I have accounts		
Blogger	User	PW & CQ
Facebook	User	PW & CQ
iTunes	User	PW & CQ
Netflix	User	PW & CQ
Pandora	User	PW & CQ
Video Game Sites	User	PW & CQ
Word Press	User	PW & CQ
My Blog Hosting	User	PW & CQ
My Registrar	User	PW & CQ

My Storage Service(s)		
Google Docs	User	PW & CQ
My Web Hosting	User	PW & CQ

Notebook: Record Detailed Information

When you finish going through the list congratulate yourself. You just saved those people who come along behind to help you a lot of needless work. Now you will list each item in your notebook. Start at the beginning of the list. You will need to include the estimated value, the detailed location and all access information. Do this for Physical Assets, Digital Assets, Debts, and Documents.

Asset or Document	Estimated Value	Physical Location	Leave to
Living Will		Top left side dresser drawer in my bedroom.	
Annuity paperwork	$125/month	Best Fund, national address, phone, FAX, contact person if known. Local address if any, phone, FAX, contact person if any. Account number, any notes. Paperwork is in **Safe Deposit Box** at Local Bank, name, address, phone, fax, contact person. The key is in my jewelry box in the top drawer.	My estate

Cell Phone	Paid $200 two years ago.	I usually have it with me. I have never bought anything using my cell phone (OR I use my cell phone for online banking, watching movies from my Netflix account, shopping at Amazon.com, and iTunes. I use it a lot for everything. email, photo sharing	It has to be cleaned of all sensitive information.
Timeshares	Paid $8,500 in 2006	The paperwork and original contract is in the lock box on the top shelf of my bedroom closet. Company name, account number, address, and phone. There is a photo copy in my safe deposit box at bank name (I only have one safe deposit box.)	I would like to leave this to my sister, name. She always looked like she needed a vacation.
Digital Assets	**Estimated Value**	**Physical Location**	**Leave to**
Family Photos	---	I have photos on my laptop computer. I have photos on CDs and DVDs that are on the shelf in the upstairs hallway. These are next to some of my photo albums. I have photos on line at name, URL(address – photophoto.com) my User name is(user). My password is (password) the challenge question is: What is my favorite color? Answer White34. I have more photos at URL (bigbearphoto.net) my User name is(user). My password is (password) the challenge question is: What is my favorite color? Answer white34. and Where were you born? Answer: the moon. I have photos on my desk computer.	

	Leave photos to:	I have hundreds of photos on my cell phone.
		I will try to have a friend copy my photos to disc. If I do not get this done please try to do this for me. If you keep the family photos together and my vacation photos separate then whoever wants some - it is OK with me.

Debt Name	Estimated Value	Physical Location	
Auto Loan Chevy truck.	Maybe $12,000 ?	It should be in the driveway. The truck title is in the safe deposit box at (name of bank). I only have the one safe deposit box and the information is listed under Annuity paperwork in this notebook. My Will is also in the box. I still owe $4,500 on the truck. If (name) wants the truck they will have to take on the debt. If they do not want my truck sell it, pay off the debt owed and put the remainder into my estate.	I want my friend (name) to have my truck. Contact information: name address, phone. I will miss them.
Electric bill is due every month	$100/ month	Name of electric company, account number, address, phone.	

Assets, Debts Documents	Estimated Value	Physical Location	Leave to
Advance Directives			
Living Will		Top left side dresser drawer in my bedroom.	

Annuity paperwork	$125/ month	My estate
	Best Fund, national address, phone, FAX, contact person if known. Local address if any, phone, FAX, contact person if any. Account number, any notes. Paperwork is in **Safe Deposit Box** at Local Bank: name, address, phone, fax, contact person. The key is in my jewelry box in the top drawer. I tagged it "dep box"	
Cell Phone	Paid $200 two years ago.	
	I usually have it with me. I have never bought anything using my cell phone or use my cell phone for online banking. **Or with a Smart Phone it might be:** I watch movies from my Netflix account, shopping at Amazon.com, and iTunes. I use it a lot for everything. Email, photo sharing and online banking.	It has to be cleaned of all sensitive information.
Timeshares	Paid $8,500 in 2006	I would like to leave this to my sister, (name). She always looks like she needs a vacation. Hi Sis!
	The paperwork and original contract is in the lock box on the top shelf of my bedroom closet. Company name, account number, address, and phone. There is a photo copy in my safe deposit box at bank name (I only have one safe deposit box.)	

Digital Assets	Estimated Value	Physical Location	Leave to
Family Photos	No real monetary value.		
	I have photos on my laptop computer. I have photos on CDs and DVDs that are on the shelf in the upstairs hallway. These are next to some of my photo albums. I have photos on line at (name, 60photo.com) my User name is (user). My password is (password) the challenge question is: What is my favorite color? Answer white34. I have more photos at URL (bigbearphoto.net) my user name is(user). My password is (password) the challenge question is: What is my favorite color? Answer white34. And Where were you born? Answer: the moon I have photos on my desk computer. I have hundreds of photos on my cell phone.		I will try to have a friend copy my photos to disc. If I do not get this done please try to do this for me. If you keep the family photos together and my vacation photos separate then whoever wants some it is OK with me.
Music	Some people have thousands of music files online that they paid for.		
Videos	Some people have thousands of Video files online that they paid for.		

Debt Name	Estimated Value	Physical Location
Auto Loan Chevy truck.	Maybe $12,000 ?	It should be in the driveway.

		The truck title is in the safe deposit box at (name of bank). I only have the one safe deposit box and the information is listed under Annuity paperwork in this notebook. My Will is also in the box. I still owe $4,500 on the truck. If (name) wants the truck they will have to take on the debt. If they do not want my truck sell it, pay off the debt owed and put the remainder into my estate.	I want my friend (name) to have my truck. Contact information: name address, phone. I will miss them.
Electric bill is due every month	$100/ month	Name of electric company, account number, address, and phone.	

Some examples are given above. What you want to do is give an estimated value unless you know the value because the item was appraised. If the item was appraised list all of the appraisal information: Appraised Value, name of appraiser, year appraisal was done, address, phone, contact person, etc. Include the location of the original paperwork if you still have it.

Take your time and be as complete as possible. You do not have to finish everything today, but you do have to finish. You are most likely the only one who knows where everything is and what it is worth. Your friends and family do not need to know what it is worth, although it helps. The government wants to know what everything is worth to determine if any tax is due. Most likely no tax is due. If you have so much stuff you are worried about the inheritance tax you should most definitely be speaking to a competent estate attorney.

Value: The list should contain all assets and all debts. Each item should be followed by its estimated worth (assets) or the current amount owed (debts).

Location: A location should be shown for each item. If a bank this should be the local branch. If you are giving the location of a Will or document this should be where it is now. Give detailed information.

Access: This should include all access information: keys, account numbers, passwords and user names, lock combinations, security access cards, secret handshakes etc.

Disbursement: Who gets what? This information then goes into your Will. It is going to help a lot when we get to writing your Will.

Health Directives

Living Will, Durable Power of Attorney or Health Care Power of Attorney

You should write this in large letters at the top of the page in your notebook. Make this large so someone can find it quickly if they need it. Do you have any health directives? Living Will, Durable Power of Attorney or Health Care Power of Attorney? Are you an Organ Donor? Did you sign the organ donor line on your driver license or did you sign onto the **First Person Consent Registry** available in some states so the family cannot overturn your decision to be an organ or tissue donor? A signed organ donation card functions legally as an advance medical directive.

If you are incapacitated and your family members can't locate a Health Care Power of Attorney, they will have to go to court to get a Guardian appointed. You then need to explain to the person you designate to act in your behalf if you are incapacitated exactly how you would like to be treated. You should also write this down or even better use a Living Will so there can be no misinterpretations. If you have a Living Will your loved ones have access to it they can honor your last wishes concerning excessive medical attention. In life and in death: take the time to do it correctly.

Will - Last Will and Testament

Do you have a current Last Will and Testament? yes/ or No. Location and access information. If this is in a safe deposit box does someone else have access? Where is the key? Include a brief description of the contents. What is the branch address where the box is located? Who is the contact person? If you place the name of another individual on your Safe Deposit Box account they will have your permission to open the safe deposit box whenever they want. They will be able to go and remove everything against your wishes. Be careful. Speak to a competent estate attorney to safe guard yourself if you are even a little concerned.

If your Will is with an attorney: list all contact information, name, address, phone number, email, name of law firm. You could attach the attorney's card to the page. It may be a good idea to include a letter of instruction with your will. This should point to your notebook so they have all of the necessary information to manage your estate properly.

Naming an Executor or Personal Representative: They are legally responsible to locate, inventory, value and disburse all items in your estate. Depending on how much you help them, it could take over a year to finish clearing your estate.

Safe Deposit Box

Check with the local Bank where you have your safe deposit box to find out exactly what their policy is concerning access to a Will and important papers after an individual's death. Some states still require the bank to "seal" safe deposit boxes for a few weeks after the death of an owner so the Tax people can stop by and look at the contents. Call their customer service and ask them. If you do not like the answer check with other banks in the area.

Digital Executor

Digital Executor: although this is not yet a legal title, it is often needed. Who does not have digital assets today? If you have a smartphone you may do online banking. You are then more prone to identity theft if this is not properly secured and wiped clean. Do you have family photos on a computer or cellphone? Have you done ANY online shopping? You most likely need a mature (not twelve years old) responsible digital executor that can work with your executor or personal representative.

Life Insurance Policies

Life Insurance Policies: Your family needs to be able to gain access to life insurance policies. In your notebook list all of the details: name, address, phone, fax, account numbers, and contact person (agent). If the original is in a safe deposit box you may want to keep a photo copy handy. Insurance Policies granted by an employer when an individual retires are most often missed. Someone else, an institution, a bank, or the state will eventually collect on this and not the family or loved one. Include all policies in your notebook. If you only have partial information, include what you have for now. Finish this up later. A little information is better than no information. Example: When I retired from (name, address, phone, and contact person) I think I got a Life Insurance policy. I can't find it. I will keep looking."

Insurance Agent: Do you have an insurance agent? Be sure to list all contact information in your notebook.

Retirement Accounts

Pensions, 401ks, Annuities, IRAs and any other retirement accounts that you have (or think you may have): List all of these in your note book. Again include all detailed information. Partial information is better than no information if you cannot recall. Could you write or call someone who could help you remember? Sometimes a few key memories can set everything else loose and bring the details back.

Many insurers say that under policy contracts, they are not required to take steps to determine if a policyholder is still alive and are only required to pay a claim when beneficiaries come forward. State treasuries hold billions of dollars in unclaimed assets. You can search for unclaimed pensions, 401ks and IRAs at **Unclaimed.com.**

Funeral Preference

Funeral Preference: How would you like your loved ones to handle your disposition? Burial or Cremation? What would you like and how would you want it done? Would you like a cremation with a rented casket for a viewing? Where would you like your ashes scattered? Would you like a burial with a closed casket? Where would you like to be buried? Would you like a direct burial or cremation with no viewing and a Memorial Service later on? List any and all preferences. Religious or non-religious service? Would you like a Eulogy? Music? A private service open only to the family? People would really like to know this. Do you have any thoughts on your obituary?

Funeral preferences should not go into the Will because it may not be accessible immediately after death. Most often your funeral decisions should be written out and left with the executor or personal representative. Also let your loved ones know what your plans are. This will allow anyone who disagrees to understand that this is what you want.

Expense: Planning ahead of time usually ends up costing less because you can make your wishes known. If you wait and make the family decide they usually spend a lot more than necessary for a variety of reasons. Also if you do not make your preferences known it can cause tremendous problems later between family members with different views.

Pre-plan or Pre-pay

Pre-plan or Pre-pay: You can pre-plan without pre-paying. If you decide to pre-pay, you are the customer. They are the funeral service business and they are in business to make money. There is nothing wrong with that, just understand it is a business. Shop around for the best service and the best price.

Did you pre-pay for anything? A Cemetery Plot, Marker, Vault, Casket or anything else? Did you pre-pay for a Cremation? Add all of this information to your notebook and include all detailed information needed to locate these and access the accounts. Most pre-paid Funeral Services are not refundable if not used so make certain those that come later to tidy up have all the necessary access to the information. Include the original paperwork with your documents.

Pets

Pets: List all information pertaining to pets. Their likes and dislikes. Do they have medical records? Record all information to locate and access to their medical records.

Marriage and Divorce

Marriage: make certain your spouse know where your note book is located and where all of the documents are kept. Make sure they have access to the marriage certificate. They may need to prove that they are really married to you to have any legal rights.

Divorce: Copies of divorce decrees or judgments usually contain a lot of information on retirement accounts, pensions, child support, alimony and property settlements. If you do not leave a copy you can be certain the divorced spouse has one. Include any and all necessary information for your estate.

Child Support

Child Support: In many, if not most states, the obligation to pay Child Support continues after death. If a Life Insurance policy benefits children from a divorce this may be used to offset child support. You really need to speak with a competent estate attorney if this gives you a lot of room for thought. Read up on the "qualified domestic relations order." This can be used to prove your spouse received a share of your retirement accounts.

Power of Attorney

Medical and Financial Powers of Attorney: Both need to be looked at as soon as possible. They may no longer be what you want. Also look at Trusts and your Will.

Expanding File Folder: You should get an Expanding File Folder. Office supply store sell these for less than ten dollars and they will help to organize your documents, papers, and billing statements. Some people make the mistake of having too much paperwork so the important things are lost. Make the important documents and paperwork easy to find.

Probate

Probate and the Estate

Probate: Probate is a legal proceeding that transfers your property following your death according to the terms of your Will or in the absence of a Will, to your heirs based on probate law. Your estate will be probated whether or not you have a Will. All states have probate and every probate court has its own detailed rules about the documents it requires, what they must contain, and when they must be filed. Probate pays debts and transfers assets to beneficiaries.

Will: If there is a valid Will then the Will determines how the estate is transferred during probate and to whom. If there is no valid Will or the Will only covers some assets, the laws where the deceased had their last legal residence or the laws where the deceased had real estate specify who gets what parts of the estate.

> Having a Will undoubtedly simplifies the distribution of property and helps speed the probate process. There are probate properties and non-probate properties. Probate handles properties distributed through probate. Having a Will may not avoid probate, but it is better than having nothing at all.
>
> **A Will declares** how individually owned assets are distributed. Assets that are owned jointly or assets that have a beneficiary designation pass to the joint tenant or beneficiary on your death. A Will controls an individually owned bank account, individually owned personal property, or individually owned investments, where there is no other joint owner and no designated beneficiary. If you want to avoid all probate you should consider a Trust. There are many, many types of Trust accounts and some are used to accomplish a specific purpose. A Revocable Living Trust and Totten Trust are both commonly used. A Non-revocable Living Trust cannot be changed at a later date in most cases.

Revocable Living Trust: A revocable living trust can definitely be a more efficient way to transfer property at death if it is not already held in joint tenancy or you live in a community property state which most likely has special laws to protect the surviving spouse.

Intestate: If there is no valid Will the probate court must appoint an administrator. The disposition of the body usually takes place long before the appointment and the funeral home or crematorium expects to be paid at the time of service. Who will pay? Where does the funding come from? Most families pay these expenses themselves and then submit the receipts to the executor for reimbursement later on. If there are no funds available to pay these expenses the executor is not obligated to reimburse the person(s) who paid them.

Probate is not inexpensive or quick. Estate attorneys usually handle probate for a flat percentage or an hourly fee. Attorney and court fees can take up to 5% of an estate's probate value. This could be $10,000 on a probate estate worth only $200,000. (The home and a few assets.) The probate process can easily take over one year and as the population ages and the courts have many more cases than they can comfortably handle it may get worse.

Probate is essentially clerical. Forms and filing deadlines. If no one contests the decisions it can proceed smoothly. Although the executor may handle the probate proceedings without an attorney, it can be very difficult in most cases, but not impossible. Without help from an attorney the executor must learn probate law for the particular area while they still distribute the non-probate assets, attend to any surviving family members, and take care of their own life, family and employer. The fewer the number of probated assets the easier it most likely should be to probate the estate. How much simpler to have a valid Will and take care of these things before it reaches this point. The executor has the authority to hire an attorney and pay them from the estate.

Avoiding Probate: If certain property is kept out of the probate estate, it may be able to avoid many of the hassles, costs, and lack of privacy concerns related to probate. There are two common and simple ways to avoid probate: 1) using joint accounts and using payable on death accounts (POD), also called transfer on death accounts (TOD), as well as in trust for accounts (ITF) and 2) Totten trusts. When assets are jointly owned they usually pass by law to the survivor, and then Probate is unnecessary. If the estate is small enough assets with little or no monetary value can usually be distributed without probate. When you reduce the probate estate (automatically transfer assets at death) you also reduce any future probate costs and ensure that the beneficiaries get some of their inheritance faster.

> More Ways you May be able to avoid probate: 1) Name beneficiaries. This could include institutions as beneficiaries. 3) Name beneficiaries for retirement accounts, vehicles, real estate, and stocks and bonds where this is practical and expedient. 4) Hold property in joint ownership. 5) Make gifts of property and money. Now may be a good time to speak with a competent estate planning attorney.

Probate Assets: In a general sense, probate assets are those you own alone.

Non-probate Assets: Assets that are generally non-probate assets will vary by state. These assets are jointly owned with others and pass automatically upon the death of a joint owner. Because they pass automatically, there is no need for probate. They may include: Property and assets that are jointly owned with rights of survivorship and assets jointly owned with the surviving spouse as tenants by the entirety (survivorship). Life insurance and investment accounts which have a specified beneficiary. Assets owned by a living trust and accounts with a specified Transfer on Death (TOD) or Payment on Death (POD) as part of the ownership. If there is a dispute over any item, no matter what the value, the item should be held over for probate. Items with little monetary value are usually distributed outside of probate.

Few Assets: If the deceased left few assets a formal probate hearing is most likely not necessary. Letters of Testamentary are issued at a formal probate hearing. Most states have informal procedures for the transfer of personal property of a relatively small value. This can be as simple as a hand written notarized statement (affidavit) stating that you are entitled to the property. If this involves a bank and they are not a lot of help try talking with another local bank to see if you can receive better information. Most professionals will be more than happy to help you in your time of need.

Simplified Procedure: Is there a simplified procedure for settling an estate with limited assets? Yes, in most states there is. There are various rules and regulations depending on the state and/or county but there will most likely be a dollar amount mentioned. An example could be: A simplified procedure for settling the estate may be available if the total value of the estate assets does not exceed ($40,000). In addition, at the time of death the decedent must not own any real estate other than survivorship property, and the estate assets must consist only of personal property and/or an unreleased interest in a mortgage with or without value etc. If a simplified procedure is available it may not be necessary to probate the estate.

Real Estate: Real estate is probated in the state where the property is actually located while there is another probate in the state where the deceased had their legal residence. If they owned another home or property in their state of residence it will be probated in that state. This means there can be more than one probate proceeding.

Probate Jurisdiction: If the individual passes while living out of state the probate court with jurisdiction is usually the court in the county where the deceased had their primary residence. This would also normally be the county in which the deceased had most of their assets. If you think another state or county should have jurisdiction call the county court in the county that you think should have jurisdiction and ask them.

Debt: The estate is responsible for the decedent's debts. Administrative costs, court costs and attorney fees are also paid by the estate. If the estate cannot pay off all of the debts they distribute as best they can. If the court approves the distribution, the debts are ended. For their services, both the lawyer and the personal representative or executors are entitled to fees from the estate. Probate fees are usually set as "reasonable" but can be as much (or more) than 5% of the value of the estate subject to probate. This could be $15,000 on a probate estate worth only $300,000. (The home and a few assets.)

Tax: The probate court also provides for the collection of appropriate state inheritance, federal estate and income taxes. A handful of other taxes must also be paid to the state before the estate can be closed.

Family Allowance: Dependent family members can ask the probate court for a "family allowance." This is primarily cash that is quickly released from the estate (and is not available to creditors) to help with short-term living expenses.

Uniform Probate Code (UPC): Not all states have adopted the UPC. Its purpose is to streamline the probate process and to standardize and modernize the various state laws governing Wills, Trusts, and Intestacy. Because the UPC has not been adopted by every state, check the code as actually adopted in that jurisdiction and do not rely on the text of the UPC in its entirety. Some states have adopted more of the code than others making a discussion of the entire code academic.

Close Probate: Do not forget to Close Probate. Documents can usually be obtained online at the Probate Court website in the county where Probate was opened.

All Taxes must be paid. All outstanding debts must be satisfied.

All Disputes Must be Settled

All Beneficiaries must be taken care of

> This is done last after all other fees, debts and taxes are paid. Some assets may have been sold to cover these other debts. Try to keep the family and heirs informed about what will be sold and why it is necessary. They may want to purchase it from the estate. You will be accountable to the court and others for the sale price.

Documents: Confirm with the courthouse which documents are required to close the estate. You may find these online at the County website. Google (name of the county where the probate court is located) (the state) close probate.

Notice to heirs and beneficiaries: You are usually required to mail or otherwise deliver a notice to heirs and beneficiaries that a final hearing is coming up. There are time limits on when to do this and you must prove to the court that you actually did this. Check with the court as to how they want this done.

Taxes: You may be required to submit copies of all taxes filed on behalf of the deceased and the estate. If a letter from the IRS is needed the estate will not be closed without it.

You may be required to prove the Will's validity by submitting the self-proving affidavit that was signed by the witnesses in front of a notary when the Will was signed. If this was not taken care of you may have to acquire notarized statements from one or more witnesses to the Will as to its validity.

Were you required to post a Bond? If you were you will also be required to show proof that you actually did this.

Proof of notification to Creditors: you will most likely need to file proof that you properly published and mailed the notice.

> You need to get the courts permission to distribute or transfer all of the remaining assets to the heirs.
>
> Remember, you will get signed, dated receipts. Notarized if you feel it is necessary or the amount of value is considered by you to be significant. see *Time Line - Receipts*, page 53
>
> Once the IRS issues a closing letter, if one is necessary, the judge will allow closure of the estate. You may now go before the court with all necessary paperwork and receipts and ask the court to close the estate and release you from your duties.

This is not intended to be all inclusive and it is not intended to be a "How To" in place of good legal advice from a competent attorney. It is, however, intended to be a window into what an executor will have to deal with should you decide to become the executor or administrator. Use this as a guide and please seek competent legal advice as needed.

Security

Security: vehicle and home alarm systems, home safes, mailboxes or gates, and locked boxes, drawers, or cabinets. For each item, note passwords, combinations, or the locations of keys.

Notify relatives and heirs that valuables will be secured. It is easier to warn Uncle Wester than to have him arrested along with your Aunt in the get-away car. "We were just having fun. It wasn't serious." We all have at least one somewhere in the family.

Bank Accounts: Protect and secure all bank accounts.

Change all locks. Call a reputable locksmith and have all door locks changed. You have no idea of who may have a key. Change codes for the garage door openers. Walk around the buildings. Lock all windows and doors. Look for places where someone could hide and break in. Secure these areas. Do not stop with the obvious. Many people own homes, condominiums, time shares, business interests, etc. in other states. These all need to be secured.

> If the residence is of the estate is in a gated community, make the necessary arrangements with security to accommodate increased traffic if necessary. Consider a house sitter for a few days if the residence is to be vacant. Notify police if the residence is to remain vacant. Keep the electric, heat and water turned on and pay the bills. Keep the lawn mowed and the insurance premiums paid. You must present the asset to the beneficiary without loss. Pay these out of estate funds. You may want to cancel cable or phone service if it is no longer necessary.

Inventory: Inventory all assets as soon as possible to prevent theft by family members. If it is not specifically left to an individual by a Will or the court it is theft. If you remove anything for safe keeping take photos and have a witness. Photograph everything.

> If the item is only worth a small amount of money it is usually all right to give it away. How much do you know about everything? A small piece of porcelain no larger than your finger may be worth thousands of dollars. A stamp. A coin. A book. A piece of glass that looks like junk to you may be worth thousands. It is always best to not give any items away, even as a keepsake, until proper procedures have been followed or the court approves. The concern here would be if the item is in fact valuable or a favorite piece that is desired by more than one family member. If the item is a favorite piece probate the item no matter the value. The court will decide who gets it.

Storage Area: You may need to store televisions, stereos, works of art, or antique furniture in a storage facility, a garage or a part of the residence that can be secured. You can by a temporary lock at home improvement stores that can be used to secure a bedroom or closet without using screws or nails. They do no damage to the residence if used properly.

Gather jewelry, collections, silver and gold, and place in a safe or storage area. As you are sorting through things collect photos, paperwork, documents etc. and begin organizing them and securing them in a safe place. Try not to throw things out until you know their value or importance.

Secure all computers, hard drives, thumb drives, DVDs, CDs, etc. There may be a digital Executor that will take care of non-monetary digital assets or monetary digital assets under the supervision of the estate's executor or personal representative. For now secure everything. Secure anything some visitor can easily walk off with. There are people who visit homes of the deceased and pretend to be a "friend" just to steal what they can.

Credit cards, bank accounts, safe deposit boxes, jewelry, real property. Change all of the locks and change the code on the garage door opener.

Household goods and Furnishings: Valuables that sit in an empty home are vulnerable to theft. Consider selling unwanted valuables in an estate sale or auction. Lock it down, keep people out, keep people from taking "a few things to remember them by," usually the best and most expensive jewelry. Tell them the pieces are listed in the Will and have to go through the attorneys. As executor you are personally responsible and libel for all assets and there disposition. If Uncle Bert is walking out with the gun collection you may find it necessary to stop him. If you need extra help, call the police. If you must, report it as a theft. It is theft and it is a crime. The personal representative or executor can be sued for the value of the assets and may have to pay this out of their own funds.

Walk through the residence with another family member to witness all items that have monetary value.

Visitation and Wakes: When opening the deceased's home for visitation secure all assets. Friends and family have just suffered a loss and thieves take advantage of this. They look very normal, dress nicely and come to rob and steal from you. We recommend that the deceased's home or anyone's home is not open for public visitation or viewing. Use a Church or local facility. Be very careful.

Automatic Payments: Locate all automatic payments for goods and services and decide if you will continue to pay these. First stop all automatic payments and then if you decide to pay these, pay them from the estate checking account you will set up.

Mail: If there is no surviving spouse you will usually have all of the mail forwarded to your address as the executor or personal representative. You still need to locate all of the deceased's assets and debts. Watch for statements. All insurance companies are required to report the status of a policy at least once a year.

Digital Executor

Digital Executor or Digital Administrator: People are naming a Digital Executor more often but state laws have not kept up with the need. The executor still has all legal responsibility for the dispensation of the estate including the distribution of all digital assets to the beneficiaries by providing them with the necessary content and/ or access information. Some digital assets may still need to be posted online after death and files may need to be deleted and hard storage scrubbed clean.

The executor has the legal responsibility for disposition of the estate. The digital executor helps with Digital Assets: online storage "in the cloud", online shopping sites, websites, blogs, videos, CD's, DVD's (some contain important documents and may be password protected or encrypted). Family photos all stored online, on DVDs or thumb drives. There are passwords, encryption, challenge codes, social networking websites. All digital Assets must be protected and distributed. The Digital Executor can be very helpful.

The executor of the estate may not know how to find or even access Digital Assets worth hundreds of thousands of dollars. They may not even be aware off their worth. Facebook's $1 billion acquisition of the mobile start-up Instagram changed a lot of things. Today something as simple (to the untrained) as an "app" could be worth a billion dollars only if it is turned into a more liquid asset quickly. If you have Digital Assets it is important to protect them with a Digital Administrator that could possibly act as executor of the estate. In any case if you have any digital assets (and we all do) you may need to allow your executor to access this information. Make them aware of your digital executor. If you name your digital executor as a beneficiary the executor is obligated by law to inform them of your death and send them a copy of your Will.

There are new business's that specialize in administering digital estates for a fee. There are few regulations so buyer beware holds true. Be careful.

Digital Assets

All digital Assets must be protected and distributed. The Digital Executor can be very helpful. Most Americans have a digital presence that needs to be located, collected, appraised, and protected. Locate all Passwords & Usernames, encryption, Keys, PINs, Combinations and challenge questions. If you are preplanning do not leave this information in your Will because it is going to be made public after your death.

There are software programs that may be able to unlock and reset current passwords. Google: password recovery

Locate: All computers, laptops, tablets, PC, Macs, eBook readers, storage, hard drives, cell phones, iPhones, iPods, iPads, answering machines, Wii, PlayStations, PSP, PS3, Xbox, thumb drives and digital cameras. Copiers are very important as they contain very sensitive information in memory.

Online Websites: Websites that may have value or contain user information that should be cleaned include but are not limited to: brokerage sites, gambling sites, online shopping sites, email accounts, blogs, photo storage sites, online subscriptions with automatic renewal, online banking, online bill paying, online credit card access, mortgage providers, college savings accounts, retirement plans, automatic bill paying for (anything) utilities and cell phones, and online tax software that may have copies of the deceased's returns. see *Identity Theft*, page 190, 246, 375

Cell Phones

Before you give away the deceased's cell phone check it for information. This is where a Digital Executor is helpful. There are companies listed online that can search the phone for you and return along with the phone a written report.

Check the Cellphone, PDA or mobile device for messages, voice mail and the phone list of contacts. Keep a copy of phone numbers, names, and contact information. It may come in handy even a year or two later. Cellphones, smartphones, PDAs and many mobile devices contain personal and sometimes sensitive information, including addresses and phone numbers, passwords, bank account numbers, email, voicemail, phone logs, even medical and prescription information. Some people pay all of their bills using their phone. They shop online, bank online, pay bills and make reservations. To date every phone operating system has been hacked. Hackers go where the money is and stay one step ahead of everyone else. Most people do not use a password on their cellphone and then they store all of their passwords on that same cellphone. All you have to do is push the login button.

Many mobile devices use a SIM Card (Subscriber Identity Module) to store contact information and data. Removing the card will not remove the information. You need to hard reset (or master reset) the device to purge this data. Google: master reset (model of phone)

Disposing of a Cellphone

Cell phones and **Personal Digital Assistants** (PDA's) may contain sensitive information, including bank account numbers, medical and prescription information, online access to shopping with credit card information, user names and passwords. Access to email accounts, both personal and business accounts. Voice mail, phone logs, contact lists containing names, address, and personal information may be available. Every type of personal electronic device operating system has been hacked. Hackers are motivated to stay ahead of everyone because they go where the money is.

Digital Assets that may be worth more than all of the liquid assets of the estate combined may be linked to these small impersonal devices. There they are. Just waiting for someone with a modicum of tech knowledge to come along and release them for any purpose. This could be distribution of the estate or theft of the assets.

All personal electronic devices should be treated as if they contain extremely sensitive information.

Sensitive Information: The first thing you need to do is Identify what information is on the device. You may need help with this. Cell Phones may use encrypting passwords and the average person may be locked out of the device. If there is a Digital Executor enlist their assistance. When the information is located it must be preserved because this may be the only existing link to a valuable asset. Locate all sensitive information. Inventory all sensitive information. Protect and secure all sensitive information. At some time in the future this information may no longer be necessary and it may be advisable to eliminate it from the device.

Even after the cellphone is no longer in service sensitive information may still be removed from it with very inexpensive software.

Check messages, voice mail and the phone list of contacts. Make and keep a copy of phone numbers, names, and contact information. It may come in handy even a year or two later. What if you find out later on that Aunt Mernnie really did have a lot of assets but left everything to the neighborhood bulldog? You may want someone who knew her to help verify she was crackers. It is always better to save it and not need it than to need it and not even have a clue where to look.

Identify Theft can be hindered by removing personal sensitive information with Permanent Data Deletion. This information is given as a basic example of what may be necessary not as a how-to. Technology changes so quickly today that more steps in the process may have already been added to the following information. In general: 1) remove the SIM card (subscriber identity module) from the phone. 2) Even if you use the Menu on the cellphone to delete information, this will only delete the references to where the information is and not the information itself. Permanent data deletion also may require you to clear data from the phone's contacts and other stored information. 3) A hard reset (or master reset) is needed to purge the device of this sensitive data. Your owner's manual, your wireless provider's website, or the manufacturer will likely provide information on how to permanently delete information. see *Identity Theft*, page 190, 246, 375

Since this device was not yours you really do not know what kinds of information it contained it is still your responsibility to dispose of it properly. It most cases it is just a cellphone or personal device and it would most likely seem reasonable to treat it as such. In most cases it still should not be given away until you can "clear" the device. When the device is "clear" and safe to give away must be determined by the executor or personal representative. Err on the side of caution.

Computers: Before you dispose of any computer you should wipe the hard drive clean of all data. When you use the "delete" function or "empty recycle bin" you do not remove data. You are only removing the sign post pointing to it. The data is still there and can be recovered. A digital executor or a knowledgeable trustworthy individual may be able to help with this. If you cannot do this you may want to remove the hard drives and dispose of them separately.

Copiers: The internal hard drives on home and office copy machines retain sensitive information. This information is almost never scrubbed clean and could be a jackpot for an identity thief. Before you dispose of any home or office copier, remove and destroy the hard drive, or internal memory. If the machine is leased, software can be purchased to scrub (wipe clean, permanently remove) the data. The executor should never give away the old copier or computers, hard drives, storage devices of any kind without first permanently removing all data so that it is considered unrecoverable. Be careful not to remove data that you need or want. A digital executor is often necessary to help in doing this.

Shredder: The executor may want to purchase a good cross-cut shredder for the purpose of disposing of bills and receipts. Shred documents containing personal information, such as credit card statements, bills and even some junk mail.

Social Security

Social Security

Social Security should be notified as soon as possible when a person dies. You will need the deceased's social security number to report the death. If the deceased person worked long enough under Social Security to qualify for benefits some of the deceased's family members may be able to receive Social Security benefits. Any family member may get in touch with the local social security office to see if they qualify for benefits. The executor usually does not handle this task but should at least inform people of the possibility of benefits available to them. The executor should notify social security of the death.

> **Identity Theft:** When you contact social security and report the death the deceased person's name goes on the Social Security Master Death Index. This helps to prevent people from collecting the deceased's social security benefits. It also helps to prevent Identity theft by flagging credit reports if someone tries to open a new credit account in the deceased's name.
>
> **Social Security Benefits:** If the deceased was receiving Social Security benefits, the benefit received for the month of death or any later months must be returned. For example, if the person dies in July, the benefit paid in August must be returned. If benefits were paid by direct deposit, the executor should contact the bank or other financial institution. Request that any funds received for the month of death or later be returned to Social Security. If the benefits were paid by check, do not cash any checks received for the month in which the person dies or later. Return the checks to Social Security as soon as possible. (This information is from the social security website in late 2012 and is believed to be accurate at this time. Check to see if it has changed). If the check was already cashed, call the local social security office and speak with

someone about how to reimburse them. Include a brief note explaining the situation. Refer to the social security contact information below.

Children and Social Security: The loss of the family wage earner can be devastating, both emotionally and financially. Social Security helps by providing income for the families of workers who die. In fact, 98 of every 100 children could get benefits if a working parent dies. And Social Security pays more benefits to children than any other federal program.

Death Benefits: Eligible family members may be able to receive death benefits for the month in which the beneficiary died.

One-Time Death Payment: A one-time payment of $255 can be paid to the surviving spouse if he or she was living with the deceased; or, if living apart, was receiving certain Social Security benefits on the deceased's record. If there is no surviving spouse, the payment is made to a child who is eligible for benefits on the deceased's record in the month of death.

Social Security Survivors Benefits for Family Members: Family members may also be entitled to monthly survivors benefits. You don't have to be of retirement age to receive benefits: dependent children, surviving spouses, and even some ex-spouses may be eligible for survivors benefits. You should apply for survivors benefits promptly because, in some cases, benefits will be paid from the time you apply and not from the time the worker died.

Certain family members may be eligible to receive monthly benefits, including:

1) A widow or widower age 60 or older (age 50 or older if disabled.)

2) A widow or widower at any age who is caring for the deceased's child under age 16 or disabled.

3) An unmarried child of the deceased who is: Younger than age 18 (or up to age 19 if he or she is a full-time student in an elementary or secondary school); or Age 18 or older with a disability that began before age 22.

4) A stepchild, grandchild, step grandchild or adopted child under certain circumstances.

5) Parents, age 62 or older, who were dependent on the deceased for at least half of their support.

6) A surviving divorced spouse, under certain circumstances.

If you are not currently getting Social Security benefits

You should apply for survivors benefits promptly because, in some cases, benefits will be paid from the time you apply and not from the time the worker died.

You can apply by telephone or at any Social Security office. They will need certain information, but do not delay applying if you do not have everything. They will help you get what you need. They need either original documents or copies certified by the agency that issued them.

The information Social Security will need includes:

1) Proof of death—either from a funeral home or death certificate.

2) Your Social Security number, as well as the deceased worker's social security number.

3) Your birth certificate.

4) Your marriage certificate, if you are a widow or widower.

5) Your divorce papers, if you are applying as a divorced widow or widower.

6) Dependent children's Social Security numbers, if available, and birth certificates.

7) Deceased worker's W-2 forms or federal self-employment tax return for the most recent year.

8) The name of your bank and your account number so your benefits can be deposited directly into your account.

If you are already getting Social Security benefits

If you are getting benefits as a wife or husband based on your spouse's work, when you report the death to social security they will change the payments to survivors benefits. If they need more information, they will contact you.

If you are getting benefits based on your own work, call or visit your local social security office and they will check to see if you can get more money as a widow or widower. If so, you will receive a combination of benefits that equals the higher amount. You will need to complete an application to switch to survivors benefits, and social security will need to see your spouse's death certificate.

If you get a pension from work where you paid Social Security taxes, that pension will not affect your Social Security benefits. However, if you get a pension from work that was not covered by Social Security— for example, the federal civil service, some state or local government employment or work in a foreign country—your Social Security benefit may be reduced.

If you work while getting Social Security survivors benefits and are younger than full retirement age, your benefits may be reduced if your earnings exceed certain limits. (The full retirement age was 65 for people born before 1938 but will gradually increase to 67 for people born in 1960 or later.) To find out what the earnings limits are this year and how earnings above those limits reduce your Social Security benefits, ask for How Work Affects Your Benefits (Publication No. 05-10069).

The Official Website of the U.S. Social Security Administration
www.socialsecurity.gov

Publications for Survivors   http://www.ssa.gov/pubs/

Social Security Teleservices

DOING BUSINESS BY TELEPHONE

You may call Social Security toll-free, 365 days a year, 24 hours a day. The number to use is 1-800-772-1213. To speak with a representative, call between the hours of 7:00am and 7:00pm on regular business days. At other times and on weekends and holidays, you may leave a message and they will call you back, in most cases, the next business day.

You may use the toll-free number to make an appointment either in a Social Security office or telephone to apply for benefits, transact other Social Security business, or just ask questions.

Supplemental Security Income (SSI)

Do not forget to check SSI for eligibility. The Supplemental Security Income (SSI) program pays benefits to disabled adults and children who have limited income and resources. SSI benefits also are payable to people 65 and older without disabilities who meet the financial limits.

http://www.ssa.gov/pgm/ssi.htm

The Supplemental Security Income (SSI) program is designed to provide a minimum monthly income to people age 65 and over, or blind and disabled people, with limited income and resources. Monthly benefits are based on need. You may be eligible even If you have never worked or paid into the social security system. Before applying for SSI, you must apply for any other benefits you are eligible for. This includes Social Security, pensions, and workman's compensation.

SSI limitations change on an annual basis. You need to contact your Social Security representative to determine if you qualify under the income and asset limits. If the Social Security Administration declares you are not eligible for SSI or reduces your SSI check, you can appeal their decision. You need to appeal within 10 days to keep your benefits at the existing rate.

Transportation

Transportation for Disposition of Remains

Funeral Transportation: Transportation expenses can include permits, transportation from out of state, and transportation from the place of death to the funeral service or crematory, and then to the church, cemetery or burial place. There can be additional charges for a hearse, chauffeured limousine, flower vehicle, service vehicle for the pallbearers, from the funeral service or crematory, and then to the church, cemetery or burial place.

Transportation from a Distance: It is not uncommon to die in one city and to be buried in another. Funeral homes and other funeral service providers can arrange transportation between cities for the deceased, even if overseas, through airlines and specialty transport companies. An individual may not make arrangements directly with an airline for the transportation of human remains due to the legal requirements for shipping, such as embalming or refrigeration.

> In most cases you may transport the body yourself. However, if you will be transporting the body across state lines, you must obtain a transit permit signed by the local medical examiner within five days of death. If you are going to transport the body overseas there will be more paperwork depending on the receiving country. Google: Mortuary Shipping

Burial-Transit Permit or Burial Permit: Transportation and disposition permission. A burial transit permit or burial permit is needed in some states for the transportation and disposition of the deceased. This document grants the holder permission to transport a body. To transport a body out-of-state you must also obtain a burial-transit permit. If the medical examiner is involved, the permit must be signed by him and by the local registrar to be valid. It is also needed at a cemetery or crematorium to bury or cremate a body.

Transportation Authorization: While most states allow non-licensed individuals to transport a body, it is necessary to have formal authorization. Be aware that transportation permits may only be valid for the state where issued. Transporting a body across state lines may require multiple permits.

In-State Transport: If a person died of natural causes, and the body is not under the jurisdiction of the medical examiner, it usually may be moved in-state without a permit. If the medical examiner must examine a body to determine cause of death, a permit is required to move it.

> In the case of death by a highly communicable disease, such as smallpox, plague, HIV, hepatitis B, rabies, or Creutzfeldt-Jakob disease, the attending physician must notify those transporting the body to use precautions to prevent the spread of disease.

Transportation, mortuary shipping: Many people move away from their state, or country, of origin, What happens in the event of death if the deceased needs to be returned back home following their death? The U.S. has a large immigrant population and many choose repatriation to their country of origin upon death.

Cost within the US: It is not difficult to transport the deceased from one place to another within the U.S. and the cost without airfare should be less than $1,500. This will usually include minimal preparation embalming, container, and transport to and from the airport.

Veterans Burial: Transportation to a National Cemetery may still be required.

Cost to transport Overseas: The cost to ship the deceased overseas from the U.S. will average $4,500 to $11,000. This includes the airfare. Costs will vary due to distance and if refrigeration will be necessary during transportation.

Cremains: The cremated ashes may be shipped by U.S. postal service within the United States if you ship by express mail, using the registered mail option with return receipt requested and indicate the contents on the outside of the package according to USPS Bulletin 52, governing the shipment of cremated remains. cremationassociation.org

UPS, FedEx and DHL do not handle the transport of cremated remains. Germany requires that a licensed cemetery receive cremated remains sent to Germany and that a licensed funeral director be involved in sending them to Germany. To bring cremains to the U.S. you will need to follow TSA guidelines.

Urns: Purchase an inexpensive traveling urn or box. Transfer the remains out of the urn into the temporary urn or box that the TSA can run through an X-ray machine.

TSA, Transportation Security Administration:

We understand how painful losing a loved one is, and we respect anyone traveling with crematory remains. Passengers are allowed to carry a crematory container as part of their carry-on luggage, but the container must pass through the X-ray machine. If the container is made of a material that generates an opaque image and prevents the Transportation Security Officer from clearly being able to see what is inside, then the container cannot be allowed through the security checkpoint.

Out of respect to the deceased and their family and friends, under no circumstances will an officer open the container even if the passenger requests this be done. Documentation from the funeral home is not sufficient to carry a crematory container through security and onto a plane without screening.

You may transport the urn as checked baggage provided that it is successfully screened. We will screen the urn for explosive materials/devices using a variety of techniques; if cleared, it will be permitted as checked baggage only.

Some airlines do not allow cremated remains as checked baggage so please check with your air carrier before attempting to transport a crematory container in checked baggage.

Crematory containers are made from many different types of materials, all with varying thickness. At present, we cannot state for certain whether your particular crematory container can successfully pass through an X-ray machine. However, we suggest that you purchase a temporary or permanent crematory container made of a lighter weight material such as wood or plastic that can be successfully X-rayed. We will continue to work with funeral home associations to provide additional guidance in the future.

U.S. Customs and Border Protection.

Requirements for importing bodies in coffins / ashes in urns. CPB info

Human remains intended for interment or subsequent cremation after entry into the United States must be accompanied by a death certificate stating the cause of death. If the death certificate is in a language other than English, then it should be accompanied by an English language translation.

Clean, dry bones or bone fragments; human hair; teeth; fingernails or toenails; or human remains that have been cremated may be admitted into the United States without restriction, regardless of the cause of death.

If the cause of death is known or suspected to be a quarantinable communicable disease (cholera, diphtheria, infectious tuberculosis, plague, smallpox, yellow fever, viral hemorrhagic fevers, severe acute respiratory syndrome, and influenza caused by novel or reemergent influenza viruses that are causing or have the potential to cause a pandemic), the Centers for Disease Control (CDC) requires that the remains are cremated; or the remains are properly embalmed and placed in a hermetically sealed casket; or the remains are accompanied by a permit issued by the CDC Director (42 Code of Federal Regulations Part 71.55). A hermetically sealed casket is one that is airtight and secured against the escape of microorganisms.

For all causes of death other than quarantineable communicable diseases, CBP may immediately admit the remains if the remains are in a leak-proof container. A leak-proof container is one that is puncture-resistant and sealed in a manner so as to contain all contents and prevent leakage of fluids during handling, storage, transport, or shipping.

If the remains are embalmed and the casket is hermetically sealed, the remains may be released under any condition.

CBP Officers will examine the death certificate to determine the cause of death and ensure that the remains are shipped in accordance with CDC requirements. If CDC requirements are not met, CBP will hold the casket and contact the appropriate quarantine station for instructions.

If a casket bearing human remains is entered at a facility with CDC Quarantine Station on site, quarantine station personnel may provide a stamped release on the Airway Bill. CBP may then admit the casket and human remains without restriction.

Additional information on the public health requirements for importation of human remains is available at the CDC Web site.

http://www.cdc.gov/quarantine/human-remains.html

U.S. Military Personal

Veterans

U.S. Veterans of the Armed Forces who received an honorable discharge may be entitled to a burial in the local National Cemetery at no cost. The Veterans Administration will reimburse a portion of the burial or cremation expenses if the veteran's death is service connected. The VA may also assist with burial, cremation, and plot expenses for eligible veterans.

Commercial Veterans Advertisements

Be very careful of commercial cemeteries that advertise so-called "veterans' specials." What are you actually paying for? In some cases the grave plot is offered free for the veteran, but an adjoining plot for the spouse is priced at a higher than normal price. If the opening and closing charges, charges for the vault or liner, record keeping fees, cost of a grave marker, fees for perpetual care and all additional fees are considered you end up paying much, much more than a competitor in the same area. They are a business. They are selling you something to make money. It is like buying a used car, some dealers are better than others.

In Service Veterans Benefits: The circumstances of a military death may never be known, but our hearts grieve at this loss. All military service branches have complete procedures to take care of the operational details related to a member's death. http://www.va.gov/

An officer or chaplain from the nearest military base will visit the surviving family. A special officer will be assigned to help with the details of the funeral and, if appropriate, transporting the loved one's body home.

Military personnel and their dependents may be buried at no cost in a government cemetery, provided there is space. The Department of Veterans Affairs' (VA) National Cemetery Administration maintains 131 national cemeteries in 39 states (and Puerto Rico) as well as 33 soldier's lots and monument sites. Burial benefits available for spouses and dependents buried in a national cemetery include burial with the Veteran, perpetual care, and the spouse or dependents name and date of birth and death will be inscribed on the Veteran's headstone, at no cost to the family. Eligible spouses and dependents may be buried, even if they predecease the Veteran.

A military service is usually at graveside, but there may be a ceremony or service at a chapel. At the grave, there will be a seven-person firing party for the salute or "volley." A bugler will play taps. There will be military pallbearers with an officer or someone of a higher rank than of the deceased.

A U.S. flag, which will later be given to a family member, will be draped over the casket. If there are flowers on the casket, a military representative will hold the folded flag. For memorial services with the cremated remains present, a military representative will hold the urn and another will hold the flag. The urn is then placed in a crypt or buried. When the flag is ceremonially given to the nearest kin, this signals the end of the ceremony.

A burial flag may be obtained through the funeral home or the local post office.

Benefits and payments are made to the designated next of kin.

The military does not issue death certificates. Instead, you will be given copies of the Report of Casualty. This report is provided whether the death occurred during combat or not. The report is used in the same way as a death certificate, for the transfer of property and settlement of life insurance benefits.

Information can be found online at: http://www.cem.va.gov/

For Burials and Emergency Requests: http://www.archives.gov/veterans/military-service-records/

Our online eVetRecs system creates a customized order form to request information from your, or your relative's, military personnel records. You may use this system if you are:

- A **military veteran**, or

- Next of kin of a **deceased**, former member of the military. The **next of kin** can be any of the following:

    Surviving spouse that has not remarried

    - Father
    - Daughter

    - Mother
    - Sister

    - Son

    - Brother

Veterans Cemeteries - States, Territories, and Tribal Governments

Many states have established state veterans cemeteries. Eligibility is similar to Department of Veterans Affairs (VA) national cemeteries, but may include residency requirements. Even though they may have been established or improved with Government funds through VA's State Cemetery Grants Program, state veterans cemeteries are run solely by the states.

http://www.cem.va.gov/cem/grants/veterans_cemeteries.asp

Discharge papers are very important in establishing eligibility. DD-214

A copy of military discharge papers can be acquired at:

National Archives: http://www.archives.gov/veterans/military-service-records/

National Personnel Records Center
1 Archives Drive, St. Louis, MO 63138

Telephone: 314-801-0800 - Fax: 314-801-9195 - E-mail: MPR.center@nara.gov

For more information online: http://www.archives.gov/st-louis/

Veterans Funeral Benefits: VA operates 131 national cemeteries, of which 72 are open for new casketed interments and 18 are open to accept only cremated remains. Burial options are limited to those available at a specific cemetery but may include in-ground casket, or interment of cremated remains in a columbarium, in ground or in a scatter garden. Contact the national cemetery directly, or visit our Web site at: www.cem.va.gov to determine if a particular cemetery is open for new burials, and which other options are available.

http://www.cem.va.gov/
http://www.va.gov/opa/publications/benefits_book/benefits_chap07.asp

Veterans Benefits Eligibility: A veteran must be discharged or separated from active duty under conditions other than dishonorable, and have completed the required period of service. U.S. Armed Forces members who die on active duty are also eligible, as are spouses and dependent children of eligible living and deceased veterans, and of current and deceased armed forces members.

Surviving Spouses of Veterans who died on or after Jan. 1, 2000, do not lose eligibility for burial in a national cemetery if they remarry. Burial of dependent children is limited to unmarried children under 21 years of age, or under 23 years of age if a full-time student at an approved educational institution. Unmarried adult children who become physically or mentally disabled and incapable of self-support before age 21, or age 23 if a full-time student, also are eligible for burial.

> Surviving spouses may not be aware of benefits that could be available to them years after their veteran spouses were engaged in military service.

Certain Eligible Parents. A new federal law passed in 2010 (Public Law 111-275) extends burial benefits to certain parents of servicemembers who die as a result of hostile activity or from training-related injuries who are buried in a national cemetery in a gravesite with available space. The biological or adopted parents of a servicemember who died in combat or while performing training in preparation for a combat mission, who leaves no surviving spouse or dependent child, may be buried with the deceased servicemember if the Secretary of Veterans Affairs determines that there is available space. The law applies to servicemembers who died on or after Oct. 7, 2001 and to parents who died on or after Oct. 13, 2010.

> http://www.va.gov/opa/publications/benefits_book/benefits_chap07.asp

Military Funeral Honors: "Honoring Those Who Served"

> The Department of Defense (DOD) is responsible for providing military funeral honors. "Honoring Those Who Served" is the title of the DOD program for providing dignified military funeral honors to Veterans who have defended our nation.

Upon the family's request, Public Law 106-65 requires that every eligible Veteran receive a military funeral honors ceremony, to include folding and presenting the United States burial flag and the playing of Taps. The law defines a military funeral honors detail as consisting of two or more uniformed military persons, with at least one being a member of the Veteran's parent service of the armed forces. The DOD program calls for funeral home directors to request military funeral honors on behalf of the Veterans' family. However, the Department of Veterans Affairs (VA) National Cemetery Administration cemetery staff can also assist with arranging military funeral honors at VA national cemeteries. Veterans organizations may assist in providing military funeral honors. When military funeral honors at a national cemetery are desired, they are arranged prior to the committal service by the funeral home.

The Department of Defense began the implementation plan for providing military funeral honors for eligible Veterans as enacted in Section 578 of Public Law 106-65 of the National Defense Authorization Act for FY 2000 on Jan. 1, 2000.

Questions or comments concerning the DOD military funeral honors program may be sent to the address listed below. The military funeral honors Web site is located at www.militaryfuneralhonors.osd.mil.

Office of the Assistant Secretary of Defense For Public Affairs
Community Relations and Public Liaison
1400 Defense Pentagon, Room 2D982
Washington, DC 20301-1400

To arrange military funeral honors, contact your local funeral home.

For more information: http://www.cem.va.gov/mhg.asp

Vital Statistics

Vital Statistics of the Deceased

Locate the original Trust and/or original Will of the decedent. This may take some time and is not usually needed right away. Keep this data safe and secure as it can be easily stolen and used for identity theft and fraud.

You will not necessarily need all of the following information. Some of it will not pertain to your current situation. Use it as a guide. Feel free to add to it. It is always better to collect as much information now when friends and family are the most agreeable. Later on you may need this information and they may have decided not to give it to you. Who gets the teapot? Little or no monetary value but it is bequeathed to the next of kin in order of linage from the county cork, in Ireland as the family immigrated to the U.S. Get any and all information you can while you still can. It is better to have too much than too little. Write everything down in a notebook. Secure the notebook and keep it safe.

Full Legal Name of the Deceased: address, phone number.

    Date of Birth:

    Place of Birth: City, state, also list the county if known.

    Driver License and number:

    Social Security Number:

    Marital Status: If divorced list all.

    Name of Spouse: If divorced list all. Include state and county of divorce.

Spouse's Maiden Name:

Children: List all children including contact information. Children of prior marriages may have a claim on the estate, especially if there is no valid Will.

Primary Emergency Contact: name, address, phone number, and email.

Education, Highest: Include the name, city and state of the school.

Citizenship: Dual citizenship?

Father's Name: address, phone number if living.

Date of Birth:

Place of Birth:

Marital Status: If divorced list all.

Name of Spouse: If divorced list all. Include state and county of divorce.

Spouse's Maiden Name: If divorced, list all.

Mother's Name and Maiden Name: address, phone number if living.

Date of Birth:

Place of Birth: City, state, also list the county if known.

Marital Status:

Name of Spouse: If divorced list all. Include state and county of divorce.

Primary Emergency Contact: name, address, phone number, and email.

Education, Highest:

Citizenship: Dual citizenship?

Pets: list all pertinent information. Pedigrees – family tree.

Email Addresses (URL) of the Deceased: include user names & passwords. Include challenge questions. Is payment involved? Monthly? Yearly? From bank account or credit card?

Online Accounts: example – PayPal, Facebook, Amazon.com, all shopping accounts, any accounts "in the cloud", cloud based service or storage. Include all user names & passwords, secure login challenge question answers.

> Is payment involved? Monthly? Yearly? From bank account or credit card? If payment is involved list the banking or credit card information: name, address, account number and type of account. If this involves a bank list the contact information for the local branch.

Names and Contact Information: of all children, step-children, grandchildren, etc. This can be time consuming but may prove invaluable later on. Much of this information may be contained in address book. Also last year's Christmas cards, birthday cards or more recent cards sent to the deceased's residence may contain contact information. This may be too much to organize right now. Just separate these cards so you can remove them and secure them for later use.

Social Security Number: social security cards and statements. This will be needed to file for social security death benefits.

Veteran: serial number or service number. Date and place of service, date of discharge. Discharge papers: DD-214.

Time at Current Residence:

Other Residences: List all that you can.

Occupation: Job title, nature of work and employment history – this information may be needed to locate any retirement accounts or pensions.

Unions: there may be life insurance to collect on.

Organizations: there may be life insurance to collect on.

Location of Work Place: address, phone number, fax and email.

Family Origin: descended from a common ancestor, or a husband, wife, and their children. Related by blood or marriage.

Medications and Drugs: all prescription medications should be located. Bedside tables and all medicine cabinets. These can be stored in a safe place for a while until you are certain cause of death was from natural causes. If there is any doubt keep all of these together in some type of container. Chain of evidence may be difficult for a later date but the information may prove invaluable.

> Current medication and prescribed medications. Check the dates on the labels. Also check for current Doctor's name. Gather up all medical records and bills. Secure these to help prevent identity theft.

Doctor's: Name, address, phone, FAX, and email. There may be more than one. Which health care provider is considered the primary provider? List all health care providers. Include suppliers of medical equipment.

Accountant: Name, address, phone, FAX, and email. There may be more than one.

Attorney: Name, address, phone, FAX, and email. There may be more than one.

Medical Equipment Suppliers: Oxygen tanks can run dry during the night. Equipment can malfunction.

> A **Red Flag** should be when **Medical Equipment Suppliers** are in a very big hurry to remove the equipment. Usually the next day after a missed appointment. Just be aware of what may happen. No one is blaming any company or person. This is a rare instance but it can and does happen. You most likely can prevent removal of medical equipment while it is in your possession. Simply do not allow the provider access and then call a friend or family member you trust to discuss your thoughts. The more the Medical Equipment Supplier tries to force you to give up the equipment the more I would be suspicious.

> **Attorney:** If the deceased had an Attorney. Record the name, address, phone, FAX, and email. List contact information for all attorneys. Estate attorneys, real estate attorneys, etc.

Family History of Major Illness or Disease: This may be important to a family member later on. It could be very important to a grandchild. Take the time and write it down.

Church, Temple or other place of Worship: Name, address, phone, FAX, and email.

> **Clergy:** name address, phone, FAX, and email.

> If the deceased had a relationship with any church, temple or other place of worship look up the number and contact person. The counsel and advice provided by experienced ministers or clergy can be a significant help. Many families may need advice on religious traditions that their parents observed, and which they would like to honor.

Current and Urgent Bills:

> Bills still need to be paid. This may or may not include out of state or rental property. Collect all mail and all bills. These are just easier to collect while you are collecting vital statistics.

Funeral Expenses:

> Are there any bank accounts set aside for this purpose? Are there any pre-paid funeral plans? Most of these are not refundable if not used at the time of death. Was a burial plot, cremation niche, or mausoleum purchased? These are just easier to collect while you are collecting vital statistics.

Documents: Gather up documents as you locate them. Birth Certificate, Social Security Card, Social Security Number and Account Information, Driver's License and number, Passport, Veteran's Affairs, etc. Anything and everything. Protect these documents to help prevent identity theft. It may be a good idea to make a quick note in your notebook of where the document was found. "Behind the blue planter in the dining room." may be valuable information later on if you are still looking for a key.

Photo albums, Photos on DVD's, old cameras or maybe even old floppy disks. These are just easier to collect now while you are going through all of the personal papers. It is difficult enough to do this once so try to include everything now. Place all photo albums and photographs in a safe place free from theft, fire and flood. You may disperses these when property is dispersed to the beneficiaries later on. There is no legal problem with giving photos to family members unless they happen to be something that has monetary value. An example would be a photo of the deceased with a famous artist who then drew a sketch on the back and signed it. If in doubt; probate it.

Document Numbers and Account Numbers: These all need to be gathered up as you find them. The general rule is to locate them, collect them in one place and protect them from theft, fire and flood. As the executor or personal representative you are responsible.

Brokerage accounts, bank accounts, bank accounts locally or anywhere in the world, checking accounts locally or anywhere in the world, credit card accounts, debit card accounts, money market accounts, trust accounts

Will - Last Will and Testament

Valid Will - Last Will and Testament

Will: Everyone should have a Will. A Will is a written document that states what you want to have happen to your property after your death. If there is a valid Will then the Will determines how the estate is transferred during probate and to whom. If there is no valid Will or the Will only covers some assets, the laws where the deceased had their last legal residence or the laws where the deceased had real estate specify who gets what parts of the estate.

Having a Will undoubtedly simplifies the distribution of property and helps speed the probate process. Your Will should ensure that your assets go to the person that you want to receive them. There are probate properties and non-probate properties. Probate handles properties distributed through probate. Having a Will may not avoid probate, but it is better than having nothing at all.

A Will declares how individually owned assets are distributed. Assets that are owned jointly or assets that have a beneficiary designation pass to the joint tenant or beneficiary on your death. A Will controls an individually owned bank account, individually owned personal property, or individually owned investments, where there is no other joint owner and no designated beneficiary. If you want to avoid all probate you should consider a Trust. There are many, many types of Trust accounts and some are used to accomplish a specific purpose. A Revocable Living Trust and Totten Trust are both commonly used. A Non-revocable Living Trust cannot be changed at a later date in most cases.

Guardianship: In addition to distribution of property, wills also allow you to provide for the guardianship of a minor child, create trusts, and save state and federal estate taxes. Creating a Will is important and it stays in effect until it is revoked by you or you draft a new Will. Your will allows you to name a personal representative or executor to make certain your wishes are carried out after you pass on. Choose wisely.

Intestate: Intestate refers to a person who has died without having written a valid Will. The state where the deceased had their permanent residence will apply its probate laws to determine how the property will be dispersed if there is no Will or it cannot be located and you essentially have no say in the distribution of your property.

Intestate Succession: The legal distribution of assets when there was no Will. The laws are similar in each state but are not all the same. Every state is different.

The executor is named in the Will. If there is no Will there is no named executor. Intestate law that covers the state and county having control of the deceased's assets, provide a priority list of individuals that are eligible to become the executor. If probate is necessary the court will appoint an Administrator based on this list. The surviving spouse or registered domestic partner is usually first; the children are next, followed by family members. If you are chosen you may or may not have to accept. see *Executor: No Thank-you*, page 144

Situations that involve legal separation or pending divorce, same-sex-marriage, or common-law marriage most likely will need the help of a competent estate attorney. This may also be true if the situation involves, step children, foster children, adopted children, children born outside of marriage and children born after the parent's death.

Executor: Personal Representative, Administrator, Exectrix, Court Appointed Administrator.

Executor: An Executor is someone who the deceased named in their Will to administer their estate: They oversee the disposition of property and possessions. If a person dies intestate, that is, without a Will, then the Personal Representative or Administrator will be appointed by the court. An Exectrix is a female executor.

> No matter what they are called, they all oversee the disposition of property and possessions of a deceased person. An executor is entrusted with the large responsibility of making sure a person's last wishes are granted with regards to the disposition of their property and possessions. They identify the estate's assets, pay off its debts and then distribute whatever is left to the rightful heirs and beneficiaries. Once the court opens a probate file and validates the Will, it gives you the authority (via the letter testamentary) to carry out the duties required to settle the estate and act on behalf of the deceased, see *Executor*, page 133

Holographic Will: A Will that has been handwritten, dated and signed by the testator. A holographic Will is valid in all states under certain conditions. State law must be checked for the state having jurisdiction.

Revoked Will: If a Will is missing or no longer valid because the decedent intentionally revoked it either an earlier Will or the laws of intestate succession are used to decide the proper distribution of the estate.

Lost or Destroyed: If the original Will has been lost or destroyed the court may (or may not) accept a photo copy of the original Will. Sometimes the decedent gives potential executors a copy of the original Will. Copies may also be in a safe deposit box. It is so simple to just tell people where you keep your Will. It also requires a great deal of trust if the person is concerned about anyone changing their Will.

> There are usually indications that there is a Will even if it cannot readily be located. It could be in a home safe kept under frozen food at the bottom of a freezer in a garage. Or just wrapped in foil, placed in a zip lock bag and kept in the bottom of a refrigerator freezer to hide it and protect it from fire. The main thing is to search but you do not have to go to extremes. It is estimated that over half of all Americans die without having taken the time to prepare a Will. You only have a fifty-fifty chance that there even is a Will.

Funeral Arrangements: Preferences or plans for funeral arraignments are usually not listed in the Will because this information needs to be readily available. Just because a Will cannot be located does not mean that funeral arraignments have not been preplanned or prepaid. It has long been recognized in common law that a person has the right to a decent burial. This is changing. States and counties no longer have the funds to provide for this beyond certain unavoidable circumstances.

Lawful Possession: It is commonly held that no one can own human remains except for their disposition. In most cases the executor has the right of possession of the deceased for disposition of the remains. If there is no Will the court appoints an administrator to take on this responsibility, but it takes time for the courts to act. The person next in line to assume the role of administrator would most likely have the right to possession for the purpose of disposition. Without a Will there is no specific person named (executor) to arrange the funeral and if family members disagree it may involve hurt feelings. If a child of divorced parents passes the parent with custody usually has right to possession. When joint custody is a factor things may change.

Lawful possession may be extended to the hospital if the person died on hospital premises. If the Coroner has jurisdiction they may have the right to possession for disposition. It depends on the circumstances.

Totten Trust: There may be any number of Trusts to cover immediate expenses. A Totten Trust is just a regular bank account with a designated "pay on death" inheritor.

When the account is opened a friend, relative (most likely named as executor) is named as the beneficiary. Whoever opens the account can also close it at any time for any reason. They may also change banks and or change beneficiaries. The beneficiary does not need to know about the arrangement, and the depositor is entitled to deposit and withdraw funds from the account as they see fit. The idea is when the person dies the beneficiary collects the account balance and pays for the funeral expenses. This can work out very well if all parties are informed and kept up to date.

Recording the Will: Depositing the Will, lodging the Will, or filing or recording the Will. Generally the most current Will is brought to the county court of the deceased's primary residence within 30 days of death where it is recorded.

Pour-over Will: A Pour-over Will transfers assets upon death to a trust account. The Pour-over Will has only one beneficiary which is the Trust Account. Assets are poured-over into the trust. This is something the executor or someone pre-planning will need to look into further and goes beyond the scope of this book. A Pour-over Will can also instruct the successor trustee to put any assets into the trust that were not put in previously. Sweet, if everything is done correctly.

Self-proving affidavit attached to a Will: An affidavit attached to a Will certifies that the witnesses and testator properly signed the Will. A self-proving will makes it easy for the court to accept the document as the true Will of the person who has died, avoiding the delay and cost of locating witnesses at the time of probate. Such Wills are legal in most states.

Joint Will: Many couples think they have a "joint Will". A mirror image Will is the same for each spouse. Each usually leaves everything to the other, surviving partner. If one of the partners is stricken with dementia either in the earliest stages or very advanced stages the other partner usually needs to correct their own Will to name a guardian or provide care if the surviving partner has dementia.

Living Will: A Living Will does not help distribute your assets it allows you to make health care decisions now in case you are unable to do so in the future. It documents instructions for your medical care in the event you are unable to communicate due to a severe injury, terminal illness or other medical condition. A Living Will can also be called a health care declaration, advance directive, or medical power of attorney.

Medical Directives, Health Care Directives or Advance Directives: An advance directive is a written statement of a person's wishes regarding medical treatment. It is a legal document detailing a person's health care wishes, including the individual to whom they give the legal authority to act on their behalf and what types of treatment they do and do not want to receive in the event they are unable to speak or communicate. The living will and the power of attorney constitute what are called advance directives. A divorce has no effect on your written directions for health care.

Medical Directives: Your last will and testament is not the document to specify how you wish to receive treatment in a medical crisis.

Dementia and Changing the Will: You are dealing with a person who is not thinking clearly. They may, and often do, change their Will often. In most cases a person with dementia can still make or change a Will if they can show that they understand what they are doing and what the effects of it will be. This needs to be addressed before a medical and financial crisis takes place. Proof of incapacity should be taken care of early.

Dementia: Dementia is a group of symptoms affecting intellectual and social abilities severely enough to interfere with daily functioning. There are many causes of dementia. Alzheimer's disease is the most common cause of a progressive dementia. In most cases a person with dementia can still make or change a Will if they can show that they understand what they are doing and what the effects of it will be.

Intestate Guardian: A guardian for minor children or the disabled is named in the Will. If there is no Will, there is no named guardian for minor children or a surviving incapacitated spouse and the court will appoint someone as guardian. This can take time.

Joint Tenancy: Any assets held in joint tenancy such as: bank accounts, safe deposit box contents, stocks and bonds, real-estate, and community property usually pass directly to the sole survivor.

Beneficiary Named: No Will is necessary for retirement accounts, IRA, 401K(s), living trust, POD (payable on death) accounts, TOD (transfer on death) accounts, or any type of plan when a beneficiary has been named. The original documents will have a section to name any beneficiary or beneficiaries. Sometimes Different beneficiaries will get a different percent of the policy or account payout. A Will does not cancel or change a beneficiary on an insurance policy, POD or TOD account or any type of plan when a beneficiary has been named. You should change the beneficiary with the plan originator.

Out of State Property: If the deceased has property in another state(s) there will be additional probate proceedings in the state(s) where the property is located. A vacation home in the desert and another at the seashore could each go through a different state probate court with each accessing fees and charges. The executor or personal representative may be required to visit the property in each state have appraisals, inspections and possible attorney fees. There may also be taxes due. How much easier it would have been to have a simple Will that read in part: "I am leaving my house in the desert to my brother Wally and my house at the seashore to my sister Wallonia," signed, Wilbur. Since probate laws vary from state to state there may be a few surprises.

Letter of Instruction: A letter of instruction may be helpful to include with a Will but it is not usually considered a legal directive. It may allow the testator to inform the executor of user names and passwords, access information and contact information that has changed since they made the Will. It can also be used to let the personal representative or executor your desires concerning your funeral arraignments. It allows you to notify your executor of updated information without having to rewrite the whole Will or include things you do not want made public. It is not a way to change beneficiaries or add assets for dispersion.

Locating a Will: This can be so simple. Executor, my Will is (and just tell them). This requires a great deal of trust. If you are worried that your executor might try to change your Will without your permission, you obviously do not want them to have access to the original document. The Will may not be in an obvious place, such as with the deceased's attorney, a desk drawer, file cabinet, or home safe. It could be stored on an external flash drive, portable hard drive, tablet device, or a smart phone. Also check for a safe deposit box at the deceased's bank. Make sure the Will is the most current version. Often, a will doesn't turn up at all, only to be found in some strange place at a later date. It could be wrapped in foil at the bottom of the freezer where it was hidden to keep it secure or in the pocket of or pined to the deceased's best suit or dress.

Name a Successor Executor: If the executor predeceases you or is no longer able or willing to fulfill the duties and obligations of executor a successor executor can be named.

Your Will becomes a Public Document when it is filed so do not put passwords or other information in it that you do not want made public.

Cost of a proper Will: There is the cost of drafting the Will and the cost of probating the estate when you are gone. Both costs must be considered. In the past codicils were added to Wills to reflect changes instead of retyping the documents. These codicils also had to be witnessed and/or notarized and could be confusing. Today it is much easier to amend the Will electronically and produce a new document. Make a new Will when any of your circumstances change, such as the birth of a child, divorce, change of property, moving to a new address etc. It should be less expensive than drafting the first Will.

Making a Will does not have to be expensive. There are some software programs available that are very good for estates worth less than one and a half million dollars. If you have had multiple marriages, a business, a recent divorce, or cannot find someone you trust to help you prepare a Will you should consider speaking with a competent estate attorney.

Making a Will does not have to be time consuming or too difficult providing you do not have unique situations or problems that need to be addressed. If you have children from a previous marriage the probate court may give them a part of your current residence instead of giving it all to your surviving spouse if you do not address this in your Will properly. Never answer an anonymous letter. Always go to other people's funerals, or they won't go to yours. (Yogi Berra) Proper wording is everything.

Risks with assets held in Joint Tenancy with Rights of Survivorship: If the asset is held in Joint Tenancy with Rights of Survivorship with a child and the child decides they do not want you to sell the asset there may be nothing you can do without their permission (signature). In some states you will also need the permission (signature) of their spouse. All of your children are angels. If they are being sued, have credit problems or are going through a divorce you may have a real problem. Now try to get your child's spouse to give you permission (signature). If you own your home jointly with a child and the child is going through bankruptcy the court may have the option to force the sale of your home or collect your assets to pay off the debt. Everything is fine: there is a red light, an accident, a lawsuit; you may lose your home in the blink of an eye and you were just sitting there minding your own business while watching *Wheel of Fortune*. Bummer.

You may have tried to do the right thing and now you are held hostage. It is always a good idea to speak with a competent estate attorney before you begin signing things away. Do not allow yourself to be pressured by relatives or family.

Probate and Joint Tenancy with Rights of Survivorship: Joint Tenancy with Rights of Survivorship automatically transfers ownership to the other spouse or business partner upon the death of the first partner and avoids probate. This is an enormous advantage for those who need the funds immediately as the probate process could make funds unavailable for months or years. How would a surviving spouse or business partner pay day-to-day expenses if the bank accounts were frozen at the death of an individual? Who would pay the mortgage, living expenses or vendors? Would everything be lost? If you still have not started to preplan your arraignments for when you pass, today would be the best day to start. see *Joint Tenancy*, page 48, 382

Digital Executor or Digital Administrator: People are naming a Digital Executor more often but state laws have not kept up with the need. The executor still has all legal responsibility for the dispensation of the estate including the distribution of all digital assets to the beneficiaries by providing them with the necessary content and/ or access information. Some digital assets may still need to be posted online after death and files may need to be deleted and hard storage scrubbed clean.

> The executor has the legal responsibility for disposition of the estate. The digital executor helps with Digital Assets: online storage "in the cloud", online shopping sites, websites, blogs, videos, CD's, DVD's (some contain important documents and may be password protected or encrypted). Family photos all stored online, on DVDs or thumb drives. There are passwords, encryption, challenge codes, social networking websites. All digital Assets must be protected and distributed. The Digital Executor can be very helpful.
>
> The executor of the estate may not know how to find or even access Digital Assets worth hundreds of thousands of dollars. They may not even be aware off their worth. Facebook's $1 billion acquisition of the mobile start-up Instagram changed a lot of things. Today something as simple (to the untrained) as an "app" could be worth a billion dollars only if it is turned into a more liquid asset quickly. If you have Digital Assets it is important to protect

them with a Digital Administrator that could possibly act as executor of the estate. In any case if you have any digital assets (and we all do) you may need to allow your executor to access this information. Make them aware of your digital executor. If you name your digital executor as a beneficiary the executor is obligated by law to inform them of your death and send them a copy of your will. see *Executor* page 133

Probate, is there a Simplified Procedure: Is there a simplified procedure for settling an estate with limited assets? Yes, in most states there is. There are various rules and regulations depending on the state and/or county but there will most likely be a dollar amount mentioned. An example could be: A simplified procedure for settling the estate may be available if the total value of the estate assets does not exceed ($40,000). In addition, at the time of death the decedent must not own any real estate other than survivorship property, and the estate assets must consist only of personal property and/or an unreleased interest in a mortgage with or without value etc. If a simplified procedure is available it may not be necessary to probate the estate. see *Probate*, page 34, 241

Parts of a Will: It is beyond the scope of this book to instruct on how to go about writing a Will. There are some good software programs, books, videos and self-help classes available that may be of assistance to you. After reading through this book you should have come to realize that it is just bad manners to leave without leaving a Will. It causes undue stress and possible financial loss and hardship for those left behind. You need to start today. see *Preplan*, page 219

CHART

APPENDIX

A GUIDE TO USUAL AND COMMON COSTS

This Chart listing **Usual and Common Costs** is to be used as a guide to reference what some of the most common costs could be. Actual cost will vary from state to state, county to county, and even week to week. We have no control over what you may or may not be charged. We recommend that you seek professional help before you sign anything.

Grieving families who don't know their legal rights are vulnerable to sales pressure, manipulation, and overspending when it comes time to plan a funeral. Most Funeral Homes and Cemeteries are honest. For those that need some help **the United States Federal Trade Commission (FTC)** enforces **The Funeral Rule.** This gives you, the consumer, specific rights to choose and pay for only the goods and services that you select. Under the law certain things may be required in one state and not another. Certain things also may be required under different circumstances. As with any law, some people and businesses will try to get around it. The Funeral Rule is a big step forward but it is not a perfect. The FTC was established in 1914 to investigate and eliminate unfair and deceptive practices in business. The Funeral Rule was written to provide consumers information and some protection concerning the purchase of goods and services from a funeral provider. You are allowed to compare prices. You do not have to purchase a "funeral package" and will most likely save money if you do not. A "funeral package" may contain many goods and services you do not need or want.

Read more: *Funeral Rule* page 178

http://business.ftc.gov/documents/bus05-complying-funeral-rule

This is an excellent U.S. Government website. Just type this URL into your browser window or Google it. As the U.S. population ages we will see more and more instances of consumer fraud within the funeral services industry simply because that is where the money is. Nothing personal.

Many consumers are under the impression they have a 3-day right to cancel any and all consumer purchases. This is not true. Do not expect a funeral service provider to help you rescind the contract. They are a business and they are in business to make a profit. Their sales staff usually works on a commission and the more you pay the more they make. This is simple business. I provide goods or a service. I charge you. You pay.

> However, if you just signed an "agreement" it is most likely a legal contract. If you now feel the need to change your mind chances are you need more help than you realize. You may be protected under a variety of laws. One such group of laws is called "Elder Law". This basically covers many areas of the law with regard to protection for the elderly or disabled. Contact a competent estate attorney immediately. If you cannot drive to see them they most likely will come to see you. Everything that you signed may be perfectly fine. Most Funeral Homes and Cemeteries are law abiding and you may have received a fair price for goods and services. Still, it is a good thing to get another opinion while you can. You may have a right to cancel the sale within a limited number of days. Make the call.
>
> The funeral provider must give you an itemized statement of the total cost of the funeral goods and services you have selected when you are making the arrangements. If the funeral provider doesn't know the cost of the cash advance items at the time, he or she is required to give you a written "good faith estimate." This statement also must disclose any legal, cemetery or crematory requirements that you purchase any specific funeral goods or services.

APPENDIX
A Guide to Usual and Common Costs.

You will always pay for these three services: Transportation from the death site to the funeral service site, a container for the body to be placed in, and basic services of the funeral home and staff

The Funeral Rule does not require any specific format for this information. Funeral providers may include it in any document they give you at the end of your discussion about funeral arrangements.

Planning for a Funeral

Shop around in advance. Compare prices from at least two funeral homes. Remember that you can supply your own casket or urn.

Ask for a price list. The law requires funeral homes to give you written price lists for products and services.

Resist pressure to buy goods and services you don't really want or need.

Avoid emotional overspending. It's not necessary to have the fanciest casket or the most elaborate funeral to properly honor a loved one.

Recognize your rights. Laws regarding funerals and burials vary from state to state. It's a smart move to know which goods or services the law requires you to purchase and which are optional.

Apply the same smart shopping techniques you use for other major purchases. You can cut costs by limiting the viewing to one day or one hour before the funeral, and by dressing your loved one in a favorite outfit instead of costly burial clothing.

Plan ahead. It allows you to comparison shop without time constraints, creates an opportunity for family discussion, and lifts some of the burden from your family.

Federal Trade commission FTC An excellent government website.
http://www.ftc.gov/bcp/edu/pubs/consumer/products/pro19.shtm

A General Guide to Prices

These Fees are so general they are almost meaningless. So why include them? We included them to give you a "ballpark" number of what the fees are. The most reputable businesses will place a Price list online at their website. Be careful of funeral service providers that say, "Just, trust me." Be careful.

ITEM	An approximate cost or price range.
Alkaline Hydrolysis	$1,000 if available in your state.
Asset Search	$400 or less
Attorney: basic estate plan	$500 to $1,000.
Bronze Grave Markers	24 x 12 $400 - $1100 / 36" x 14" $1100 - up
Burial Clothes	Men's: $150 and up Woman's $100 and up
Burial containers: Vaults, Grave Liners or Concrete Box,	Wooden shell $200 - $300 Plastic vault $750 - $950 Concrete vault $1,150 - $1,350 Steel vault $1,250 - $1,450 Stainless steel $2,000
Casket	$2,300
Casket pine or cedar	$500

APPENDIX
A Guide to Usual and Common Costs.

Celebrant Fee	$200 to over $800 depending on type of service, location, travel and other expenses
Ceramic Pictures & Headstone Photos	$175 and up
Clergy	
Columbarium Niche	$1,500
Cremation: A direct cremation package usually includes transportation, brief storage of the body, document processing (permits, death certificate), a container (usually cardboard) for the body prior to and during cremation, and a basic container (cardboard or plastic) for the ashes.	$1,000 without casket rental and viewing
Cremation container. A simple unlined and unfinished container or casket.	Prices start around $20 -$250 for hardboard, softwood caskets covered with fabric cost $200 -$1,000; and a hardwood casket can be $1,200 -$8,000
Crypt eBay Crypt in a community mausoleum	$100,000 double to less than $6,000 double
Crypt in a community mausoleum	$2,000
Custodian	$50.00
Death Certificate —certified copy	$8 - $60 each

Embalming and body preparation	$750 and up
First call fee to pick up and transport the deceased to the funeral home or crematory	$150 - $500
Flat Lawn Marker Granite	$600 and up
Flowers	$100 and up
Funeral director's basic services fee	$1,500
Funeral ceremony and Viewing (as an add on)	$1,000
Viewing (usually includes a time limit.)	Additional time may be billed at $100 an hour and up
Grave marker	$1,000
Grave space single grave plot	$1,000 - $2,000 and up
Pillow Top Granite	$400 20Lx10Wx6H
Upright Granite	$1,200 18 H with a 24L x 6H
Guest Register Book	#12 and up
Hairdressing	$35 and up

APPENDIX
A Guide to Usual and Common Costs.

Headstone	$500 and up $2,000 is common
Hearse	$150 - $600
Chauffeured Limousine	$250 - $700
Honorarium	$50 - $300
Honorarium to Clergy	$200 and up (it is OK to ask)
Mausoleum: Free-standing single and double crypt granite	$12,000 delivered to the site and assembled.
Living Trust	Attorney fee: $600-$1200 Do it yourself book $30, software $50
Mausoleums	$30,000 - $300,000 and up
Memorial Book	$40 - $80
Memorial tribute or remembrance cards no photo	$1.00 each or less With photo about $1.50 each
Music	$150 - $250
Obituary	Some are free $300 is average for twenty lines of type.
Opening and closing costs of the burial/cremation space	$1,000

Preparation Fees	$150 - $550
Refrigeration Fees	$50 - $100 a day
Transportation within the US excluding airfare	$1,500
Transportation of the remains Overseas	$4,500 - $11,000 includes airfare
Cremains it is usually easiest to fly with the cremains using a travel urn or box.	Cost of airfare.
Vaults, Grave Liners or Concrete Box, Burial containers	$300 and up
Vault, grave liner installation fees	$100 and up
Vases Granite	$45 and up
Receiving the remains from another funeral home can range in price from	$450 – $2,000
Forwarding the remains to another funeral home can range in price from	$800 – $2,000

Glossary & Index

A

Administrator: A person appointed by a court to take charge of the estate of a decedent, but not appointed in the decedent's will.

Executor, Personal Representative, Administrator, Exectrix, Court Appointed Administrator.

An Executor is someone who administers an estate of a person who left a valid Will. If a person dies intestate, that is, without a Will, then the Personal Representative or Administrator will be appointed by the court. An Exectrix is a female executor.

> No matter what they are called, they all oversee the disposition of property and possessions of a deceased person. An executor is entrusted with the large responsibility of making sure a person's last wishes are granted with regards to the disposition of their property and possessions. They identify the estate's assets, pay off its debts and then distribute whatever is left to the rightful heirs and beneficiaries. see *Executor*, page 133

Medical Directives, Health Care Directives or Advance Directives: An advance directive is a written statement of a person's wishes regarding medical treatment. It is a legal document detailing a person's health care wishes, including the individual to whom they give the legal authority to act on their behalf and what types of treatment they do and do not want to receive in the event they are unable to speak or communicate. The living will and the power of attorney constitute what are called advance directives. A divorce has no effect on your written directions for health care.

Special Administrator: A special administrator is a person appointed by the court in a probate proceeding to administrate in the same or similar capacity as executor. A special administrator may be appointed when there is a dispute between beneficiaries or other situations arise. A special administrator can be appointed whether or not there is a Will (intestate).

Advance Directives: Living Will and Durable Health Care Power of Attorney and Organ Donor Cards are a few.

Affidavit: A statement in writing and sworn to in the presence of someone authorized to administer an oath, such as a notary public. An affidavit can be used as evidence in court.

Aging: Commission on Law and Aging, American Bar Association.

> http://www.americanbar.org/groups/law_aging.html

Alkaline Hydrolysis Disposition: Alkaline Hydrolysis is also called **Water Cremation**, **Bio Cremation** or **Green Cremation.** It is sold as being good for the environment. This will most likely depend on the legislation that is yet to be enacted in most states. The process has been in use for many years but is new to the funeral industry.

> The natural processes of breakdown by the environment is accelerated by a gently flow of water held to specific temperatures and alkalinity until the body has been dissolved in water. At the end of the process the only solid remains are an ash similar to cremation. This ash is then returned to the family in an urn.

> Alkaline Hydrolysis Disposition protects the living from deadly organisms, viruses and bacteria. It consumes less than a tenth the fossil fuel and emits ninety-four percent fewer greenhouse gases compared to cremation.

> **No casket is legally required** for a dignified disposition using this process. Like other forms of cremation a casket can be rented for a viewing or service. The ashes can be scattered anywhere but you should get permission before scattering on someone else's property. Laws may also vary for city, state and country. Many parks also have rules and permit requirements so you will want to check into the requirements. A little known but extremely dangerous contamination is mercury left from dental amalgam.

GLOSSARY & INDEX
Terms and Definitions

Amalgam Fillings, sometimes called "silver amalgams," are actually half mercury. Mercury is toxic. Some studies show that amalgam is not stable after it is implanted into human teeth and it constantly releases toxic mercury vapor. There is special equipment to be used and special masks to be worn when dentists remove amalgam (silver) fillings. There are special requirements to dispose of the amalgam and to keep the patient from more contamination. Mercury bio-accumulates. The mercury in amalgam is a neurotoxin and when released into the environment, dental mercury most often converts to its even more toxic form, methyl mercury. The most common concerns of cremation by fire are energy consumption and mercury emissions from vaporized dental fillings. It has been reported by the United Nations Environment Programme that close to thirty-two tons of mercury are used annually by the dental industry in the U.S. It is well worth your time to look into this.

> There are patient support organizations for people with chronic mercury conditions and people looking for advice about dental mercury issues. Google: Dental Amalgam Mercury.

Alternative Container: An unfinished wood box or other non-metal receptacle without ornamentation, often made of fiberboard, pressed wood or composition materials, and generally lower in cost than caskets.

Amendment: a change made by addition, correction, or deletion.

Annuity: An insurance policy or annuity is a contract between the company that sold it and the person who bought it and is designed to meet retirement and other long-range goals. The individual makes a lump-sum payment or series of payments. In return, the insurer agrees to make periodic payments to them beginning immediately or at some future date. The proceeds do not go through the probate process.

> Annuities typically offer tax-deferred growth of earnings and may include a death benefit that will pay a beneficiary a specified minimum amount, such as the total purchase payments. As a financial product, annuities are primarily used as a means of securing a steady cash flow for an individual during their retirement years.

Appraisal: To evaluate and estimate the quality and value of an object. Appraisals are made for estates to determine the value of objects, memorabilia and collections.

Arrangement Conference: The meeting between the customer and the sales person at the funeral home when service(s) and merchandise are purchased. A binding contract for the funeral goods and services selected by the family is drawn up and signed. An arrangement conference can also be held at a hospital or the family's home.

Arrangement Room: A room at the funeral home used to make the necessary funeral arrangements with the family of the deceased. It is used for an arrangement conference where the customer and the sales person meet to draw up a binding contract for goods and services.

Ashes: Cremated remains or cremains.

Asset: A resource with economic value. Any item of monetary value owned by an individual or corporation, especially that which could be converted to cash. Assets are both **Intangible** such as investments and **Liquid** such as cash and bank accounts.

> **Probate Asset:** A probate asset is one in which title to the property does not transfer by operation of law upon the death of the owner and therefore requires court involvement.
>
> **Commingling of Assets:** An account consisting of assets from several different accounts that are mixed together. The executor or personal representative should always keep the decedent's assets separate from their own.
>
> **Transfer on Death Assets:** Many assets (such as bank accounts) or benefits such as retirement savings accounts (e.g., IRAs) have their own beneficiary designations that allow the asset to pass payable on death (POD) or transfer on death (TOD). Check any trusts. Trusts should be mentioned in the Will but the executor may have to read the details of the trust in the trust documents available from the attorney who set up the trust. Joint ownership deeds and retirement statements that include beneficiary names and directives also need to be checked.

Assisted Living: Assisted living facilities are usually state-licensed programs offered at senior residential communities with services that include meals, laundry, housekeeping, medication reminders, and assistance with daily living activities. The legal definition varies from state to state with a few states not even licensing assisted living facilities.

Auto Titles: A state issues a title to provide a vehicle owner with proof of ownership. Each title has a unique number.

Autopsy: An autopsy is a medical examination performed on the body of someone who died in order to determine the cause of death. It may also be referred to as a post-mortem examination. The medical examination could take a couple of days to complete.

> In most cases a physician cannot order an autopsy on a patient without the consent of the next-of-kin. Physicians may request an autopsy and a medical examiner or a coroner may order an autopsy without the consent of the next-of-kin. If permission from the next-of-kin is necessary they can also limit the extent of the autopsy to include only certain organs or areas of the body.
>
> Sudden or violent deaths usually warrant an autopsy.
>
> Photographs are usually taken along with body and tissue samples.

Autopsy, who pays? In many cases the federal government pays for autopsies through Medicare funding to hospitals. Health Insurance covers the costs in some cases and autopsies are paid for by the family if they want to place liability for the death. The hospital may also directly bill the estate of the deceased if the patient dies at home or in a nursing home. If the patient dies in the hospital, the autopsy is often free to the family.

B

Bank Levy: An order that enables the creditor to attach the debtor's bank account.

Basic Arrangements Fee: The Funeral Rule allows funeral providers to charge a basic services fee that customers cannot decline to pay. The basic services fee includes services that are common to all funerals, regardless of the specific arrangement. These include funeral planning, securing the necessary permits and copies of death certificates, preparing the notices, sheltering the remains, and coordinating the arrangements with the cemetery, crematory or other third parties. The fee does not include charges for optional services or merchandise.

http://www.ftc.gov/bcp/edu/pubs/consumer/products/pro19.shtm

Note: If you select direct burial or direct cremation, the arrangements fee cannot be added since it is already figured into the prices for these services.

Beneficiary: A person or group entitled to receive funds or other property under a trust, a Valid Last Will and Testament, or insurance policy. see *Beneficiary*, page 38, 87

Beneficiary Named: No Will is necessary for retirement accounts, IRA, 401K(s), living trust, POD (payable on death) accounts, TOD (transfer on death) accounts, or any type of plan when a beneficiary has been named. The original documents will have a section to name any beneficiary or beneficiaries. Sometimes Different beneficiaries will get a different percent of the policy or account payout.

Bequest: Any gift of property made in a Will.

Bereaved: A person who has suffered the death of someone they loved. The immediate family of the deceased.

Bill Collectors: It used to be when someone died they had some assets. Not so today. Many boomers will be in debt when they pass. They will leave this burden to family, friends or the state. Many children are concerned that if they serve as the executor of the Will or as Trustee of their parents Trust that may be held responsible for this debt. That is not likely. If you share debt you can be held libel. If the deceased was the sole debtor the estate is responsible for paying the creditor in almost all situations. If there are insufficient assets or there are no assets, the Trustee or the executor is not going to be held personally responsible. However, many bill collectors may try to manipulate the executor into paying the debt themselves. Bill collectors also try to get friends or relatives to pay the debt. Collectors that try to appeal to a consumer's moral obligation to pay the debt could be in violation of federal law.

FTC Consumer Alert: Paying the Debts of a Deceased Relative: Who Is Responsible? After a relative dies, the last thing grieving family members want are calls from debt collectors asking them to pay a loved one's debts. As a rule, those debts are paid from the deceased person's estate.

According to the Federal Trade Commission (FTC), the nation's consumer protection agency, family members typically are not obligated to pay the debts of a deceased relative from their own assets. What's more, family members – and all consumers – are protected by the federal Fair Debt Collection Practices Act (FDCPA), which prohibits debt collectors from using abusive, unfair, or deceptive practices to try to collect a debt.

Under the FDCPA, a debt collector is someone who regularly collects debts owed to others. This includes collection agencies, lawyers who collect debts on a regular basis and companies that buy delinquent debts and then try to collect them.

Does a debt go away when the debtor dies? No. The estate of the deceased person owes the debt. If there isn't enough money in the estate to cover the debt, it typically goes unpaid. But there are exceptions to this rule. You may be responsible for the debt if you: co-signed the obligation; live in a community property state, such as California; are the deceased person's spouse and state law requires you to pay a particular type of debt, like some health care expenses; or were legally responsible for resolving the estate and didn't comply with certain state probate laws.

If you have questions about whether you are legally obligated to pay a deceased person's debts from your own assets, talk to a lawyer.

http://www.ftc.gov/bcp/edu/pubs/consumer/alerts/alt004.shtm

Bio-ethicists: Bio-ethicists work with dying people and have grappled with the dilemma of what is reasonable care for a dying person.

Birth Certificate: An official document issued to record a person's birth.

Blanket Levy: This process involves the serving of a Writ of Execution and a Bank Levy on every bank in the debtor's home area and assumes that the debtor's bank of record is located within a short distance of home or work, which is usually the case.

Brokerage Accounts: An account at a firm that conducts transactions on behalf of a client for a fee. A stock broker charges a fee to act as intermediary between buyer and seller.

Brokerage Firm: A firm that conducts transactions on behalf of a client for a fee. A stock broker charges a fee to act as intermediary between buyer and seller. There are several kinds of brokers: A bill-and-note broker, a commercial or merchandise broker, an insurance broker, and a Real estate broker are some examples.

Bereavement Fare: In most instances it seems like the current sale price of an airline ticket is less expensive than the standard discount on the regular airfare for a bereavement fare if it is even available.

Burial

Ground Burial: The action or practice of interring a dead body in an underground chamber. Also called a funeral or interment.

Traditional, Full-service Burial: A traditional funeral usually includes a viewing or visitation and formal funeral service, use of a hearse to transport the body to the funeral site and cemetery, and burial, entombment or cremation of the remains.

A traditional funeral service is generally the most expensive type of funeral. In addition to the funeral home's basic services fee, costs often include embalming, dressing the body, rental of the funeral home for the viewing or service and use of vehicles to transport the family if they don't use their own. Cemetery costs for the plot, mausoleum or niche, opening and closing the grave, headstone or marker, and perpetual maintenance are most likely not included.

GLOSSARY & INDEX
Terms and Definitions

Direct Burial or **Green Burial:** Direct Burial is the most common final disposition and is also called a Green Burial. It is the process of burying a body without the use of chemical preservation in a simple container to help preserve the earth. Costs associated with direct burial include grave opening and closing and perpetual care (maintenance) of the grave site. There are also charges for the purchase of a grave site.

Burial at Sea: Burial at sea when the deceased has not been cremated shall take place at a minimum of three nautical miles from land in water at least six-hundred feet deep. Certain environmentally protected areas such as the coast of central Florida to the east, and the coast of Florida to the west in most areas require a water depth of at least one-thousand, eight-hundred feet deep. The body must be prepared to sink to the bottom rapidly and permanently.

Permits from may be required. Check with local law and customs first. The EPA requires information concerning the name of the deceased, the type of remains (cremated or non-cremated), date of burial, location of burial (longitude and latitude, depth of water and distance from shore, name of the port from which you departed, name of the vessel, and photo copies of any other necessary permits.

Burial of Cremated remains at Sea: The disposition of Cremated ashes follow some of the same procedures as to permits. Always confirm what you think is alright with local laws. Cremated ash is a lot heavier than most people realize. It does not just blow away in a breeze but is more the consistency of a sand and dust. Be aware of the wind direction so the ashes do not blow back into the mourners faces. This does happen quite a lot unless you are prepared.

Burials in Inland Waters are regulated by the Clean Water Act and permits are required from the proper state agency. Any flowers or wreaths must be made of natural materials which readily decompose in the marine environment.

Burial Certificate or Permit: A legal paper issued by the local government authorizing burial or cremation. This is part of the process required for transporting a body out of the area in which they died. The body is generally embalmed before transport and the burial permit is a type of proof that the body will be buried at its end destination.

Burial-Transit Permit or Burial Permit: Transportation and disposition permission. A burial transit permit or burial permit is needed in some states for the transportation and disposition of the deceased. This document grants the holder permission to transport a body. To transport a body out-of-state you must also obtain a burial-transit permit. If the medical examiner is involved, the permit must be signed by him and by the local registrar to be valid. It is also needed at a cemetery or crematorium to bury or cremate a body.

Transportation Authorization: While most states allow non-licensed individuals to transport a body, it is necessary to have formal authorization. Transportation permits may only be valid for the state where issued. Transporting a body across state lines may require multiple permits.

Burial Containers: Vault, Grave Liner or Concrete Box. Most states do not have laws requiring an outer burial container. The cemetery may require this because it does help prevent the ground from collapsing around the grave site. Also the human body has lots of hazardous materials that need to be contained and it makes for easier maintenance of the grounds.

The Outer Burial Container Price List: Information and Use. If you sell outer burial containers and do not list the retail price of each such container on your General Price List, you must prepare a separate printed or typewritten Outer Burial Container Price List (OBC Price List).(12) The term "outer burial container" refers to any container designed to be placed around the casket in the grave. Such containers may include burial vaults, grave boxes, and grave liners. From the *Funeral Rule*, page 178.

Burial Vault: A burial vault completely contains the casket, while a grave liner generally covers only the top and sides of the casket and allows the bottom of the casket to be in contact with the earth. Purchased online it may be sent directly to the cemetery, but because cemeteries are not covered by the FTC's Funeral Rule, the cemetery may charge a fee for using a burial vault or grave liner you purchased elsewhere. Eventually water or dirt from may find a way to get inside the casket which is not necessarily a bad thing.

> The cost of a grave liner is a few hundred dollars and up to a few thousand dollars. Then you pay a fee to have it lowered into the ground. This lowering fee is usually another $100. You bury it. You almost never dig it back up. It deteriorates. If it is required, purchase the least expensive grave liner that you

can find. Plastic and wood are also options. Plastic is strong, less susceptible to water seepage, and durable. Stainless steel liners can be painted and decorated with gold, silver or bronze trims.

Decent Burial: Common Law recognizes there is a duty to both the deceased and to society for what is referred to as a "decent burial" without unnecessary delay.

Burial Garments: Clothing used to cover a body in preparation for burial. This includes undergarments, glasses and jewelry. If the Burial garments are too large the professionals at the funeral home will adjust them to look as if they fit.

Burial Insurance: A basic type of life insurance that is used to pay for funeral goods and services rather than cash. When someone passes away, their debts do not disappear, that is what funereal insurance is for. Burial insurance does not all have to be spent for the burial.

Business Ownership: Sole Proprietorship, limited liability corporation (LLC), partnership or corporate operating agreements. The deceased may have had an active role in a business or just a financial stake as a part owner. The executor should have access to clients or work contacts. Include the name, email address and phone number of each current client, or your manager if you are employed by others.

C

Canopy: A portable canvas shelter used to cover the grave area during a burial. Also called a tent.

Care Fund: A care fund is made up of a portion of the monies collected from the sale of interment spaces and invested for future care.

Caregivers

Caregivers: A caregiver is a family member or paid helper who provides direct care for a child or a sick, elderly, or disabled person. Caregivers are family, friends, partners, and neighbors. The roles of a caregiver change as the patient's needs change. They may just need a little assistance with the shopping and maybe a ride to the doctor or the local library or to visit with friends. Younger patients need the same basic help that seniors need.

Caregivers are part of the health care team and should be responsive to this role. They should have phone numbers and contact information in case of an emergency.

Family Member Caregiver: More often today, a family member provides care for a loved one and they sometimes need to cut back on their regular employment to do this. In many cases the caregiver would like to be compensated for the time they spend caring for the loved one. If the individual needing care goes into a nursing home at a later time, Medicare/Medicaid will access any payments made to family members. If payments to the family member are not done correctly the patient could be denied Medicaid latter on. In some states all that is necessary is a formal contract detailing goods and services provided for payment rendered. The law changes constantly and this really needs to be looked into to stay legal. It is not a matter of getting away with anything. It is simply dealing with government and being certain you did every little thing just like they want it.

Stress: Due to the stress involved in being a caregiver their health is 40% more likely to fail than a non-caregiver. Should they be compensated? Most often only one child will be in a position to act as the primary caregiver and the other children tend to think everything is taken care of. This is hard on their health, hard on their marriage and hard on their family. Friends and families should address this situation before it becomes necessary. How will the caregiver(s) be compensated? It is best to write things down to avoid misunderstandings later on. A simple Caregivers Agreement listing goods and services for payment rendered will help jog memories next year. Look into Medicare/Medicaid to see what is necessary to put in writing and plan ahead.

Sometimes there are no funds available to compensate the caregiver while the patient is alive and an agreement may be needed to provide for the caregiver from the estate of the loved one through assets, life insurance or pensions that are available. Put everything in writing. Now would be a really good time to consult with a competent estate attorney.

Alzheimer's: Alzheimer's disease is just one of many reasons a family member would provide care to a loved one. More than 15 million Americans provide unpaid care valued at $210 billion for persons with Alzheimer's and other dementias. Payments for care are estimated to be $200 billion in the United States in 2012. One in eight older Americans has Alzheimer's disease. In 2012, the direct costs of caring for those with Alzheimer's or other dementias to American society will total an estimated $200 billion, including $140 billion in costs to Medicare and Medicaid. see - alz.org

Caskets

Caskets: A casket or coffin is often the single most expensive item to be purchased. Prices can range from less than one thousand dollars to more than ten thousand dollars.

Materials and Cost: Caskets are made from almost any material. Common materials are wood, metal and plastic. Copper or bronze caskets can cost over ten thousand dollars. Wood caskets constructed from mahogany, walnut, oak or cherry have a higher markup and are the ones most funeral homes will show customers. A pine or cedar casket can be purchased for $500. The eighteen gauge steel caskets that most people are familiar with can cost $5,000 or more at a local funeral home. The same casket can be purchased online for $995 and this price includes free shipping to your local funeral home. Caskets and other funeral service supplies can be purchased online from Wal-Mart, Costco, Sears, other online retailers or direct from the manufacturer. Everyone should shop online first to get an idea of cost and quality while you are under no pressure to purchase anything. When you have some facts you will be in a much better position to make an informed decision.

Casket for Direct Burial: The body is buried shortly after death, usually in a simple container. No viewing or visitation is involved, so no embalming is necessary. A memorial service may be held at the graveside or later. Direct burial usually costs less than the "traditional," full-service funeral. Costs include the funeral home's basic services fee, as well as transportation and care of the body, the purchase of a casket or burial container and a cemetery plot or crypt. If the family chooses to be at the cemetery for the burial, the funeral home often charges an additional fee for a graveside service.

http://www.ftc.gov/bcp/edu/pubs/consumer/products/pro19.shtm

Casket for Direct Cremation: The body is cremated shortly after death, without embalming and the cremated remains are placed in an urn or other container. No viewing or visitation is involved, although a memorial service may be held. Many families that opt to have their loved ones cremated rent a casket from the funeral home for the visitation and funeral. The deceased is then removed from the casket before cremation. If direct cremation without viewing or visitation is chosen the provider must offer an inexpensive unfinished wood box or alternative container that is cremated with the body.

The remains can be kept in the home, buried or placed in a crypt or niche in a cemetery, or buried or scattered in a favorite spot. Direct cremation usually costs less than the "traditional," full-service funeral. Costs include the funeral home's basic services fee, as well as transportation and care of the body. A crematory fee may be included or, if the funeral home does not own the crematory, the fee may be added on. There also will be a charge for an urn or other container. The cost of a cemetery plot or crypt is included only if the remains are buried or entombed. Small urns are available if more than one family member would like an urn containing the deceased's ashes.

http://www.ftc.gov/bcp/edu/pubs/consumer/products/pro19.shtm

Alternative Container: Funeral providers who offer direct cremations also must offer to provide an alternative container that can be used in place of a casket.

Casket Rental: It is very common to rent an appropriate casket for a graveside or memorial service to be held before cremation or burial. The remains are then transferred before cremation or burial. Jewelry is returned to the family if requested. To avoid problems, request this in writing; have it signed and keep a copy.

Airtight Seals and Gaskets: Protective gaskets are sometimes sold as add-ons for up to several thousand dollars in additional charges. What is accomplished by an airtight seal? The consumer is often told that this seal will help to preserve the body of the loved one. A casket sealed with a tight rubber gasket creates an environment that helps bacteria thrive. When placed in a tightly sealed container most bodies have a tendency to liquefy and create bloating gas which explodes the container releasing noxious gasses into the crypt or mausoleum. Most cemetery workers pop the seal to allow air to vent into the casket to keep the remains from exploding. The seal is also broken to allow air to vent when the casket is placed above ground.

Without this airtight gasket there is normal dehydration and deterioration of the body.

Funeral Rule: To protect consumers, the Federal Trade Commission wrote and enforces The Funeral Rule. The funeral rule clearly says funeral homes must accept delivery of merchandise purchased from other retailers at no extra charge to the consumer. Cemeteries are not under the funeral rule and can charge you a fee for using merchandise from another retailer. see page 178

Casket Price List: The casket price list (CPL) is a required printed list which the funeral service provider presents to you before you discuss or are shown a casket. This list will provide a brief description of each casket and alternative container (such as a cardboard or pressed wood box) regularly offered by the funeral home. The Funeral Rule states funeral homes must give you a written list with all the prices and services offered, including the least expensive. It must state the retail price of each item offered.

The Funeral Rule states funeral homes must give you a written list with all the prices and services offered, including the least expensive. From The Funeral Rule, FTC website.

FTC . gov - Instructions for funeral homes and funeral service directors.

http://business.ftc.gov/documents/bus05-complying-funeral-rule

The Casket Price List: Information and Use

If you do not list the retail price of each casket on your General Price List, you must prepare a separate printed or typewritten Casket Price List (CPL).(11)

Information to be Included

The CPL must include the following basic information:

- the name of your business;
- the caption: "Casket Price List;"
- the effective date for the Casket Price List; and
- the retail price of each casket and alternative container that does not require special ordering, with enough information to identify it.

You must give enough descriptive information about each casket on the CPL to enable consumers to identify the specific casket or container and understand what they are buying. For example, the CPL could describe the exterior appearance (including the gauge of metal or type of wood), the exterior trim, and the interior fabric. You also may give any other information, such as a photograph or manufacturer name and model number. However, a photograph or model number alone is not a sufficient description under the Rule.

According to the Funeral Rule:

- you have the right to choose the funeral goods and services you want (with some exceptions).
- the funeral provider must state this right in writing on the general price list.
- if state or local law requires you to buy any particular item, the funeral provider must disclose it on the price list, with a reference to the specific law.
- the funeral provider may not refuse, or charge a fee, to handle a casket you bought elsewhere.

- a funeral provider that offers cremations must make alternative containers available.

Casket Veil: A silk or net transparent covering for the casket for the purpose of keeping flies and other insects from the remains.

Catafalque: A decorated wooden framework supporting the casket of a distinguished person during a funeral or while lying in state.

Cash Advance Items: Cash Advance Items are service or merchandise for which the funeral home pays directly to a third party, such as fees for the cemetery or crematory, death certificates and clergy. Some funeral homes require payment for these items before the funeral service. You may be able to pay some of these fees directly, if you choose. Do not forget to get receipts for any money you spend, whether it is to the funeral home or to third parties. These should be paid back to you by the estate. If you are not the executor, personal representative or administrator of the estate it may be best if you allow the person in charge of administrative responsibilities for the estate to pay for all items. You may or may not be reimbursed by the estate, depending on whether or not the estate is solvent.

Cash Card: These can access bank accounts using a PIN (personal identity number). Also called a debit card or bank card.

Celebrant: A Celebrant tries to meet the needs of the family during their time of loss. They serve by providing a personalized funeral service that reflects the personality and lifestyle of the deceased. It is considered an alternative to the traditional religious service.

Cell Phone

Before you give away the deceased's cell phone check it for information. This is where a Digital Executor is helpful. There are companies listed online that can search the phone for you and return along with the phone a written report.

Check the Cellphone, PDA or mobile device for messages, voice mail and the phone list of contacts. Keep a copy of phone numbers, names, and contact information. It may come in handy even a year or two later. Cellphones, smartphones, PDAs and many mobile devices contain personal and sometimes sensitive information, including addresses and phone numbers, passwords, bank account numbers, email, voicemail, phone logs, even medical and prescription information. Some people pay all of their bills using their phone. They shop online, bank online, pay bills and make reservations. To date every phone operating system has been hacked. Hackers go where the money is and stay one step ahead of everyone else. Most people do not use a password on their cellphone and then they store all of their passwords on that same cellphone. All you have to do is push the login button.

Many mobile devices use a SIM Card (Subscriber Identity Module) to store contact information and data. Removing the card will not remove the information. You need to hard reset (or master reset) the device to purge this data. Google: master reset (model of phone)

Disposing of a Cell phone and **Personal Digital Assistant** (PDA's) may contain sensitive information, including bank account numbers, medical and prescription information, online access to shopping with credit card information, user names and passwords. Access to email accounts, both personal and business accounts. Voice mail, phone logs, contact lists containing names, address, and personal information may be available. Every type of personal electronic device operating system has been hacked. Hackers are motivated to stay ahead of everyone because the go where the money is.

Digital Assets that may be worth more than all of the liquid assets of the estate combined may be linked to these small impersonal devices. They are just waiting for someone with a modicum of tech knowledge to come along and release them for any purpose. This could be distribution of the estate or theft of the assets.

All personal electronic devices should be treated as if they contain extremely sensitive information.

GLOSSARY & INDEX
Terms and Definitions

Sensitive Information: The first thing you need to do is Identify what information is on the device. You may need help with this. Cell Phones may use encrypting passwords and the average person may be locked out of the device. If there is a Digital Executor enlist their assistance. When the information is located it must be preserved because this may be the only existing link to a valuable asset. Locate all sensitive information. Inventory all sensitive information. Protect and secure all sensitive information. At some time in the future this information may no longer be necessary and it may be advisable to eliminate it from the device.

Even after the cellphone is no longer in service sensitive information may still be removed from it with very inexpensive software.

Check messages, voice mail and the phone list of contacts. Make and keep a copy of phone numbers, names, and contact information. It may come in handy even a year or two later. What if you find out later on that Aunt Bernie really did have a lot of assets but left everything to the neighborhood bulldog? You may want someone who knew her to help verify she was crackers. It is always better to save it and not need it than to need it and not even have a clue where to look.

Identify Theft can be hindered by removing personal sensitive information with Permanent Data Deletion. This information is given as a basic example of what may be necessary not as a how-to. Technology changes so quickly today that more steps in the process may have already been added to the following information. In general: 1) remove the SIM card (subscriber identity module) from the phone. 2) Even if you use the Menu on the cellphone to delete information, this will only delete the references to where the information is and not the information itself. Permanent data deletion also may require you to clear data from the phone's contacts and other stored information. 3) A hard reset (or master reset) is needed to purge the device of this sensitive data. Your owner's manual, your wireless provider's website, or the manufacturer will likely provide information on how to permanently delete information.

Since this device was not yours you really do not know what kinds of information it contained it is still your responsibility to dispose of it properly. It most cases it is just a cellphone or personal device and it would most likely seem reasonable to treat it as such. In most cases it still should not be given away until you can "clear" the device. When the device is "clear" and safe to give away must be determined by the executor or personal representative. Err on the side of caution. Google wallet and AT&T, Inc. are both experimenting with digital money.

Cemetery

Cemetery or Memorial Park: An area of ground set aside for burial or entombment of the deceased. Most often Memorial parks allow only flat markers, while cemeteries allow markers of varying heights. Cemeteries can be large landscaped lawns or small architected memorial gardens. A body can be buried directly in the ground (green burial), in a casket, in a vault: above or below ground, individually or communally. Most often Memorial parks allow only flat markers, while cemeteries allow markers of varying heights.

County Cemetery: Does your county have a cemetery that is still in use and not just of historic significance? Most county cemeteries have more lenient regulations covering eligibility. General rules can be as simple as: 1) Primary residence in County for five years. 2) Tax payer in County for five years. 3) Or having a request in granted in writing by the Cemetery Board. Google: public burial cemetery (your county) (your state)

State Cemetery: Some state cemeteries are restricted to former members of the legislature or a member who dies in office; a former elective state official or an elective state official who dies in office or other "prominent" people.

State Veterans Cemeteries: Many states have established state veterans' cemeteries. The regulations vary from state to state. Google: veteran cemetery (your state of choice).

National Cemetery: All veterans are entitled to a free burial in a national cemetery and a grave marker if space is available. Benefits also extend to their spouse and families. Be sure to check on transportation costs, if any, to the National Cemetery. There are usually no charges for opening or closing the grave, for a vault or liner, or for setting the marker in a national cemetery. see *Veterans*, page 263, 447.

Green Cemetery, Green Burial: The purpose of a green burial is to return the body to the earth in a way that does not hinder decomposition. There are few green cemeteries in the U.S., but many existing cemeteries are allowing green burial. It is not only "green" it usually saves the consumer thousands of dollars.

Cemetery Deed: Also known as Certificate of Interment Rights or Deed for Interment Rights. The cemetery deed is the document from the cemetery that proves your right to burial or entombment or inurnment in an interment space. If the funeral director has the deed they must return it to you after the funeral. A cemetery deed can be difficult to replace so keep it in a safe place with your other important documents.

Cemetery Property: A grave, crypt or niche.

Owner of Burial Space: The owner is the person to whom the cemetery operator or his authorized agent has transferred the right of use of burial space.

Cemetery Services: Opening and closing graves, crypts or niches; setting grave liners and vaults; setting markers; and long-term maintenance of cemetery grounds and facilities.

Cenotaph: An empty tomb or monument erected in memory to someone buried elsewhere.

Certificate of Deposit: A certificate of deposit is a deposit of a specified amount of money in a bank, usually for a specified period of time at a fixed rate of interest. If it is a joint account it may pass to the survivor automatically. The account can be cleared with a certified copy of the death certificate any time. There may or may not be penalties for withdrawal or closing this account. Check with customer service at the bank where the account is located.

Certified Public Accountant, (CPA): A CPA is a professional accountant licensed by the state. They have taken and passed the uniform CPA examination administered by the American Institute of Certified Public Accountants, and have received state certification to practice accounting.

Chapel: A large room of the funeral home in which the farewell service is held.

Charity

Charitable Pledges: A charitable pledge is a legally binding contract between a donor and a charity (this may be a religious institution) in which the donor pledges to pay a certain amount of money in the future. We find these particularly reprehensible from a religious organization because they are not required by the Bible unless one goes out of their way to weave a specific set of conditions that would lead the unschooled to believe that they are in fact required. Under traditional contract law a charitable pledge may be enforceable. If you are the executor and this involves an amount that you consider significant this may be a good time to speak with a competent estate attorney. If the charity has taken an action based on the expectation of receiving the pledge than it can become a bit tricky. Not all states recognize "promissory estoppel" or "detrimental reliance". Ask your attorney because in most cases if the donor dies before fulfilling the pledge, the pledge is also enforceable under the donor's estate.

Faith Promise: A better way to "pledge" is called a Faith Promise. Tithing is and always should be a voluntary act. If you are required (forced) to tithe by a "church" or organization it is not a tithe. It is a TAX. Like joining the country club, you are paying dues and have signed a legal contract if you pledge. Tithing always needs to be done with the right attitude. A Faith Promise is a commitment to give a certain amount IF the Lord provides it. Too many

GLOSSARY & INDEX
Terms and Definitions

people today badger and continually ask for "Tithes" and then sit on the very committees that decide where this money is spent. Sometimes it goes directly to favorite "ministries". The executor or personal representative should never allow themselves to be badgered into giving sums of money they feel is in excess of normal fees for services just to use the "church" building or have this "religious person" say a few words at the service. Watch their eyes; the true vipers are just waiting to collect on what they now consider a previous customer. Sorry to have to tell you this. Google: Faith Promise /or pledge - for much more information. We are living in perilous times.

Charitable contributions made to qualified organizations may help lower your tax bill. If your goal is a legitimate tax deduction, then you must be giving to a qualified organization. Donations of stock or other non-cash property are usually valued at the fair market value of the property. There are many types of Trust accounts available that are beyond the scope of this book.

Charitable Transfers: Many states limit the amounts that may be transferred to charity at the expense of close family relatives.

Charitable Trust: For those of you in the planning or estate pre-planning stage a charitable remainder trust in which your spouse receives payments may actually increase the value of your spouse's estate so much that estate taxes are now due. If you are in this situation ask your competent estate attorney.

Charitable Lead Trust: If you are the executor a Charitable Lead Trust can be used to make a series of payments to a charitable organization and at some time in the future the remaining property in the trust reverts back to the donor or someone else as specified in the trust.

Charitable Remainder Trust: In a charitable remainder trust the beneficiary receives a specific amount of money for a specified time. At the end of that time whatever is left goes to the charity.

There are many, many types of Trust accounts that may be set up. As executor you may be dealing with one of these now. First Google the type of trust to see what you can find out. Then it may be a good time to seek the advice of a competent estate attorney.

Child Support: In many, if not most states, the obligation to pay Child Support continues after death. If a Life Insurance policy benefits children from a divorce this may be used to offset child support. You really need to speak with a competent estate attorney if this gives you a lot of room for thought. Read up on the "qualified domestic relations order." This can be used to prove your spouse received a share of your retirement accounts.

Children

Children and Grief: A child's understanding and reaction to death depends on their closeness to the deceased, their stage of development and the interactions with family and friends at the time of a loved one's death. Even babies can sense the emotions of those caring for them. Children are aware of death.

Young children have a growing curiosity about death and a vague understanding of what it means. They tend to think it is temporary and reversible. As they get older they begin to understand that death is permanent. At the age of nine they understand clinical death somewhat but think of it as something a long way off that may not touch them personally.

Acknowledge their feelings and understand that children deal with grief in many different ways. They go through the same process of denial, anger and sadness. Stay close and give them time to process all of the new information. They may be afraid the surviving parent will also leave them. Sometimes children will just be children and run and play. That is still all right. They may then come and tell you they want to go and be with the deceased. Listen to them and take them seriously. They are going through the loss without the knowledge and understanding an adult should have. Now is the time to answer their questions and help them develop a strong base to deal with this grief. If you think their behavior is extreme, talk to a counselor or other professional who can help.

When children return to school they face the added stress of answering questions from curious classmates. These children may have never experienced death themselves and do not understand exactly what happened. They are curious. It is Ok for the grieving child to keep things simple and acknowledge someone died without going into details. Inform their teacher before they return to class about the situation so they will be understanding and available to help.

When children reach their teens a death may cause others to shun them simply because they do not know what to say or what to do in this situation. The child is grieving and hurt while their friends may put them at some distance. Talk to them and listen to their feelings about what they are going through. It is going to pass very soon. Something different will focus their school mates attention next week but for right now, it can be painful. A child's grief can be spread over a few years.

When a Child Dies: The death of a child is particularly tragic. The family and friends are grieving. The other children must not be burdened with unrealistic expectations. It is common for children to idealize the deceased and feel very guilty for surviving. Talk to them and listen to their concerns. They will grieve in a way that is determined by their stage of maturity and the understanding they have of death and love. Allow them to ask questions but do not give them more information than they can process at their age level. Try to be sensitive, listen and accept their feelings and try to answer their questions in a brief, simple manner. None of us has all of the answers. It is Ok to say that you do not know or fully understand.

When a child passes it is natural for a parent to be very worried about the welfare of surviving children. They may be over protective and fearful. This is an extremely difficult time for the whole family and you may want or need to get professional help in dealing with your loss.

If a family's baby was stillborn it is just as much of a loss. The grieving process is the same and the sadness can reoccur from time-to-time for years. This is normal. Parents need to mourn the loss and each individual will grieve in their own way. Some individuals will show more emotion than others and some will be in denial for a much longer period of time. There are many support groups that help people deal with their loss.

Sometimes when a child dies, the grieving parents are told they can have more children. Anyone who has lost a child to death knows that a child cannot be replaced by having another baby.

Procreation: If a child is conceived by using posthumous sperm retrieval, is the deceased still considered to be the father of the child?

Citizenship Papers: Citizenship papers are documents confirming that someone has been awarded citizenship of a country he or she was not born in. A green card is a document showing evidence of lawful permanent resident status in the United States. They were originally green in color. It allows aliens to work legally in the United States. If the executor finds a green card this may signify employment by the deceased. If there was employment there may be insurance connected with the employer.

Clearing Title: A clear title is a title that is free of liens and legal questions as to ownership of the property. It is a requirement for the sale of real estate. The name of the deceased has been legally removed from the deed of the property and replaced with the name(s) of the beneficiaries or heirs.

Clergy, Religious Leadership, all faiths & ethnicities

Religious leadership should be contacted as soon as possible. Many religions have time constraints on the disposition of the deceased's remains. Did the deceased have any religious affiliation? Is there a Church, Synagogue or religious institution listed in the deceased's address book? Are there any contact numbers? If there are; call and explain the situation and ask what the normal procedure is. Write things down and make a decision latter on as to what course of action you will follow.

If there is no religious affiliation the person taking care of the funeral or cremation usually has someone on call to take care of the funeral service, graveside service or memorial service. The service leader does not have to be ordained or licensed and can be of your own choosing.

GLOSSARY & INDEX
Terms and Definitions

Honorariums for Religious Leaders: A payment given to a professional person for services for which fees are not legally or traditionally required. The honorarium for the individual clergy to perform a graveside service or memorial service range from $50 to $500. The fee for a Celebrant is usually between $300 and $900. The fee for the building where the service is to take place is additional. The fee for an organist, pianist, or soloist is an additional $100 to $300 each.

Close the Estate: The duties of the executor begin from the time of death and continue until the Probate Court releases them from their duties. The executor or personal representative must complete all of their duties before the court will close the estate and release the executor. see *Time Line*, page 54, *Executor*, 138

Codicil: A codicil is a modification, supplement or amendment. Applied to a Will it is in addition to and not necessarily disposing of the entire estate but modifying, explaining, or otherwise qualifying the Will in some way. When admitted to probate, the codicil becomes a part of the Will.

Coffin: A coffin, by definition, is a case or receptacle for the disposition of human remains which has six or eight sides. A casket has straight sides.

Columbarium: A columbarium is a structure with niches (small spaces) for placing cremated remains in urns or other approved containers. It may be outdoors or part of a mausoleum. They may have marble, granite or even glass fronts for viewing the cremation urns.

Commingling of Assets: An account consisting of assets from several different accounts that are mixed together. Issues about commingling of assets, personal property and bank accounts are more likely with unmarried couples living together. If they were married and a spouse dies without a Will or a Trust, under the probate laws the surviving spouse will be entitled to inherit most, if not all of that spouses assets. If you are cohabitating with another individual and they die, you are entitled to none of their assets if there is no Will or Trust. If the two unmarried partners have children from a previous relationship, there are issues as to whether the children will inherit anything or whether it will pass to the surviving partner or next of kin. If there is commingling of assets now may be a good time to speak with a competent professional.

Committal Service: The final portion of the funeral service at which time the deceased is interred or entombed.

Community Mausoleum: A mausoleum above ground, or partially above and partially below ground, containing crypts and niches for use by members of the general public to inter remains.

Community Niche: A community niche is a common area where several cremation containers may be placed.

Community Property: In some community property states assets are considered to be joint property under certain conditions and debts are also considered to be joint debt under certain conditions. In some community property states even if there is only one name on the title to property the law may limit what you can now do with it. Depending on state law you may be able to only transfer one half of the interest in such property. Some states have additional protection for spouses.

Laws change every day. It is always your responsibility to use due diligence and review the laws in your state and county. Check the state law.

Companion Lawn Crypts: A companion or multiple lawn crypts are an interment space in the Cemetery which contains a vault capable of holding two or more caskets.

Companion Lawn Niche: A companion or multiple lawn niches is a space in an urn garden, designed to accommodate two cremated remains. Companion Lawn Urn: A companion lawn urn is a receptacle usually made of bronze or granite in which two cremated remains may be placed.

Computers and Copiers: Computer hard drives and copier memory may hold vast amounts of personal information. These need to be scrubbed clean. see *Digital Assets*, page 40, 250, 333

Computer Security: Do not give computers away without first scrubbing the drives or removing them. see *Digital Assets*, page 40, 250, 333

GLOSSARY & INDEX
Terms and Definitions

Condolence Letter

Condolence: Most people do not know what to say. This is a very confusing time for the family and friends. No matter how you express your sympathy, it is important to clearly identify yourself to the family. The fact that you care is more important than your exact words. The family receives great comfort from reading engaging and heartfelt letters and notes acknowledging their loss.

Even though many of us feel awkward and uncomfortable when faced with the death of a loved one a letter of condolence should be written and sent promptly within two weeks. If you write the letter in a normal manner, the same way you would speak to the person it should be fine. You want to let them know they are in your thoughts.

Condolence Letter or Sympathy Letter: A condolence letter can be as short as a few sentences and should be written on good stationary. It is an expression of sympathy to a person who has experienced grief or misfortune and is usually greatly appreciated by those who are grieving. They are very thankful that other people are thinking about them and this helps in their healing process. Mention the name of the deceased and acknowledge the loss. You may use the word death or passed away and if you can include a happy memory of the deceased. Close with something like: (Name of deceased) will be missed.

Do not try to explain the loss. Do not make comparisons. Do not tell them that you understand what they are going through unless you have had the exact same situation. Losing a child is not the same as losing a pet. Do not share private information the deceased never told anyone. They never told anyone for a good reason. Respect that.

Do not express relief that the person passed after a very long illness. There are a lot of emotions that must be dealt with now. Saying the surviving spouse or family member is blessed because the long ordeal is now over is not the most tactful thing to say. You may feel a need to offer assistance, but do not make offers that you are not able and willing to fulfill. Do not ask about the Will.

When you are finished writing the condolence letter, read it out loud. It should sound like you are just talking to the person. Keep it simple.

Condolence Card: Condolence or sympathy card. Just a short note expressing your sympathy for someone who has suffered a loss.

Congressman: If you feel like you are being lied to or treated unfairly Google: congressman, (your county) (your state) get your congressman's phone number and call them. Your local congressman and their staff will be more than happy to assist you in your time of need.

Conservator or Guardian: A Guardian or Conservator may be appointed to handle a person's financial affairs if they become incapacitated. see *Guardian*, page 366

Coroner: A coroner or medical examiner is similar but not exactly the same in all circumstances. The designation, duties and qualifications vary from state to state. A coroner or medical examiner is a public official that investigates any death thought to be of other than natural causes or if there was no physician in attendance for a long time prior to death.

Corpse: Who owns the body? Common law appears to say the corpse is the same as the person and cannot be owned. In most cases, the person in charge of the disposition of the body has a right to possess for disposition. The surviving spouse usually has the principal right to custody of the remains and to burial. In the case of the death of a child of divorced parents, the right to possess for disposition is usually awarded to the parent who had custody.

> In many cases right to possess for disposition will fall upon the personal representative or executor of the deceased. If a person is not named in the Will to oversee the estate, the rights of possession for disposition are usually held by the surviving spouse or next of kin. Following burial, the body is considered part of the ground in which it is placed and the law owns the body and has jurisdiction over it. An exception may be when an organ donor gives body parts away at death. It should be obvious they could not be reclaimed if they were in use.

At times, the need to perform an autopsy or postmortem examination gives the local coroner a superior right to possess the dead body until such an examination is performed.

If the person dies in a medical facility such as a hospital or hospice, the attending medical personnel will sign the death certificate and release the body for disposition. Hospitals, may release the deceased to a funeral home without input from the decedent's legal representative in order to conserve space. The legal representative has a right to move the body.

A corpse may not be retained by a funeral home as security for unpaid expenses. They may not hold a body without authorization and demand payment as a condition precedent to its release.

Copiers: The internal hard drives on home and office copy machines retain sensitive information. This information is almost never scrubbed clean and could be a jackpot for an identity thief. Before you dispose of any home or office copier, remove and destroy the hard drive, or internal memory. If the machine is leased, software can be purchased to scrub (wipe clean, permanently remove) the data.

Cortege: A cortege is referring to the funeral procession.

Cosmetology and Hairstyle: Utilization of cosmetics to restore a life-like appearance to the deceased.

Costco: Caskets, urns, and funeral items. http://www.costco.com Search/funeral

Cot: The stretcher-like carrier used to remove deceased persons from the place of death to the funeral home.

Court Fees: Court fees are dictated by state law and can range anywhere from a few hundred dollars to over a thousand dollars.

Credit Cards, Charge Cards: Identify authorized users for each credit card and account. If another person is added to the account as an authorized user, depending upon the company specific terms, he or she may be agreeing to repay all of the debt when using the card.

Creditors: A person or institution to which money or assets are owed.

Credit Report: A credit report contains detailed information on a person's credit history, including identifying information, credit accounts, loans, bankruptcies and late payments. The executor should get a current credit report from the big three credit reporting agencies in the United States: Experian, Transunion & Equifax. This may help locate assets.

Cremation

Cremation: Reduction of the body to ashes, (cremains), by fire. The ashes may be buried, placed in a columbarium, or kept in your home. An urn may be purchased for the cremains rather than use the container provided by the crematory. You may also dispose of the cremains in any manner that complies with local health department or other regulations.

Cremation Authorization Form: Since cremation is irreversible a cremation authorization form must be filled out and signed by the executor, the personal representative or the next of kin agreeing to the process of cremation for the deceased. In most states, individuals are allowed to sign their own authorization prior to death.

Stopping a Cremation: In most all states at any time after executing a cremation authorization form and prior to the beginning of the cremation process, the authorizing agent who executed the cremation authorization form may modify the arrangements for the final disposition of the cremated remains of the decedent set forth in the authorization form or may, in writing, revoke the authorization, cancel the cremation, and claim the decedent's body for purposes of making alternative arrangements for the final disposition of the decedent's body. So if you or someone else changes their mind you may stop the cremation in most cases if it has not already been started.

Cremains: Also called cremains are another term for the decedent's ashes. Who owns cremation ashes? Common law appears to say the ashes are the same as the person and cannot be owned. In most cases, the person in charge of the disposition of the body has a right to possess the ashes for disposition.

GLOSSARY & INDEX
Terms and Definitions

Cremated Remains, Ashes, or Cremains: The portion of a body remaining after cremation.

Cremation Permit: A certificate issued by local government authorizing cremation of the deceased.

Crematory: A building housing a furnace for cremating remains.

Cremation Vault: A cremation vault is a container for an urn. They can be made from marble, granite, metal or concrete.

Crypt: A crypt is usually beneath the floor of a church. A crypt can also be any underground space in a mausoleum or other building to hold cremated or whole remains.

Custodial Care: Custodial care is a service of a nonmedical nature provided on a long-term basis. It is also a fee the funeral home may charge for days that the body is being held and no other services are being provided. This fee must be disclosed and identified as a daily, weekly or one-time fee.

Customer: A customer is the person making funeral arraignments. The customer may be a family member, legal representative or a friend legally designated by the decedent. The customer will be legally responsible for the payment of the funeral bill.

Customer's Designation of Intentions: a specific form that the funeral director will complete if you select cremation. Cremation is not reversible so you must sign a form. In most states there is a time limit for the executor or personal representative to pick up the cremains or the funeral service has the right to dispose of them. You must be given a copy of everything you sign before you leave the funeral service provider.

D

Dying

What to Expect: In 2012 the process of death seems to be a lot lonelier. Many people no longer die in their homes, but die instead in hospitals or nursing homes. Their loved ones may be living in a distant state and the dying become isolated.

With nearly 80,000,000 boomers approaching the end of life the world will see more unprepared deaths even when they are of natural causes and a normal part of life. Assets will be striped. Homes will still have mortgages. Bank accounts that were once full will be close to empty.

People that should know better are going to be leaving without a Will or tipping the doorman.

Instead of leaving another burden for someone else to clean up have the decency to leave with a certain amount of grace and consideration. Prepare a notebook with information needed by their executor (access to assets, an inventory and appraisal of assets, a list of all documents and there location, keys, codes, passwords, usernames, the list is longer. If you do not finish, we understand, but at least start today. Do not put this off any longer.

Death Experience: As we go through the death experience we must cope with many different emotions: scared, angry, sad, worried, shocked, unprepared, or confused. We are sometimes angry and then relieved and at peace. Anxiety is perfectly normal and quite common.

Physical Changes to look for include: the body temperature lowers slightly, the blood pressure lowers slightly, and the pulse becomes irregular and may slow down or speed up. The body is having a more difficult time maintaining itself. There may be an increase in perspiration. The skin color will change as the circulation of blood becomes slower. The lips and nails may become pale and bluish. Breathing often becomes more rapid and labored. Congestion may also occur causing a rattling sound and cough. Speaking decreases and eventually stops altogether.

Death

Pre-Death: As a person prepares for death there are some outward signs that bodily systems are slowing down. The person begins sleeping more to conserve the little energy that is left. They may lose the desire to eat and then to drink. Swallowing becomes difficult and the mouth becomes very dry. Wet the lips with a cool cloth dipped in water. They will lose bladder and bowel control, but accidents will occur less frequently as they consume less.

The person may be overly communicative to see if you are ready to let them go. Gently tell them what you most need to say and let them go.

The night before a person dies can be difficult to watch. The person often is disoriented and seems like they cannot find a comfortable position. There is also labored breathing, shortness of breath and gasps for air. Elevating the head, and/or turning the person onto their side may bring comfort.

Most experts believe the process is not painful and the person has a sense of well-being and peace as the body begins to shut down. The person's hands and arms, feet and then legs become increasingly cool to the touch as blood circulation slows. The person may speak or claim to have spoken with others who have already died. This is very real to them even if you cannot see or hear it. This is a normal experience. They will begin to withdraw from the surroundings but can hear right up to the end. Holding their hand and speaking gently to them will help them to let go.

Death: Even though the death is expected and people are prepared for the death process they may not be prepared for the actual death. It can be difficult and the process of acceptance can be different for everyone. When death occurs there will be no response. Breathing will stop and there will be no pulse. The eyelids may be open or closed and the eyes will be fixed in one direction. There may be loss of control of the bladder or bowel.

The body does not have to be moved until you are ready. If the family wants to assist in preparing the body by bathing and dressing, that may be done. Make the First Call.

Harvard Medical School newly defined death as irreversible damage to the brain, or brain death, in 1968.

Expected Death: If no further medical intervention is required.

No further medical intervention is normally required if the person passed while in a hospital, or under a doctor's care at a nursing home, assisted living facility or at a home residence with Hospice. You will most likely not need to call 911, the Police, or the Fire department after death has occurred.

First Call: If you have health care professionals involved in the care of the dying person they should be notified of the death, where the death took place and the circumstances of death. You will need to call the Doctor, Hospice Nurse or the health care professionals involved. Phone numbers can sometimes be found on the patient's medication.

Medical Facility or Hospice: If the person dies in a medical facility such as a hospital or hospice, the attending medical personnel will sign the death certificate and release the body for disposition.

Unexpected Death

If the person dies anywhere else call the police by dialing 911.

First Call: If you are not sure what to do, call 911. What happens next will be determined by state law. In most cases a medical examiner or coroner, will be dispatched. If the medical examiner or coroner determines the person died of natural causes they will sign a death certificate and the body will be released.

If the medical examiner or coroner cannot determine the cause of death the body will be moved for an autopsy. When the autopsy is completed the medical examiner or coroner will sign the death certificate and the body will be released for disposition.

Remain in communication with the medical examiners, (coroners) office to determine the status of the death certificate and release date of the body.

Death Certificate

Death Certificate: A death certificate is a legal document issued by a medical practitioner certifying a person as deceased. It is signed by the attending physician showing the date, location, cause of a person's death and other vital statistical data pertaining to the deceased. The death certificate is usually filled with the clerk in the county where the death took place within twenty-four hours of the death and may still be open to correction for six months.

Certified Death Certificate: A certified death certificate is a legal copy of the original death certificate issued by the local government and certified to be a true copy of the original. It is used mostly for the purpose of substantiating claims by the estate or family of the deceased. In most cases a relative or someone with a proven financial interest in an individual's death can legally obtain a certified copy of the death certificate. This most often includes (but not in every instance) a member of the immediate family, which includes wife, husband, son, daughter, mother, father, brother, sister, grandmother, grandfather, grandchild, aunt, uncle, niece, nephew and in-law. This does not include cousins in most locals. Others may include a guardian, foster parent, step-parent and attorney acting on behalf of the registrant or family and as we mentioned, anyone with a proven financial interest.

Number of Copies: Arrange to receive several copies of the death certificate. Twelve is not too many in most cases (the Funeral Home can request these for you). To estimate how many you need get one each for every bank or investment account, real estate owned either solely or jointly, each life insurance policy, each pension and retirement plan, and one for passport cancellation (if you cancel the passport).

Certified Copies are necessary to claim insurance proceeds and to transfer money out of bank, brokerage and mutual fund accounts. It is much easier to get a few too many than to try to get one or two more later on. Twenty is not an unreasonable number as it can be very time consuming to try to get these later. Death certificates cost between $8.00 and $25.00 per copy depending on where they are filled in the US. You may request them from the funeral director (if you are using the services of one) or directly from the Bureau of Vital Statistics.

Photocopies of the certificate are sufficient in many cases to cancel a driver's license, voter's registration, or to request a presidential memorial certificate. You may request that companies return all original documents including death certificates once they have reviewed them for authenticity. You may then reuse these as necessary.

Bureau of Vital Statistics: You can request certified copies of the death certificate from the Bureau of Vital Statistics in the state or county where the death took place.

Information Needed: To obtain copies you will need the following information:

1) The full name of the deceased.

2) Male or Female

3) Date and place of death. The place of death should include the city or town, county and state.

4) The deceased's relationship to the person filling the request and the reason the certified copies are needed. (To settle the deceased's estate.)

5) The person making the request will provide their name, address and some proof of identity. A driver license or similar identity card is most often used. The person making the request then signs the form. In all cases an I.D. is not required to request certified copies.

Death Notice: A published notice of a death, sometimes with a brief biography of the deceased. An obituary can be considered a death notice.

Death Records: official records of deaths.

A Directory of links to websites with online death indexes, listed by state and county. Included are death records, death certificate indexes, death notices &

GLOSSARY & INDEX
Terms and Definitions

registers, obituaries, probate indexes, and cemetery & burial records.
http://www.deathindexes.com/

A Guide to Finding Death Records and Databases on the Internet
http://death-records.net/

Death Public Records Search Guide: The Free Guide for How and Where to Find death records and Certified death certificates in all 50 states.
http://deathrecordsonline.org/

Social Security Death Index (SSDI): http://ssdi.rootsweb.ancestry.com/

Debts: There are debts to collect and debts to pay. If a probate estate is opened, the probate estate is primarily liable for decedent's debts.

Unsecured Debt: see *Debt*, page 112

Debtor's Examination: A legal proceeding in which the creditor is allowed to ask the debtor questions about current income and assets. Unfortunately, the debtor has time to withdraw funds from the account prior to the examination, but an examination of the bank's records may reveal information regarding a possible transfer of funds to another account.

Deceased: A person who has died.

Decedent: A person who has died.

Dementia

Dementia: A group of symptoms affecting intellectual and social abilities severely enough to interfere with daily functioning. There are many causes of dementia. Alzheimer's disease is the most common cause of a progressive dementia. One in eight older Americans has Alzheimer's disease. More than 15 million Americans provide unpaid care valued at $210 billion for persons with Alzheimer's and other dementias. Alzheimer's disease is the sixth-leading cause of death in the United States and the only cause of death among the top

10 in the United States that cannot be prevented, cured or even slowed. alz.org

In most cases a person with dementia can still make or change a Will if they can show that they understand what they are doing and what the effects of their actions are going to be.

Joint Will: many couples think they have a "joint Will" because it is a mirror image Will that is the same for each spouse. Each usually leaves everything to the other surviving partner. If one of the partners is stricken with dementia either in the earliest stages or very advanced stages the other partner usually needs to correct their own Will to name a guardian or provide care if the surviving partner has dementia.

Dementia and Changing the Will: You are dealing with a person who is not thinking clearly. They may, and often do, change their Will often. In most cases a person with dementia can still make or change a Will if they can show that they understand what they are doing and what the effects of it will be. This needs to be addressed before a medical and financial crisis takes place. Proof of incapacity should be taken care of early.

If there is a named Durable Power of Attorney, successor trustee or Medical Advocate. They need to get the individual showing signs of dementia to a doctor as soon as possible and obtain the necessary signatures from the doctors verifying the individual should no longer be able to make medical and financial decisions for themselves or others. This then allows the person with power of attorney or the person named as trustee or medical advocate to begin serving. If you wait, things only get worse. This can be time consuming, expensive and very painful to the loved one. If there are any problems with the necessary paperwork they can be addressed while you still have a little time. Do not wait for a crisis to occur. You are no longer dealing with the same person you may have known for most of, or all of your lifetime. They are sick.

Designation of Patient Advocate: A written statement of a person's wishes regarding medical treatment. A health care directive.

GLOSSARY & INDEX
Terms and Definitions

Digital Assets

Many of the assets are the same as those listed under Assets page 57 but the access is online. Sometimes a bank account or a brokerage account is located in another state and access is online with passwords, user names and challenge questions. Locate all Passwords & Usernames, encryption, Keys, PINs, Combinations and challenge questions. If you are preplanning do not leave this information in your Will because it is going to be made public after your death.

Software: There are software programs that may be able to unlock and reset current passwords. Google: password recovery

Locate: All computers, laptops, tablets, PC, Macs, eBook readers, storage, hard drives, cell phones, iPhones, iPods, iPads, answering machines, Wii, PlayStations, PSP, PS3, Xbox, thumb drives and digital cameras. Copiers are very important as they contain very sensitive information in memory.

Computer Software can cost thousands of dollars and must be considered an asset. Sometimes you may not just move software from one computer to another. If you do not understand the legal ownership and rights of possession of computer software find a friend or family member who is competent in handling digital accounts.

Online Websites: Websites that may have value or contain user information that should be cleaned include but are not limited to: brokerage sites, gambling sites, online shopping sites, email accounts, blogs, photo storage sites, online subscriptions with automatic renewal, online banking, online bill paying, online credit card access, mortgage providers, college savings accounts, retirement plans, automatic bill paying for (anything) utilities and cell phones, and online tax software that may have copies of the deceased's returns.

Online Billing: There are more people than ever using paperless billing and statements online. These and all online accounts need to be analyzed. Make copies of everything and then most accounts will need to be cleaned and closed. Be careful before you clear or close accounts. Do they have any special privileges like ordering season tickets? Can this be resold or reassigned to someone else? In any case, be careful before you delete or clear anything. If you need help now would be a good time to seek out a competent individual.

Media: There may also be videos of other assets, movie videos, mp3 files, mp4 files, and social networking websites. Collect All CD's DVD's do not assume it is a movie just because someone printed "Movie" on the disk with a marker. These will all have to be viewed by someone. They may contain ANYTHING! They may contain video of hidden collections, documents or a whole other life no one ever knew about. They may contain maps and directions to hidden treasures that the loved one was keeping safe for their beneficiary(s).

Royalties, Copyrights or Patents: Much of the information necessary to locate these can be found online in documents or statements.

Stocks and Bonds: Today electronic transfers are most common. Hard copies are less common but you may still find them. Most people would leave the actual certificate with a broker or agent. Some old certificates are worth more to collectors than their actual monetary worth. An original stock certificate for Joe Namath's New York restaurant registers 100 shares, is green and white like the New York Jets colors, and includes a small football player graphic (approximate worth $99.) Certificates from old gold mines, land companies and railroads may be worth millions or a few hundred dollars. It is up to the executor to show due diligence in valuing these.

All digital Assets must be protected and distributed. The Digital Executor can be very helpful. Most Americans have a digital presence that needs to be located, collected, appraised, and protected.

Computers: Before you dispose of any computer you should wipe the hard drive clean of all data. When you use the "delete" function or "empty recycle bin" you do not remove data. You are only removing the sign post pointing to it. The data is still there and can be recovered. A digital executor or a knowledgeable trustworthy individual may be able to help with this. If you cannot do this you may want to remove the hard drives.

GLOSSARY & INDEX
Terms and Definitions

Copiers: The internal hard drives on home and office copy machines retain sensitive information. This information is almost never scrubbed clean and could be a jackpot for an identity thief. Before you dispose of any home or office copier, remove and destroy the hard drive, or internal memory. If the machine is leased, software can be purchased to scrub (wipe clean, permanently remove) the data. The executor should never give away the old copier or computers, hard drives, storage devices of any kind without first permanently removing all data so that it is considered unrecoverable. Be careful not to remove data that you need or want. A digital executor is often necessary to help in doing this.

Born-digital Assets: Assets that began in a digital form such as digital art, photographs, manuscripts, some documents etc.

Digital Estate: All digitally stored content and accounts owned by an individual at death. The digital estate of the deceased needs to be located, reviewed and distributed as required by a valid Will or the probate court.

Digital Executor or Digital Administrator: People are naming a Digital Executor more often but state laws have not kept up with the need. The executor still has all legal responsibility for the dispensation of the estate including the distribution of all digital assets to the beneficiaries by providing them with the necessary content and/ or access information. Some digital assets may still need to be posted online after death and files may need to be deleted and hard storage scrubbed clean.

The executor has the legal responsibility for disposition of the estate. The digital executor helps with Digital Assets: online storage "in the cloud", online shopping sites, websites, blogs, videos, CD's, DVD's (some contain important documents and may be password protected or encrypted). Family photos all stored online, on DVDs or thumb drives. There are passwords, encryption, challenge codes, social networking websites. All digital Assets must be protected and distributed. The Digital Executor can be very helpful.

The executor of the estate may not know how to find or even access Digital Assets worth hundreds of thousands of dollars. They may not even be aware off their worth. Facebook's $1 billion acquisition of the mobile start-up

Instagram changed a lot of things. Today something as simple (to the untrained) as an "app" could be worth millions of dollars only if it is turned into a more liquid asset quickly. If you have Digital Assets it is important to protect them with a Digital Administrator that could possibly act as executor of the estate. In any case if you have any digital assets (and we all do) you may need to allow your executor to access this information. Make them aware of your digital executor. If you name your digital executor as a beneficiary the executor is obligated by law to inform them of your death and send them a copy of your Will.

There are new business's that specialize in administering digital estates for a fee. There are few regulations so buyer beware holds true. Be careful.

Digital Wallet: software that allows you to pay for things using your cell phone. An individual's bank account is usually linked to the digital wallet.

Direct Burial: Have the funeral home place the deceased in the least expensive casket available or have one shipped to the funeral home from an outside vendor, online or local. Then ask for the body to be sent directly to the cemetery for burial. Embalming is not required or necessary. If a refrigeration charge is added that is substantial, use another funeral home or call your state representative for advice in this time of need.

Direct Cremation: A direct cremation package usually includes transportation, brief storage of the body, document processing (permits, death certificate), a container (usually cardboard) for the body prior to and during cremation, and a basic container (cardboard or plastic) for the ashes. This is the type (not guaranteed) of container the TSA suggests for airline passengers to carry on. The cost averages $1,000.

Disability Claims: Filing a claim for disability. An executor may find evidence of disability claims that were providing benefits to the deceased and will have to be stopped. Even if you can work in another occupation, you still receive disability benefits. The definition of disability under Social Security is different than other programs. Some insurance policies pay disability benefits.

Disbursement Fees: Disbursement fees are charges the crematorium or funeral service provider makes on the behalf of others such as a doctor's office or clergy. If you do not understand what you are being charged for ask for a written good faith estimate itemizing all fees and charges.

Discharge Papers: Discharge papers are very important in establishing eligibility for Veteran's benefits. DD-214 see *Veterans*, page 263, 447

Disinter: To remove the remains from a burial place.

Disinterment and Reburial: State law varies from state to state and even within a state but the cost for disinterment and reburial is generally the responsibility of the person who caused it to be done.

Display Room: A room in the funeral home for the display of caskets, urns, and burial garments. Sometimes expensive vaults are displayed.

Disposition: Disposition of remains is in the public interest: health, safety and welfare. There is much room for personal expression and religious beliefs but it is governed by state and federal law. Legal disposition includes burial, cremation or alkaline hydrolysis.

Disposition Permit: A disposition permit is required prior to burial, entombment or cremation of a body. This document is signed by a medical professional or a medical examiner and releases a body for disposition either in the form of burial or cremation. A cemetery will also require this document for burial even if a cremation was performed.

Direct Burial: The body is buried shortly after death, usually in a simple container. No viewing or visitation is involved, so no embalming is necessary. A memorial service may be held at the graveside or later. Direct burial usually costs less than the "traditional," full-service funeral. Costs include the funeral home's basic services fee, as well as transportation and care of the body, the purchase of a casket or burial container and a cemetery plot or crypt. If the family chooses to be at the cemetery for the burial, the funeral home often charges an additional fee for a graveside service.

Direct Cremation: The body is cremated shortly after death, without embalming. The cremated remains are placed in an urn or other container. No viewing or visitation is involved, although a memorial service may be held, with or without the cremated remains present. The remains can be kept in the home, buried or placed in a crypt or niche in a cemetery, or buried or scattered in a favorite spot. Direct cremation usually costs less than the "traditional," full-service funeral. Costs include the funeral home's basic services fee, as well as transportation and care of the body. A crematory fee may be included or, if the funeral home does not own the crematory, the fee may be added on. There also will be a charge for an urn or other container. The cost of a cemetery plot or crypt is included only if the remains are buried or entombed.

Funeral providers who offer direct cremations also must offer to provide an alternative container that can be used in place of a casket.

Documents, Signing: Know what you are signing. If you are the spouse of someone with a medical situation you need to know and understand the implications of what is going to happen if: 1) everything goes as planned with no surprises. 2) Surprise! You do not qualify for the benefit and now you must pay the bill because you signed. 3) Surprise! Your spouse qualifies for Medicare or Medicaid but you do not and now you must pay the bill from your own funds because by signing you took responsibility for paying the debt. If you had talked with a professional well versed in the area of health care where you need assistance this may have been avoided. At the very least you would not be surprised.

Most people do not understand anything about what they are signing; they are just told to, "Sign Here" and they do it. Most people who are telling you to, "Just sign here." do not understand what it is that you are signing or what they are required to explain to you by law. Their job is to have you sign the documents. Remember what happened with all of the foreclosure documents that employees were told to sign? I do not know of anyone except a professional that is working in the area that actually understands what the document means you are legally libel for once you sign. You could have a lien placed on your home and it is a real concern that your home could be taken from you if you made an error in judgment. Be careful. Get some help.

Do-Not-Resuscitate (DNR): If a medical emergency occurs, this form alerts emergency personnel that you do not wish to receive cardiopulmonary resuscitation (CPR). Your doctor can add a DNR order to your medical record if you are in a hospital. You may also create a pre-hospital DNR to alert paramedics. You should also obtain an easily identifiable Medic Alert bracelet, anklet, or necklace.

Domestic Relations Order: A qualified domestic relations order is usually found in a divorce agreement and recognizes that an ex-spouse is entitled to receive a predefined portion of the former spouse's retirement plan. In most cases the QDRO assigns 50% of the value of the assets gained from the beginning of the marriage to the time of the divorce to the ex-spouse. The executor must be aware of previous marriages.

Donor: A person who donates something.

Donor Card: A card that you carry with you to alert medical personal of your intentions regarding organ and/or tissue donation at the time of your death.

Direct Disposition: Arraignments made for the disposition of the body without formal viewing, visitation, or ceremony.

Department of Motor Vehicles (DMV)

Driver's License: The Department of Motor Vehicles (DMV) tries to make it easy to clear settle the vehicle and driver's license records when someone passes away. This is not difficult but the law varies as to the exact procedure from state to state. In some states it may be all right for the Heir to sign for the deceased and in other states a clerk at the DMV may want to witness the Heir as they sign for the deceased. Google: dmv deceased (the state in which the vehicle was titled or your state of residence.). Call them first and follow the instructions.

Cancel the driver's license or identification Card.

Cancel license plates (Tags). The Tags usually remain valid until the end of the current registration period or ownership is transferred.

Cancel Disabled Placard. Also call or visit customer service at the DMV office.

Transfer vehicle ownership, Titles: Usually the executor will need a certified copy of the death certificate, the vehicle title a court-issued document or Will appointing the executor or administrator and payment of appropriate fees.

Transfer vehicle registrations.

In almost all cases you will need a copy of the death certificate and the driver's license or ID card. Changing or removing the name of the deceased may help to prevent identity theft.

Joint Owner with the Right of Survivorship: You are usually considered a joint owner with the right of survivorship if: 1) your name is listed on the title as one of the vehicle owners and "or" appears between the names listed, 2) the words "or survivor" appear after the names, or the words "Tenants by the Entireties" or "Tenants by the Entirety" appear after the names.

Durable Financial Power-of-Attorney: Without a durable financial power-of-attorney it is extremely difficult if not impossible to make financial decisions in a timely manner on your behalf if you are incapacitated.

Durable Power of Attorney: In estate planning, a durable power of attorney is often chosen as a way to plan for those times when you are incapacitated. With a durable power of attorney, you are able to appoint an agent to manage your financial affairs, make health care decisions, or conduct other business for you during your incapacitation A durable power of attorney may be general or limited. A general durable power of attorney may allow your agent to do every act which may legally be done by you. A limited durable power of attorney cover specific events, like selling property, making investments, or making health care decisions.

The durable power of attorney for health care is a limited durable power of attorney created only for the purpose of making health care decisions. There may be slight legal differences depending on the state you reside in or become incapacitated in.

The durable power of attorney for health care can do everything that a living will can do. In addition, it gives your agent the power to actively remind your physician of your wishes. Your agent will make all of your health care decisions in the event you become incapacitated. The agent must follow your wishes and must consider your physician's recommendations. Any decision must also be within the range of accepted medical practice.

In most instances the durable power of attorney ends when the person dies but many states are now allowing the agent permission to oversee the final disposition of the body, including authorizing an autopsy and following your wishes for organ and tissue donation.

Possible Liability: As the Durable power of attorney you will most likely be the first in line to be held, legally responsible to pay for the disposition of the body in the event of death. Even if there are no assets in the estate after taxes and fees are paid you may be next in line to pay from your own resources. Now might be a good time to speak with a competent estate attorney. Yes, a few states can compel someone to pay for a funeral under certain circumstances.

E

Elder Law: Elder law is a specialty in legal practice, covering estate planning, Wills, trusts, arrangements for care, social security and retirement benefits, protection against elder abuse (physical, emotional and financial), and other concerns of older people.

Embalming

Embalming is generally not necessary or legally required if the deceased is to be buried or cremated shortly after death except under special circumstances. Most states do not allow disposition prior to two days, to allow time to determine and document the cause of death. Usually bodies are refrigerated for temporary preservation but each state specifies how many days a body can be kept without embalming, usually 2-5 days. Foregoing embalming can save hundreds of dollars and most loved ones can be presented very nicely without it if you have the viewing within a few days of death.

Refrigeration: If a funeral home or service provider does not have a refrigerated holding room or they charge an excessive fee for its use look for another funeral home that can meet your needs at less cost.

Embalming: Embalming is the process of preserving a dead body by means of circulating a preservative embalming fluid through the veins and arteries and must be performed by a licensed death care professional. The funeral service provider must disclose in writing that you usually have the right to choose a disposition, such as direct cremation or immediate burial that does not require embalming if you do not want this service. The Centers for Disease Control has consistently shown that embalming does not serve any public health purpose.

Embalming Authorization: Embalming authorization allows a body to be embalmed by a licensed death care professional.

Unauthorized Embalming: Unauthorized embalming of a body, by and of, itself does not necessarily support a cause of action for damages based upon mutilation or mishandling. Legal action might be brought if unauthorized embalming occurs, combined with the resulting mental suffering of the next of kin and other such factors. Now would be a good time to speak with a competent attorney.

Funeral Rule: The Funeral Rule prohibits funeral providers from claiming that any process or product can preserve remains in the grave indefinitely. They may not state that embalming or a particular casket or liner will preserve the body of the deceased for an unlimited time.

Many funeral homes require embalming if you're planning a viewing or visitation. But embalming generally is not necessary or legally required if the body is buried or cremated shortly after death. Eliminating this service can save you hundreds of dollars.

Under the Funeral Rule, a funeral provider:

- may not provide embalming services without permission.

- may not falsely state that embalming is required by law.

- must disclose in writing that embalming is not required by law, except in certain special cases.

- may not charge a fee for unauthorized embalming unless embalming is required by state law.

- must disclose in writing that you usually have the right to choose a disposition, such as direct cremation or immediate burial, that does not require embalming if you do not want this service.

- must disclose in writing that some funeral arrangements, such as a funeral with viewing, may make embalming a practical necessity and, if so, a required purchase.

http://www.ftc.gov/bcp/edu/pubs/consumer/products/pro19.shtm

Employment ID's: A photo ID card can be used by employees to gain access to a secure building. It is an identification card bearing a photographic image of the cardholder. The image can be an actual photograph or one captured wholly electronically.

Employee Retirement Income Security Act of 1974, (ERISA): ERISA is a federal law that sets minimum standards for retirement plans in private industry. It protects the assets of millions of Americans so that funds placed in retirement plans during their working lives will be there when they retire.

Employer Identification Number, (EIN): www.irs.gov If a tax return is required, obtain an Employer Identification Number. It is also needed to set up an estate checking account to pay bills from the estate. Using this account will also give you a record of bills paid which you will need to close probate.

Endowment Care Fund: Money collected from cemetery property purchasers and placed in trust for the maintenance and upkeep of the cemetery.

Endowment Care: A cemetery endowment care trust fund is designed to ensure that income will always be available for the continued maintenance and upkeep of the cemetery, even when all the interment spaces are sold. The cemetery owner should not be permitted to withdraw the principal of the endowment care trust fund. They should receive the income earned by the principal to offset maintenance expenses. This is good in a growing economy but what happens when the economy is stagnant and the owner has had enough?

Entombment: Entombment is the placement of human remains in a crypt. There may or may not be a separate fee for this.

Epitaph: Epitaphs are words engraved on a person's tomb or on a grave marker. The words could have been written by people close to the deceased or by the person themselves. An epitaph should speak a lot about the deceased and this is a final occasion to communicate to the world the significance of our loved one. An Epitaph should reflect on one's existence highlighting their personality traits or accomplishments in life. They are a meaningful way to show respect to the deceased.

> **Popular forms of Epitaph:** Many families chose a Biblical verse that may have been special to the deceased. Others choose to write about accomplishments of the decedent's life. Some are just funny.
>
> **In 1925 W. C. Fields,** a film actor and comedian purposed this epitaph for himself. Here lies W. C. Fields. I would rather be living in Philadelphia.

Escheat: When the state takes over an estate due to no beneficiaries or heirs. It serves to ensure that property is not left in limbo without recognized ownership.

Estate Attorney: An attorney certified to practice law specializing in estate issues. They are often referred to as a probate attorney.

Estate Checking Account: This is a checking account set up by the personal representative or executor for the safe keeping and distribution of assets for the estate. Funeral bills, taxes and other fees and expenses are paid out of this account in a manner described by your local probate laws. The executor will usually need an Employer Identification Number, a copy of the death certificate, Letters testamentary and two forms of ID, to authorize the transfer of account funds for the estate.

Estate's EIN: The personal representative must apply for an employer identification number (EIN) for the estate.

Estate Taxes: The estate is subject to the federal estate tax if it is worth (more than $5.12 million for someone who dies in 2012. An individual may pass tax free a specific amount at the time of death. This amount changes often.

Tax: a final 1040 must be filled for the deceased for the year of their death. This includes the time from January 1, through the date of death. You may also have to file state income-tax return and a state estate-tax return. see Tax, page 433

Estate's Income Tax: It may be necessary to file an estate income tax return if income generated by the deceased's holdings after death is now part of the estate. This is different that the estate tax listed above.

Estate Liquidation Company: Estate sales are used to liquidate the contents of both modest homes and mansions. Professional estate liquidators define the term "Estate Sale," to mean: 1) The liquidation of the personal property of a decedent. 2) An on-site sale of the personal property of someone who for whatever reason is downsizing or liquidating.

Eulogy: A brief speech that offers praise and celebrates the life of the person who has died. It can be considered as an honor to give and a gift to the deceased and their loved ones.

> **A member of the family, clergy, a close personal friend** or a business associate of the deceased, may give a eulogy. It may be a good idea to have a backup to give the Eulogy if the person becomes too emotional or just cannot do it at the time. It should be less than five minutes, offer praise and commendation and reflect the life of the person who has died. It should help the spirit of the deceased live on in the memories of the listeners. Do not use clichés. Name the deceased and explain your relationship. Summarize in a few sentences the deceased's life and what they meant to you and others. Be honest and focus on the person's positive qualities. Finish by saying goodbye to the deceased (directly or indirectly). Write as you normally speak and ask for help if you want it. Do not focus on yourself and the deceased. Include remembering the deceased and others also. When you are finished, read it out loud to see how it sounds. If you would rather use notes it may sound more natural. A eulogy is a way to honor, commemorate and express love for the deceased.

It is all right to show emotion but if you are really having a difficult time the backup person should be allowed to take over. Have some tissues or a handkerchief and a glass or bottle of water available.

You may ask if anyone would like to share a short memory. Once you allow someone to speak you may have to also stop them later. "Thank you for sharing that. I see (anyone) would like to say something."

Some denominations either discourage or do not permit eulogies at services to maintain respect for traditions.

Euthanasia and Assisted Suicide

Euthanasia and Assisted Suicide: Physician-assisted suicide (dying), doctor-assisted dying (suicide), and more loosely termed mercy killing. Under most state laws assisting in suicide is a crime with criminal penalties. Assisted-suicide advocates are promoting their agenda in the name of personal choice and they meet with many who are not in favor of this approach. At the same time "bean counters' and "experts" are attempting to limit medical treatment or care even if the patient requests it. Times, they are a-changing. . .

Passive Euthanasia: Passive euthanasia is when life-sustaining medical treatment is withheld. Passive euthanasia could also refer to a Doctor who prescribes increased doses of pain medication to a dying patient while understanding the increased dose may prove to be toxic.

Active Euthanasia: Active euthanasia is when a course of action is undertaken to end a patient's life.

Hippocratic Oath: The Hippocratic Oath has been modified on a number of occasions to make it more acceptable. To "do no harm" can be argued both for and against assisted suicide. Is the glass half empty or half full?

Washington State: May 14, 2012. A new report from the Washington state health department shows the number of people killing themselves in assisted suicides is on the rise for the second straight time since the state followed Oregon in legalizing assisted suicide.

Montana Assisted Suicide: On Thursday, February 10, 2011, Montana state lawmakers in Montana defeated a bill that would have allowed and regulated assisted suicide. The Senate Judiciary Committee defeated SB 167 that would set up rules and protections for doctors who write lethal prescriptions for drugs that patients can use to kill themselves.

Oregon: On October 27, 1997 Oregon enacted the Death with Dignity Act which allows terminally-ill Oregonians to end their lives through the voluntary self-administration of lethal medications, expressly prescribed by a physician for that purpose. The Oregon Death with Dignity Act requires the Oregon Health Authority to collect information about the patients and physicians who participate in the Act, and publish an annual statistical report. http://public.health.oregon.gov

Health Care Providers: Health care providers are not required to honor any and all decisions made by a patient or their designated agent if the provider conscientiously objects to such care or treatment. However, federal law requires that the patient or the patient's decision-maker be provided with written policies at the time of admission of any limitations on carrying out such decisions, including the range of medical conditions or procedures affected by the conscience objection. Additionally, the notification must cite state law that relates to permitting those limitations.

More Information: There are many "right-to-die" agencies around the world. Most Americans demonstrate support for the concept of a doctor helping a patient end a life with painless means, but support immediately drops if the word "suicide" is used instead. People, in general, just do not want to give up what they believe is control of their lives.

Palliative Care: Other end-of-life decisions include palliative care when medicine shifts from a course of action trying to cure a person to a treatment that can provide comfort and control pain.

Evicting a Family Member

Evicting a Family Member: Most administrators do not anticipate having to evict a family member from the home. An increasing number of children are moving back into their parents' home after a divorce or job loss. The average age the adult male leaves home in the U.S. is now estimated to be 27 years old. It is very possible one of the beneficiaries of the estate may be living in the home at the time of death. They are not the sole beneficiary of the home and are in no position to purchase the home from the estate. They also may be quite argumentative and refuse to leave the home so it may be sold. The executor or administrator may have to go through the eviction process. If the family member has been living in the home for some time they may be considered a month to month tenant and throwing all of their personal items out on the lawn may be a violation of their rights. The family may feel it is less expensive and kinder to resettle the individual in an apartment in the individual's name. Do not sign a lease in your name for someone else. As executor you may have to formally evict the family member. Go to your local sheriff's department and get information on what forms to fill out and how long it takes in your area. Someone will still have to get the home ready for sale after it is empty.

Executor: Personal Representative, Administrator, Exectrix, Court Appointed Administrator.

Executor: An Executor is someone who the deceased named in their Will to administer their estate: They oversee the disposition of property and possessions. If a person dies intestate, that is, without a Will, then the Personal Representative or Administrator will be appointed by the court. An Exectrix is a female executor.

No matter what they are called, they all oversee the disposition of property and possessions of a deceased person. An executor is entrusted with the large responsibility of making sure a person's last wishes are granted with regards to the disposition of their property and possessions. They identify the estate's assets, pay off its debts and then distribute whatever is left to the rightful heirs and beneficiaries

Executor: The executor must determine who is entitled to assets when an heir has died. If the heir was one of the deceased's children and they have already passed but have left a spouse and grandchildren, the spouse and/or grandchildren may now be entitled to all or part of what the parent would have received.

Exhume: To dig up the remains; to remove from the place of burial.

F

Family Allowance: Dependent family members can ask the probate court for a "family allowance." This is primarily cash that is quickly released from the estate (and is not available to creditors) to help with short-term living expenses.

Family Burial Estate: This is an area within a cemetery where the use is restricted to a group of persons related to each other by blood or marriage.

Family Car: The lead limousine in the funeral procession set aside for the use of the immediate family.

Family Limited Partnership (FLP): A family limited partnership is a strategy for asset protection and estate planning created to transfer ownership of assets to family members with a minimum of tax consequences.

Family Members: The executor should try to include everyone, not just traditional family members. You may need to include previous family members (they may now be beneficiaries). Children from a prior marriage and former spouses may have assets they are entitled to. This may be especially true if there is no valid Will. Retirement funds may have a valid claim by a former spouse up until the time of divorce and also a valid claim by a present spouse. You may need to seek the counsel of a competent estate attorney.

Family (Private) Mausoleum: A family mausoleum is a structure above ground, or partially above and partially below ground, containing crypts for a single family.

Family Room: A specially arranged room in the funeral home, which affords the family privacy at the time of the funeral service.

Federal Employment Benefits: If the deceased worked for the Federal Government benefits may be available to a beneficiary or to the family.

FTC (Federal Trade Commission): Facts for Consumers.
Funerals: A Consumer Guide.
http://www.ftc.gov/bcp/edu/pubs/consumer/products/pro19.shtm

Federal Employment Benefits: If the deceased worked for the Federal Government benefits may be available to a beneficiary or to the family.

Fiduciaries: An individual, corporation or association holding something in trust for another party.

Final Disposition: The last process the remains go through; usually burial or cremation.

Final Rites: The funeral service.

Financial Power of Attorney: A financial power of attorney gives a trusted person authority to handle your finances and property if you become incapacitated and unable to handle your own affairs. In most cases this is a good idea and if you have wisely chosen an agent they will manage your financial affairs as you would have. Can they steal from you? Yes. You are giving them the right to act in your place. It would be a good idea to see a competent attorney to discuss this. If you do not have a durable financial power of attorney and you are alone and incapacitated your family may have to go to court to have a guardian or conservator appointed. This can be expensive and take time. Even if you are married, have a living trust or joint tenancy a durable power of attorney may make it easier for your family if you become incapacitated. In many situations property may not be sold without the joint tenant's signature because an incapacitated spouse cannot consent to a sale

> If you have assets that you are concerned about, you should most likely discuss this with a competent attorney.

First Call: First call usually establishes the beginning of the duties of the funeral director to pick up and transport the deceased.

First Person Consent Laws: Laws being passed in states to make it easier for an Organ Donor to have their wishes fulfilled after death. It is now the practice in many states to disallow an organ donor without the families consent. This is being done to limit liability issues with the family.

First Person Consent Registry: A first person consent registry is available in some states so the family cannot overturn your decision to be an organ or tissue donor.

Flag Cases: Flag cases are mainly used to preserve and display the American flag of a veteran who has passed away.

Flowers: Flowers have played an important role at funeral and memorial services in many cultures throughout history. Sending a floral tribute is a very appropriate way of expressing sympathy to the family of the deceased unless the family has expressed a desire for donations in lieu of flowers. This should have been mentioned in the obituary.

> **What types** of flowers are appropriate? Are some flower arraignments more suited to a funeral? Not really. Even bright floral arrangements are now acceptable at a funeral. The florist where you are purchasing your flower arraignment will be able to help you make good decisions. They understand what the usual custom for the area is. The florist places an identification card on the floral tribute. The cards are removed from the floral tributes and given to the family at the funeral home so they may acknowledge the tributes sent. You do not have to overspend. Simple can be very elegant and dignified.
>
> The casket could have a floral wreath placed near the end whether the casket is open or closed. If there is an urn, a flower wreath may be placed on a stand next to the urn display. Flowers add a symbolic and aesthetic element to a funeral. They represent life and beauty. A funeral without flowers is a more mournful event while flowers extend a feeling of sympathy for the mourners.

Flower Bearer: A flower bearer is an individual who walks before or behind the casket carrying flower tributes sent to the family.

Flower Car: A vehicle used for the transportation of flower displays, mementos and other things located from the funeral home to the church and/or cemetery or grave site. There is usually an additional charge for this service.

Flower Racks and Stands: Wooden or metal stands and racks of varying heights used for banking flowers around the casket.

Food Stamps: For over 40 years, the federal Food Stamp Program, now officially named SNAP – the Supplemental Nutrition Assistance Program – has served as a mainline federal social assistance program designed to help low-income families and individuals buy the food they need for good health. The SNAP (Food Stamp) program now helps put nutritious food on the tables of 28 million people every month.

> **Emergency Food Assistance:** The Emergency Food Assistance Program (TEFAP) is a Federal program that helps supplement the diets of low-income needy individuals and families, including elderly people, by providing them with emergency food assistance at no cost.
>
> **Temporary Assistance for Needy Families (TANF):** Temporary Assistance for Needy Families (TANF) is federally funded - state administered - financial assistance program for low income families with dependent children and for pregnant women in their last three months of pregnancy. TANF provides temporary financial assistance while also helping recipients find jobs that will allow them to support themselves.
>
> **HUD Public Housing Assistance Program:** The HUD Public Housing assistance program was established to provide decent and safe rental housing for eligible low-income families. Public housing comes in all sizes and types, from scattered single family houses to high-rise apartments for elderly families. As of 2009, there were approximately 1.2 million households living in public housing units, managed by some 3,300 local public housing agencies (HAs).

Forensic: Forensic is the application of scientific knowledge to legal problems.

Forensic Science: the body of knowledge for the application of scientific knowledge to legal problems used by medical examiners or crime scene technicians, crime lab technicians, and forensic engineers to name a few.

Forgiveness: Forgiveness benefits the giver as much or more than the person being forgiven. Your blood pressure lowers, your immune system strengthens and there is less stress. You also reduce the anger, bitterness, depression, and resentment that accompany unforgiveness. Forgiveness does not mean that you deny the other persons responsibility and it does not justify the wrong. Forgiveness is an act of your free will that gives up your right to be angry, hurt, bitter and resentful. It does not condone the act but sets the person free from the act as far as you are concerned. Take the time to forgive yourself, this is often more difficult.

Funeral Arrangements: Preferences or plans for funeral arraignments are usually not listed in the Will because this information needs to be readily available. Just because a Will cannot be located does not mean that funeral arraignments have not been preplanned or prepaid. It has long been recognized in common law that a person has the right to a decent burial. This is changing. States and counties no longer have the funds to provide for this beyond certain unavoidable circumstances.

> **Many people don't realize that they are not legally required to use a funeral home** to plan and conduct a funeral. However, because they have little experience with the many details and legal requirements involved and may be emotionally distraught when it is time to make plans, many people find the services of a professional funeral home to be a comfort.
>
> **Consumers often select** a funeral home or cemetery because it's close to home, has served the family in the past, or has been recommended by someone they trust. But people who limit their search to just one funeral home may risk paying more than necessary for the funeral or narrowing their choice of goods and services.
>
> **Comparison shopping need not be difficult,** especially if it's done before the need for a funeral arises. If you visit a funeral home in person, the funeral provider is required by law to give you a general price list itemizing the cost of the items and services the home offers. If the general price list does not include specific prices of caskets or outer burial containers, the law requires

the funeral director to show you the price lists for those items before showing you the items.

Sometimes it's more convenient and less stressful to "price shop" funeral homes by telephone. The Funeral Rule requires funeral directors to provide price information over the phone to any caller who asks for it. In addition, many funeral homes are happy to mail you their price lists, although that is not required by law.

When comparing prices, be sure to consider the total cost of all the items together, in addition to the costs of single items. Every funeral home should have price lists that include all the items essential for the different types of arrangements it offers. Many funeral homes offer package funerals that may cost less than purchasing individual items or services. Offering package funerals is permitted by law, as long as an itemized price list also is provided. But only by using the price lists can you accurately compare total costs.

Federal Trade commission (FTC)   An excellent government website.
http://www.ftc.gov/bcp/edu/pubs/consumer/products/pro19.shtm

Funeral Expenses and Who Pays: Even in the absence of contract or statute, a person may be liable for funeral or burial expenses based on his or her relationship to the decedent, such as a husband and wife, or a parent and child. Statutes may also dictate liability. Some statutes designate the persons charged with the duty of burial but do not impose financial responsibility for burial or funeral expenses. Others impose financial liability on designated people in the order in which they are named in the statute.

Unclaimed Bodies: The number of bodies that are left unclaimed is increasing every year. Bodies are being abandoned in hospital morgues and the funeral home that picked up the person who died at home. The families of the deceased used to ask for a few days and somehow collect the money for a decent burial or cremation. Now more often they call within a day or two and say there is nothing they can do. When you abandon the body you usually give up any inheritance and rights to the disposition of the body. The county or state has a dignified burial or cremation of the body without any service.

GLOSSARY & INDEX
Terms and Definitions

Liability for burial expenses is not ordinarily imposed on someone merely because that person received a financial benefit as a result of the decedent's death. Usually a joint tenant will not be charged with funeral expenses merely as a result of the joint ownership of property with the deceased.

Funeral Insurance Policy: The vast majority of final expense life insurance policies will typically have a cash value of somewhere in between $5,000 and $50,000. You do not have to spend all of this money on a funeral. It should be spent by the survivors to help them financially through this time of need. Do not sign over an insurance policy to a funeral service provider for any more than the "Good Faith estimate". It is our suggestion that you never sign over an insurance policy to anyone without the advice of a competent estate attorney. Some people "overspend" on a funeral or burial because they think of it as a reflection of their feelings for the deceased.

> Purchase a good quality funeral insurance policy from a reputable insurance company. You can check prices, complaints and reviews online. Your actual cost may vary due to your age and health. Read the fine print and check for restrictive clauses that may limit or eliminate the payout. If you are paying premiums and only get back what you paid in you may be better off rethinking this particular policy.

Funeral Programs, Prayer Cards, and Keepsakes: Although this is still considered an obituary it is usually more detailed and longer, containing three or four paragraphs. This type of obituary will include the full name, area of residence. They sometimes refer to the circumstances of death in a general way, such as, "prolonged illness." There may or may not be a need for information on a memorial service, wake or viewing and internment. Due to the proliferation of identity theft it is recommended that many personal details no longer be given. Do not include: Mothers maiden name, address, ancestry, occupation, date-of-birth and date-of-death or any personal information that can be used to steal an identity. You can still honor the person without giving up their personal information. The FTC estimates that as many as 9 million Americans have their identities stolen each year. This is a very real, serious problem for millions of Americans. Please do not allow yourself to become a victim. see *Identity Theft*, page 190, 246, 375

Funeral, Green Funeral

A green funeral is one that is friendlier to the earth. Many of the green" options are also less costly. There are cemeteries that agree to avoid toxins and harmful materials.

Direct Burial or Green Burial: Direct Burial is the most common final disposition and is also called a Green Burial. It is the process of burying a body without the use of chemical preservation in a simple container to help preserve the earth. Costs associated with direct burial include grave opening and closing and perpetual care (maintenance) of the grave site. There are also charges for the purchase of a grave site

Embalming is almost never required. The two-three gallons of formaldehyde used is toxic and can seep into the soil and ground water.

Biodegradable Containers: A simple wood casket, cardboard box, or shroud is dignified, less costly and can be less of a hazard. There are also biodegradable urns for ashes that will be buried. By law in most every state and county you are allowed to use whatever type of container you choose. You may even use a homemade container. The funeral service industry is a business that wants to make a profit. You are the customer that needs to be "sold" goods or services. It is like shopping for a used car except most people are also dealing with the death of a close friend, relative or family member and are not really paying close attention. Green Funerals have a legitimate purpose to be dignified and less harmful to the environment.

Vaults: Try to avoid cemeteries that insist that you use (and pay for) a vault. They are of some benefit to the cemetery for ease of landscaping and maintenance, but at seven hundred dollars to several thousand dollars do not seem to be worth the cost.

Cremation: Cremation uses the least amount of resources, is dignified and much less expensive than burial. There is the risk of mercury pollution from amalgam fillings (silver fillings) a toxic substance.

GLOSSARY & INDEX
Terms and Definitions

Alkaline Hydrolysis is also called Water Cremation, Bio Cremation or Green Cremation. It is sold as being good for the environment. This will most likely depend on the legislation that is yet to be enacted in most states. The process has been in use for many years but is new to the funeral industry.

Home Funerals

Home Funerals: Most states allow individuals to act entirely on their own and bury their deceased at home. The cost is dramatically lower. Wal-Mart and Costco now sell caskets and urns online and will deliver to almost any location that is on a regular service route. Funerals are big business and some states try their best to discourage home funerals. These laws are changing all of the time and vary from state to state and county to county. It is always best if you check the local laws for the rules that apply in the location you are planning to have a home funeral. If you run into a lot of obstacles that seem to go against the "spirit of the law" do not be shy about calling your local Congressman. They have people on staff that would love to help you in your time of need. Home funerals can help in the grieving process.

Organizations: There are organizations where you can find more information. We do not endorse or recommend any of them, so you must use your own due diligence. The Green Burial Council is a nonprofit organization that promotes sustainable after-death practices. They also provide a list of some Green Cemeteries. http://www.greenburialcouncil.org/

Funeral Director: A trained and certified professional who prepares for the burial or other disposition of the deceased, supervises such burial or disposition, maintains a funeral establishment for such purposes and counsels with survivors. They are also called a mortician or undertaker. Funeral directors are business people.

Funeral Etiquette

Funeral Etiquette: It is often difficult to know what to say or do when there is a loss but there are certain things that need to be done when someone passes away. It is proper to pay your respects to the grieving family in the form of a condolence visit within the first few weeks. Letting them know that you care and offering to offer sympathy and assistance only if you are going to follow through with your offer are appreciated. This does not have to be a long visit; fifteen to thirty minutes will give you enough time. There is no need to hide your emotions unless they really become unmanageable, then it would be best if you excuse yourself and leave.

Close friends will offer to help with food preparation and childcare. It is appropriate to express sympathy and relate fond memories of the deceased. Sometimes family members just need someone to listen. It is almost never appropriate to ask the cause of death. When attending a wake or a visitation you should approach the family and express your sympathy. If you were acquainted with the deceased but not the family, introduce yourself. If you are attending the viewing it is customary to show your respects by viewing the deceased. Children may or may not want to view the deceased or even go to the viewing. As a parent or guardian, use your best judgment as to what you feel is best for the child. How long you stay at a wake or visitation is up to you. It need not be long. If prayer or speeches are in progress it will be considered disrespectful to leave in the middle of them. There is usually a memorial book or guest book to sign.

Flowers: You may send flowers to the family home or to the funeral home or memorial service at any time unless the family has requested donations in lieu of flowers. Florists know what is appropriate to send. Flowers generally are not sent to Jewish synagogues and Catholic churches. Even if you don't make a gift, a note or card to the deceased's family expressing your thoughts of the deceased is a welcome gesture, especially if you were not able to attend the funeral.

Funeral Service Etiquette: Although black dress is no longer required, at least wear something business casual in a darker color. Bright colors and busy patterns are inappropriate for mourning. Use some uncommon sense. If you have none, borrow some.

When seating yourself, please leave the first few rows empty for family members, who may come in following the casket. If there is a ceremony it is usually conducted by a religious leader but it isn't at all uncommon for friends and family to say a few words about the deceased or read poems or even sing a song. After the ceremony is over you will proceed to your car to drive to the burial site. Cars are usually arranged when you enter the service. You will just follow the car in front of you. When following the funeral procession, be sure to turn on your headlights. This is to let the other cars on the road know you're part of the procession. The family will most likely ride in the funeral coach and funeral service vehicles. Pallbearers and honorary pallbearers may all be riding in a vehicle provided by the funeral service provider so they arrive at the same time. Someone will offer a prayer or a few words of comfort. Many families do not stay to watch the casket lowered into the ground while it is customary for some families to do so.

Do Not Say: Do not say anything to the family that the deceased would not have wanted you to say if they were there. Now is not the time or the place (if there is ever a time or place). Do not say: "You'll get over it"; "They are better off now"; "You can have more children"; "I know how you feel"; "You have to keep busy"; "How are you financially?"; "Time heals all wounds"; "Life goes on"; "There number was up"; or "You look terrible". Do not tell them stories of families that have had it even worse. If you are at a viewing do not say how great the deceased looks. Use some uncommon sense.

Be respectful and you will be fine. It is important for the family to know that you care.

Statement of Funeral Goods and Services Selected: Cost Information and Disclosures. The Statement of Funeral Goods and Services Selected (Statement) is an itemized list of the goods and services that the consumer has selected during the arrangements conference. (13) The Statement allows consumers to evaluate their selections and to make any desired changes. From the Funeral Rule.

Funeral Home: A building used for the purpose of embalming, arranging and conducting funerals. Also called a Mortuary.

Home Funeral: see *Home Funeral*, page 92, 357, 373

Funeral Memorial Book: A funeral memorial book may contain any of or all of the following: A dedication page for recording the name, birth and death dates, family record, eulogy notes, final resting place, photos, floral memories, friends and relatives pages. Do not make personal information available to the public (or even all family members) to help prevent identity theft. see *Memorial Book*, page 396

Funeral Procession: When the funeral ceremony and the burial are both held within the local area, friends and relatives might accompany the family to the cemetery. Immediate family members may be riding in a limousine at the front of the procession. see *Funeral Procession*, page 176

Funeral Prepaid: There are two kinds of prepaid funeral contracts: revocable and irrevocable.

> **Revocable means** you may cancel the contract and get most of your money back. There may be cancelation fees.

> **Irrevocable means** you cannot cancel the contract, but you may be able to transfer it to another funeral home. Even irrevocable preneed funeral contracts may be canceled in many states. Some states allow three days and some states allow ten days. This would be a good time to speak with a competent estate attorney. New laws are written every day and things change. If you need to rescind a contract do not waste time. Make that call now.

Funeral Rule: The Funeral Rule was written for the Protection of consumers, you and me. The Funeral Rule requires the funeral provider to give consumers accurate, itemized price information and various other disclosures about funeral goods and services. see *Funeral Rule*, page 178

> **The Funeral Rule, enforced by the FTC,** makes it possible for you to choose only those goods and services you want or need and to pay only for those you select, whether you are making arrangements when a death occurs

or in advance. The Rule allows you to compare prices among funeral homes, and makes it possible for you to select the funeral arrangements you want at the home you use. (The Rule does not apply to third-party sellers, such as casket and monument dealers, or to cemeteries that lack an on-site funeral home.) Some "package" deals are more expensive than single item purchases.

Funereal Service Providers: Funeral service providers take care of the final disposition of human remains. The religious or other rites conducted immediately before final disposition of the dead human body are conducted by clergy or other religious leaders.

Funeral Services: Services provided by a funeral director and staff, which may include consulting with the family on funeral planning; transportation, shelter, refrigeration and embalming of remains; preparing and filing notices; obtaining authorizations and permits; and coordinating with the cemetery, crematory or other third parties.

Funeral Societies: Funeral societies used to be a place where you could find information on reputable funeral homes, explanation of legal rules and advice on how to make final arrangements. The funeral service industry provides services to them at a small discount. Some are better than others. Be careful and shop around.

Funeral Spray: A funeral spray is a collective mass of cut flowers sent to the residence of the deceased or to the funeral home as a floral tribute to the deceased.

G

Gaskets, Airtight Seals and Gaskets: Protective gaskets are sometimes sold as add-ons for up to several thousand dollars in additional charges. What is accomplished by an airtight seal? The consumer is often told that this seal will help to preserve the body of the loved one. A casket sealed with a tight rubber gasket creates an environment that helps bacteria thrive. When placed in a tightly sealed container most bodies have a tendency to liquefy, creating gas which may force the lid off of the container releasing noxious gasses into the crypt or mausoleum. Most cemetery workers pop the seal allowing air to vent into the casket to keep the remains from forcing the lid off the casket. The seal is also broken to allow air to vent when the casket is placed above ground.

Without this airtight gasket there is normal dehydration and deterioration of the body. Many of the newer Green Cemeteries do not allow seals or gaskets.

The General Price List: The General Price List (GPL) is the key stone of the Funeral Rule. It must contain identifying information (see page 6), itemized prices for the various goods and services that you sell (see pages 9-13), and other important disclosures (see pages 6-9). The GPL enables consumers to comparison shop and to purchase, on an itemized basis, only the goods and services they want see *Funeral Rule*, page 178

Gift Cards: A gift card enables the recipient to receive goods or services of a specific value from the card issuer.

Gifting: To give away assets while you are alive to legally avoid taxes and probate. There are statutory limits on the value of gifts in any given year before estate or inheritance taxes will be imposed. Medicaid and Tax laws are most often in conflict when it comes to dumping assets to qualify.

God Parents: A godparent is someone who sponsors the child's baptism. This is not a legal responsibility. see *Guardian*, page 366

Google Search: "name" state. Enter the person's name in quotation marks and add any defining information such as occupation or the State where they last lived. http://www.google.com/

Government Search: Direct access to searchable information from the United States government, state governments, and local governments.   http://www.usa.gov/

Grantor: A grantor is usually a person who transfers ownership of property.

Gratitude: A dying person will often experience extreme gratitude for their life. They will be grateful for experiences they had and the people they shared them with. Death is a natural process that will happen to each and every one of us. When the dying person accepts this they allow the natural order of life and death to complete the cycle.

Grave: A space in the ground in a cemetery for the burial of human remains.

GLOSSARY & INDEX
Terms and Definitions

Owner of Burial Space: The owner is the person to whom the cemetery operator or his authorized agent has transferred the right of use of burial space.

Find a Grave: You can search 83 million grave records. Find famous graves. Search by date, location, and various data bases. http://www.findagrave.com/

Grave Liner: A receptacle made of concrete, metal or wood into which the casket is placed. A grave liner is a cover that fits over a casket in a grave. Some liners cover tops and sides of the casket while others, referred to as vaults, completely enclose the casket. Grave liners minimize ground settling and this allows easier maintenance of the cemetery grounds.

Grave Marker: A method of identifying the occupant of a particular grave. Permanent grave markers are usually of metal or stone, which gives such data as the name of the individual, date and place of birth, date and place of death. Check the spelling and dates before it is ordered.

Grave Site Service: Some cultures consider it a sign of respect to deposit a ceremonial shovel of earth into the grave. This ceremony is initiated by a member of the family and followed by others. If you were close to the deceased, you may take your turn.

Graveside Service: A service to commemorate the deceased held at the cemetery before burial.

Green Burial: The purpose of a green burial is to return the body to the earth in a way that does not hinder decomposition. There are few green cemeteries in the U.S., but many existing cemeteries are allowing green burial. It is not only "green" it usually saves the consumer thousands of dollars.

Grief

Grief: Deep sorrow caused by someone's death. Grief is a way of coping with the death of a loved one.

Grief and How to Cope with Death: Grief and mourning are natural responses to loss. The way in which an individual copes with tragedy is deeply personal and people react to death differently. When the death is unexpected, the usual reaction is disbelief. When you know someone is going to die, and you have had time to mentally prepare for this, you probably went through denial when the person became sick or injured.

Changes: Physical, behavioral, emotional, mental, social, and spiritual changes and challenges can occur. Some people have trouble concentrating, studying, sleeping, or eating when they are coping with a death. Others lose interest in activities they used to enjoy and some people feel numb, as if nothing has happened.

It is all right to cry. Crying is a normal human response to loss. Crying, it has been said, is pain leaving the body.

Stay connected to people. Do not stop taking calls or having people visit. Even if your friends and family do not know what to say or do, they usually mean well.

Saying Good-bye: We all have to let go and say good-bye. This allows the person the comfort of knowing you are ready for them to go. While we may never be fully ready, we need to allow them to do what is necessary and your words will most likely result in a relaxation response from them. Saying good-bye is painful and the loved one does not immediately pass away. It may be hours or days later. Most often the act of letting go and saying good-bye is repeated over many days by different people.

Touch the loved ones hands or gently hug them in a comforting way. Tell your loved one that you love them and if they cannot respond answer for them. "I know you love me too."

Children and Grief: Children often do a very good job at grieving intensely for a time and then taking a break. The break is usually in the form of play and adults often mistake a child's play as a sign that the child is not grieving. The child will grieve again and rest again.

GLOSSARY & INDEX
Terms and Definitions

Children and Funerals: Whether or not children attend the funeral is up to the parent or guardian. Do not allow yourself to be pressured into doing something that you do not feel is in the best interest of the child. Attending the funeral may be fine for some children and not the best thing for others. Encouraging children to talk about their feelings is still one of the best ways to allow them to grieve.

Time and Grief: Even after months or years the loved one may still be on your mind as you continue to move forward with your life. If they were loved or hated it seems they are remembered. Talking about them with someone is a way of letting go. Birthdays, anniversaries, Christmas, they all hurt, especially the first year. The grieving person does not return to being the same person they were before the loss. Their lives are different. After a while you will remember a fond memory and smile. This happens at different times for everyone. There are free grief support groups. Google: grief support group (your city or county)

Sudden Grief: When the death of a loved one is sudden and without warning there can be exaggerated reactions and strong emotional release.

Helping Someone Cope: If you are helping someone cope with the death of a loved one, listen to them. Listen to them without judgment or interruption. They may need to tell the story again and again as a way to begin to process their grief. Clichés, religious platitudes or easy answers do not help. Do not be too quick to share your opinions.

Even if you are uncomfortable, try to stay with the grieving friend. Do not judge and understand that you cannot fix anything and you are not supposed to. Your being there as a friend to listen and be supportive is important and will be appreciated.

Coping with a Baby's Death: When an unborn baby dies or a miscarriage occurs is a profound loss. In time you will learn to live with the loss and deal with the loss but you may never get over the loss completely. Grief is usually not something one recovers from because the loss is never regained or replaced. When death is because of a stillbirth, an aborted pregnancy, through miscarriage or the result of an ectopic or tubal pregnancy, it may feel as if you have no one to talk with. Some parents and grandparents of the baby report it feels socially unacceptable to discuss the death after about a week or two of the event. While this is totally false, it makes grief more difficult. It is as if the baby did not exist at all and that is simply not true. Many parents report they feel like they are in a fog the first few weeks after the death. This is nature's way of protecting you. Crying, sobbing and wailing or some other deeply emotional release usually marks the end of the initial period of shock.

There may or not be a funeral. There may or not be a spouse or close friend to talk with. There may or may not be family that is supportive. You may feel like you are alone because you really are alone right now. There are others that feel similar and a grief support group may be a good place to start. There are free groups associated with hospitals and religious organizations. Google: grief support group (your city or county) This is difficult to get through with the help of a caring spouse. I can only imagine what it would be like to go through this alone. Pretending like it did not happen can be counterproductive making closure very difficult. You are not alone. Find some help, you deserve it.

Guardian

Guardian: A legal guardianship is a relationship established by the court where one person acts for the benefit and protection of another person. A guardian is legally responsible for the child's physical care, health, education, and welfare until he or she reaches 18 years of age. A "ward" is the person receiving the services of the guardian. This is usually a minor child. Persons with mental or physical handicaps may also have a legal guardian appointed to look after them. There are several different types of legal guardianships, such as temporary guardianships, emergency guardianships, and adult guardianships.

In most cases if a child's other parent survives, then that parent assumes the guardianship without any other special actions.

Guardian Selection: There should be a section of the Will that deals with guardianship. A judge will make the final determination about guardianship so

GLOSSARY & INDEX
Terms and Definitions

you should write down your reason for choosing this particular guardian. If you want to name a guardian other than the next of kin or other parent you can do this but you most likely will want to discuss this with a competent estate attorney.

Always discuss your choice with the person you select and be certain they are willing to accept the responsibility should it become necessary. You would want the same common courtesy if someone was designating you and the guardian you appoint does not have to accept the responsibility. Because a guardian is not legally obligated to serve, an alternate choice is recommended in case the first choice refuses or is unable to serve.

Guardian(s): Naming one guardian is usually a better idea than naming co-guardians. Co-guardians can disagree on childrearing issues or decide to go their separate ways. For example, naming a husband and wife as co-guardians could get complicated if there is later a divorce that results in a custody battle. If couples are named as co-guardians be specific as to what you want to happen in the event they separate or divorce later on. Another person may be the guardian or Conservator of the child's assets.

Guardian Removal: If the executor or personal representative has any misgivings about the named guardian(s) they should speak with a qualified attorney or other professional as soon as possible.

Guardians and Godparents: If minor children are involved and the deceased has not named a guardian in the event something happens to both parents the court may use the selection of the godparent(s) to help determine the parent's wishes. This may not be what the deceased intended. Guardianship papers should be drawn up and the Will should nominate guardians for the children.

A Guardian or Conservator may be appointed to handle a person's financial affairs if they become incapacitated. The Conservator for the child's financial affairs can be the same person or a different person than the children's Guardian. A guardian or conservator is appointed by the court and anyone can petition the court for appointment of a guardian or conservator, but it is usually done by a relative or by the person or facility that has assumed responsibility for the person's care. Any interested person, including the

Department of Health or the Department of Social Services, may petition to have a guardian appointed to someone. The court might appoint more than one guardian or conservator.

Guest Book: A guest book, Register Book or Book of Condolence allows friends and family to leave their name and a brief note of condolence. One line such as, "You will be missed;" is often enough. A guest book can be a source of comfort for the family when they read the guests' names and comments later. If the funeral service is small and restricted to close friends and family a register may not be necessary. It is a personal choice.

H

Headstone: Check the spelling and dates before it is ordered.

Hearse: A Hearse or Funeral Coach is a specially designed vehicle used to transport the casket from the funeral service to the cemetery. There is only room for the driver and funeral director to ride in the hearse.

Health Care Directives or Advance Directives: An advance directive is a written statement of a person's wishes regarding medical treatment. It is a legal document detailing a person's health care wishes, including the individual to whom they give the legal authority to act on their behalf and what types of treatment they do and do not want to receive in the event they are unable to speak or communicate. The living Will and the power of attorney constitute what are called advance directives. A divorce has no effect on your written directions for health care.

Health Care Proxy: An advance directive is a written statement of a person's wishes regarding medical treatment. A health care directive or advance directive.

Health Care Power of Attorney: A health care power of attorney gives someone you choose the power to make decisions if you if you are incapacitated. These papers should be readily accessible. If you are incapacitated and your family members cannot locate a health care power of attorney, they may have to go to court to have a guardian appointed.

Companies like http://www.docubank.com/ offer immediate access to healthcare directives & emergency medical information. They keep all of your health care directives online for you to access 24/7 We are not recommending any company, just pointing out they exist and may be beneficial.

Heir: When there is no Will. Heirs denote those persons, including the surviving spouse, who are entitled under the statutes to the estate of the decedent who dies intestate. A person or group entitled to receive funds or other property when they are named by the court. Sometimes potential Heirs attempt do-it-yourself distribution and find out later they cannot clear titles or clear other legal problems.

Heirs and Probate: Probate law generally defines heirs to be the spouse; their children and later heirs; parents; brothers and sisters; grandparents; and then others also considered next-of-kin. The exact order may vary from state to state. After going through a fairly long list of possible heirs the estate goes to the state if no heirs can be found. For instance a "laughing heir" statute exists in a few states. This statute names a person so remotely connected to the deceased that they would not feel any sorrow at the mention of the death.

Home Health Care: Home health care is usually considered to be skilled nursing care services rendered by members of the health professions for the benefit of a patient in a home setting.

Home Care: Home care is usually considered to be non-medical services rendered in a home setting for the benefit of a patient.

HIPPA

Health Insurance Portability & Accountability Act of 1996 (HIPPA)

HIPAA is a federal law that gives you rights over your health information and sets rules and limits on who can look at and receive your health information.

The HIPAA Privacy Rule provides federal protections for personal health information held by covered entities and gives patients an array of rights with respect to that information. At the same time, the Privacy Rule is balanced so that it permits the disclosure of personal health information needed for patient care and other important purposes.

The Security Rule specifies a series of administrative, physical, and technical safeguards for covered entities to use to assure the confidentiality, integrity, and availability of electronic protected health information.

What Rights Does The Privacy Rule Give Me Over My Health Information?

You have a right to:

• Ask to see and get a copy of your health records

• Have corrections added to your health information

• Receive a notice that tells you how your health information may be used and shared

• Decide if you want to give your permission before your health information can be used or shared for certain purposes, such as for marketing

• Get a report on when and why your health information was shared for certain purposes

• If you believe your rights are being denied or your health information isn't being protected, you can

• File a complaint with your provider or health insurer

• File a complaint with the U.S. Government

You should get to know these important rights, which help you protect your health information.

You can ask your provider or health insurer questions about your rights.

Who Must Follow These Laws? We call the entities that must follow the HIPAA regulations covered entities.

Covered entities include:

• Health Plans, including health insurance companies, HMOs, company health plans, and certain government programs that pay for health care, such as Medicare and Medicaid.

• Most Health Care Providers—those that conduct certain business electronically, such as electronically billing your health insurance—including most doctors, clinics, hospitals, psychologists, chiropractors, nursing homes, pharmacies, and dentists.

• Health Care Clearinghouses—entities that process nonstandard health information they receive from another entity into a standard (i.e., standard electronic format or data content), or vice versa.

What Information Is Protected?

• Information your doctors, nurses, and other health care providers put in your medical record

• Conversations your doctor has about your care or treatment with nurses and others

• Information about you in your health insurer's computer system

• Billing information about you at your clinic

• Most other health information about you held by those who must follow these laws

Who Can Look at and Receive Your Health Information?

The Privacy Rule sets rules and limits on who can look at and receive your health information

To make sure that your health information is protected in a way that does not interfere with your health care, your information can be used and shared:

• For your treatment and care coordination

- To pay doctors and hospitals for your health care and to help run their businesses

- With your family, relatives, friends, or others you identify who are involved with your health care or your health care bills, unless you object

- To make sure doctors give good care and nursing homes are clean and safe

- To protect the public's health, such as by reporting when the flu is in your area

- To make required reports to the police, such as reporting gunshot wounds

Your health information cannot be used or shared without your written permission unless this law allows it. For example, without your authorization, your provider generally cannot:

- Give your information to your employer

- Use or share your information for marketing or advertising purposes

- Share private notes about your health care

U.S. Department of Health & Human Services

www.HHS.gov   Health Information Privacy
http://www.hhs.gov/ocr/privacy/hipaa/understanding/consumers/index.html

Every hospital and insurer must publish a copy of practices and privacy rules in compliance with HIPAA and must make them available upon request.

Holographic Will: A Holographic Will has been handwritten, dated and signed by the testator. A holographic Will is valid in all states under certain conditions. State law must be checked for the state having jurisdiction.

Home Funeral

Home funeral: In many areas of the United States, there is no formal requirement that burial be done in a cemetery. Without any local restrictions and the permission of the landowner burial is legal and acceptable on most private property. Some states require a licensed funeral director for the disposition of remains. Home funerals may not be allowed when death involves certain infectious diseases. It is still your responsibility to check all state and local death and home funeral regulations in your state and county.

Preparing the body, transporting it, and arranging the memorial service do not require special training or professional certificates. These tasks can be performed by the families. Yes, you will have to touch, wash, handle, bathe and dress the deceased. This may be awkward even when the weight is only one-hundred pounds. Home health care may help with the grieving process but that does not mean that it is easy.

In-State Transport: If a person died of natural causes, and the body is not under the jurisdiction of the medical examiner, it may be moved in-state without a permit in most cases. If the medical examiner must examine a body to determine cause of death, a permit is required to move it. see *Transportation*, page 259

Disease: In the case of death by a highly communicable disease, such as smallpox, plague, HIV, hepatitis B, rabies, or Creutzfeldt-Jakob disease, the attending physician must notify those transporting the body to use precautions to prevent the spread of disease.

Rigor mortis, stiffening of the body, begins around 3 hours after death and will peak around 12 hours. Then the body gradually relaxes. You will need to get some information to prepare yourself and your family for this task. Moving a body will take some strength. It usually takes four adults to move an average adult body on a professional gurney.

Embalming: Funeral service providers like to require embalming because it can only be performed by someone licensed to do so. However, embalming is generally not necessary or legally required if the deceased is to be buried or cremated shortly after death except under special circumstances. Most states do not allow disposition prior to two days, to allow time to determine and document the cause of death and bodies are usually refrigerated for temporary preservation. Each state specifies how many days a body can be kept without embalming, usually 2-5 days. Foregoing embalming can save hundreds of dollars and most loved ones can be presented very nicely without it if you have the viewing within a few days of death.

Home Funerals were Common: Home funerals were normal while most people still lived on farms. It was during the civil war that undertakes became necessary because so many bodies had to be transported long distances back home and needed to be preserved for the journey. Over the last one hundred years this practice has become less common. PBS made a documentary a few years ago called "A Family Undertaking" about home funerals.

Home funerals allow the family to participate in the death care of the loved one and the decedent may have requested a home funeral. Even with professional death care, it may still be possible to participate in some parts of the process. Death midwifes are professionals that can assist in home funerals. There are also books and videos available: home funeral guides for family directed funerals, memorials, with cremation or green burials. Google: home funeral

Cremation: A less complicated home funeral may be a direct cremation. The cost is $1,000 or less. The memorial service can be held in someone's home or on their property with or without a viewing. A casket can be rented for the viewing from the crematorium.

Honorariums: A payment given to a professional person for services for which fees are not legally or traditionally required. The honorarium for the individual to perform a graveside service or memorial service can be from $50 to $500. The fee for a Celebrant is usually between $300 and $900. The fee for the building where the service is to take place is additional. The fee for an organist, pianist, or soloist is an additional $100 to $300 each.

Hospice: Hospice is a philosophy of care that focuses on patient comfort rather than curing illnesses. Choosing hospice care in no way means a patient is giving up hope.

Hospice care neither prolongs life nor hastens death. Hospice offers a variety of bereavement and counseling services to families before and after a patient's death. Hospice includes pain management.

Hospital Cards: A hospital card or health care card is used by countries other than the U.S. They are now being considered for use in the U.S.

House Sitter: A house sitter is considered to be a reliable person who lives in a residence for a period of time to provide security to the property and contents. They may be paid or just receive free use of the house for their services. It is becoming more common for homes to be stripped of complete kitchens and/or bathrooms in the middle of the night.

I

Identity Theft

Identity Theft: Identity theft occurs when someone uses your personally identifying information, like your name, Social Security number, or credit card number, without your permission, to commit fraud or other crimes.

The FTC estimates that as many as 9 million Americans have their identities stolen each year. In fact, you or someone you know may have experienced some form of identity theft.

The crime takes many forms. Identity thieves may rent an apartment, obtain a credit card, or establish a telephone account in your name. You may not find out about the theft until you review your credit report or a credit card statement and notice charges you didn't make—or until you're contacted by a debt collector.

Identity theft is serious. While some identity theft victims can resolve their problems quickly, others spend hundreds of dollars and many days repairing damage to their good name and credit record. Some consumers victimized by identity theft may lose out on job opportunities, or be denied loans for education, housing or cars because of negative information on their credit reports. In rare cases, they may even be arrested for crimes they did not commit.

This website is a one-stop national resource to learn about the crime of identity theft. It provides detailed information to help you deter, detect, and defend against identity theft.

http://www.ftc.gov/bcp/edu/microsites/idtheft/

Immediate Burial: see *Direct Burial*, page 95, 337

Immediate Cremation: see *Direct Cremation*, page 104, 337

Incapacitated: A person is legally incapacitated when they are temporarily or permanently impaired by mental and/or physical disability, illness, or by the use of drugs to the extent they lack sufficient understanding to make rational decisions or engage in responsible actions.

Independent Living Facility: An independent living facility is a multi-unit senior housing development that may provide supportive services such as meals, housekeeping, social activities, and transportation. They encourage socialization with central dining facilities.

Inpatient Care: Inpatient care is medical treatment provided in a hospital or other facility that requires at least one overnight stay.

Inquest: An official inquiry or examination to determine the cause of death.

Insolvent: One is considered insolvent when their obligations (debts) exceed their assets.

Insurance: Insurance is a contract that promises to pay the insured for a covered loss if the insured prepays for the contract. The executor must review and pay the decedent's automobile, homeowner's liability, and other insurance to assure coverage continues until assets are distributed. If you locate an agent associated with any policy talk to them and see if they have any additional information on other policies the decedent may have had. Life insurance was never intended to be spent on a fancy funeral. It was to help the survivors continue with their lives after someone's death. You should not allow the funeral to become a family burden. see *Insurance*, page 198

Insurance Cards: A card that you may carry on your person proving that you carry a type of insurance. It could be for auto insurance or medical insurance.

Interment: The act of burying a dead body in a grave. Interment is the burial, or entombment of human remains.

Inurnment: The placing of cremated remains in an urn or the placement of cremated remains in a niche, crypt, grave or other suitable location in the Cemetery.

Interment Space or Inurnment Space: An interment space or inurnment space is a grave, crypt, niche or plot.

Intestate

Intestate: Intestate refers to a person who has died without having written a valid Will. The state where the deceased had their permanent residence will apply its probate laws to determine how the property will be dispersed if there is no Will or it cannot be located.

Holographic Will: A Will that has been handwritten, dated and signed by the testator. A holographic Will is valid in all states under certain conditions. State law must be checked for the state having jurisdiction.

Funeral Arrangements: Preferences or plans for funeral arraignments are usually not listed in the Will because this information needs to be readily available. Just because a Will cannot be located does not mean that funeral arraignments have not been preplanned or prepaid. It has long been recognized in common law that a person has the right to a decent burial. This is changing. States and counties no longer have the funds to provide for this beyond certain unavoidable circumstances.

Lawful Possession: It is commonly held that no one can own human remains except for their disposition. In most cases the executor has the right of possession of the deceased for disposition of the remains. If there is no Will the court appoints an administrator to take on this responsibility, but it takes time for the courts to act. The person next in line to assume the role of administrator would most likely have the right to possession for the purpose of disposition. Without a Will there is no specific person named (executor) to arrange the funeral and if family members disagree it may involve hurt feelings. If a child of divorced parents passes the parent with custody usually has right to possession. When joint custody is a factor things may change.

Lawful possession may be extended to the hospital if the person died on hospital premises. If the Coroner has jurisdiction they may have the right to possession for disposition. It depends on the circumstances.

Totten Trust: Even if there is no valid Will there may be a Trust fund to cover expenses. A Totten Trust is just a regular bank account with a designated "pay on death" inheritor. When the account is opened a friend, relative (most likely named as executor) is named as the beneficiary. Whoever opens the account can also close it at any time for any reason. They may also change banks and or change beneficiaries. The beneficiary does not need to know about the arrangement, and the depositor is entitled to deposit and withdraw funds from the account as they see fit. The idea is when the person dies the beneficiary collects the account balance and pays for the funeral expenses. This can work out very well if all parties are informed and kept up to date.

Intestate: If there is no valid Will the probate court must appoint an administrator. The disposition of the body usually takes place long before the appointment and the funeral home or crematorium expects to be paid at the time of service. Who will pay? Where does the funding come from? Most families pay these expenses themselves and then submit the receipts to the executor for reimbursement later on. If there are no funds available to pay these expenses the executor is not obligated to reimburse the person(s) who paid them.

Intestate Succession: The legal distribution of assets when there was no Will. The laws are similar in each state but are not all the same. Every state is different.

GLOSSARY & INDEX
Terms and Definitions

Executor: The executor is named in the Will. If there is no Will there is no named executor. Intestate law that covers the state and county having control of the deceased's assets, provide a priority list of individuals that are eligible to become the executor. If probate is necessary the court will appoint an Administrator based on this list. The surviving spouse or registered domestic partner is usually first; the children are next, followed by family members. If you are chosen you may or may not have to accept. see Executor, page 144

Divorce: Situations that involve legal separation or pending divorce, same-sex-marriage, or common-law marriage most likely will need the help of a competent estate attorney. This may also be true if the situation involves, step children, foster children, adopted children, children born outside of marriage and children born after the parent's death.

Intestate Guardian: A guardian for minor children or the disabled is named in the Will. If there is no Will, there is no named guardian for minor children or a surviving incapacitated spouse and the court will appoint someone as guardian. This can take time.

Joint Tenancy: Any assets held in joint tenancy such as: bank accounts, safe deposit box contents, stocks and bonds, real-estate, and community property usually pass directly to the sole survivor.

Beneficiary Named: No Will is necessary for retirement accounts, IRA, 401K(s), living trust, POD (payable on death) accounts, TOD (transfer on death) accounts, or any type of plan when a beneficiary has been named. The original documents will have a section to name any beneficiary or beneficiaries. Sometimes Different beneficiaries will get a different percent of the policy or account payout.

Out of State Property: If the deceased has property in another state(s) there will be additional probate proceedings in the state(s) where the property is located. A vacation home in the desert and another at the seashore could each go through a different state probate court with each accessing fees and charges. The executor or personal representative may be required to visit the property in each state have appraisals, inspections and possible attorney fees. There may also be taxes due. How much easier it would have been to have a simple Will that read in part: "I am leaving my house in the desert to my brother Wally and my house at the seashore to my sister Wallonia," signed, Wilbur. Since probate laws vary from state to state there may be a few surprises.

Revoked Will: If a Will is missing or no longer valid because the decedent intentionally revoked it either an earlier Will or the laws of intestate succession are used to decide the proper distribution of the estate.

Lost or Destroyed: If the original Will has been lost or destroyed the court may (or may not) accept a photo copy of the original Will. Sometimes the decedent gives potential executors a copy of the original Will. Copies may also be in a safe deposit box. It is so simple to just tell people where you keep your Will. It also requires a great deal of trust if the person is concerned about anyone changing their Will.

There are usually indications that there is a Will even if it cannot readily be located. It could be in a home safe kept under frozen food at the bottom of a freezer in a garage. Or just wrapped in foil, placed in a zip lock bag and kept in the bottom of a refrigerator freezer to hide it and protect it from fire. The main thing is to search but you do not have to go to extremes. It is estimated that over half of all Americans die without having taken the time to prepare a Will. You only have a fifty-fifty chance that there even is a Will.

Living Will: A Living Will allows you to make health care decisions now in case you are unable to do so in the future. It documents instructions for your medical care in the event you are unable to communicate due to a severe injury, terminal illness or other medical condition. A Living Will can also be called a health care declaration, advance directive, or medical power of attorney.

Dementia and Changing the Will: You are dealing with a person who is not thinking clearly. They may, and often do, change their Will often. In most cases a person with dementia can still make or change a Will if they can show that they understand what they are doing and what the effects of it will be. This needs to be addressed before a medical and financial crisis takes place. Proof of incapacity should be taken care of early.

GLOSSARY & INDEX
Terms and Definitions

Dementia: Dementia is a group of symptoms affecting intellectual and social abilities severely enough to interfere with daily functioning. There are many causes of dementia. Alzheimer's disease is the most common cause of a progressive dementia. In most cases a person with dementia can still make or change a Will if they can show that they understand what they are doing and what the effects of it will be.

In-State Funeral: An in-state funeral or state funeral is the practice of honoring elected or military officials with a public viewing of their casket before burial.

Intangible Assets: Intangible assets are not physical in nature. Examples of some intangible assets are your reputation, a brand, franchise, trademark, or patent.

Itemized Statement of Services and Merchandise: An itemized statement of services and merchandise can be a detailed outline of the specific goods and services you have chosen, the price of each item, and a total cost. This itemized statement may also be a contract. Be careful what you sign. If someone tells you they just need your "OK, here" while handing you a pen and pointing to a blank line, it most likely is a contract and you will be held responsible to pay the debt if you sign.

Inter: To inter is to bury a dead body in the ground, a grave or a tomb.

IRA: A tax-deferred retirement account that allows individuals to direct pretax income toward investments. An Individual Retirement Account is considered dormant or unclaimed if no withdrawal has been made by age 70½.

Irrevocable Trust: An irrevocable trust transfers asset ownership to the trust fund, making the fund the legal owner of those assets. They are more private and harder to dispute. Once the trust is set up as an irrevocable trust it cannot be amended, modified, changed, or revoked. However, some Irrevocable Trusts are written with instructions to the Trustees or beneficiaries to allow for the terms of the trust to be modified under specific limited circumstances. Now is an excellent time to speak with a competent legal professional.

Irrevocable: Irrevocable in a legal sense most often means that it is almost impossible or much too expensive to undo or change something.

J

Joint Tenancy: Joint Tenancy with Rights of Survivorship

Joint Tenancy: Any assets held in joint tenancy such as: bank accounts, safe deposit box contents, stocks and bonds, real-estate, and community property usually pass directly to the sole survivor.

Joint tenancy creates a Right of Survivorship. This is a type of account that is owned by at least two entities (people or a business entity in some cases). Joint tenancy is a way that more than one person can own property together. All tenants have an equal right to the account's assets and are afforded survivorship rights in the event of the death of another account holder. It is a common practice for couples and business partners to take title to each other's bank accounts, brokerage accounts, real estate and/or personal property as joint tenants with rights of survivorship. When one owner dies, the other owners automatically inherit the deceased person's share of the property.

Under the right of survivorship, the death of one joint tenant automatically transfers the remainder of the property to the survivor(s).

Joint Property: Joint property or joint tenancy with rights of survivorship usually transfers on death to the joint survivor. This is not always the case, even with joint bank accounts. In Texas, which is a community property state, it has been held in court that the bank signature cards are not in and of themselves sufficient in all cases to establish "joint tenancy with rights of survivorship."

Community Property States: In some community property states property held during marriage takes its status as separate property or community property at the time it is acquired. Such status is fixed by the facts or circumstances existing at that time.

Assets held in Joint Tenancy with Rights of Survivorship: Both tenants bear responsibility for the asset. They both share in the increase in value or the debt of the asset. If the relationship is unstable or one of the individuals is unstable this can be a dangerous way to hold assets.

Risks with assets held in Joint Tenancy with Rights of Survivorship: If the asset is held in Joint Tenancy with Rights of Survivorship with a child and the child decides they do not want you to sell the asset there may be nothing you can do without their permission (signature). In some states you will also need the permission (signature) of their spouse. Ok, all of your children are angels but if they are being sued, have credit problems or are going through a divorce you may have a real problem. Now try to get your child's spouse to give you permission (signature). If you own your home jointly with a child and the child is going through bankruptcy the court may have the option to force the sale of your home or collect your assets to pay off the debt. Maybe everything is fine: there is a red light, an accident, a lawsuit; you may lose your home in the blink of an eye and you were just sitting there minding your own business while watching Wheel of Fortune. Bummer.

If you become incapacitated, the other joint tenant owners have very limited authority over your share of the joint tenancy property. A person who is incapacitated cannot agree to the sale of property.

You may have tried to do the right thing and now you are held hostage. It is always a good idea to speak with a competent estate attorney before you begin signing things away. Do not allow yourself to be pressured by relatives or family.

Probate and Joint Tenancy with Rights of Survivorship: automatically transfers ownership to the other spouse or business partner upon the death of the first partner and avoids probate. This is an enormous advantage for those who need the funds immediately as the probate process could make funds unavailable for months or years. How would a surviving spouse or business partner pay day-to-day expenses if the bank accounts were frozen at the death of an individual? Who would pay the mortgage, living expenses or vendors? Would everything be lost? If you still have not started to preplan your arraignments for when you pass, today would be the best day to start. see *Preplan*, page 219

Control of the Asset held in Joint Tenancy with Rights of Survivorship: At death the surviving spouse or business partner assumes control over the joint asset. They may sell it or give it away. The deceased loses control of the final disposition of the asset if they would have preferred to leave it to someone else. In a business relationship they may have preferred to leave their part of the business to a family member. If held jointly it may pass out of the family forever.

Clear Title: If you are clearing an estate and you come across property that does not have clear title from when the first Joint Tenant died you will now need to go back and clear the title from the first joint tenant. Then clear the title from the deceased. Then you may transfer the title to the new owner.

Frozen Assets: If the deceased is heavily in debt and the court feels the surviving joint tenant will liquidate the asset to avoid paying the debt, the court may freeze the account. In some cases the joint account may be frozen.

Tenancy in Common: Tenancy in common is an alternative to Joint Tenancy with Rights of Survivorship. Each owner owns the asset or a percentage of the asset. They may legally sell or share their part of the asset without the other party's consent or approval. The asset is transferred at death according to the deceased's Will. If there is no Will, the asset will pass to heirs according to probate law. While the asset is being probated the other owner(s) still have use of their share of the asset. In most cases they may sell their share or dispose of it without waiting for the probate court.

Joint Will: Many couples think they have a "joint Will". A mirror image Will is the same for each spouse. Each usually leaves everything to the other, surviving partner. If one of the partners is stricken with dementia either in the earliest stages or very advanced stages the other partner usually needs to correct their own Will to name a guardian or provide care if the surviving partner has dementia.

K

Keogh: A type of profit-sharing plan used by small business owners. Include the name of institution, contact information, account number and the amount of funds being paid out, if any.

L

Law of Cadavers: There is an undeniable recognition of the rights of the dead and the living to have respected the peaceful and inviolate sanctity of the grave. It may be generally said that once a person is buried, the law, having a proper respect for the dead, a just regard for the sensibilities of the living, and a care for the due preservation of the public health, jealously guards the grave against ruthless or unjustifiable intrusion. The Law of Cadavers by Percival Jackson (1936).

Lawful Possession: It is commonly held that no one can own human remains except for their disposition. In most cases the executor has the right of possession of the deceased for disposition of the remains. If there is no Will the court appoints an administrator to take on this responsibility, but it takes time for the courts to act. The person next in line to assume the role of administrator would most likely have the right to possession for the purpose of disposition. Without a Will there is no specific person named (executor) to arrange the funeral and if family members disagree it may involve hurt feelings. If a child of divorced parents passes the parent with custody usually has right to possession. When joint custody is a factor things may change.

Lawful possession may be extended to the hospital if the person died on hospital premises. If the Coroner has jurisdiction they may have the right to possession for disposition. It depends on the circumstances.

Lawsuits: Lawsuits for wrongful death may be filed against an incompetent doctor, health care provider, careless driver or someone committing a crime among others. These lawsuits must be filed within a certain amount of time after death. Speak with a competent attorney. It can be important to gather and secure evidence.

Lawn Crypts: A lawn crypt is usually a burial vault or other permanent container for a casket which is permanently installed below ground prior to the time of the actual interment. A lawn crypt may permit single or multiple interments in a grave space.

Lawn Niche: A lawn niche is an interment space in an urn garden in the cemetery used for the burial of cremated remains.

Lawn Space: A lawn space is grave space in the cemetery already in use or to be used for the burial of human remains.

Lawn Urn: A lawn urn is a receptacle for the burial of cremains. They are usually made of bronze, marble or granite.

Lawn Vase: A lawn vase is a receptacle for the placement of flowers on a grave, lawn crypt, lawn niche, or memorial.

Lead Car: A funeral service vehicle that the funeral director and sometimes the clergyman ride. The lead car leads the procession to the church and/or cemetery.

Legally Incapacitated: A person is legally incapacitated when they are temporarily or permanently impaired by a mental and/or physical disability, illness, or by the use of drugs to the extent they lack sufficient understanding to make rational decisions or engage in responsible actions.

Letters of Administration: Letters of Administration is a document issued by the probate court to authorize the administrator of an estate when there is no Will. The appointed person must sign an acceptance statement that describes his or her duties and acknowledges that the court can fine or remove an administrator or executor for failure to perform those duties faithfully. In most cases the administrator or executor must also post a bond to cover potential losses that the estate might suffer. If the Will states there is no bond necessary the state may still require a bond. This varies from state to state. The executor should always request additional copies of the Letters of Administration from the court as they are necessary to prove the executor has been assigned by the court to distribute the estate.

Letters Testamentary: Letters Testamentary proves that a person is the executor of a Will. They are issued by the court with jurisdiction over the estate to authorize the executor of an estate when there is a Will. They are issued by the court with jurisdiction over the estate. The executor should always request additional copies of the letters testamentary from the court as they are necessary to prove the executor has been assigned by the court to distribute the estate. Certified copies of the letters are often required by banks and other financial institutions, the federal government, stock transfer agents or other courts before transfer of money or assets to the executor of the estate.

> If the person who passed away had a valid Will and you are the executor of the estate, you can obtain letters testamentary from the local courthouse in the county where the deceased was living when they died. You usually must take the official Will to the court, along with a certified death certificate, and file a probate petition.

Liability: One is libel or has liability when they are responsible for something by law.

Lien: A legal claim against an asset which is used to secure a loan. This must be paid when the asset is sold.

Life Insurance: Life insurance pays a specific amount of money either on the death of the insured person or after a set period. If you locate an agent associated with any policy talk to them and see if they have any additional information on other policies the decedent may have had.

Life Insurance Policies: Each policy should be located. Include name of the carrier, policy number, named beneficiary, all access information and policy amount. These are most often missed when they are from a former employer. If you locate an agent associated with any policy talk to them and see if they have any additional information on other policies the decedent may have had.

Limited Liability Company, (LLC): A business structure that can be used to protect an individual's assets while engaging in business. An LLC provides statutory limits to liability without all of the requirements of a corporation as well as favorable tax treatment.

Limousine: A limousine is an automobile designed to seat five or more persons behind the driver's seat. They are usually driven by a chauffeur.

Liner: A liner is a container made of concrete, fiberglass, or steel with or without any bottom to be used for the burial of a casket.

Liquidation: Liquidation of an estate is usually when a its assets are sold and the proceeds pay creditors.

Living Trust: In most cases a living trust allows someone to distribute assets at the time of your death but does not allow for someone to make financial decisions for you if you become incapacitated.

> **Revocable Living Trust:** A revocable living trust can definitely be a more efficient way to transfer property at death if it is not already held in joint tenancy or you live in a community property state which most likely has special laws to protect the surviving spouse.

Living Will: A Living Will allows you to make health care decisions now in case you are unable to do so in the future. It documents instructions for your medical care in the event you are unable to communicate due to a severe injury, terminal illness or other medical condition. A Living Will can also be called a health care declaration, advance directive, or medical power of attorney. It is not a Last Will and Testament or a Living Trust.

Living Will Declaration: A Living Will. The actual document.

Liquid Assets: Liquid assets can be cash or accounts that can be converted to cash: Money Market Funds, Promissory Notes, Certificates of Deposit, Treasury Bills, Savings Bonds, are some examples 401K accounts, IRAs, annuities, savings bonds and mutual funds.

Long Term Care: Many people become more fearful of long term health care as they age. Medicaid is an option but too many people believe that an individual can transfer all of their assets to family members and then qualify for Medicaid. This is not the case. Medicaid is a program, funded by the federal and state governments, which pays for medical care for those who cannot afford it. The program typically helps low-income individuals or families, as well as elderly or disabled individuals. The state and federal government closely scrutinizes what people do with their money prior to entering a nursing home and applying for Medicaid.

If a person successfully transfers assets to an adult child there may be events not planned on such as divorce or medical bills that will change the future amount of these funds.

Lot: A lot can refer to a grave, crypt, niche or plot in a cemetery.

Lowering Device: A lowering device is a piece of cemetery equipment used to lower the casket into the ground.

Low Income Home Energy Assistance Program: If you cannot afford to pay your home energy bill, your home may not be safe, and you and your family may be at risk of serious illness or injury. The federal Low Income Home Energy Assistance Program (LIHEAP) may be able to help keep you and your family safe and healthy.

M

Mail: The U.S. Postal Service does not need to be informed of a person death. The mail needs to be forwarded to the executor's home address or a post office box for at least a year. The bills and financial statements that come in the mail are often the most reliable way to find all of the deceased person's assets and debts. All insurance companies are required by law to send a statement once a year and this may identify previously unknown policies and accounts.

All mail should be sent certified, return receipt requested and keep copies of everything including notes on what was mailed and when.

The U.S. Postal Service has change of address cards that may be filled out.

A Change of Address (COA) request must be submitted by the addressee or by someone authorized to file on behalf of the addressee. When submitting a COA request, please note the following:

The person who submits this COA request states that he or she is the person, executor, guardian, authorized officer, or agent of the person for whom mail would be forwarded under this request form.

Anyone intentionally submitting false or inaccurate information on a COA request form is subject to punishment by fines or imprisonment or both under Sections 2, 1001, 1702 and 1708 of Title 18, United States Code (U.S.C.).

Marker: A grave marker is usually a flat headstone set flush to the ground. Most cemeteries have limitations on the size and type of grave marker that is permitted.

Monument: A monument at a grave site is usually a headstone, measuring at least two feet by one foot that extends above the surface of the ground. A single monument is usually allowed on a designated "monument lot" or subdivision. Monuments may not be permitted on single graves. Every cemetery may have different rules that you will need to follow. Before you purchase anything check with the cemetery you have chosen.

Marriage License: The spouse may not be able to claim anything if they cannot prove they were married to the deceased. Be certain the spouse has immediate access to all documents.

Marriage: Many people are not getting remarried after a divorce. In some states if you die intestate (without a Will) your married spouse does not receive everything from the estate if you have children from a previous marriage. State laws vary and there are community property states and non-community property states. When two people are living together without benefit of marriage it becomes more complicated. If one person owns the home and dies will the surviving significant other be able to continue living in the home? Will the home pass to children from a previous marriage? Will stepchildren, foster children or adopted children inherit anything? Will they be left with nothing?

Remarriage: If a person has remarried and a son or daughter from a previous marriage is the financial power of attorney and executor of the estate and there is conflict between the various households it can be expense and time consuming to straighten things out.

Mass Cards: Mass cards can be sent either by Catholic or non-Catholic friends. The offering of prayers is a valued expression of sympathy to a Catholic family. A card indicating that a Mass for the deceased has been arranged may be obtained from any Catholic parish.

GLOSSARY & INDEX
Terms and Definitions

Mausoleum: A mausoleum a large tomb: an external free-standing building constructed as a monument. It contains burial chamber of a deceased person or persons. They are usually built above ground in cemeteries and are more common in areas with a high water table. Community mausoleums in cemeteries or churches can have hundreds of crypts, which are purchased individually. Many mausoleums are prefabricated and delivered to the site where they are assembled. There are additional fees. Entombment fees are charged to open and close the crypt or mausoleum. These range from $500 - $2,000, depending on the cemetery and time of entombment, with weekends and holidays being extra. Engraving the date of death can cost $50 to $200 or more. There may be perpetual care fees and record keeping fees. Be certain that all of this is understood before you sign the contract.

Mausoleum Trust Fund: In some cases a Trust Fund must be established with the Cemetery's Association before a Mausoleum can be built. The income from this Trust Fund will be used exclusively to maintain and care for the mausoleum. The amount of the fund will be determined by the cemetery's management, but will not be less than 10 percent of the total cost of the lot and structure.

Mausoleum Crypt: A mausoleum crypt is a space in a mausoleum capable of holding a casket.

Mausoleum Niche: A mausoleum niche is a space in a mausoleum or columbarium to for inurnment of cremated human remains in an urn.

Mausoleum Vase: A mausoleum vase is a receptacle for the placement of flowers on a crypt or niche.

Medicaid

Medicaid: Medicaid is a need-based program that provides health-care benefits to families based on income and other criteria. Each state operates a Medicaid program that provides health coverage for lower-income people, families and children, the elderly, and people with disabilities. The eligibility rules for Medicaid are different for each state, but most states offer coverage for adults with children at some income level. In addition, beginning in 2014, most adults under age 65 with individual incomes up to about $15,000 per year will qualify for Medicaid in every state. Less than 10% of seniors typically have long term care insurance, yet 90% worry about long term care costs. see *Medicaid*, page 207

Medicare

Medicare: Medicare does not cover all health care services, nor does it pay the entire cost of all the services that it does cover. http://www.medicare.gov

Hospice Care: To get payment from Medicare, the agency must be approved by Medicare to provide hospice services.

Generally, Medicare does not cover long term "custodial" care and is designed to cover only those medical expenses deemed necessary.

Medicare and Funeral Expense: The average funeral in 2012 is over $8,500. Medicare may, under certain circumstances, pay a benefit of a few hundred dollars. The Medicare program may also cover some bereavement services if they are provided by a qualifying hospice in connection with hospice care.

People eligible for the program include:

1) People 65 or older.

2) People under 65 with certain disabilities.

3) People of any age with End-Stage Renal Disease (ESRD) (permanent kidney failure requiring dialysis or a kidney transplant).

Medicare Part A (Hospital Insurance)

Medicare Part B (Medical Insurance)

Medicare Part C (also known as Medicare Advantage)

Medicare Advantage Plans are health plans that are approved by Medicare and provided by private companies. Medicare sets the rules for Medicare Advantage Plans and regulates the private companies who operate the Plans.

Medicare Part D (Medicare Prescription Drug Coverage)

The Original Medicare Plan is available nationwide and is a pay-per-visit health plan. There are usually coverage "gaps" or costs that you must pay, such as deductibles, copayments and coinsurance.

Help is available. If you have limited income and resources, you may qualify for help paying your Medicare health care and/or prescription drug coverage costs.

http://www.medicare.gov/publications/pubs/pdf/10050.pdf (Medicare & You 2012)

For more information, visit www.socialsecurity.gov,

Call Social Security at 1-800-772-1213,

Or apply for help at your State Medical Assistance (Medicaid) office.

If you have questions about Medicare, visit www.medicare.gov, or call 1-800-MEDICARE (1-800-633-4227). TTY users should call 1-877-486-2048.

Medicaid Hospice: In 1986, laws were passed to allow the states to develop coverage for hospice programs. Most states have a Medicaid hospice benefit, which is patterned after the Medicare hospice benefit.

Medicaid and Trusts: Funds placed in a trust designated to pay for a funeral and burial expenses may be exempt in determining Medicaid eligibility.

Medical Directives, Health Care Directives or Advance Directives: An advance directive is a written statement of a person's wishes regarding medical treatment. It is a legal document detailing a person's health care wishes, including the individual to whom they give the legal authority to act on their behalf and what types of treatment they do and do not want to receive in the event they are unable to speak or communicate. The living will and the power of attorney constitute what are called advance directives. A divorce has no effect on your written directions for health care.

Medical Examiner: A medical examiner and a coroner are similar but not exactly the same in all circumstances. The designation, duties and qualifications vary from state to state. A medical examiner or coroner is a public official that investigates any death thought to be of other than natural causes or if there was no physician in attendance for a long time prior to death.

Medical Intervention: Medical intervention is usually a procedure used to modify a process or situation. Someone undergoing a drug overdose would most likely need medical intervention to survive.

Medical Power of Attorney: A written statement of a person's wishes regarding medical treatment. A health care directive.

Medigap: Medigap is an insurance policy offered by private insurance companies to fill the gaps in coverage for original Medicare. Medigap is also known as Medicare supplement insurance. When purchasing Medigap insurance, shop around. Policies offering the same benefits can vary greatly in price.

Medical Information Bureau (MIB): MIB Group, Inc. ("MIB") is a membership corporation owned by approximately 470 member insurance companies in the US and Canada. Organized in 1902, MIB's Fraud Protection/Risk Assessment Services protect insurers, policyholders and applicants from attempts to conceal or omit information material to the sound and equitable underwriting of life, health, disability income, critical illness and long-term care insurance.

> MIB is committed to the principle that every consumer should be entitled to know the contents of his or her consumer file maintained by MIB and to correct any inaccurate or incomplete information in the record. The executor can contact the MIB to see what is on file for the deceased. An insurance company will have most likely searched the individual's data before a policy was issued.
>
> The Medical Information Bureau (MIB) "Will Provide One Free MIB Consumer Report Every Year" Under the Fair and Accurate Transactions Act (FACTA), at your request, MIB will provide you one free MIB disclosure report every 12 months.

To request your free report: Call 1-866-692-6901 OR

Visit our on-line disclosure request form on our website.
http://www.mib.com/html/request_your_record.html

Memorial Service: A memorial service can be held with or without the body present and can vary in ceremony and procedures according to the community and religious affiliations. Some families prefer public visitations followed by a private or graveside service with a memorial service later at the church or funeral home.

Memberships: Some memberships can be sold or transferred and are valuable assets. Some examples are country clubs, local annual golf memberships, theme parks, museums, travel, and health clubs, season tickets and annual passes to almost anything. Look for any documentation pointing to these assets. It is up to the executor to show due diligence in valuing memberships.

Memorial: A memorial is any monument, tombstone, grave marker, or headstone identifying a grave or graves. It can also refer to a name plate, name bar, or inscription identifying a crypt or niche.

Memorial Book: This is a type of scrapbook in memory of the deceased. Friends, family and loved ones can all contribute to it. It could be reproduced later on in a hardcover edition by companies like LuLu.com one copy or a few copies at a time.

> You may add photos, copies of the Obituary and favorite memories. The purpose is to honor and memorialize the deceased.

Memorial Card: A memorial card is a small credit card sized card on which a poem or scripture is printed, along with the deceased name and related information. They are sometimes called memorial tribute or remembrance cards.

Memorial Donations

Memorial Donations: Donations instead of Flowers. Many people today are suggesting that friends contribute to a memorial fund set up in the name of the deceased instead of sending flowers. Setting up a memorial fund is fairly easy, and many banks and foundations will help you set up the fund free of charge.

Memorial donations provide financial support for various projects. If recognized as a charitable institution, some gifts may be deductible for tax purposes.

If you do set up a Memorial fund get some consensus as to what charity the fund will benefit. It can benefit more than one charity. As with anything else, if the scale of the fund is large enough it will affect taxes down the road.

When you name the memorial fund you should include the name of the individual to whom the fund is dedicated. Create a brief description of the fund and its purpose and set up the memorial fund as soon as possible so people can donate. The executor or personal representative would most likely be the person named as the fund's administrator. A little more work, but one less person to be held accountable. see *Charity*, page 314

Obituary: The obituary could include a mailing address for the memorial fund and ask people to donate to the fund rather than contribute flowers at a viewing or funeral.

Memorial Garden: A memorial garden is usually a church garden with a section in which the cremated ashes are poured directly into the ground, and covered by grass or a ground-cover vine. These ashes are commingled with other ashes and with soil, in a tangible symbol of the communion of saints. A plaque on which the names and dates can be inscribed is usually nearby. A fountain in the memorial garden symbolizes Baptism in living water and is often comforting to the bereaved. It is also common to have some benches, so people can sit and meditate.

Memorial Park: Most often memorial parks allow only flat markers, while cemeteries allow markers of varying heights.

Memorial Service or Tribute Service

Memorial Service or Tribute Service: A memorial service is conducted in memory of the deceased without the remains being present. It can vary in ceremony and procedure according to community and religious affiliations. If the decedent's remains are present at a service held more than a few days after death it is almost always necessary to preserve the body through embalming. If there is an open casket the body will also need to be prepared for viewing with wardrobe and make-up. This is one reason a casket or urn is usually not present. A memorial service is not mandatory. Some people prefer to allow loved ones to be remembered in personal and private ways.

The memorial service is less formal than a funeral and is most often held within a week of the death. It is simply a gathering of family and friends to honor and recognize the deceased. It can also be postponed for weeks until family members can be gathered together. If the memorial service is postponed for a few weeks a graveside service or wake is usually held within a week of death.

Registry Book: It is customary to sign a registry book. Include a brief note and your full name and complete address so the family can contact you at a later date if necessary. They may just want to say thank you. Your note should be a very short remembrance; "He/she was well thought of. We will miss him/her." Or "He/she was so much help at – we will all miss him/her." Keep it short and simple.

Food: A memorial service held for family and close friends close to the time of death most likely will not be catered. The last thing the family wants to deal with right now is preparing meals so it is always nice to bring food. Just use good sense and you will be fine. Place food in a disposable container so the family does not have to clean it and return it to you. A casserole, plate of cookies or quiche is always appreciated. Ethnic food is fine if you know the family preferences. If you cannot bring food do not worry about it. It is more important for the family to see you than to have you bring something.

Dress: We should definitely dress respectfully for all services, wakes, visitations and viewings. Maybe not as formal as for funerals but use some uncommon sense: No ratty cut offs, t-shirts, bare midriffs or flip flops. Stay away from all denim (jeans). Dress respectfully. Business casual is what we would expect.

There may also be Clergy, Religious Leaders or others who may want to say or read something. This is always up to the family to decide. This is not a time to try to impose your will on their wishes.

Memorial Society: An organization that provides information about funerals and disposition, but is not part of the state-regulated funeral service industry.

Mercury Amalgam Dental Fillings: Along with energy consumption, mercury emissions from vaporized dental fillings are a common concern associated with cremation.

> According to the United Nations Environment Programme, the use of mercury in tooth fillings represents some 10% of global mercury consumption, thus being among the largest consumer uses of mercury in the world (AMAP/UNEP 2008). In the U.S., as demonstrated in this report, mercury use in dentistry amounts to over 32 tons[3] annually, which is considerably more than some recent estimates.[4] For comparison, in the European Union dental applications comprise the second largest use of mercury, amounting to some 20-25% of the annual consumption of mercury in the EU. With something less than twice the population of the U.S., the EU use of mercury in dentistry is somewhat more than twice the U.S. consumption (BIO 2012).
>
> www.chem.unep.ch/mercury/Atmospheric_Emissions/Technical_background_report.pdf
>
> http://www.zeromercury.org

Dental Mercury: The significant releases to the environment of dental mercury in waste and through other pathways, as well as its persistence once it reaches the environment, are well established.

Environment: Once in the environment, dental mercury can convert to its even more toxic form, methyl mercury.

> The answer seems to be in the continued filtration systems at crematories that reduce or eliminate the toxic chemicals contained in the deceased.

Microprocessor Card: A microprocessor card is a type of smart card. They contain memory and are used for identification and to secure confidential files among other things.

Miscarriage: stillbirth, an unborn baby's death. Generally, in the United States, when fetal death occurs after 20 weeks of pregnancy, it is referred to as stillbirth or Sudden Antenatal Death Syndrome. A fetal death prior to 20 weeks is a miscarriage.

Missing Money: State treasurers currently hold $32.9 billion in unclaimed bank accounts and other assets. You can search for unclaimed assets at MissingMoney.com

Monetary Value: Monetary value refers to the U.S. dollar value of an asset. Sometimes you will need an appraisal to ascertain a valid monetary value.

Money Market Accounts: A type of bank account in which the bank pays a higher than usual interest rate in exchange for a high minimum balance and a restriction on the number of transactions made in any given month. Usually a Certified Copy of the Death Certificate and Letters of Administration or a Letter of Testamentary is necessary to gain access to the account if it is not a joint account with right of survivorship.

Monument: A monument usually refers to a memorial made principally of stone which extends above the surface of the earth, in upright form.

Morgue: Places in which human remains are kept until identified and claimed or until arrangements for burial have been made.

Mortgage: When a person dies the mortgage passes to the joint tenant if there is one. Real property held in joint tenancy can be transferred by recording an affidavit of death of a joint tenant with the local county recorder's office. A home solely titled in the name of the decedent will require probate to transfer title of the home. Probate can easily take a year or more if there are no situations (someone contesting a decision made by the executor, for example).

Married, Community Property: Some states limit a spouse's ability to transfer property acquired during the marriage as an extra protection for the surviving spouse. Even if only the decedent's name is listed on the property title, depending on state law, they may be able to transfer only one half interest in the property. The surviving spouse may also be able to claim a forced share of the estate if this amount is more than what is provided in the Will.

Intestate: If the decedent left no Will and the property is held in joint tenancy it passes to the joint tenant in almost all cases. If the decedent owned property in joint tenancy in more than one state, who inherits the property is determined by the intestacy laws of two or more different states. If one state is a joint property state and one state is not and the property was not held in joint tenancy, now may be a good time to speak with a competent professional. Usually any assets held in joint tenancy such as: bank accounts, safe deposit box contents, stocks and bonds, real-estate, and community property usually pas directly to the sole survivor.

Assume the Mortgage: Not all lenders allow assumptions by family members following the death of original mortgagors, but many do. Unless other arraignments are made the lender will foreclose on the house if payments stop.

Mortuary: Also called a funeral home. A mortuary is a building specifically designed and constructed for caring for the dead.

Mortuary Science: Mortuary science is the part of the funeral service industry dealing with the proper preparation of the body for final disposition. All funeral directors must have either an associate's degree in funeral science or an associate's degree in mortuary science. Many states require students to complete a practicum with a licensed funeral home while enrolled in school.

Mortician: A funeral director.

Mourner: One who is present at the funeral out of affection or respect for the deceased.

Mourning: Mourning is the process one takes when grieving and moving towards healing.

Mutual Funds: Mutual funds are an investment program funded by shareholders that invest in stocks, bonds or other assets. Each investor in the fund owns shares, which represent a part of these holdings.

N

Niche: A space in a columbarium or mausoleum for placing Urns containing cremated ashes. Not all niches are the same size and not all urns will fit in all niches. You need to be certain the urn will fit in the niche.

Niche Garden: An outdoor garden containing structures with niches for urns.

Notify

Notify the Immediate Family: Call immediate family members first. Parents, Children, Brothers, Sisters and Grandparents of the deceased. People from out of state will have to make arrangements if they are planning to attend a Funeral or Memorial Service. After a divorce or separation things can become more challenging. Do your best and try not to forget anyone. While you are calling ask about other members of the family and get their contact information. Predetermine where cards, flowers, or donations will be sent.

Do not worry about waking others. Research has shown that when people are not notified immediately they feel left out. The initial reaction from most people is shock. Have others assist you in notifying everyone, this is a lot to do right now by yourself.

Funeral Home, Crematory or Home Funeral: You will need to know exactly where the decedent will be moved for final disposition. Will this be a funeral provider or a crematory? It could also be a Home Funeral. If there is a Will the decedent's wishes should have been made known. If there was no Will (intestate) you should already have gathered contact information and have some idea of the funeral plans.

Ask for help. Decide who will look after minor children. Arrange for the immediate care of a surviving spouse, children, pets, and anyone living with the deceased while you call. Keep a list of names and phone numbers of anyone who says they will help. You will need these later and will not remember where everything is located, so make a list now. Consider transportation, medical, and dietary needs. Keep a list of who was contacted and when. People will need to know how to follow up to obtain information regarding funeral and or other arrangements.

Notify the executor or administrator and any trustee named in a Will or Trust. The executor usually has full responsibility with regards to the funeral arrangements and should be named in the Will. If the deceased dies intestate (no Will) or there is no executor then an administrator, or the person in priority to be the administrator, has the right to possession of the body for the purpose of disposing of the remains. This will usually be the surviving spouse and then the next of kin.

Priority: What is the usual order of priority for disposition of remains? 1) An agent under a power of attorney for health care who has the right and duty of disposition. 2) The competent surviving spouse. 3) The sole surviving competent adult child of the decedent or, if there is more than one competent adult child of the decedent, the majority of the surviving competent adult children. (if they can all be notified and are able). 4) The sole surviving competent adult sibling of the decedent or, if there is more than one surviving competent adult sibling of the decedent, the majority of the surviving competent adult siblings (if they can all be notified and are able). 5) The surviving competent adult person or persons respectively in the next degrees of kinship. Next of kin. This is meant to be a general order but always check with your state statutes for a proper legal explanation.

Notify the Beneficiaries. They should each be sent a copy of the will.

Notify the Employer: If the deceased was working someone needs to call their employer immediately. Ask about the deceased's benefits and any pay due, including vacation or sick time, disability income, etc. Find out if any dependents are still eligible for benefit coverage through the company. Find out if there is a life insurance policy through the employer, who the beneficiary is and how to file a claim. Get copies of the paperwork in case you cannot readily locate them.

Call all Life Insurance Companies: As you are going through the deceased's documents or preplan notebook, collect all insurance contact information and have someone start calling and ask how to file a claim. Write down all information and if you do not understand ask them to repeat it. There may be payment options.

Obituary: Publish an Obituary in the local newspaper. With the decline of readership in local newspapers publishing an obituary is no longer a guarantee of informing most people in the area. Families are now located in several states or overseas and a phone call is the best way to inform people. In a short time it will most likely be considered "proper" to use a social network or text the news. For the time being it is more considerate to phone someone and tell them. Email is still acceptable, but not everyone still looks at their email on a daily basis.

Notify all clubs and organizations the deceased was a member of. Civic Organizations, Fraternal Organizations and Clubs. Do not just close memberships without first checking to see if there are certain benefits such as reduced dues and fees or season tickets that may be sold or transferred to someone else.

Non-domicile State: A person's state of domicile is the state in which they have their permanent residence. It is possible to have a permanent residence in one state, move to another state and still have taxes owed to the first state. You most likely need to change your domicile and become a non-resident of the first state for tax purposes. This is sometimes tricky to do because the first state wants your money. **Non-recourse Loan: Underwater Homes:** A home is said to be "underwater" when more is owed on the home than the home is worth. A reverse mortgage is a "non-recourse" loan which means that the HECM borrower (or their estate) will never owe more than the loan balance or value of the property, whichever is less; and no assets other than the home must be used to repay the debt. Non-recourse means simply that if the borrower (or estate) does not pay the balance when due, the mortgagee's remedy is limited to foreclosure and the borrower will not be personally liable for any deficiency resulting from the foreclosure.

Non-Recourse Loans: With the HUD (Department of Housing and Urban Development), FHA-insured (Federal Housing Administration) HECM (Home Equity Conversion Mortgage) reverse mortgage, the borrower can never owe more than the value of the property and cannot pass on any debt from the reverse mortgage to any heirs. The sole remedy the lender has is the collateral, not assets in the estate, if applicable.

> **The executor may sell the home.** If a member of the family or an heir chooses to pay off the loan in order to prevent selling the house the full amount of the loan has to be repaid even if the balance of the loan is higher than the value of the house. However, if the heirs decide to sell the house to repay the loan, the HECM product has a non-recourse policy which states that the heirs will not be required to pay more than the value of the home, even if the loan balance exceeds the value of the home. Now may be a good time to consult a competent professional.

Nursing Home: A nursing home is a private residential institution equipped to care for persons unable to look after themselves entirely as they age or are chronically ill.

O

Obduction: The act or instance of performing a postmortem examination.

Obituary

> **Obituary:** An obituary is a notice of the death of a person that contains a biographical sketch of the deceased person. It is sometimes referred to as a Death Notice and is recorded in a newspaper or online.

> **Obituary, how to notify Friends and Family:** With the decline of readership in local newspapers publishing an obituary is no longer a guarantee of informing most people in the area. Families are now located in several

states or overseas and a phone call is the best way to inform people. In a short time it will most likely be considered "proper" to use a social network or text the news. For the time being it is more considerate to phone someone and tell them. Email is still acceptable, but not everyone still looks at their email on a daily basis.

Writing an Obituary: For many people an Obituary may be the only thing that was ever written about them. A simple paragraph or two will be fine. You want to inform the public that your loved one has died. It acknowledges the loss while expressing the joy their presence brought and includes information on the upcoming funeral or memorial service. Today an obituary should only include the full name, and plans for a memorial service and internment. Families are now located in several states or overseas and a phone call is the best way to inform people. see *Identity Theft*, page 190

Do Not Include: It is recommended to not include any of the following facts about the deceased. Yes, Times, they are a changing. **Do not include:** Mothers maiden name, address, ancestry, occupation, date-of-birth and date-of-death or any personal information that can be used to steal an identity. You can still honor the person without giving up their personal information. see *Identity Theft*, page 190

Identity theft and Obituaries: Identity theft continues to be one of the fastest growing crimes in the United States. The FTC estimates that as many as 9 million Americans have their identities stolen each year. Due to this proliferation of identity theft it is recommended that the full date of birth or even the year of birth not be given. Unfortunately there are people who read through obituaries for names and addresses and then buy social security numbers, credit histories and other personal data online. They will apply for and get credit cards in the name of the deceased and run up charges quickly. Surviving family members are unlikely to be held liable for the debt but may still spend a lot of time and money straightening out the fraud. Why is the Federal Government allowing this to not only persist, but get worse? We will most likely lose some of our freedom as our society becomes more digital and no one wants to step up. The FTC estimates that as many as 9 million Americans have their identities stolen each year. This is a very real, serious problem for millions of Americans. Please do not allow yourself to become a victim see *Identity Theft*, page 190

An Excellent Free Government Resource:
http://www.ftc.gov/bcp/edu/microsites/idtheft/consumers/about-identity-theft.html

Another excellent resource: http://www.idtheftcenter.org/

Modern Obituary: 1) Announce the death. "Jop Jopne", passed away, died, went to be with his Lord, after a long struggle with health problems, surrounded by their family, in peace, etc. **2)** You may list some important events, qualities, or accomplishments: married for 5o years, worked with youth baseball leagues, baked for friends and family, was always a joy to be around, etc. **3)** Is survived by: spouse, immediate family, relatives all want to be remembered and mentioned. You may do this as long as you do not give personal details that will help in identity theft. This takes some though and planning. We all have paper trails. Our purpose is to respect and honor the deceased and their family without doing any harm. **4)** Service time and place. **5)** Any special message about donations, flowers or charities.

If you make it difficult to steal the identity of the deceased by "hardening the target" it is hoped the thief will go somewhere else where it is easier to steal. It is still more considerate to phone someone and tell them. Perhaps obituaries will disappear altogether except for the rich and famous.

Obituaries Online: Online obituaries may contain Guest Books that allow comments to be added. This can benefit both the family and friends of the loved one and the person writing the memory. Expressing condolences online is also less personal than a private note or in person. Nothing can replace a hug. There have been many cases of thieves obtaining the home address of the deceased and the date of the service from the obituary. They then burglarize the home of the deceased while people are away attending the service. It is like sending the thief an invitation to steal. Things are not even the same as they were five years ago. Burglars, thieves, scam artists are digital. How well is the surviving spouse or family member able to handle a liar and thief in the coming weeks? You may be able to help for a few weeks but what happens when everyone is gone and a "friend" of the deceased drops in on the surviving spouse or family? They can and do rob them for as much as they can get. It is suggested that you have a realistic view of the world and understand that it is the day-to-day job of some people to rob, steal and kill. Be careful.

Obituaries Online, How to Find: The National Obituary Archive ™ is the world's largest repository of obituaries and death records with more than 55 million individual entries on file. Visitors may search the archive freely to learn about the deaths of friends or family or to explore relationships when building family trees or doing genealogical research. http://www.arrangeonline.com/

Opening and Closing the Grave or Crypt: Opening and Closing Fees: Cemetery fees for the digging and refilling of a grave.

Optical Card: An optical card contains information recorded on an optical memory stripe, similar to compact disks. These are not very common but still need to be secured.

Online log-in Information: User name, password, pin number if needed and challenge questions. While these are not strictly documents, they access documents and assets that are sometimes worth than everything else combined. see *Digital Assets*, page 40, 41, 333

Opening and Closing Fees: Cemetery fees for the digging and refilling of a grave.

Organ and Tissue Donations

Organ and Tissue Donation: Even if someone signs a donor card, it is essential that their family also knows their wishes regarding organ donation. Let them know as soon as possible. The family may still be asked to sign a consent form in order for the donation to occur. If they say no, the hospital may refuse to accept the organ(s). If the donor has taken the time to register with the Secretary of State or with the Gift of Life, then their family does not have the right to object once they are in the registry. Sign the organ donor space on your driver license and carry an organ donor card. Make this information available to health care workers.

Anyone over eighteen years of age can become an organ or tissue donor. This will not interfere with their own health care and it will not, within reason, delay their own funeral arrangements. You may change your mind at any time, simply notify people you have changed your mind and if you have checked Organ Donor on your driver's license, contact the department of motor vehicles in the state where the license was issued to change the designation. The most important thing to do is to sign up as an organ and tissue donor in your state's donor registry. www.organdonor.gov

For reasons why you should think about this before making a decision read:

What You Lose When You Sign That Donor Card, By Dick Teresi
http://online.wsj.com/article/SB10001424052970204603004577269910906351598.html

http://blog.beliefnet.com/watchwomanonthewall/2012/03/what-you-lose-when-you-sign-that-donor-card.html

Google: What You Lose When You Sign That Donor Card, By Dick Teresi (you will get some good pro and con)

Organ transplantation is a twenty billion dollar a year business. Organ transplantation—from procurement of organs to transplant to the first year of postoperative care—is a $20 billion per year business. Recipients of single-organ transplants—heart, intestine, kidney, liver, single and double lung and pancreas—are charged an average $470,000, ranging from $288,000 for a kidney transplant to $1.2 million for an intestine transplant, according to consulting firm Milliman. Neither donors nor their families can be paid for organs.

Your Cost: Your family pays for your medical care and funeral costs, but not for organ donation. Costs related to donation are paid by the recipient, usually through insurance, Medicare or Medicaid. Costs for the donation of organ or tissues are covered by the local organ procurement organization in many cases and the assumption is they are reimbursed.

First Person Consent: Recently, several states have passed legislation establishing "first-person consent" whereby the family cannot override an individual's documented desire to be an organ donor. Some states have established first-person consent registries for people interested in being deceased organ donors.

Organ Donor Cards: Many Organ Donor Cards can be downloaded, printed, signed and carried with you. On Facebook Time Line, under Life Event there is a Health and Wellness section with a place for the individual to indicate that they have decided to be an organ donor, provide their state and/or country and even a story about why they have chosen to be an organ donor.

Out of State Property: If the deceased has property in another state(s) there will be additional probate proceedings in the state(s) where the property is located. A vacation home in the desert and another at the seashore could each go through a different state probate court with each accessing fees and charges. The executor or personal representative may be required to visit the property in each state have appraisals, inspections and possible attorney fees. There may also be taxes due. How much easier it would have been to have a simple Will that read in part: "I am leaving my house in the desert to my brother Wally and my house at the seashore to my sister Wallonia," signed, Wilbur. Since probate laws vary from state to state there may be a few surprises.

Outer Interment Receptacle: Another term for a vault or grave liner. Not all cemeteries require them. Shop around. The funeral service provider is required under the Funeral Rule to provide you with a price list. see *Funeral Rule*, page 178

Owner of Burial Space: The owner is the person to whom the cemetery operator or his authorized agent has transferred the **right of use** of burial space.

P

Package Deals: A package of services may be more expensive than just purchasing the goods and services that you actually want or need. Ask to see the price list and make an informed decision.

You do not need to spend a lot of money to have a meaningful dignified service. Who owns the local funeral service provider? Many local family-owned service providers are owned by corporate chains. They often keep the original name but change pricing and policy after the buyout.

Pain Control: Hospice care and palliative care both favor pain control. see *Hospice Care*, page 187

Pallbearers

Pallbearers: Carrying a casket for a loved one is one of the highest honors that can be bestowed upon a family member or close friend. There are usually six to eight pallbearers selected from family, friends or business associates. In some instances pallbearers are hired because there are no able bodied individuals who can perform the service.

Someone will tell the pallbearers exactly what to do. Sometimes you do not actually carry anything. You just walk alongside the casket as it rolls on a gurney or cart. Ask if you are uncertain because of your age or health. The casket will be moved from the funeral home to the hearse outside and then from the hearse to the grave site.

Often the pallbearers will be asked to ride in one of the vehicles driven by someone on staff at the funeral home. This ensures the pallbearers and the hearse all arrive at the cemetery at the same time.

GLOSSARY & INDEX
Terms and Definitions

Military Escort: If there is a military escort they will be responsible at the grave site for honors (rifle salute) folding of the flag, and presentation to the selected family member.

Pallbearers Selection: If the casket will actually be carried the selection criterion is different. Age, health and the size and weight of the deceased and the casket must now be considered.

Honorary Pallbearers: Honorary Pallbearers do not actively assist in carrying the casket. They usually walk in front of the casket.

All pallbearers, ushers and other parts of the funeral service should be scheduled to arrive 30 minutes before the funeral service takes place to receive directions. When arriving at the funeral home or religious facility someone will arrange for the cars of the pallbearers to be parked in front so they can all arrive together at the cemetery. As the time nears the start of the funeral service cars will be arranged as they arrive.

Palliative Care (Pain Relief): If you chose not to have life-prolonging intervention it does not mean that you cannot alleviate pain or be made comfortable. Instead of prolonging life, palliative care focuses on quality of life and dignity by helping a patient remain comfortable and free from pain until life ends naturally.

Palliative Care Programs: Palliative care is a program of action to make a patient comfortable by treating the person's symptoms from an illness. Hospice and palliative care both focus on helping a person be comfortable by addressing issues causing physical or emotional pain, or suffering. The goals of palliative care are to improve the quality of a seriously ill person's life and to support that person and their family during and after treatment.

Hospice care focuses on relieving symptoms and supporting patients with a life expectancy of months not years. Palliative care may be given at any time during a person's illness, from diagnosis on and is being used by other healthcare providers, including teams in hospitals, nursing facilities and home health agencies in combination with other medical treatments to help people who are seriously ill. Most hospices have a set of defined services, team members and rules and regulations for palliative care.

Passport and/or Passport Card: According to the NPIC, National Passport Information Center, you do not have to do anything with the passport or passport card of the deceased. The passport of a person who has died can be kept as a memento if you choose, or you can return it for cancellation.

> If you choose to have the passport cancelled and returned to you or destroyed, you may return the passport to the Consular Lost and Stolen Passport - CLASP unit. A copy of the Certificate of Death is required along with the passport. **If you want the cancelled passport returned, you must include a letter stating that request.** Mail the passport, Certificate of Death, and letter requesting cancelled/returned passport (if applicable) to the following address:
>
> Attention CLASP, 1111 19th St NW, Suite 500, Washington, DC 20036

Payable-on-Death Account (POD): You can set up a payable-on-death account at your bank and deposit funds into it to pay for your funeral and related expenses. A payable on death bank account is a regular bank account that names a specific person as the beneficiary. The immediate transfer of assets is triggered by the death of the client.

Pension Plans: A regular payment made during a person's retirement from an investment fund to which that person or their employer has contributed during their working life. Also a regular payment made by the government to some individuals who are disabled or of retirement age. A pension may be paid by a private company, government agency, or union. Each should name a beneficiary.

> Some pensions end at death while others are extended in whole or in part to the part to a surviving spouse or dependent children.
>
> If you are looking for a lost pension try: http://www.pbgc.gov/

People Search and Public Information Search Engine: People Search. Honestly Free! Search by Name. Find People in the USA. Free People Finder. A search tool that focuses on finding data related to individual people: names, addresses, and phone numbers.   http://www.zabasearch.com/

Perpetual Care Charge: A perpetual care charge may be included as part of the funeral and burial costs or it may be a separate charge. Cemeteries are maintained by perpetual care funds.

Personal Property Memorandum: Memorandum of Tangible Personal Property. This details how you want your personal effects distributed. It may include gun collections, stamps or coins, antiques, art, digital assets: websites, blogs, etc. The Memorandum can be more convenient because it can be changed at a later date without your having to amend the Will or Trust. State law determines if a Memorandum is legally binding on your beneficiaries. You may need to consult with a competent estate attorney.

Personal Representative

> **Executor, Personal Representative, Administrator, Exectrix, Court Appointed Administrator, Independent Executor, Independent Administrator, Temporary Administrator, Guardian and Temporary Guardian, together with their successors.**
>
> **An Executor is** someone who administers an estate of a person who left a valid Will. If a person dies intestate, that is, without a Will, then the Personal Representative or Administrator will be appointed by the court. An Exectrix is a female executor.
>
> No matter what they are called, they all oversee the disposition of property and possessions of a deceased person. An executor is entrusted with the large responsibility of making sure a person's last wishes are granted with regards to the disposition of their property and possessions. They identify the estate's assets, pay off its debts and then distribute whatever is left to the rightful heirs and beneficiaries.

Pets: Many people with terminal illness avoid bringing up a discussion of their pets because they are afraid the pet will be "put down." If you have a loved one with pets take the time to reassure them that the pets will be taken care of in the event of their death. Find someone to take on the responsibility of permanent care of the deceased person's pets.

Not all airlines accept pets. When traveling with a pet on an airplane, be sure to contact the airline directly for reservations and specific travel instructions. You do not always have to travel with the pet. There are pet transportation companies that will take care of this for you. You may need a copy of the animal's health certificate.

There are companies that specialize in transporting pets. These businesses are licensed and inspected by USDA/APHIS's Animal Care Unit. Many of the licensed animal transporters are listed on the member pages of the International Pet Animal Transportation Association (IPATA) web pages.

Phone Card: A phone card stores a specific cash amount that allows the user to access telephone networks via a PIN number.

Photo ID Card: A photo ID card can be used by employees to gain access to a secure building. It is an identification card bearing a photographic image of the cardholder. The image can be an actual photograph or one captured wholly electronically.

Physician, Attending: a physician who is mainly responsible for a patient at a particular time.

Physician, Primary Care: A physician, such as a family practitioner or internist who is chosen by an individual to provide continuous medical care.

Plaque: Check for any size requirements. Check the spelling and the dates before ordering.

Plot: A plot is a piece of property to be used or in use as a place for burial within a cemetery.

Plot, Burial Plot: A specific area of ground in a cemetery. A plot usually contains two or more graves. This is the space used to bury the casketed body or an urn containing cremains (ashes).

> In the U.S., at one time rights in burial plots were perpetual. The relatives of the deceased had a perpetual right to visit and maintain a grave and headstone and to sue to prevent desecration, neglect, or removal of the body. These rights persisted even if the property where the grave is located was sold,

provided the grave site was dedicated as such or was in an area dedicated as a cemetery. Some states have changed these rules by statute, permitting easier abandonment of cemeteries. Everything changes so check the local laws.

Pour-over Will: A Pour-over Will transfers assets upon death to a trust account. The Pour-over Will has only one beneficiary which is the Trust Account. Assets are poured-over into the trust. This is something the executor or someone pre-planning will need to look into further and goes beyond the scope of this book. A Pour-over Will can also instruct the successor trustee to put any assets into the trust that were not put in previously. Sweet, if everything is done correctly.

Power of Attorney: A written document in which one person (the principal) appoints another person to act as an agent on their behalf. They may legally sign a document for the principle. A limited power imposes limits on exactly what the representative may do in place of the principle. With a durable power of attorney, you are able to appoint an agent to manage your financial affairs, make health care decisions, or conduct other business for you during your incapacitation. a durable power of attorney is often chosen as a way to plan for those times when you are incapacitated.

Durable Power of Attorney: A durable power of attorney differs from a traditional power of attorney in that it continues the relationship if the principle becomes incapacitated. You will most likely be the first in line to be held, legally responsible to pay for the disposition of the body in the event of death. Even if there is are no assets in the estate after taxes and fees are paid you will be next in line to pay from your own resources for the funeral or cremation. An Authorization to Release Protected Healthcare Information form should also be filled out.

Prayer Cards, Funeral Programs and Keepsakes: Although this is still considered an obituary it is usually more detailed and longer, containing three or four paragraphs. This type of obituary will include the full name, area of residence. They sometimes refer to the circumstances of death in a general way, such as, "prolonged illness." There may or may not be a need for information on a memorial service, wake or viewing and internment. Due to the proliferation of identity theft it is recommended that many personal details no longer be given. Do not include: Mothers maiden name, address, ancestry, occupation, date-of-birth and date-of-death or any personal information that can be used to steal an identity. You can still honor the person without giving up their personal information. The FTC estimates that as many as 9 million Americans have their identities stolen each year. This is a very real, serious problem for millions of Americans. Please do not allow yourself to become a victim. see *Identity Theft*, page 190, 246, 375

Prearranged Funeral: Funeral arrangements that were completed by an individual prior to their death.

Prearranged Funeral Trust: A method by which an individual can pre-pay their funeral expenses.

Precious Metals: Just because it looks like gold, tastes like gold and smells like gold does not necessarily mean that it is gold. Many, many people have been fooled over the years by what appears to be valuable metals, jewelry, art, or artifacts. Have the item assayed or appraised. Keep an eye on it.

Pre-need: purchasing cemetery property in advance of actual need. The Cemetery property may be developed or undeveloped.

Prenuptial Agreement

A Prenuptial Agreement is a contract between two people before they are married and usually handles issues relating to property. The agreement will usually declare who owns what in the event of a divorce or separation and who will receive certain property when one of the spouses dies. A prenuptial agreement may take priority over a Last Will and Testament if it contains specific statements to that effect.

Prenuptial Agreements and Wills: If the terms of a prenuptial agreement conflict with the terms of either spouses valid Will, a probate court may choose to uphold the prenuptial agreement. In the past, Probate courts have usually ruled in favor of a prenuptial agreement when it appears that the agreement was fairly negotiated between the spouses.

Prenuptial Agreements and Intestacy: A prenuptial agreement may be used to distribute the estate if one spouse dies intestate (without a valid Will). The probate court may use the prenuptial agreement to distribute the property. Most states will not allow a spouse to completely disown the other spouse in a Will but with a prenuptial agreement this could happen, leaving the entire estate to someone else.

Prenuptial Agreements and Death: A prenuptial agreement should be written to leave little room for interpretation. It should declare which state laws should be applied to interpret it. If a spouse dies out of state there will be less conflict between state laws. Otherwise, the law in the state where the spouse died will control, even if that was not the law the couple had in mind when they made the Will.

Prenuptial Agreements and Sunset Clauses: A sunset clause sets an expiration date for the agreement. If that date has passed, the agreement is no longer legally binding in most cases.

Prepaid Card: A prepaid card is any one of many cards paid for at point of sale allowing the holder to purchase goods or services in an amount up to the prepaid value. The identity of the purchaser is not always known.

Prepay Funeral Expenses: see *Funeral Prepay*, page 216

Preparation Room: A preparation room in a funeral home is designed and equipped for preparing the deceased for final disposition.

Prepay for Funeral Services: Is it a good idea to prepay for your funeral services? Usually it is a better idea to set up a trust to cover your expenses. A Totten Trust seems to work out very well for most. It may also be advisable to prepay for some services like a cemetery plot, direct burial or direct cremation and set aside money in a trust for the cost of a service and other expenses. When you finish with this book you should have a much better idea of what you want to do.

Prepaid Card: A prepaid card is any one of many cards paid for at point of sale allowing the holder to purchase goods or services in an amount up to the prepaid value. The identity of the purchaser is not always known.

Pre-plan or Pre-pay: You can pre-plan without pre-paying. If you decide to pre-pay, you are the customer. They are the funeral service business. They are in business to make money. There is nothing wrong with that, just understand it is a business. Shop around for the best service and the best price.

Private Service: A private service is by invitation only and may be held at a place of worship, a funeral home or a family home. Only selected relatives and a few close friends attend a private funeral service. Sometimes a public viewing is held either earlier or later in the day.

Priority for Disposition of Remains: What is the usual order of priority for disposition of remains? 1) An agent under a power of attorney for health care who has the right and duty of disposition. 2) The competent surviving spouse. 3) The sole surviving competent adult child of the decedent or, if there is more than one competent adult child of the decedent, the majority of the surviving competent adult children. (if they can all be notified and are able). 4) The sole surviving competent adult sibling of the decedent or, if there is more than one surviving competent adult sibling of the decedent, the majority of the surviving competent adult siblings (if they can all be notified and are able). 5) The surviving competent adult person or persons respectively in the next degrees of kinship; Next of kin. This is meant to be a general order but always check with your state statutes for a proper legal explanation.

> Before the court issues official Letters Testamentary naming an administrator (or executor), the appointed person must sign an acceptance statement that describes his or her duties and acknowledges that the court can fine or remove an administrator (or executor) for failure to perform those duties faithfully. This varies by state. Most states require the executor, personal representative or administrator to post a Bond covering their actions. Although the executor may not be officially assigned until the court appointment, that person should be made available immediately to secure assets, gather information and make arraignments for final disposition.

Priority for Administrator of the Estate: If there is no Will (intestate) the probate court will appoint an administrator for the estate. The court will usually appoint the surviving spouse of the decedent, of if none, or if the spouse declines, the court will appoint one of the next of kin of the decedent. Before the court issues official Letters

Testamentary naming an administrator (or executor), the appointed person must sign an acceptance statement that describes his or her duties and acknowledges that the court can fine or remove an administrator (or executor) for failure to perform those duties faithfully. This varies by state. Most states require the executor, personal representative or administrator to post a Bond covering their actions. Although the executor may not be officially assigned until the court appointment, that person should be made available immediately to secure assets, gather information and make arraignments for final disposition.

Priority for Debt: This varies from state to state. Generally funeral expenses, costs and expenses of administering the estate, and taxes must be paid first. After paying taxes and creditors, the executor must give a full accounting to the court, detailing everything they did. Record expenses YOU paid using personal funds as these can add up fast. You need to be reimbursed by the estate. Your priority will be costs and expenses of administering the estate in most instances. The order of priority may change from state to state. The purpose of this book is to point you in the right direction and not to answer every question for every situation.

Private Service: A private service is by invitation only and may be held at a place of worship, a funeral home or a family home. Only selected relatives and a few close friends attend a private funeral service. Sometimes a public viewing is held either earlier or later in the day.

Probate Attorney: an attorney certified to practice law specializing in estate issues.

Probate: Probate is a legal proceeding that transfers your property following your death according to the terms of your Will or in the absence of a Will, to your heirs based on probate law. Your estate will be probated whether or not you have a Will. All states have probate and every probate court has its own detailed rules about the documents it requires, what they must contain, and when they must be filed. Probate pays debts and transfers assets to beneficiaries.

Renounce Probate: An Executor can renounce probate, which means they no longer wish to be an Executor. If an Executor does not apply for Probate, family members, beneficiaries and other interested parties can apply to the Court to be appointed an Executor. This could include a creditor as they have an interest in the estate.

Simplified Procedure: Is there a simplified procedure for settling an estate with limited assets? Yes, in most states there is. There are various rules and regulations depending on the state and/or county but there will most likely be a dollar amount mentioned. An example could be: A simplified procedure for settling the estate may be available if the total value of the estate assets does not exceed ($40,000). In addition, at the time of death the decedent must not own any real estate other than survivorship property, and the estate assets must consist only of personal property and/or an unreleased interest in a mortgage with or without value etc. If a simplified procedure is available it may not be necessary to probate the estate.

Probate Asset: A probate asset is one in which title to the property does not transfer by operation of law upon the death of the owner and therefore requires court involvement.

Uniform Probate Code (UPC): Not all states have adopted the UPC. Its purpose is to streamline the probate process and to standardize and modernize the various state laws governing Wills, Trusts, and Intestacy. Because the UPC has not been adopted by every state, check the code as actually adopted in that jurisdiction and do not rely on the text of the UPC in its entirety. Some states have adopted more of the code than others making a discussion of the entire code academic.

Tax: The personal representative or executor is responsible for paying all taxes. This includes, but is not limited to, the deceased's income taxes for the last year they were alive. This is from January 1 until the date of death. see *Tax*, page 433

Close Probate: Do not forget to Close Probate. Documents can usually be obtained online at the Probate Court website in the county where Probate was opened. see *Probate*, page 34, 241

Procession: The funeral procession is the vehicular movement of the funeral from the place where the funeral service was conducted to the cemetery.

Property Search Companies: A property search company can sometimes assist in finding and reclaiming safe deposit boxes and other assets. Contact the unclaimed property department at the institution first before approaching a property search company. Start with customer service.

Protected Memory Card: A protected memory card is a smart card that requires a secret code or PIN number to be entered before data can be sent or received from the chip.

Protective Medical Decisions Document (PMDD): A durable power of attorney for health care designed to meet state requirements and protect the signer. It is available from the "Patients Rights Council." Federal regulations require every hospital and health program that receives any Medicare or Medicaid funds to inform you, upon admission, of your rights regarding an advance directive. As a result, many facilities are giving patients a Living Will or Durable Power of Attorney to sign at the time of admission. They feel this "covers" them. The PMDD specifically prohibits euthanasia and assisted suicide.

Proximity Card: A proximity card or Key Card is placed near a reader and the information is read from the card. They are used for mainly for employee security access control.

Public Records Search: http://www.censusfinder.com/ For the United States, Canada, and the United Kingdom, a free public records search site. Track down vital records.

R

Railroad Retirement Act: If the deceased worked for a railroad and was covered by the federal railroad retirement act the family may be eligible for benefits.

Real-estate: Some states require the title to real estate be transferred to the surviving spouse in order for title insurance to remain in force. Many people assume that if they own their home together with a spouse that the surviving spouse will inherit the home at the time of their death. This is not always true. If the deceased spouse left a valid Will they can leave their half of the house to the surviving spouse which would make the surviving spouses share 100% If the spouse dies intestate (without a valid Will) the property passes 100% to the surviving spouse only if the property is community property and the deceased had no children from a previous marriage. This scenario is not true in all states. It is true in some community property states. Check the law in your state. It may also be a good time to consult with a competent estate attorney.

Real Property: Real property includes land and buildings, and anything affixed to the land.

Recording the Will: Recording the Will is also called Lodging the Will or Depositing the Will. This is usually done by the executor within a short time of death in the deceased's at the county courthouse where the deceased had their primary residence.

Refrigeration Fee: A refrigeration fee is charged by some funeral homes for cooling the body when embalming is not selected. If such a fee is charged, it must be stated up front, on both the General Price List and the Itemized Statement. This service is not always necessary and can cost from $50 to over $100 a day. If a funeral service provider tells you they have no refrigeration facilities they are trying to get you to pay for embalming which is also not generally required if the funeral takes place within a few days except under some circumstances. Embalming can cost $750 or more. Shop around for another service provider.

Register: A book made available for recording the names of people visiting the Funeral Home, Memorial Service or other Visitation to pay their respects to the deceased. Also has space for entering other data such as name, dates of birth and death of the deceased, name of the officiating clergyman, place of interment, time and date of service, list of floral tributes, etc.

Religious Leadership, all Faiths and Ethnicities

Religious leadership should be contacted as soon as possible. Many religions have time constraints on the disposition of the deceased's remains. Did the deceased have any religious affiliation? Is there a Church, Synagogue or religious institution listed in the deceased's address book? Are there any contact numbers? If there are; call and explain the situation and ask what the normal procedure is. Write things down and make a decision latter on as to what course of action you will follow.

If there is no religious affiliation the person taking care of the funeral or cremation usually has someone on call to take care of the funeral service, graveside service or memorial service. The service leader does not have to be ordained or licensed and can be of your own choosing.

Honorariums: A payment given to a professional person for services for which fees are not legally or traditionally required. The honorarium for the individual clergy to perform a graveside service or memorial service can range from $50 to $500. The fee for a Celebrant is usually between $300 and $900. The fee for the building where the service is to take place is additional. The fee for an organist, pianist, or soloist is an additional $100 to $300 each.

Renounce Probate: An Executor can renounce probate, which means they no longer wish to be an Executor. If an Executor does not apply for Probate, family members, beneficiaries and other interested parties can apply to the Court to be appointed an Executor. This could include a creditor as they have an interest in the estate.

Report of Casualty: The military does not issue death certificates. Instead, you will be given copies of the Report of Casualty. This report is provided whether the death occurred during combat or not. The report is used in the same way as a death certificate, for the transfer of property and settlement of life insurance benefits.

Reposing Room: A reposing room at the funeral home is where a body lies in state from the time it is casketed until the time of the funeral service.

Retail Store Cards: Retail store cards are used by some grocery stores to track purchases. Not ever card refers back to a customer name, address, phone number and email. The store expects the customer to fill out the information but many customers just use the card without ever doing so.

Retirement Accounts: IRAs, 401Ks, and any other pensions or retirement accounts. An IRA is considered dormant or unclaimed if no withdrawal has been made by age 70½. Each should name a beneficiary so any money due will pass directly to the beneficiaries named, without the hassles and expense of probate court. Many plans require the spouse to be named as beneficiary unless they sign a form giving up that right. A Certified Copy of the death certificate will be necessary to access the account.

Restorative Art: Restorative Art is a mix of techniques used to ensure the deceased looks natural and restful during the funeral proceedings employing wax, creams, plaster.

Reverse Mortgage (HECM): A reverse mortgage is a special type of home loan available to homeowners age 62 or older that lets you convert a portion of the equity in your home into cash. The equity that you built up over years of making mortgage payments can be paid to you. FHA's Home Equity Conversion Mortgage (HECM) program may be available to you. The reverse mortgage can become due when all homeowners have passed away or moved out of the home for 12 consecutive months. Taxes and insurance must be paid.

Fraud Alert: If you are interested in a reverse mortgage, beware of scam artists that charge thousands of dollars for information that is free from HUD! see *Reverse Mortgage*, page 211

Revocable Living Trust: A revocable living trust can definitely be a more efficient way to transfer property at death if it is not already held in joint tenancy or you live in a community property state which most likely has special laws to protect the surviving spouse.

Revoked Will: If a Will is missing or no longer valid because the decedent intentionally revoked it either an earlier Will or the laws of intestate succession are used to decide the proper distribution of the estate.

Retirement Accounts: IRAs, 401Ks, and any other pensions or retirement accounts. There are several types of IRAs.

> An IRA is considered dormant or unclaimed if no withdrawal has been made by age 70½. Each should name a beneficiary so any money due will pass directly to the beneficiaries named, without the hassles and expense of probate court. Many plans require the spouse to be named as beneficiary unless they sign a form giving up that right. A Certified Copy of the death certificate will be necessary to access the account. see *Assets*, page 41, 57, 75

S

Safe Deposit Boxes: There could be more than one. Include all information as to the location, keys, contents list, contact person and all access information.

Savings Accounts: There could be more than one. Include all information as to the location, keys, contents list, contact person and all access information.

Savings Bonds: Savings bonds with a named beneficiary are not part of the estate. The beneficiary may cash the bond if they possess a certified copy of the death certificate.

> Savings bonds without a named beneficiary may be cashed or reissued in the names of beneficiaries if stated in the Will.

Scattering Garden: A scattering garden is an area set aside for the scattering of cremains. There may be a charge for using a scattering garden.

Seals and Gaskets: Protective gaskets are sometimes sold as add-ons for up to several thousand dollars in additional charges. What is accomplished by an airtight seal? The consumer is often told that this seal will help to preserve the body of the loved one. A casket sealed with a tight rubber gasket creates an environment that helps bacteria thrive. When placed in a tightly sealed container most bodies have a tendency to liquefy and create bloating gas which explodes releasing noxious gasses into the crypt or mausoleum. Most cemetery workers pop the seal allowing air to vent into the casket to keep the remains from exploding the lid off the casket. The seal is also broken to allow air to vent when the casket is placed above ground.

> Without this airtight gasket there is normal dehydration and deterioration of the body. The newer Green Cemeteries do not allow seals or gaskets.

Season Tickets: These can be very valuable. Do any rights pass to heirs on death or do they expire at death?

Security Deposits: There are many different kinds from the electric company and other utility companies to property rentals.

Search Google: "name" state. Enter the person's name in quotation marks and add any defining information such as occupation or the State where they last lived. You may uncover assets. http://www.google.com/

Search the Government: Direct access to searchable information from the United States government, state governments, and local governments. http://www.usa.gov/

Search Missing Money: State treasurers currently hold $32.9 billion in unclaimed bank accounts and other assets. You can search for unclaimed assets at MissingMoney.com.

Unclaimed Property: Go directly to a government unclaimed property program by clicking on a state, territory, or province from the map or drop box below. You should search in every state where you have lived.   http://www.unclaimed.org/

Social Security Search: The Social Security Death Index (SSDI) is a database containing the names and dates of birth and death for over 77 million Americans. This massive database is a wonderful resource for genealogists, and is available in many online locations for free.

> http://www.ssa.gov/   or   http://www.archives.com/collections

Search Vital Records: One of the most comprehensive resources for locating vital records online. United States Birth Certificates, Death Records & Marriage Licenses. Some Local Libraries allow you to use this and other websites for free. Call your local library for details.   http://www.vitalrec.com/

Free People Search and Public Information Search Engine. People Search. Honestly Free! Search by Name. Find People in the USA. Free People Finder. A search tool that focuses on finding data related to individual people: names, addresses, and phone numbers.   http://www.zabasearch.com/

Find a Grave: You can search 83 million grave records. Find famous graves. Search by date, location, and various data bases. http://www.findagrave.com

Self-proving affidavit attached to a Will: An affidavit attached to a Will certifies that the witnesses and testator properly signed the Will. A self-proving Will makes it easy for the court to accept the document as the true Will of the person who has died, avoiding the delay and cost of locating witnesses at the time of probate. Such Wills are legal in most states.

Senior Citizens Information: Are you looking for housing options for yourself, an aging parent, relative, or friend? Do some research first to determine what kind of assistance or living arrangement you need; what your health insurance might cover; and what you can afford. Then check here for financial assistance resources and guides for making the right choice. Talk to a HUD-approved housing counselor if you have questions about your situation.

http://portal.hud.gov/hudportal/HUD?src=/topics/information_for_senior_citizens

Senior Centers: A senior center is a community focal point where older adults come together for services and activities that reflect their experience and skills, respond to their diverse needs and interests, enhance their dignity, support their independence, and encourage their involvement in and with the center and the community. Senior centers are designated as community focal points through the Older Americans Act.

Service Car: A service car is a funeral service vehicle used to transport chairs, lamps, flower stands, etc.

SIM card: A SIM card (Subscriber Identification Module) is a smart card that connects to a GSM (Global System for Mobile Communication) and establishes a user's identity and account number.

Slumber Room: A room containing a bed on which the deceased lies until being placed in a casket.

Smart Card, Contact Smart Card, or IC card: A smart card has an embedded microchip that may be used to store information about the cardholder or record card transactions as they occur. They are the size of a credit card and contain one or more semiconductor chips.

Social Security Many funeral directors voluntarily provide death information directly to Social Security. But, family members of a deceased individual still have the legal responsibility to notify Social Security. see *Social Security*, page 254

Social Security: The Social Security Death Index (SSDI) is a database containing the names and dates of birth and death for over 77 million Americans. This massive database is a wonderful resource for genealogists, and is available in many online locations for free. http://www.ssa.gov/ or http://www.archives.com/collections

Social Security One-Time Death Payment: A one-time payment of $255 can be paid to the surviving spouse if he or she was living with the deceased; or, if living apart, was receiving certain Social Security benefits on the deceased's record. If there is no surviving spouse, the payment is made to a child who is eligible for benefits on the deceased's record in the month of death. Ninety eight of every one hundred children could get benefits if a working parent dies. And Social Security pays more benefits to children than any other federal program.

Social Security Numbers: For every account the deceased had they were required to give their social security number and address. For any accounts that paid interest or a dividend, the institution is required to send to the deceased and to the IRS statements of the payments made so that taxes can be calculated and paid. Have all of the deceased's mail forwarded to the executor where they can watch for other assets.

Special Administrator: A special administrator may be appointed by the probate court when there is a dispute between beneficiaries.

Special Needs: Special needs are not just for people who may have a mental or physical disability and need to be protected.

Find a Guardian. If you are living with someone and not legally married who will take care of the child? The named guardian may take care of the child while a conservator may take care of the child's assets. They do not have to be the same person. One person may just be much better with finances and the other much better in raising children.

Trust Fund: A trust is a good way to set up financing for someone with special needs.

Medicaid and Beneficiaries: If an individual is receiving Medicaid or Supplemental Security Income (SSI) they are only authorized to have $2,000 or less in their bank account. If they then inherit a substantial amount of money, that money will become part of their estate and if the amount exceeds $2,000 they will most likely lose their government benefits. If they try to refuse the inheritance that could be considered a divestment and may affect their benefits. It may be best to have those funds go directly into a special needs trust for the individual with a guardian to oversee the funds.

Spiritual Banquet: A Roman Catholic practice involving specific prayers, such as Masses and Rosaries.

GLOSSARY & INDEX
Terms and Definitions

Split Property Interests: Property can be transferred by a Will that is split between heirs. For example a vacation cabin can be split between heirs with one group using it for six months and then the other group using it for the next six months. If there is a surviving spouse and the estate is filing an individual income tax return a distinction must be made as to what percent of the property is taxable for each.

Savings Bonds: Who Owns the Bond?

- If only one person is named on a savings bond, and that person is deceased, the bond becomes the property of their estate.
- If both people named on a bond are deceased, the bond is the property of the estate of the person who died last.
- If one of two people named on a bond is deceased, the surviving person is automatically the owner as if that survivor had been the sole owner from the time the bond was issued.

http://www.treasurydirect.gov/tdhome.htm

Successor Trustee: the person who takes over as trustee in the event of the original trustee's death. It is usually a good idea to name a successor trustee as a precaution.

Suicide

Legality: Under most state laws, suicide is not a crime, but assisting in suicide is. When a suicide takes place the "criminal" is dead so there would be no one to prosecute but the law is not neutral when it comes to suicide. The reason people are taken into custody when they attempt suicide is because they are breaking other laws: public disturbance, obstruction of a thoroughfare, or endangerment to themselves and/or others. Attempted suicide may also be grounds for a psychiatric exam.

Suicide is not chosen, it happens when pain exceeds resources for coping with pain.

People do get through whatever they are going through.

People often turn to suicide because they are seeking relief from pain. Remember that relief is a feeling. And you have to be alive to feel it. You will not feel the relief you so desperately seek, if you are dead.

If you are feeling suicidal now, please stop long enough to read this. It will only take about five minutes. Before you decide, take a look at this website.

http://www.metanoia.org/suicide/

Suicide, Euthanasia and Assisted Suicide

Euthanasia and Assisted Suicide: Physician-assisted suicide (dying), doctor-assisted dying (suicide), and more loosely termed mercy killing. Under most state laws assisting in suicide is a crime with criminal penalties. Assisted-suicide advocates are promoting their agenda in the name of personal choice and they meet with many who are not in favor of this approach. At the same time "bean counters' and "experts" are attempting to limit medical treatment or care even if the patient requests it. Times, they are a-changing. . .

Passive Euthanasia: Passive euthanasia is when life-sustaining medical treatment is withheld. Passive euthanasia could also refer to a Doctor who prescribes increased doses of pain medication to a dying patient while understanding the increased dose may prove to be toxic.

Active Euthanasia: Active euthanasia is when a course of action is undertaken to end a patient's life.

Hippocratic Oath: The Hippocratic Oath has been modified on a number of occasions to make it more acceptable. To "do no harm" can be argued both for and against assisted suicide. Is the glass half empty or half full?

Washington State: May 14, 2012. A new report from the Washington state health department shows the number of people killing themselves in assisted suicides is on the rise for the second straight time since the state followed Oregon in legalizing assisted suicide.

Montana Assisted Suicide: On Thursday, February 10, 2011, Montana state lawmakers in Montana defeated a bill that would have allowed and regulated assisted suicide. The Senate Judiciary Committee defeated SB 167 that would set up rules and protections for doctors who write lethal prescriptions for drugs that patients can use to kill themselves.

Oregon: On October 27, 1997 Oregon enacted the Death with Dignity Act which allows terminally-ill Oregonians to end their lives through the voluntary self-administration of lethal medications, expressly prescribed by a physician for that purpose. The Oregon Death with Dignity Act requires the Oregon Health Authority to collect information about the patients and physicians who participate in the Act, and publish an annual statistical report. http://public.health.oregon.gov

Health Care Providers: Health care providers are not required to honor any and all decisions made by a patient or their designated agent if the provider conscientiously objects to such care or treatment. However, federal law requires that the patient or the patient's decision-maker be provided with written policies at the time of admission of any limitations on carrying out such decisions, including the range of medical conditions or procedures affected by the conscience objection. Additionally, the notification must cite state law that relates to permitting those limitations.

More Information: There are many "right-to-die" agencies around the world. Most Americans demonstrate support for the concept of a doctor helping a patient end a life with painless means, but support immediately drops if the word "suicide" is used instead. People, in general, just do not want to give up what they believe is control of their lives.

Palliative Care: Other end-of-life decisions include palliative care when medicine shifts from a course of action trying to cure a person to a treatment that can provide comfort and control pain.

Surname: The surname is the family name (last name).

Survivors: The persons outliving the deceased, particularly the immediate family.

Sympathy Cards or Condolence Card: A card sent to the family to express their sympathy.

T

Taphonomy: The study of the conditions and processes by which organisms decay and become fossilized. There is also Forensic Taphonomy and Archeological Taphonomy.

Tangible Personal Property List: This can be a list in the deceased's own handwriting that is dated and signed with witnesses attesting to your signature. This may or may not be valid for distribution of some assets depending on state and local laws.

Tax Returns, all: Tax returns can supply personal information and social security numbers may list assets that you should be looking for. A final personal income tax return most likely needs to be filled from January 1, through the date of death. There may also be a revocable living trust return that needs to be filed.

Tax

    1) Federal Income Tax: payable for the year from January 1 up to the date of death. The return is due on the standard date, meaning April 15, 2013 for someone who dies in 2012. If the decedent was married the final 1040 may be filled as a joint return. The final joint return includes the decedent's income and deductions up to the time of death plus the surviving spouse's income and deductions for the entire year. This is one reason you already have gathered all medical bills, statements and receipts.

    2) State Income Tax: payable for the year from January 1 up to the date of death. Many states also tax an individual's income.

    3) Business Tax: if the decedent owned a business. There may be Federal, State and Local taxes.

2) Federal Estate Tax: Not the same as estate income tax. Federal Estate Tax is a tax on the estate of the deceased. For deaths occurring in 2012, up to $5,120,000 can be passed from an individual upon his or her death without incurring federal estate tax. Married couples can transfer up to twice the exempt amount tax-free, and property left to a spouse (as long as the spouse is a U.S. citizen) or tax-exempt charity is exempt from the tax.

3) State Estate Tax: many states also impose an estate tax or inheritance tax.

4) Estate Income Tax: Did the estate earn any income? If yes, a tax is due.

5) Gift Tax: A gift tax may be due if monetary gifts were given before death.

6) Property tax: may be due on real-estate.

Taxes: The personal representative or executor must apply for an employer identification number (EIN) for the estate. They must pay the all tax due up to the date of discharge from duties. This could easily take more than a year. They may also be required to submit to the court copies of all taxes filed on behalf of the deceased and the estate. Keep good records of what you did and when you did it. Keep copies of everything in a safe, secure location. The executor or personal representative is legally responsible until the estate is cleared and they are discharged from their duties. Any taxes the deceased or their estate owes are priority claims against the assets during probate. The personal representative or executor usually pays these first to ensure that there is enough money in the estate to do so.

Federal Estate Tax Return: If an estate tax return has to be filed the executor must wait for a closing letter from the IRS before they can close the estate.

IRA: An IRA or other asset that has been tax deferred and held until the individuals death have most likely appreciated in value. When those assets pass to heirs the heirs get a "step-up in basis." Any increase in value is irrelevant and the IRS only looks at the current date of death value. If the beneficiary liquidates the asset at the date of death value there are usually no capital gains.

Trust and Taxes: Trust income tax rates are higher than individual tax rates. Annual income above a certain amount in a child's trust is taxed at the higher trust tax rates. A trustee for a child's trust must file yearly income tax returns for the trust.

Annuity: The earnings on annuities are usually not taxed until they are distributed.

UGMA (Uniform Gift to Minor's Act) and UTMA (Uniform Transfer to Minor's Act) Custodial Accounts are often used to take advantage of the "kiddie tax." The kiddie tax allows a certain amount of a minor's income to go untaxed and an equal amount to be taxed at the child's tax rate. **Now would be a good time to seek the advice of a professional.**

IRS.gov

Part 5. Collecting Process
Chapter 5. Decedent Estates and
Estate Taxes
Section 1. Decedent and Estate Tax Accounts
This IRM section provides information to explain differences between decedent accounts, estate tax accounts, legal terms used in probate, documents used in probate proceedings and general information regarding probate proceedings.

http://www.irs.gov/irm/part5/irm_05-005-001.html

Telephone Price Disclosures: You must give consumers who telephone your place of business and ask about your prices or offerings accurate information from your General Price List, Casket Price List, and Outer Burial Container Price List. You also must answer any other questions about your offerings and prices with any readily available information that reasonably answers the question. (17) From the Funeral Rule

GLOSSARY & INDEX
Terms and Definitions

Temporary Assistance for Needy Families (TANF): Temporary Assistance for Needy Families (TANF) is federally funded - state administered - financial assistance program for low income families with dependent children and for pregnant women in their last three months of pregnancy. TANF provides temporary financial assistance while also helping recipients find jobs that will allow them to support themselves.

> **Food Stamps (SNAP):** For over 40 years, the federal Food Stamp Program, now officially named SNAP – the Supplemental Nutrition Assistance Program – has served as a mainline federal social assistance program designed to help low-income families and individuals buy the food they need for good health. The SNAP (Food Stamp) program now helps put nutritious food on the tables of 28 million people every month.

> **Emergency Food Assistance:** The Emergency Food Assistance Program (TEFAP) is a Federal program that helps supplement the diets of low-income needy individuals and families, including elderly people, by providing them with emergency food assistance at no cost.

> **HUD Public Housing Assistance Program:** The HUD Public Housing assistance program was established to provide decent and safe rental housing for eligible low-income families. Public housing comes in all sizes and types, from scattered single family houses to high-rise apartments for elderly families. As of 2009, there were approximately 1.2 million households living in public housing units, managed by some 3,300 local public housing agencies (HAs).

Temporary Marker: A temporary identifying marker may be used by the cemetery at the time of burial. It will be removed shortly thereafter.

Tenancy in Common: Tenancy in common is an alternative to Joint Tenancy with Rights of Survivorship. Each owner owns the asset or a percentage of the asset. They may legally sell or share their part of the asset without the other party's consent or approval. The asset is transferred at death according to the deceased's Will. If there is no Will, the asset will pass to heirs according to probate law. While the asset is being probated the other owner(s) still have use of their share of the asset. In most cases they may sell their share or dispose of it without waiting for the probate court.

Terminal Illness: A terminal illness is an active and malignant disease that cannot be cured and there is no expectation of recovery.

Testator: A testator is a person who makes a Will or dies leaving a valid Will.

Thank You Cards: It is not necessary to send a thank-you to everyone who attended the funeral or visitation.

> Although it is not necessary to send thank you notes for a funeral, it is appropriate to send special thanks to those who were really there to assist you in your time of need, and those who made funeral donations. If the family received sympathy cards, flowers, Mass cards, contributions to charity and offers of help, these should be acknowledged with a thank-you. When you thank someone for a donation do not mention the money. Say something like, "Thank-you for the generous gift."
>
> **Remember Clergy, pallbearers and ushers.** If flowers or a donation was from a group, send the card to the leader of the group. As a rule, just keep it simple. Preprinted Thank-you cards are fine. Write the thank-you when you can and if you can. Do not feel pressured into writing them when you don't want to. Make it from your heart and be polite. Traditional etiquette is to send a thank-you note within two months after a funeral.

Tomb: A tomb is a place for burial that is most often underground.

Topical Disinfectant: A topical disinfectant is a chemical used to inhibit or prevent the growth of microbes on living tissue. Denatured alcohol is an example.

Totten Trust: A Totten trust is just a regular bank account with a designated "pay on death" inheritor. When the account is opened a friend, relative (most likely named as executor) is named as the beneficiary. Whoever opens the account can also close it at any time for any reason. They may also change banks and or change beneficiaries. The idea is when the person dies the beneficiary collects the account balance and pays for the funeral expenses. This can work out very well if all parties are informed and kept up to date.

Traditional Funeral: A traditional funeral is usually considered a three part funeral where there is a viewing or visitation followed by a funeral, which is the church or religious aspect of the funeral, and finally a grave side service, where the family members meet at the final resting place of the body whether that be a grave, a niche wall, or another location. A traditional funeral can be used for burial or cremation.

> **A traditional funeral service is generally the most expensive** type of funeral. In addition to the funeral home's basic services fee, costs often include embalming, dressing the body, rental of the funeral home for the viewing or service and use of vehicles to transport the family if they don't use their own. Cemetery costs for the plot, mausoleum or niche, opening and closing the grave, headstone or marker, and perpetual maintenance are most likely not included.
>
> **Cremation:** A traditional funeral can also be used with cremation. It may include a viewing or visitation with a rented casket followed by a funeral, which is the church or religious aspect of the funeral, and finally a grave side service, where the family members meet at the final resting place of the body whether that be a grave, a niche wall, or another location where the cremains may be scattered.
>
> **Direct Burial** or **Green Burial:** Direct Burial is the most common final disposition and is also called a Green Burial. It is the process of burying a body without the use of chemical preservation in a simple container to help preserve the earth. Costs associated with direct burial include grave opening and closing and perpetual care (maintenance) of the grave site. There are also charges for the purchase of a grave site.

Transfer of Remains Fee: A transfer of remains fee is a charge for the transportation of the body from the place of death to the funeral home or crematory.

Transfer on Death Assets: Many assets (such as bank accounts) or benefits such as retirement savings accounts (e.g., IRAs) have their own beneficiary designations that allow the asset to pass payable on death (POD) or transfer on death (TOD). Check any trusts. Trusts should be mentioned in the will but the executor may have to read the details of the trust in the trust documents available from the attorney who set up the trust. Joint ownership deeds and retirement statements that include beneficiary names and directives also need to be checked.

Transfer on Death Account, (TOD): A contractual option that allows an owner of certain property to designate a beneficiary that will receive the property upon their death. The property should, in most cases, pass directly to the beneficiary.

Transit Permit: Burial-Transit Permit or Burial Permit: Transportation and disposition permission. A burial transit permit or burial permit is needed in some states for the transportation and disposition of the deceased. This document grants the holder permission to transport a body. To transport a body out-of-state you must also obtain a burial-transit permit. If the medical examiner is involved, the permit must be signed by him and by the local registrar to be valid. It is also needed at a cemetery or crematorium to bury or cremate a body.

Transportation Authorization: While most states allow non-licensed individuals to transport a body, it is necessary to have formal authorization. Be aware that transportation permits may only be valid for the state where issued. Transporting a body across state lines may require multiple permits.

Transportation, Mortuary Shipping: Many people move away from their state, or country, of origin, however what happens in the event of death if the deceased needs to be returned back home following their death? U.S. has a large immigrant population and many choose repatriation to their country of origin upon death.

Transportation Permission: In-State Transport: If a person died of natural causes, and the body is not under the jurisdiction of the medical examiner, it usually may be moved in-state without a permit. A Burial-Transit Permit is used to transport a body out-of-state. If the medical examiner is involved, the permit must be signed by him and by the local registrar to be valid. Many states allow people other than death care professionals to transport a body.

Trust

Trust Agreement: A trust agreement is a legal document that allows the Trustor (person creating the trust) to transfer property or assets for the benefit of someone else (beneficiaries). Beneficiaries can be individuals, businesses, or charitable organizations who act as managers and distribute assets under the terms of the trust. The estate or trust accounts are set up to provide a safe haven for assets as they are passed on or used on the behalf of the beneficiaries. They are intended to keep the assets safe for the beneficiaries use at a later time without being delayed by probate court. To help in locating a trust account the executor should check the deceased's federal tax returns for any 1099 forms reporting interest earned from a trust account. The 1099 should also contain information naming who holds the account.

Because there are so many variations and reasons for creating a Trust it now may be a good time to speak with a competent professional. For example: If you create a living trust to avoid probate, it is generally not a good idea to name the trust as the beneficiary of your retirement accounts. Retirement funds are in most cases already exempt from probate, and by naming your trust as beneficiary, inheritors are likely to lose some of the benefits. Laws are always changing.

Making Changes: When making changes to Trust Accounts a hand written note placed between the pages is not the best way to go about this. You may be creating a lot of future legal problems. It would be best to seek the advice of an estate attorney and make formal legal changes to the documents.

Types of Trust Accounts: Some examples are: Asset Management Trust, Beneficiary Trust, Catastrophic Illness Trust, Charitable Remainder Trust, Children's Trust, Generation Skipping Trust, IRA and Qualified Plan Trusts, Irrevocable Life Insurance Trust, Insurance Preservation Trust, Irrevocable Trust, Land Trust, Personal Property Trust, Private Annuity Trust, Qualified Personal Residence Trust, Revocable Living Trust, Special Needs Trust and a Totten Trust. There is no one right approach for everyone. Too much depends on individual circumstances and wishes. Some trusts have an advantage over a Will, and some do not.

Wills and Trusts: A Will becomes public record when it is submitted for probate. The terms of a living trust do not need to be made public. A living trust is not a complete substitute for a Will. A living trust and a pour-over Will are used to limit or avoid probate. A pour-over Will is a Will with only one beneficiary, which is the living trust.

Should there still be a Will? Yes. If there is a living trust there still needs to be a Will. If there is no Will, assets that are not included in the trust will most likely have to be probated. A pour-over Will is different but it is still a Will.

Pour-over Will: A Pour-over Will transfers assets upon death to a trust account. The Pour-over Will has only one beneficiary which is the Trust Account. Assets are poured-over into the trust. This is something the executor or someone pre-planning will need to look into further and goes beyond the scope of this book. A Pour-over Will can also instruct the successor trustee to put any assets into the trust that were not put in previously. Sweet, if everything is done correctly.

Assets in Trust: Real-estate and other property with title documents must usually be retitled in the name of the trust. The process is most often not difficult or complicated but must be done correctly or the titled property could end up in probate. A living trust will most likely not reduce any estate taxes owed.

Children: Except for items of little value, children under the age of eighteen cannot legally own property. Any property that is left to a minor must be managed by an adult until the minor reaches legal age. A trust can be used to accomplish this. A Will is used to name a guardian for minor children. A trust cannot be used to do this.

Special Needs: A minor or any person with special needs can be taken care of with the use of a trust and their government benefits can be protected. If the person will remain living in the property, this as well as taxes and insurance payments can also be dealt with in a living trust. Statistics show autism is on the rise and families need to preplan. Since government assistance to people with special needs is typically in the form of Medicaid and Social Security which are needs based programs the recipient of these benefits is not allowed to retain more than $2,000 of assets in their own bank account. If a guardian or parent does not do the necessary estate planning during their lifetime and they leave a large sum of money to a person with special needs they may automatically lose their benefits. If the money is left to the individual in a trust it can be used to cover additional expenses not otherwise covered. Since the individual with special needs does not own the funds and cannot access them individually, the money set aside will not affect their government benefits.

Charitable Trust: Setting up a charitable trust to leave property to a qualified charitable organization can reduce your estate taxes similar to the way giving gifts to charitable organizations offers the charitable deduction to reduce gift taxes.

Reporting Requirements: A trustee for a minor child must file a yearly income tax return for the trust in most cases and trust income tax rates are generally higher than individual income tax rates. A Trustee is required to report and account annually to all beneficiaries for which he or she is managing money.

Irrevocable Trust: An irrevocable trust (contract) in most cases cannot be canceled or refunded. An irrevocable trust transfers asset ownership to the trust fund, making the fund the legal owner of those assets. They are more private and harder to dispute. Once the trust is set up as an irrevocable trust it cannot be amended, modified, changed, or revoked. However, some Irrevocable Trusts are written with instructions to the Trustees or beneficiaries to allow for the terms of the trust to be modified under specific limited circumstances. Now is an excellent time to speak with a competent legal professional. Sometimes if you move to a different town or state the money in trust cannot be moved prior to death.

Revocable Trust: A revocable living trust can be changed anytime during your lifetime and they are more private and harder to dispute. You retain ownership of the trust assets and can dissolve or change the trust as needed.

Living Trust: Trusts designed to take effect while the individual is still alive. Property left through a living trust can pass to beneficiaries without probate. Many feel that Probate may be all together avoided with proper planning. The idea is to place assets in a Revocable Living Trust, allowing the individual to determine who gets their assets when they die. A revocable living trust allows the individual to change the trust as their circumstances or wishes change. A living trust does not generally protect assets from creditors.

Testamentary Trusts: Trusts designed to take effect when the individual dies. In many cases the assets must then pass through probate which is what the individual was trying to avoid in the first place. Many Wills that were done years and years ago had a provision for this type of trust. If your does it would be wise to see if it is accomplishing what you intend. Wills should be updated periodically.

Totten Trust: A Totten Trust is just a regular bank account with a designated "pay on death" inheritor. When the account is opened a friend, relative (most likely named as executor) is named as the beneficiary. Whoever opens the account can also close it at any time for any reason. They may also change banks and or change beneficiaries. The beneficiary does not need to know about the arrangement, and the depositor is entitled to deposit and withdraw funds from the account as they see fit. The idea is when the person dies the beneficiary collects the account balance and pays for the funeral expenses. This can work out very well if all parties are informed and kept up to date.

Medicaid and Trusts: Funds placed in a trust designated to pay for funeral or burial expenses may be exempt in determining Medicaid eligibility.

Trustee: The person in charge of the trust is called the Trustee. The trustee is in general legally responsible to understand the rules for the type of trust they are managing and act responsibly to cause no harm or lose through negligence. The trustee is usually the person making the trust while they are still alive and then becomes the named (successor) trustee when the individual dies. When a death occurs the trustee usually has between thirty to sixty days to notify all beneficiaries and supply them with a copy of the trust documents. If the executor is not the trustee the executor has an obligation to notify the trustee and follow up to be certain they are taking care of their duties to the estate. If you were chosen as a trustee it was most likely because the beneficiary needed to be protected and you were chosen because they trusted you to do the right thing.

Trustor: The person who creates the trust is called the trustor, settlor or grantor.

Professional Trustees: There are Fees involved and most estates do not require the services of a professional trustee. All trustees are responsible for managing the trust property. In many situations, trustees also make distribution decisions. Experience, professionalism and avoiding family issues are some good reasons to choose a professional. Attorneys, CPAs, banks, and trust companies are just some of the types of professional trustees.

Close the Trust: The trust should be closed once the assets have been distributed. This may also depend on the status of probate. State laws vary widely.

Turnover Order: A turnover order is a court order requiring the debtor to turn over specified property. In some cases the property is then sold to pay the creditor.

U

Underwater Homes

Underwater Homes: A home is said to be "underwater" when more is owed on the home than the home is worth. A reverse mortgage is a "non-recourse" loan which means that the HECM borrower (or their estate) will never owe more than the loan balance or value of the property, whichever is less; and no assets other than the home must be used to repay the debt. Non-recourse means simply that if the borrower (or estate) does not pay the balance when due, the mortgagee's remedy is limited to foreclosure and the borrower will not be personally liable for any deficiency resulting from the foreclosure.

Non-Recourse Loans: With the HUD (Department of Housing and Urban Development), FHA-insured (Federal Housing Administration) HECM (Home Equity Conversion Mortgage) reverse mortgage, the borrower can never owe more than the value of the property and cannot pass on any debt from the reverse mortgage to any heirs. The sole remedy the lender has is the collateral, not assets in the estate, if applicable.

The executor may sell the home. If a member of the family or an heir chooses to pay off the loan in order to prevent selling the house the full amount of the loan has to be repaid even if the balance of the loan is higher than the value of the house. However, if the heirs decide to sell the house to repay the loan, the HECM product has a non-recourse policy which states that the heirs will not be required to pay more than the value of the home, even if the loan balance exceeds the value of the home. Now may be a good time to consult a competent professional.

Uniform Probate Code (UPC): Not all states have adopted the UPC. Its purpose is to streamline the probate process and to standardize and modernize the various state laws governing Wills, Trusts, and Intestacy. Because the UPC has not been adopted by every state, check the code as actually adopted in that jurisdiction and do not rely on the text of the UPC in its entirety. Some states have adopted more of the code than others making a discussion of the entire code academic.

Unions: A few unions provide death benefits.

Union Cards: may hold account information, Insurance Policy Information, or any other information depending on the card and its purpose.

Urn: An urn is a container to hold cremated remains. It can be placed in a columbarium or mausoleum, or buried in the ground. It is not necessary to purchase an Urn for the Ashes, a white colored dust, of a loved one. They are available from the service provider or online in many sizes and materials priced from around $75. An Urn can be made of any material. Metal, wood and stone are the most common. Sets of six mini Urns are also available. An Urn from a third party retailer may be purchased and shipped directly to the funeral home. The funeral home may not charge a fee for using these.

If a Columbarium or Niche is going to be used remember not all Urns will fit inside every Niche. It is important to measure the Niche or Columbarium first.

Who owns the ashes? The answer – You can't own them. You may only take possession for their legal disposition.

Urn Garden: A garden containing urn burial sites.

Unsecured Debt: Unsecured debts in the deceased's name only are not owed by the spouse. The estate will most likely be held responsible. Community estate property is usually liable for any debt incurred by either spouse during marriage (if the couple was living separate and apart before entry of a judgment of marital dissolution or legal separation). If you are concerned about a situation involving a beneficiary you should do more research or speak with a competent estate attorney. Credit cards are unsecured debt. The Credit CARD Act of 2009 requires credit card issuers to stop adding fees and penalties during the time the estate is being settled.

V

Vault, Grave Liner or Concrete Box, Outer Burial Container

Outer Burial Container: Most states do not have laws requiring an outer burial container. The cemetery may require this because it does help prevent the ground from collapsing around the grave site. Also the human body has lots of hazardous materials that need to be contained and it makes for easier maintenance of the grounds.

A burial vault completely contains the casket, while a **grave liner** generally covers only the top and sides of the casket and allows the bottom of the casket to be in contact with the earth. Purchased online it may be sent directly to the cemetery, but because cemeteries are not covered by the FTC's Funeral Rule, the cemetery may charge a fee for using a burial vault or grave liner you purchased elsewhere.

Cost: The cost of a grave liner is a few hundred dollars and up to a few thousand dollars. Then you pay a fee to have it lowered into the ground. This is usually another $100. You bury it. You almost never dig it back up. It deteriorates. If one is required, purchase the least expensive grave liner that you can find. Plastic and wood are also options.

Veteran

Veterans: U.S. Veterans of the Armed Forces who received an honorable discharge may be entitled to a burial in the local National Cemetery at no cost. The Veterans Administration will reimburse a portion of the burial or cremation expenses if the veteran's death is service connected. The VA may also assist with burial, cremation, and plot expenses for eligible veterans.

Veteran's Discharge Certificate: DD-214

Discharge papers are very important in establishing eligibility.

A copy of military discharge papers can be acquired at:
National Archives: http://www.archives.gov/veterans/military-service-records/

National Personnel Records Center
1 Archives Drive, St. Louis, MO 63138

Telephone: 314-801-0800 - Fax: 314-801-9195 - E-mail: MPR.center@nara.gov

For more information online: http://www.archives.gov/st-louis/

Veterans Health Care Program: Veterans Medical Care Benefits provide outpatient medical services, hospital care, medicines, and supplies to eligible US military veterans.

Veteran's Discharge Certificate: A veteran's discharge certificate is a Certificate of Release or Discharge from Active Duty (DD Form 214).

Viatical: pertaining to the purchase of insurance policies from terminally ill policy holders.

Viewing: Making the deceased available to be visited and seen by relatives and friends prior to or after the funeral service.

Vigil: A Roman Catholic religious service held on the eve of the funeral service.

Visitation

Visitation: An opportunity for survivors and friends to view the deceased in private usually in a special room within the funeral home. It is often difficult to know what to say or do when there is a loss but there are certain things that need to be done when someone passes away. When attending a wake or a visitation you should approach the family and express your sympathy. If you were acquainted with the deceased but not the family, introduce yourself. If you are attending the viewing it is customary to show your respects by viewing the deceased. Children may or may not want to view the deceased or even go to the viewing. As a parent or guardian, use your best judgment as to what you feel is best for the child. How long you stay at a wake or visitation is up to you. It need not be long. If prayer or speeches are in progress it will be considered disrespectful to leave in the middle of them. There is usually a memorial book or guest book to sign.

What to Wear: Although black dress is no longer required, at least wear something business casual in a darker color. Bright colors and busy patterns are inappropriate for mourning. Use some uncommon sense. If you have none, borrow some.

Do Not Say: Do not say anything to the family that the deceased would not have wanted you to say if they were there. Now is not the time or the place (if there is ever a time or place). do not say: "You'll get over it"; "They are better off now"; "You can have more children"; "I know how you feel"; "You have to keep busy"; "How are you financially?"; "Time heals all wounds"; "Life goes on"; "There number was up"; or "You look terrible". Do not tell them stories of families that have had it even worse. If you are at a viewing do not say how great the deceased looks. Use some uncommon sense.

Be respectful and you will be fine. It is important for the family to know that you care.

Visitation Room: A room in a funeral home where the body lies prior to the funeral service so that people may view the deceased.

Vital Records: One of the most comprehensive resources for locating vital records online. United States Birth Certificates, Death Records & Marriage Licenses. Some Local Libraries allow you to use this and other websites for free. Call your local library for details.   http://www.vitalrec.com/ see Search

Voter Registration: request a cancellation for a deceased voter.

W

Wake

Wake: A wake is a ceremony held to honor and recognize the deceased. It is usually held in the afternoon or early evening a few days or the night before a funeral People come to visit with the family and pay their respects for a few hours. The deceased may be laid out in their home or the home of a family member. Sometimes this is done at a funeral home or other location. It is not mandatory but viewing the body is often seen as a sign of respect. In some cases there is no casket or viewing at the wake but there may be photographs of the deceased placed around the room.

Wakes may also be called a Visitation or Viewing. People eat, exchange stories about the deceased, sing traditional songs and laments, and support the family members. The decision to have a wake is up to the family. It may be public or private and the details surrounding the wake or visitation should be published in the obituary.

Registry Book: It is customary to sign a Registry Book. Include a brief note and your full name and address so the family may contact you or send thanks later. Your note should be a very short remembrance; "He/she was well thought of. We will miss him/her." Or "He/she was so much help at – we will all miss him/her." Keep it short and simple.

Children: Children often accompany their parents to the wake or visitation. The children may or may not want to view the body and the parents may or may not feel the need to bring them to the wake. Sometimes an older person will say they want the grandchildren to see the deceased one last time and you know in your heart this is not the best thing for the child at this time in their life. This decision is up to the parents of the children. Just do your best with these decisions. People handle grief differently and attitudes change over time. Make the best decisions based on what you feel is best for your children and you will be fine.

Food: It is always nice to bring food. The family does not want to deal with this right now. Just use good sense and you will be fine. Place food in a disposable container so the family does not have to clean it and return it to you. A casserole, plate of cookies or quiche is always appreciated. Ethnic food is fine if you know the family preferences. If you cannot bring food do not worry about it. It is more important for the family to see you than to have you bring something.

Dress: we should definitely dress respectfully for wakes, visitations and viewings. Maybe not as formal as for funerals but use some uncommon sense: No ratty cut offs, t-shirts, bare midriffs or flip flops. Stay away from all denim (jeans). Dress respectfully. Business casual is what we would expect.

Wal-Mart: Find funeral items, caskets, urns, pet urns, and more for everyday low prices at Walmart.com.   http://www.walmart.com/cp/Funeral/1058564

Will - Last Will & Testament

Will: If there is a valid Will then the Will determines how the estate is transferred during probate and to whom. If there is no valid Will or the Will only covers some assets, the laws where the deceased had their last legal residence or the laws where the deceased had real estate specify who gets what parts of the estate.

Having a Will undoubtedly simplifies the distribution of property and helps speed the probate process. There are probate properties and non-probate properties. Probate handles properties distributed through probate. Having a Will may not avoid probate, but it is better than having nothing at all.

A Will declares how individually owned assets are distributed. Assets that are owned jointly or assets that have a beneficiary designation pass to the joint tenant or beneficiary on your death. A Will controls an individually owned bank account, individually owned personal property, or individually owned investments, where there is no other joint owner and no designated beneficiary. If you want to avoid all probate you should consider a Trust. There are many, many types of Trust accounts and some are used to accomplish a specific purpose. A Revocable Living Trust and Totten Trust are both commonly used. A Non-revocable Living Trust cannot be changed at a later date in most cases.

Intestate: Intestate refers to a person who has died without having written a valid will. The state where the deceased had their permanent residence will apply its probate laws to determine how the property will be dispersed if there is no Will or it cannot be located.

Holographic Will: A Will that has been handwritten, dated and signed by the testator. A holographic Will is valid in all states under certain conditions. State law must be checked for the state having jurisdiction.

Revoked Will: If a Will is missing or no longer valid because the decedent intentionally revoked it either an earlier Will or the laws of intestate succession are used to decide the proper distribution of the estate.

Lost or Destroyed: If the original Will has been lost or destroyed the court may (or may not) accept a photo copy of the original Will. Sometimes the decedent gives potential executors a copy of the original Will. Copies may also be in a safe deposit box. It is so simple to just tell people where you keep your

Will. It also requires a great deal of trust if the person is concerned about anyone changing their Will.

Locating a Will: There are usually indications that there is a Will even if it cannot readily be located. It could be in a home safe kept under frozen food at the bottom of a freezer in a garage. Or just wrapped in foil, placed in a zip lock bag and kept in the bottom of a refrigerator freezer to hide it and protect it from fire. The main thing is to search but you do not have to go to extremes. It is estimated that over half of all Americans die without having taken the time to prepare a Will. You only have a fifty-fifty chance that there even is a Will.

Pour-over Will: A Pour-over Will transfers assets upon death to a trust account. The Pour-over Will has only one beneficiary which is the Trust Account. Assets are poured-over into the trust. This is something the executor or someone pre-planning will need to look into further and goes beyond the scope of this book. A Pour-over Will can also instruct the successor trustee to put any assets into the trust that were not put in previously. Sweet, if everything is done correctly.

Self Proving Will: Self-proving affidavit attached to a Will: An affidavit attached to a Will certifies that the witnesses and testator properly signed the Will. A self-proving will makes it easy for the court to accept the document as the true Will of the person who has died, avoiding the delay and cost of locating witnesses at the time of probate. Such Wills are legal in most states.

Joint Will: Many couples think they have a "joint Will". A mirror image Will is the same for each spouse. Each usually leaves everything to the other, surviving partner. If one of the partners is stricken with dementia either in the earliest stages or very advanced stages the other partner usually needs to correct their own Will to name a guardian or provide care if the surviving partner has dementia.

Living Will: A Living Will allows you to make health care decisions now in case you are unable to do so in the future. It documents instructions for your medical care in the event you are unable to communicate due to a severe injury, terminal illness or other medical condition. A Living Will can also be called a health care declaration, advance directive, or medical power of attorney.

Medical Directives, Health Care Directives or Advance Directives: An advance directive is a written statement of a person's wishes regarding medical treatment. It is a legal document detailing a person's health care wishes, including the individual to whom they give the legal authority to act on their behalf and what types of treatment they do and do not want to receive in the event they are unable to speak or communicate. The living Will and the power of attorney constitute what are called advance directives. A divorce has no effect on your written directions for health care.

Dementia: a group of symptoms affecting intellectual and social abilities severely enough to interfere with daily functioning. There are many causes of dementia. Alzheimer's disease is the most common cause of a progressive dementia. In most cases a person with dementia can still make or change a Will if they can show that they understand what they are doing and what the effects of it are going to be. see *Will*, page 274

Dementia and Changing the Will: You are dealing with a person who is not thinking clearly. They may, and often do, change their Will often. In most cases a person with dementia can still make or change a Will if they can show that they understand what they are doing and what the effects of it will be. This needs to be addressed before a medical and financial crisis takes place. Proof of incapacity should be taken care of early.

Recording the Will: Depositing the Will, lodging the Will, or filing or recording the Will. Generally the most current Will is brought to the county court of the deceased's primary residence within 30 days of death where it is recorded.

Writ of Execution: A writ of execution is a court order authorizing the seizure of an asset. Usually a local sheriff is charged with taking possession of property owned by the debtor. The property can be sold at auction to satisfy the debt.

Women: Estate Planning: Women are still not taking control of their lives when it comes to estate planning. A recent survey suggests that women care more about losing weight then protecting their financial assets. Women live longer than men. They are most often widowed and find themselves with all of the couple's assets and should decide who the beneficiaries are going to be. When many older women are widowed they do not want to do the estate planning by themselves. This is why they should begin to make a plan while they are younger and can still get the help and assistance they need. Women have been considered care givers but do not take into account their own care which includes financial maintenance and estate planning. Show your husband this book. No one can read this book and walk away with the idea that "We do not need to plan. Everything is going to work itself out." If you are reading this you should already have a Will and an estate plan or you should begin working on one now. At the very minimum you should have a Will, an asset list with access information and a good friend to help out. You danced with the monkey and now it is time to toss a banana in the box.

Wrongful Death: When somebody dies due to consequences of a wrongful act of a person or business or government body, either by negligence or by a deliberate act. If someone dies due to the negligent, reckless, or deliberate behavior of someone or something else, then the surviving family members may be able to file a wrongful death lawsuit in order to collect damages for their loved one's untimely death. It is the executor or personal representative's responsibility to file a wrongful death lawsuit for the estate of the deceased. Now would be a good time to speak with a competent attorney that can assist in such an action if it is necessary.

We sincerely hope this book has been a help to you. While it does not answer all of your questions it should help you through this difficult time.

www.ingramcontent.com/pod-product-compliance
Lightning Source LLC
Chambersburg PA
CBHW080833230426
43665CB00021B/2825